English File

Advanced
Teacher's Guide

WITH TEACHER'S RESOURCE CENTRE

Christina Latham-Koenig
Clive Oxenden
Jerry Lambert
Kate Chomacki

with Anna Lowy
Amanda Begg

Contents

Syllabus checklist

SPEAKING	LISTENING	READING
half-agreeing and politely disagreeing	understanding names and dates	interpreting a questionnaire
talking about work	listening for detailed information	identifying attitude and implied meaning
developing a long turn	using existing knowledge to make sense of information	expressing a response to a creative text / literature
conveying the main ideas in a text	understanding accents	reading notes and expanding them into a spoken explanation
expressing ideas with precision	inferring attitudes and emotions	inferring general meaning / skimming
conveying the main ideas in a text	understanding a complex topic	scanning for specific information
giving background details to an experience	understanding opinions and explanations	understanding the plot of a novel / reading for pleasure
contributing to a group discussion	understanding attitudes and finer details	identifying benefits
discussing and interpreting information in a questionnaire	understanding comparisons	understanding reasons and consequences
categorizing information	understanding how a business works	categorizing information

SPEAKING	LISTENING	READING
giving a well-structured presentation and taking questions	understanding a lecture or talk	understanding advice
discussing behaviour, showing sensitivity to different perspectives	distinguishing between positive and negative effects	distinguishing between positive and negative effects
using persuasive language	making notes	inferring meaning
exchanging complex information to solve a problem	separating the factual details (names, dates, measurements, etc.) from what the art represents	understanding a complex text
discussing issues showing sensitivity to different viewpoints	understanding the results of research	identifying reasons and understanding explanations
telling an anecdote	understanding an anecdote	identifying negative reactions
discussing contentious issues diplomatically	understanding contrasting points of view, agreement / disagreement / partial agreement	understanding complex language
relaying precise instructions	extracting and understanding the main points of an argument	following instructions / a recipe, reading and explaining, rebuilding instructions from notes
reacting to a speaker and relating your own ideas	listening for detail	scanning for specific information
highlighting key information	inferring attitude	understanding the sequence in a complex text

Course overview

Introduction

Our aim with *English File fourth edition* has been to make every lesson better and to make the package more student- and teacher-friendly. As well as the main A and B Student's Book lessons, there is a range of material that you can use according to your students' needs, and the time and resources you have available. Don't forget:

- videos that can be used in class in every File: Colloquial English, Video Listening, and Can you understand these people?
- Quick Tests and File tests for every File, as well as Progress Tests, an End-of-course Test, and an Entry Test, which you can use at the beginning of the course
- photocopiable Grammar and Communicative activities for every A and B lesson, and a Vocabulary activity for every Vocabulary Bank

Online Practice and the **Workbook** provide review, support, and practice for students outside the class.

The **Teacher's Guide** suggests different ways of exploiting the Student's Book depending on the level of your class. We very much hope you enjoy using *English File fourth edition*.

What do Advanced students need?

When students reach an advanced level of English, they are, by definition, successful learners and they typically feel positive about the language and their classes. However, it can be hard to make them feel they are actually making progress and improving.

It is important to challenge students with material that they feel is relevant to their needs and which they can see a purpose to. They want to see and hear material from the real world, which respects their intelligence, but also need support to help them use what they know to overcome new challenges and to set realistic and positive expectations of what they can achieve.

Grammar

- A wide range of structures to express different concepts
- Fluency using more sophisticated grammar structures
- Awareness of the register of different structures

At this level, students will have already studied most of the common grammatical structures. However, students will still need to work with more complex areas such as past modals and they will also meet several new structures, such as inversion and ellipsis. Grammar is often presented functionally, e.g. the structures to use for distancing, or for adding emphasis, which allows students to revise and extend certain structures without feeling that they are retracing their steps. There is often a focus in the **Grammar Banks** on the register of structures to make students aware of the different levels of formality and informality. Students can look again at the grammar presented in the lesson on **Online Practice**. The **Workbook** provides a variety of practice exercises and the opportunity for students to use the new grammar to express their own ideas.

Vocabulary

- Systematic expansion of their vocabulary
- A focus on idioms, synonyms, phrasal verbs, and collocation
- A focus on register and appropriacy

At this level, expanding students' vocabulary is the most visible and motivating measure of their progress. Many lessons are linked to the **Vocabulary Banks** which help present and practise the vocabulary in class, give an audio model of each word or phrase, and provide a clear reference so students can revise and test themselves in their own time. Students can review the meaning and the pronunciation of new vocabulary on **Online Practice**, and find further practice in the **Workbook**. Reading and listening exercises include the **Language in Context** feature, which focuses on naturally-occurring advanced words and phrases.

Pronunciation

- 'Fine-tuning' of pronunciation of difficult sounds
- The ability to use appropriate rhythm and intonation
- Continue to develop their instinct for rules and patterns

Clear, *intelligible* pronunciation (not perfection) should be the goal of students at this level. There is a pronunciation focus in every lesson, which integrates a focus on individual sounds with regular work on word and sentence stress, as well as on areas that students might not have studied before, such as secondary stress, intonation, linking, and features of accents. **Online Practice** contains the Sound Bank videos which show students the mouth positions to make English vowels and consonants. They can also review the pronunciation from the lesson at their own speed. There is more practice of pronunciation in the **Workbook**, with audio, which can be found on **Online Practice**.

Speaking

- To learn to adapt their spoken English to a variety of situations and registers
- Practice in recognizing and using discourse markers in speech
- Improvement in accuracy as well as further development of their fluency

We believe that a good topic or text is very important in motivating students to speak in class. Every lesson has a speaking activity which enables students to contribute their own knowledge, opinions, or experience. Students can use **Online Practice** to develop their writing skills further.

Listening

- Motivating, integrated listening material
- Achievable tasks but with an increasing level of challenge
- Exposure to longer listenings and a wide variety of accents
- Exposure to authentic and colloquial spoken language

For most students, listening is still the hardest skill and it is vital that listening material is both interesting and provides the right level of challenge. *English File Advanced* includes more unscripted authentic listening alongside more controlled material in the main lessons to provide challenge and support appropriate to the level. These recordings expose students to a wider variety of language, accent and speed of speech with achievable but challenging tasks. The Colloquial English lessons give students practice in listening to unscripted authentic speech. On **Online Practice**, for each File students can find further listening practice related to the topic. They can also access the listening activities from every lesson, to practise in their own time, and to read the script to check anything that they have found difficult.

Reading

- Engaging topics and stimulating material
- Exposure to a wide variety of authentic text types
- Challenging tasks which help them read more skillfully

Many students need to read in English for their work or studies, and reading is also important in helping to build vocabulary and to consolidate grammar. The key to encouraging students to read is to provide material where they feel there is a reason to read and tasks which help them to get the most out of a text. This level contains a variety of readings from real sources (the British press, magazines, websites, forums, infographics) and have been chosen for their intrinsic interest and potential to generate a reaction. The opinions expressed in these texts do not necessarily reflect the view of the *English File* authors or of Oxford University Press.

Writing

- Practice in planning, organizing, writing, and checking
- An awareness of register, structure, and fixed phrases
- A focus on 'micro' writing skills

It is often difficult to motivate students to write at this level. Each guided writing activity flows out of a main lesson to ensure that students have plenty of ideas to start with and focuses on key areas of language, style, and organization to help break the writing process down into a series of achievable tasks.

Students can use **Online Practice** to develop their writing skills further. The Discussion board also provides opportunities for informal written interaction.

Colloquial English

- Further exposure to authentic colloquial speech
- The ability to deal with different speeds and accents
- Exposure to high-frequency colloquial phrases and idioms
- Techniques and strategies for participating in a conversation

The five *Colloquial English* lessons focus on an unscripted interview with a person who is an expert in his / her field and a spontaneous conversation between three people answering a question related to the lesson topic. There is also a 'Looking at Language' focus, which looks at a particular aspect of functional language as used by the speaker. On **Online Practice**, students can use the interactive video to record themselves and hear their own voice as part of the conversation. The **Workbook** provides practice of all the language from the Colloquial English lessons.

Revision

- Regular review
- Motivating reference and practice material
- A sense of progress

The higher the level, the harder it is to see your progress. Advanced students need to feel they are increasing their knowledge, improving their skills, and using English more fluently and effectively. After every two Files there is a two-page Revise & Check section. The left-hand page revises the grammar, vocabulary, and pronunciation of each File. The right-hand page provides a series of skills-based challenges, including street interviews, and helps students to measure their progress in terms of competence. These pages are designed to be used flexibly according to the needs of your students.

On **Online Practice**, for each File, there are three **Check your progress** activities. The first is a multiple choice activity for students to test themselves on the Grammar and Vocabulary from the File. The second is a dictation related to the topic and the language of the File for students to practise the new language in context. Finally, there is a **Challenge** activity, which involves a mini-research project based on a topic from the File. After every two Files, the **Workbook** contains a *Can you remember...?* page, which provides a cumulative review of language students have covered in the **Student's Book**.

Course overview

For students

Student's Book

The Student's Book has 10 Files. Each File is organized like this:

A and B lessons

Each File contains two four-page lessons which present and practise **Grammar**, **Vocabulary**, and **Pronunciation** with a balance of reading and listening activities, and lots of opportunities for speaking. Every two Files (starting from File 2), the B lesson ends with a **Video Listening** section. All lessons have clear references to the **Grammar Bank** and **Vocabulary Bank**.

Colloquial English

Every two Files (starting from File 1) there is a two-page lesson where students develop their ability to listen to authentic English and look at elements of natural language. Integrated into every *Colloquial English* lesson is an interview with an expert in his / her field and a conversation.

Revise & Check

Every two Files (starting from File 2) there is a two-page section revising the **Grammar** and **Vocabulary** of each File and practising **Reading** and **Listening**. The *'Can you…?'* section challenges students with engaging reading texts and street interview videos, which give students exposure to real-life English.

The back of the Student's Book

Communication, Writing, Listening, Grammar Bank, Vocabulary Bank, and Sound Bank.

The Student's Book is also available as an eBook.

Online Practice

For students to practise and develop their language and skills or catch up on a class they have missed.

- **Look again:** students can review the language from every lesson.
- **Practice:** students can develop their skills with extra Reading, Writing, Listening, and Speaking practice.
- **Check your progress:** students can test themselves on the main language from the lesson and get instant feedback, and try an extra challenge.
- **Interactive video** to practise the language from the Colloquial English lessons.
- **Sound Bank videos** to learn and practise pronunciation of English sounds.
- **Resources:** All Student's Book audio, video, scripts, wordlists, dyslexia-friendly texts, and CEFR Language Portfolio.

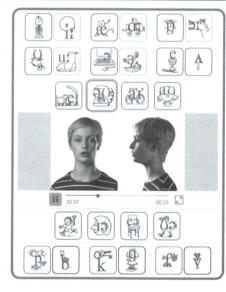

Workbook

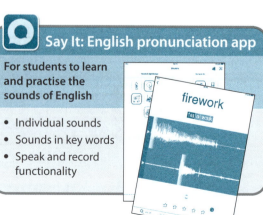

For language practice after class.

- All the Grammar, Vocabulary, and Colloquial English
- Pronunciation exercises with audio. The audio can be accessed on **Online Practice**
  - *Can you remember…?* exercises for students to check their progress
  - Available with or without key

Say It: English pronunciation app

For students to learn and practise the sounds of English

- Individual sounds
- Sounds in key words
- Speak and record functionality

firework

For teachers

Teacher's Guide

Step-by-step procedural notes for all the lessons including:

- an optional 'books-closed' lead-in for every lesson.
- **Extra challenge** suggestions for ways of exploiting the Student's Book material in a more challenging way if you have a stronger class.
- **Extra support** suggestions for ways of adapting activities or exercises to make them work with weaker students.
- **Extra ideas** for optional activities.

All lesson plans include answer keys and audio scripts.

Over 50 pages of photocopiable activities.

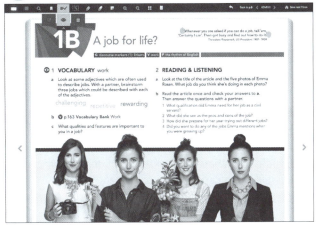

Grammar

see pp. 165–186

- An activity for every Grammar Bank, which can be used in class or for self-study extra practice

Communicative

see pp. 187–213

- Extra speaking practice for every A and B lesson

Vocabulary

see pp. 214–231

- An activity for every Vocabulary Bank, which can be used in class or for self-study extra practice

There is more information on page 164 of this Teacher's Guide about the photocopiable worksheets and tips on how best to use them.

Teacher's Resource Centre

- All the Student's Book audio/video files and scripts
- Detailed lesson plans from the Teacher's Guide
- Answer keys
- All the photocopiable activities from the Teacher's Guide, including customisable versions
- All the Workbook audio files and scripts
- Tests and assessment material, including: an Entry Test; Progress Tests; an End-of-course Test; a Quick Test for every File; and complete test for every File. There are A and B versions of all the main tests and audio files for all the Listening tests
- CEFR documents

 Classroom Presentation Tool

- The complete Student's Book
- Photocopiable activities from the Teacher's Guide
- All class audio and video, with interactive scripts
- Answer keys for exercises in the Student's Book and photocopiable activities
- Dyslexia-friendly texts
- The Workbook is also available as a Classroom Presentation Tool.

Class audio

All the listening materials for the Student's Book can be found on the **Teacher's Resource Centre**, **Classroom Presentation Tool**, **Online Practice**, **Student's eBook**, and the **Class Audio CDs**.

Video

Video listening

- Short documentaries for students at the end of even-numbered B lessons (2B, 4B, 6B, etc.)

Colloquial English

- Interviews and conversations that go with the Colloquial English lessons in the Student's Book

Revise & Check video

- Street interviews filmed in London and Oxford to accompany the Revise & Check section

All the video materials for the Student's Book can be found on the **Teacher's Resource Centre**, **Classroom Presentation Tool**, **Online Practice**, **Student's eBook**, and the **Class DVD**.

G *have*: lexical and grammatical uses
V personality
P using a dictionary

Lesson plan

In the first File, the grammar has a revision element, but groups and presents key structures again in a challenging way. Each lesson has a substantial input of new vocabulary, which reflects the importance of lexis at this level.

This lesson has two main contexts. In the first half of the lesson, the focus is family. The context is an exhibition of period family photos of well-known people. After speculating about the people and their relationship with the other people in the photos, Sts listen to an audio guide to find out more information. This leads to Sts talking about aspects of their own family and then discussing family-related issues in general, where they are encouraged to use more sophisticated expressions for half-agreeing and politely disagreeing. This is followed by a grammar focus on different uses of *have* as a main and auxiliary verb, and expressions and idioms with *have* and *have got*.

In the second half of the lesson, Sts revise previously learned words and phrases to describe personality, and learn some new ones. This is followed by a pronunciation focus on using a dictionary to check pronunciation, so it would be helpful to make sure Sts have paper or online dictionaries with them. In Reading & Speaking, Sts focus on how to look up phrasal verbs and idioms and then they read and answer a quiz assessing personality, based on the well-known Myers-Briggs test.

More materials

For teachers

Photocopiables
Grammar *have*: lexical and grammatical uses *p.167*
Communicative Families *p.193* (instructions *p187*)
Vocabulary Personality *p.218* (instructions *p.214*)

For students
Workbook 1A
Online Practice 1A

OPTIONAL LEAD-IN – THE QUOTE

Write the quote at the top of *p.6* on the board (books closed) and the name of the person who said it, or get Sts to open their books and read it.

Point out that Leo Tolstoy (1828–1910) was a Russian writer. His most famous works are *War and Peace* and *Anna Karenina*.

Ask Sts what they think the quote means and whether they agree with it.

1 LISTENING understanding names and dates

a Focus on the photos and task, and explain / elicit that a *statesman* means an experienced political leader. Put Sts in pairs and get them to answer questions 1–3.

EXTRA IDEA Do the questions as a whole-class activity.

Elicit some opinions, but <u>don't</u> tell Sts if they are correct or not.

b 🔊 **1.2** Tell Sts that they should imagine that they are at the exhibition and listening on headphones to the audio guide, in English, giving information about the photos. Point out the information they need to listen for. Tell Sts not to worry about the spelling of the names.

Play the audio once the whole way through, pausing after each photo is mentioned to give Sts time to make notes.

Get Sts to compare with a partner.

Check answers and write the names on the board to help Sts with **c** later. You could elicit / explain the use of *Junior* (= used after the name of a man who has the same name as his father, to avoid confusion) in the part about JFK.

Finally, find out how many answers Sts got correct in **a**.

EXTRA SUPPORT Read through the script and decide if you need to pre-teach any new lexis before Sts listen.

Photo 1	**Anastasia, daughter of Tsar Nicholas II**, with her **sisters** in **1906**
Photo 2	John **Kennedy**, the **US President**, with his **children** (John Junior and Caroline) in **1963**
Photo 3	Pablo **Picasso**, the **artist**, with his **partner** (Françoise Gilot) and their **son** (Claude) in **1952**
Photo 4	Mohandas **Gandhi**, the **statesman**, with his **wife** (Kasturba) in **1915**
Photo 5	Leo **Tolstoy**, the **writer**, with his **grandchildren** (Ilya and Sonia) in **1907**
Photo 6	Albert **Einstein**, the **scientist**, with his **sister** (Maja) in **1886**

🔊 **1.2**
(script in Student's Book on *p.130*)
1
These four children would never grow old. The photo, taken around nineteen oh six, shows the four daughters of Tsar Nicholas the second of Russia. After the Russian Revolution in nineteen seventeen, they and their parents and brother were arrested and imprisoned in a house in Yekaterinburg. There, on the seventeenth of July nineteen eighteen, they were executed on the orders of Lenin. For many years after their assassination, there were rumours that the youngest daughter, Anastasia, on the right of the photo, had managed to escape. Several women claimed to have been Anastasia; the best-known impostor was Anna Anderson, a woman living in Germany, whose claims, though rejected by most surviving members of the Tsar's family, were widely believed. In nineteen seventy-nine, the bodies of the Tsar and his wife and three of their daughters were discovered near Yekaterinburg, which fuelled the myth that Anastasia had escaped. However, in July two thousand and seven, an amateur historian discovered bones near Yekaterinburg belonging to a boy and a young woman, and in April two thousand and eight, DNA tests proved that they belonged to two children of Nicholas the second, a son and a daughter – Anastasia. As a result, the story of her survival was conclusively disproved.

2

In this rather touching photo, showing his softer family side, US President John F Kennedy is greeted by his children, John Junior and Caroline, on his arrival to spend the weekend with them at their summer home in Massachusetts on the twenty-third of August, nineteen sixty-three. His natural joy at seeing them may well have been intensified on this occasion by the fact that, a few weeks previously, his third child, a son named Patrick, had died at just a few days old. Almost exactly three months later, on the twenty-second of November, Kennedy was assassinated in Dallas. His son John Junior, as so many of this ill-fated family, also died young in a plane crash in nineteen ninety-nine, and Caroline is the only surviving member of the family.

3

Spanish artist Pablo Picasso is seen here with Françoise Gilot and their son, Claude, in around nineteen fifty-two. Françoise met Picasso in nineteen forty-three, when she was twenty-one and he was over forty years older. Although they never married, they spent nearly ten years together and had two children, Claude and Paloma. However, Françoise and Picasso's relationship was not a happy one, and in nineteen sixty-four, eleven years after their separation, she wrote a damning description of him in her book called *Life with Picasso*. Picasso tried to stop its publication, but he failed, and it went on to sell over one million copies in dozens of languages. From then on, Picasso refused to see Claude or Paloma ever again.

4

In May eighteen eighty-three, the thirteen-year-old Mohandas Gandhi was married to fourteen-year-old Kasturba, following the arranged marriage custom of their region at the time. This photo was taken in nineteen fifteen, when Gandhi was beginning his thirty-two-year struggle for Indian independence, and it is the earliest known photo of Gandhi and his wife. In the first years of their marriage, Gandhi is said to have been a very controlling husband, but writing many years later, he described the feelings he felt for Kasturba at the time: 'Even at school I used to think of her, and the thought of nightfall and our subsequent meeting was ever haunting me.' Despite frequently being apart, their shared beliefs in national independence and education, not to mention a deep emotional attachment, held them together, and their marriage lasted for over sixty years.

5

The importance of family to the great Russian writer Leo Tolstoy apparently influenced his work, especially his two most famous novels, *War and Peace* and *Anna Karenina*. This photo, taken in nineteen oh nine, shows him telling a story to two of his grandchildren, Ilya and Sonia. Although his relationship with his children and grandchildren was very close, for most of his marriage he and his wife, Sofia, did not get on. She was strongly opposed to many of his views, especially the idea of giving away his private property, and was also jealous of the attention he gave to his many followers. Shortly after this photo was taken, at the age of eighty-two and after nearly fifty years of marriage, Tolstoy finally made up his mind to separate from her. He left home in the middle of winter, in the dead of night. He took a train south, but when he arrived at Astapovo station a day later, he became ill and died of pneumonia. According to some sources, he had spent the last hours of his life preaching love and non-violence to his fellow passengers on the train.

6

This photo, taken around eighteen eighty-six, is of scientist Albert Einstein with his sister, Maja, as small children. They resembled each other physically, and were extremely close – according to Albert, she was his only friend. After Maja's marriage, she and her husband Paul bought a villa in Italy, near Florence, and Albert frequently visited her. In nineteen thirty-nine, at the outbreak of World War Two, she was forced to leave Italy because she was Jewish. She sought refuge with her beloved brother in the USA, but she had to leave behind her husband, who could not get a visa. Tragically, in nineteen forty-six, just after the war had ended, she had a stroke, and was unable to travel. She never saw her husband again, and Albert cared for her until her death in nineteen fifty-one.

---

c Focus on the task and give Sts time to read questions 1–5. You might want to tell them that there is more than one answer for some of the questions.

Play the audio again the whole way through.

Get Sts to compare with a partner, and then check answers.

1 Tolstoy and his wife (Sofia), Picasso and his partner (Françoise Gilot)
2 Tolstoy and his grandchildren; Gandhi and his wife (Kasturba); Einstein and his sister (Maja)
3 John Kennedy (assassinated); John Junior (plane crash); Anastasia and her sisters (assassinated)
4 Caroline Kennedy
5 Anastasia

d Focus on the phrases from the listening and make sure Sts know what a *collocation* is (= a combination of words that happens very often and more frequently than would happen by chance).

Give Sts time to discuss who each item refers to and what the **bold** collocations mean.

Check answers.

1 Anastasia; **conclusively disproved** = completely and finally proved wrong
2 John Junior / the Kennedy family (The *as* refers to John Junior, the *this* refers to the family); **ill-fated family** = unlucky family
3 Picasso's partner Françoise Gilot, and Picasso; **a damning description** = a very critical and negative description
4 Gandhi and his wife, Kasturba; **shared beliefs** = things that they both believed
5 Tolstoy's wife, Sofia; **strongly opposed** = completely disagreed
6 Tolstoy; **in the dead of night** = in the middle of the night
7 Einstein's sister, Maja; **sought refuge** = she went to the USA to be safe

EXTRA SUPPORT If there's time, you could get Sts to listen again with the script on *p.130*, so they can see exactly what they understood / didn't understand. Translate / Explain any new words or phrases.

e Focus on the question and make sure Sts understand *draws you in* (= attracted to).

Do this as a whole-class activity, or put Sts in pairs and then get some feedback. You could tell the class which photo draws you in the most and why.

EXTRA IDEA Get Sts to bring in some old family photos to show each other and explain who the people are, with a bit of background detail.

2 SPEAKING

a Put Sts in small groups of three or four and focus on the task. Make sure they understand *framed or displayed* in the first set of questions. Highlight the pronunciation of *close* /kləʊs/ as an adjective in the third set of questions and compare with the pronunciation of *close* /kləʊz/ as a verb. A *close family / friend* suggests intimacy and trust as well as enjoyment in each other's company.

! If you think your Sts might not want to answer who they don't get on with, you could tell them they can politely refuse to answer a question by saying *I'd rather not talk about that.*

Give Sts time to answer the questions.

Monitor and help with any words or phrases Sts need.

Get some feedback for each set of questions.

b Focus on the statements and make sure Sts understand them, e.g. that *the only person who should be allowed to criticize your family is you* = it's OK for you to criticize your own family, but other people shouldn't do so in front of you. Remind Sts of the meaning of *dedicated* (= working hard at sth because it is very important to you) and *inevitably* (= is certain to happen).

Give Sts time to think about each statement as well as reasons or examples to back their opinion.

❗ Don't start the discussion yet – this will be done in **e**.

EXTRA SUPPORT Get Sts to mark each one with either *A* (agree), *HA* (half agree), or *D* (disagree), depending on their opinion. They should also think of reasons and examples to support their opinion.

EXTRA IDEA If you want to expand the activity, or think your Sts might not want to discuss one or more of the statements, you could provide them with some alternatives, e.g.:

It's better to be an only child than to have brothers and sisters.

You should always defend members of your family against the police, even if they have done something wrong.

Mothers and daughters have a more difficult relationship than mothers and sons.

If a couple don't get on, it's better for their children for them to divorce than to stay together but constantly argue.

If we want to save the planet, no couples should be allowed to have more than two children.

Your 'family' are the people who care about you, not necessarily your blood relatives.

Your parents brought you up, so it's your responsibility to take care of them when they're old.

c 🔊 **1.3** Focus on the **Half-agreeing and politely disagreeing** box and go through it with the class.

Now focus on the task and tell Sts to concentrate on the polite intonation in the expressions in the box.

Play the audio once the whole way through.

🔊 **1.3**

1
A I absolutely don't think that parents should try to be their children's friends. Friends and parents are completely different things.
B I see what you mean, but I think children should have a more friendly relationship with their parents than my generation did.

2
A I think people who are very dedicated to their work rarely manage to have a happy family life. I think they can sometimes be quite selfish and they don't have enough time for their family.
B I agree up to a point, but I do think there are exceptions, for example…

3
A I think it's true that young children should be looked after by one or other of their parents.
B I agree in theory, but what happens if they can't afford to live on one salary?

4
A I think it's true that marrying very young almost inevitably ends badly. I think marrying in your thirties is probably the best age.
B I'm not sure I agree with you. My parents got married when my dad was twenty and my mum was eighteen, and they're still happily married.

5
A I think you have to love your family, but you don't have to like them. I love my sister, but she drives me mad most of the time.
B I don't really think that's right. It's impossible to love somebody that you don't like.

d 🔊 **1.4** Play the audio again, pausing after each expression for Sts to repeat, copying the rhythm and intonation.

🔊 **1.4**
See expressions in the information box in Student's Book on *p.7*

Finally, you could repeat the activity, eliciting responses from individual Sts.

EXTRA SUPPORT Give Sts time to practise saying the expressions in pairs.

e Focus on the task. Sts should work in the same groups as they were in for **a**. You might want to set a time limit for each discussion, e.g. two or three minutes. Sts take turns in their groups to talk about the statements in **b**. The student starting the discussion should give their opinion on the topic and try to give clear reasons and examples to justify their point of view. Then the rest of the group give their opinion and discuss the statement. If you are timing the discussions, say *Next!* when the time limit is up, and another student starts the next discussion in their group, etc. Remind Sts before they start to try to use the expressions for half-agreeing and politely disagreeing during the discussions.

Monitor and help with any words or phrases Sts need.

Get some feedback from various groups. If there's time, you could choose one statement and do it as a whole-class activity.

3 GRAMMAR *have*: lexical and grammatical uses

a Focus on the task and highlight that groups 1–4 all contain sentences with different uses of *have*. Make sure Sts understand that they need to answer the two bulleted questions for each group. Elicit / Explain the meaning of *register* (= the level of formality or informality of a word in a piece of writing or speech).

Put Sts in pairs and give them time to discuss the questions.

Check answers.

1 Yes, all three options are possible.
There is no difference in meaning or register between *haven't got* and *don't have*, but in *haven't got, have* = auxiliary; and in *don't have, have* = main verb.
The use of *haven't* on its own, without *got*, is possible, but not very common, except in a few fixed expressions like *I haven't time* and *I haven't a clue*.
2 Yes, both options are possible.
There is a difference in meaning. *I've been making* emphasizes the duration of the action, and it may not be completed, i.e. there may still be food being made. *I've made* emphasizes that the action is completed.
In both cases *'ve* = auxiliary verb.
3 Yes, both options are possible. There is no difference in meaning; however, *have we got to* is less common in American English.
Have we got to is more informal.
Have we got to = auxiliary verb; *Do we have to* = main verb.

4 Yes, both options are possible. There is a difference in meaning:
I've had some lovely photos taken = a photographer has done it for me
I've taken some lovely photos = I've taken them myself
In *I've had … taken*, *I've* = auxiliary and *had* = main verb; and in *I've taken*, *have* is an auxiliary verb.

b Tell Sts to go to **Grammar Bank 1A** on *p.142*. If your Sts have not used the *English File* series before, explain that all the grammar rules and exercises are in this part of the book.

Grammar notes

The verb *have*, because of its different meanings and uses, often causes problems, even for advanced Sts. Here the uses and meanings are pulled together and revised.

When explaining that *have* in its meaning of *possess* is a stative verb, you may want to go into the concept of stative and dynamic verbs in more detail. Stative verbs refer to states or conditions which continue over a period of time, not actions, and are not normally used in continuous tenses (e.g. *We have a new car* NOT ~~We are having a new car~~). Dynamic verbs refer to actions and are commonly used in continuous tenses.

Sts sometimes try to manipulate *have got* in the same way as *have*. It may help to point out that although the meaning of *have got* is present, the form is present perfect, which is why it is *Have you got…?* NOT ~~Do you have got…?~~

Have to and *must* for obligation are gone into in more detail in **7A**, and *get* as an alternative to *have* in *have sth done* is studied in **3A**.

Focus on the example sentences for **different uses of *have* as a main verb** and go through the rules with the class.

Repeat for **different uses of *have* as an auxiliary verb** and **have or *have got* in idioms and expressions**.

Focus on the exercises and get Sts to do them individually or in pairs. If they do them individually, get them to compare with a partner.

Check answers, getting Sts to read the full sentences.

a
1 ✓
2 ✓
3 ✗ Does your husband have to work tomorrow? / Has your husband got to work tomorrow?
4 ✓
5 ✗ How long have you had your flat in London?
6 ✓
7 ✗ My parents had a lot of problems with my sister when she was a teenager.
8 ✗ I haven't had a holiday for 18 months.
9 ✓

b
1 She **doesn't have / hasn't got** brothers or sisters.
2 We used **to have a family photograph taken** every year.
3 All **drivers have to have** car insurance.
4 He **hasn't seen him for** two years.
5 He **doesn't have / hasn't got the right qualifications** for this job.
6 We **don't have to / haven't got to do it now**; we can do it later.

7 The sea was amazingly clear and warm – we **had a swim** every morning.
8 How long **have you been getting on** badly?
9 I need **to have the central heating fixed**.

c
1 him   2 laugh   3 on   4 got   5 had

Tell Sts to go back to the main lesson **1A**.

EXTRA SUPPORT If you think Sts need more practice, you may want to give them the **Grammar** photocopiable activity at this point.

c This is an oral grammar activation exercise. Demonstrate the activity by telling Sts if the first sentence is true for you and why (not).

Now put Sts in pairs and get them to go through each statement one by one and take turns to say if they are true for them or not, and why.

Monitor and help.

Get some feedback by asking some Sts whether a sentence was true for them or not.

4 VOCABULARY personality

a Focus on the task and make sure Sts know what all the adjectives mean and what they have to do. You might want to check that Sts know what a *partner* is in this context (= the person that you are married to or having a sexual relationship with).

EXTRA SUPPORT Go through the list of adjectives as a whole class and elicit / explain their meaning and whether they are positive or negative traits. Also elicit or model their pronunciation.

b Put Sts in pairs to compare what they underlined and circled in **a**. Tell them to also discuss the question, reminding them that the word *partner* here means romantic partner and not class partner.

Elicit some answers from the class for **a**. If you have any parents in the class, ask them their opinion. You could also tell the class what you think.

Finally, ask Sts which adjectives they thought might make someone a difficult parent or partner, and why. Again, if you have any parents in the class, you could ask them if they agree.

c Tell Sts to go to **Vocabulary Bank Personality** on *p.162*.

Vocabulary notes

Sts at this level may think they have 'done' adjectives of personality before. This is almost certainly true, in that they will have learned one or two groups; however, there are a huge number of adjectives and idioms used in English to describe personality, and here Sts will expand their vocabulary, enabling them to use a wider range of words and expressions, and improve their ability to describe people.

Useful phrases when describing personality

You might want to tell Sts that we often use *a bit / a bit of a* before negative adjectives or idioms to 'soften' them, e.g. *She can be a bit sarcastic. He's a bit of a pain in the neck*. We also often use *not very* + positive adjectives, rather than using negative ones, e.g. *He's not very bright* rather than *He's stupid*.

Focus on **1 Adjectives** and get Sts to do **a** individually or in pairs.

🔊 **1.5** Now focus on **b**. Play the audio for Sts to listen and check.

Check answers.

🔊 **1.5**
Personality
1 Adjectives
1 resourceful
2 thorough
3 bright
4 straightforward
5 determined
6 self-sufficient
7 sympathetic
8 conscientious
9 gentle
10 steady
11 spontaneous
12 sarcastic

Now either use the audio to drill the pronunciation of the adjectives, or model and drill them yourself. Give further practice of any words your Sts find difficult to pronounce.

Now focus on the **False friends** box and go through it with the class. You may want to ask Sts if they know any other adjectives of personality which are false friends, e.g. *sensible* for Spanish and French speakers.

Focus on **2 Useful phrases when describing personality** and get Sts to do **a** individually or in pairs.

🔊 **1.6** Now focus on **b**. Play the audio for Sts to listen and check.

Check answers. You could get Sts to read the full sentence and explain the meaning of the phrase.

🔊 **1.6**
2 Useful phrases when describing personality
1 My father tends to avoid conflict – he never argues with my mother, he just leaves the room.
2 **On the surface** he seems self-confident, but **deep down** he's quite insecure.
3 I worry about my grandmother. She's **a bit too** trusting, so it's easy for people to take advantage of her.
4 **On the whole** he's pretty laid-back, though he can sometimes get very stressed about work.
5 She's **a bit of a** control freak – she always needs to organize everything and everybody.
6 He **comes across** as quite sarcastic, but in fact he's really friendly.

Highlight any words your Sts may have problems pronouncing correctly, e.g. *surface* /ˈsɜːfɪs/.

Now focus on **3 Idioms** and make sure Sts know what an *idiom* is (= a group of words whose meaning is different from the meanings of the individual words).

Get Sts to do **a** individually or in pairs.

🔊 **1.7** Now focus on **b**. Play the audio for Sts to listen and check.

Check answers and make sure Sts are clear about the meaning of the idioms.

🔊 **1.7**
3 Idioms
1 B
My dad's got a heart of gold. He's incredibly kind to everyone he meets.
2 I
My brother-in-law is very down to earth. He's very sensible and practical.
3 A
My boss is a bit of a cold fish. She's unfriendly and she never shows her emotions.
4 C
My brother's a real pain in the neck. He's so annoying – he's always taking my things.
5 E
My mum's a soft touch. I can always persuade her to give me extra pocket money.
6 H
My uncle has a very quick temper. He gets angry very easily.
7 J
I know I shouldn't criticize your family, but your sister is really full of herself. She thinks she's the most important member of the family.
8 G
He comes across as aggressive, but in fact he wouldn't hurt a fly. He's the gentlest person I know.
9 F
My brother never lifts a finger around the house. He expects the rest of us to do everything.
10 D
My cousin's always the life and soul of the party. She's great at telling jokes and making people laugh.

Finally, focus on **Activation** and give Sts time to think of their answers.

EXTRA SUPPORT Demonstrate the activity to show Sts what they need to do.

Put Sts in pairs and get them to tell their partner about the people they have thought of.

Get some feedback from the class.

Tell Sts to go back to the main lesson **1A**.

EXTRA IDEA Get Sts to play *The Describing Game* with words and phrases from the **Vocabulary Bank**.

Put Sts in pairs, **A** and **B**, and tell Sts **B** to turn their chairs round or cover their eyes so that they can't see the board.

Write six adjectives or idioms on the board. Then tell Sts **A** they have one minute to define the words to **B**, without using any part of the word or phrase itself.

When one minute is up, see how many pairs managed to communicate all six items.

Now get Sts to swap roles and repeat with six more adjectives or idioms.

EXTRA SUPPORT If you think Sts need more practice, you may want to give them the **Vocabulary** photocopiable activity at this point.

5 PRONUNCIATION using a dictionary

Pronunciation notes

At this level, Sts usually have a well-developed ability to predict the pronunciation of new words from their spelling, and it is important to encourage them to do this every time they learn a new word. However, it is also important for Sts to be able to use a dictionary to check pronunciation in the case of words which have a very irregular sound–spelling relationship. Even if Sts are using an online dictionary or app and can hear the pronunciation, the phonetics will help them to distinguish between individual sounds.

Sts who have previously used *English File* will be familiar with the 'sound pictures' used throughout the course to provide them with a clear model of all the sounds of English and to familiarize them with the phonetic symbol for that sound. If your Sts have not used *English File* before, this would be a good moment to introduce them to the **Sound Bank** on *pp.174–175*, which provides common sound–spelling rules. Highlight that this resource will help them to check the pronunciation of new words in the dictionary, by using the phonetic transcription, and predict pronunciation from spelling. It will also help them to 'fine-tune' their own pronunciation. There are also Sound Bank videos on *Online Practice*.

a 🔊 **1.8** Do this as a whole-class activity, or put Sts in pairs and then elicit answers. You might want to explain that *NAmE* means *North American English*.

Play the audio for Sts to listen and check.

Check answers.

dete<u>r</u>mined
In American English the *r* is pronounced.

🔊 **1.8**
British English: determined
American English: determined

---

b Focus on the task, and if your Sts haven't used *English File* before, point out how the eight adjectives have been divided into syllables.

Give Sts time to underline the stressed syllable in each adjective. Remind them that this kind of exercise is easier if they say the words aloud to themselves. <u>Don't</u> check answers at this stage.

EXTRA SUPPORT Get Sts to do **b** and **c** in pairs. You could check answers to **b** first to help Sts with **c**. Alternatively, you could get Sts to work individually and use dictionaries to look up each adjective and find out which syllable is stressed.

c Now tell Sts to look at the syllables they underlined in the adjectives in **b** and match the vowels to the sound pictures.

Get Sts to compare answers to both **b** and **c** with a partner.

EXTRA SUPPORT Focus on each sound picture and elicit the word and sound.

d 🔊 **1.9** Play the audio for Sts to listen and check their answers to **b** and **c**.

Check answers by eliciting the pronunciation of the adjectives one by one and making sure Sts remember what they mean.

1 consci<u>e</u>ntious /e/ egg
2 re<u>sou</u>rceful /ɔː/ horse
3 sar<u>ca</u>stic /æ/ cat
4 <u>tho</u>rough /ʌ/ up
5 spont<u>a</u>neous /eɪ/ train
6 straight<u>fo</u>rward /ɔː/ horse
7 <u>stea</u>dy /e/ egg
8 self-su<u>ffi</u>cient /ɪ/ fish

🔊 **1.9**
See words in Student's Book on *p.8*

Now play the audio again, pausing after each item for Sts to listen and repeat the adjective and sound.

Then repeat the activity, eliciting responses from individual Sts.

EXTRA CHALLENGE Ask Sts which words have an extra *r* sound in American English (*resourceful, straightforward*).

EXTRA SUPPORT If these sounds are difficult for your Sts, it will help to show them the mouth position. You could model this yourself or use the Sound Bank videos on the *Teacher's Resource Centre*.

e Focus on the task and then put Sts in pairs and get them to complete the task.

Check answers, getting Sts to spell each adjective. Elicit or model their pronunciation.

1 anxious = feeling worried or nervous
2 lively = full of life and energy
3 nosy = too interested in things that don't concern you, especially other people's affairs
4 sociable = enjoying spending time with other people
5 stingy = not generous, especially with money

f Do this as a whole-class activity.

6 READING & SPEAKING interpreting a questionnaire

a You could do this as a whole-class activity, or put Sts in pairs or small groups.

If Sts worked in pairs or small groups, get some feedback for each way of predicting personality types. You could also ask Sts if they know any other ways of predicting personality types.

b Focus on the task and make sure Sts understand what they have to do. You could ask Sts if they know the artist, and elicit / tell them that it is Salvador Dalí (1904–1989) – a surrealist painter.

Give Sts exactly 30 seconds to write what they see.

LANGUAGE IN CONTEXT

c This is the first of a regular exercise type focusing on useful lexical items that occur in reading and listening texts. Focus on the instructions.

Put Sts in pairs and get them to read the *What's your personality?* questionnaire. As they go through it, they should try to work out the meaning of the highlighted phrasal verbs and idioms.

! Make sure Sts don't actually do the questionnaire (i.e. answer the questions) or use dictionaries.

EXTRA SUPPORT Before Sts read the questionnaire the first time, check whether you need to pre-teach any other vocabulary, but not the highlighted phrasal verbs and idioms.

d Focus on the **Looking up phrasal verbs and idioms in a dictionary** box and go through it with the class. Phrasal verbs are always shown after the main verb, e.g. *get off* and *get over* would be under *get*. The rule of thumb regarding looking up idioms in the dictionary is to look under the first 'full' word (e.g. verb, noun, adverb, adjective, etc.) and if it isn't there, then try under the other word(s). Phrasal verbs and idioms are not listed under prepositions and articles in a dictionary. You might want to point out to Sts that *English File* mentions phrasal verbs with an object, but their dictionary might call these *transitive phrasal verbs*.

Highlight that if it is an idiom involving a very common verb, e.g. *get*, then you may need to look under the next 'full' word, e.g. *get into trouble* would be under *trouble*. However, a phrasal verb like *get on with sb* would be under *get*.

Highlight also that when Sts look up an idiom, it is a good idea to copy down, as well as the definition, a clear example if one is given.

This would be a good moment to make sure that your Sts have a good monolingual Advanced dictionary, such as the *Oxford Advanced Learner's Dictionary*, as well as a good bilingual dictionary.

Now give Sts time to look up the highlighted phrasal verbs and idioms, and check whether they worked them out correctly in **c**.

Check answers.

puts things off = delays things until a later time or date
to the letter = paying attention to every detail
get stuck = be unable to continue
put together = to make or prepare sth by fitting or collecting parts or information together
catches your eye = attracts your attention
go round = follow a route
head-on = in a direct way
your gut feeling = your natural feelings that make you react in a particular way
a white lie = a harmless or small lie, especially one that you tell to avoid hurting sb
carry on = continue

Deal with any vocabulary problems that arose.

e Now get Sts to do the personality test individually.

EXTRA IDEA You could get Sts to compare answers and give reasons or examples to support their choices.

f Focus on the task and the eight types (*planner*, *spontaneous*, etc.).

Now give Sts time to work out which type they are for each section of the questionnaire.

g Tell Sts to go to **Communication What's your personality?** on *p.106*. Here they follow the instructions to identify their overall personality (*Realist, Supervisor*, etc.). Finally, they read the description of their personality.

Get Sts to ask their partner for his / her personality and read their description, too. Sts then tell each other how accurate they think the description is.

Get some feedback from the class. With a show of hands, you could find out how many Sts think their description is accurate.

1B A job for life?

G discourse markers (1): linkers
V work
P the rhythm of English

Lesson plan

The topic of this lesson is work.

In the first half of the lesson, Sts expand their lexis related to the world of work. Sts then read an article and listen to an interview about a woman who decided to try 25 different jobs before she turned 25. Pronunciation focuses on the rhythm of English. The first half ends with a Speaking activity in which Sts talk about two people they know, one who likes and one who dislikes their job. The context provides an opportunity for Sts to discuss how they would feel about doing all the different jobs their classmates have mentioned.

In the second half of the lesson, Sts read three articles taken from a weekly series in *The Guardian* newspaper, where ordinary people write a short paragraph showing how they really feel about their jobs. Extracts from more articles provide a lead-in to the grammar focus, which is on linkers expressing reason, result, purpose, and contrast. Finally, Sts write a covering letter to accompany a job application.

More materials

For teachers

Photocopiables

Grammar discourse markers (1): linkers *p.168*

Communicative Have I got the job? *p.194* (instructions *p.187*)

Vocabulary Work *p.219* (instructions *p.214*)

For students

Workbook 1B

Online Practice 1B

OPTIONAL LEAD-IN – THE QUOTE Write the quote at the top of *p.10* on the board (books closed) and the name of the person who said it, or get Sts to open their books and read it.

Point out that Theodore Roosevelt (1858–1919) was the President of the United States from 1901 to 1909. He is often ranked among the top five US presidents, and many people consider him to have established America's place in the modern world.

Get Sts to discuss with a partner whether they agree with the quote or not, and why.

Open the discussion to the whole class and elicit ideas and opinions.

1 VOCABULARY work

a Focus on the task and make sure Sts know the meaning of the three adjectives:

- a *challenging* job tests your abilities and energies in a positive way
- *repetitive* = saying or doing the same thing many times, so that it becomes boring

- *rewarding* is a synonym of *satisfying*, but with an even more positive meaning. It suggests the work is hard but worth it. Point out that the adjective comes from the noun *reward* (= sth you are given for doing sth good, working hard, etc.).

   Put Sts in pairs and give them time to think of three jobs for each of the adjectives.

   Elicit some answers.

Possible answers

challenging – journalist, firefighter, police officer

repetitive – supermarket checkout assistant, factory worker, cleaner

rewarding – teacher, doctor, musician

b Tell Sts to go to **Vocabulary Bank Work** on *p.163*.

Vocabulary notes

Adjectives

Highlight:

- the difference between a *challenging* job and a *demanding* job (which has more negative connotations).
- that *monotonous* and *repetitive* are very similar in meaning, but *monotonous* stresses that a job is both repetitive and boring.
- that *tedious* and *boring* have the same meaning.

Collocations

Highlight that *career* refers to the series of jobs that a person has in a particular area of work, usually involving more responsibility as time passes, e.g. *a career in journalism*. It can also refer to the period of your life that you spend working, e.g. *He had a long career as a tennis player*. A *career ladder* is a series of stages by which you can make progress in your career. Other collocations with *ladder* include *social ladder* and *property ladder*.

Highlight the meaning of:

- *maternity leave* (= period of time when a woman temporarily leaves her job to have a baby – *paternity leave* is for a father).
- *compassionate leave* (= time that you are allowed to be away from work because sb in your family is ill or has died).
- *freelance* (= earning money by selling your work or services to several different organizations, rather than being employed by one particular organization).
- *a temporary contract* (= a contract for a job you may do only for a few months) and *a part-time contract* (= a contract for a job where you only work some hours a day, or some days a week).
- *fixed-term* (= a fixed-term contract is one that only lasts for an agreed period of time)
- *zero hours* (= in a zero-hours contract, the employer is not obliged to provide any minimum working hours, and the worker is not obliged to accept any work offered).

The same or different?

Tell Sts when they read a formal text, they will find words and phrases which the dictionary will list as formal. When they record them, they should make a note of the neutral / informal alternative, e.g. *resign* (neutral), *quit* (informal).

Highlight that:
- *be sacked* is more informal than *be fired*.
- *hire* is more common in American English.
- *perks* is more informal than *benefits*. You might also want to point out that *perks* is generally used in the plural.

Focus on **1 Adjectives** and get Sts to do **a** individually or in pairs.

▶ **1.10** Now focus on **b**. Play the audio for Sts to listen and check.

Check answers and make sure Sts understand the explanations in A–H.

▶ **1.10**
Work
1 Adjectives
1 C
  My job as a divorce lawyer is very challenging. It tests my abilities in a way that keeps me interested.
2 A
  Working as a checkout assistant can be a bit monotonous and repetitive. I have to do exactly the same thing every day.
3 F
  I'm a primary school teacher. I find working with children very rewarding. It makes me happy because it's useful and important.
4 B
  I work in a small design company and my job's really motivating. I never mind having to work overtime.
5 H
  Being a surgeon is very demanding. It's very high pressure and you have to work long hours.
6 E
  I always wanted an exciting job, but sadly mine is incredibly tedious. It's really boring and it makes me feel impatient all the time.
7 G
  He's in a dead-end job in the local factory. The wages are low and there's no hope of promotion.
8 D
  She's got a very high-powered job in finance. It's important and comes with a lot of responsibility.

Highlight any words your Sts may have problems pronouncing correctly, e.g. *tedious* /ˈtiːdiəs/.

Focus on **Activation** and give Sts time to think of their answers.

Put Sts in pairs and get them to tell their partner the jobs they have thought of for each adjective.

Elicit a few jobs for each adjective.

EXTRA SUPPORT Do the **Activation** exercise as a whole-class activity.

Focus on **2 Collocations** and remind Sts that collocations are words that often go together. You could remind them of the collocation *rough itinerary*, which they saw in the personality quiz in the previous lesson. Explain that these two words combine to provide natural-sounding speech and writing – we wouldn't say *approximate itinerary*.

Get Sts to do **a** individually or in pairs.

▶ **1.11** Now focus on **b**. Play the audio for Sts to listen and check.

Check answers by getting Sts to read the full sentences.

▶ **1.11**
2 Collocations
1 I'm hoping it'll be a good **career move** to go from publishing to advertising.
2 I've been unemployed for six months now, so I spend most of my time **job-hunting**.
3 My brother works as an **events manager**, organizing conferences.
4 I left school at fifteen, so I had to look for a job that didn't require any **academic qualifications**.
5 My problem is that all the jobs I want to apply for ask for some **work experience**, and as I've just finished university, I don't have any.
6 I'm a junior doctor, and if I want to move up the **career ladder**, I need to work in several different hospitals and departments.
7 In Britain, people who work for government departments are called **civil servants**.
8 In some careers, people with very good qualifications are put onto a **fast track**, so they get promoted more quickly.

Tell Sts that noticing and recording words that go together will improve the accuracy and fluency of their speaking and writing.

Focus on the instructions for **c** and get Sts to do it individually or in pairs.

Check answers and elicit the meaning of each collocation.

1 leave   2 contract

Focus on **3 The same or different?** and get Sts to do **a** individually or in pairs.

▶ **1.12** Now focus on **b**. Play the audio for Sts to listen and check, and to check the pronunciation.

Check answers and get Sts to explain the ones that are different.

1 *Colleagues* and *co-workers* mean the same thing, but *co-workers* is American English.
2 *Quit* and *resign* mean the same thing, but *quit* is more informal.
3 *Staff* and *workforce* mean the same thing.
4 *Laid off* and *made redundant* mean the same thing, but *laid off* can be temporary and *made redundant* can't.
5 *Out of work* and *off work* are different. *Out of work* means you don't have a job or have lost the one you had, and *off work* means a temporary absence because of illness or if you are having a baby.
6 *Be sacked* and *be fired* mean the same thing, but *be fired* is more common in American English.
7 *Get promoted* and *get a pay rise* are different. *Get promoted* means get a better job in the same company. *Get a pay rise* means get an increase in salary.
8 *Skills* and *qualifications* are different. *Skills* are particular abilities; *qualifications* are exams you have passed or studies you have completed.
9 *Hire* and *employ* mean the same thing, but *to hire somebody* can be for the first time or temporary, for example *to hire a detective*, *to hire a lawyer*.
10 *Perks* and *benefits* mean the same thing, but *perks* is more informal.

▶ **1.12**
3 The same or different?
1 *Colleagues* and *co-workers* mean the same thing.
2 *Quit* and *resign* mean the same thing.

3 *Staff* and *workforce* mean the same thing.

4 *Laid off* and *made redundant* mean the same thing.

5 *Out of work* and *off work* are different. *Out of work* means unemployed. *Off work* means away from work because of illness or another reason.

6 *Was sacked* and *was fired* mean the same thing.

7 *Get promoted* and *get a pay rise* are different. *Get promoted* means get a better job in the same company. *Get a pay rise* means get an increase in salary.

8 *Skills* and *qualifications* are different. *Skills* are particular abilities, for example, IT skills. *Qualifications* are exams you have passed or studies you have completed.

9 *Hire* and *employ* mean the same thing.

10 *Perks* and *benefits* mean the same thing.

Tell Sts to go back to the main lesson **1B**.

EXTRA SUPPORT If you think Sts need more practice, you may want to give them the **Vocabulary** photocopiable activity at this point

c This is a quick revision exercise on the lexis Sts have just studied in the **Vocabulary Bank**. Do this as a whole-class activity, or put Sts in pairs and then get some feedback.

2 READING & LISTENING

a Do this as a whole-class activity. Tell Sts to look at what Emma is wearing and holding in each photo. Elicit the jobs, but <u>don't</u> tell Sts if they are correct or not.

b Focus on the task, making sure Sts know the meaning of *pros and cons*.

Now focus on the **Glossary** and go though it with the class. You might want to tell Sts that the definition of *millennial* might be different in their country. You could also tell them that *bucket list* comes from the expression *to kick the bucket*, which means *to die*.

Put Sts in pairs and give them time to read the article.

When they have finished, tell them to check their answers to **a** and discuss questions 1–4 with their partner.

Check answers and elicit opinions for question 4.

EXTRA SUPPORT Before Sts read the article the first time, check whether you need to pre-teach any vocabulary.

The jobs Emma is doing in the photos are wedding photographer, archaeologist, landscape gardener, journalist, and TV producer.

1 A degree

2 pros: a job for life
cons: commuting, sitting in an office all day, she didn't see the point of the job

3 She wrote a bucket list of jobs she wanted to try; she organized two-week placements; she saved money.

Deal with any other new vocabulary. Elicit or model and drill the pronunciation of any tricky words.

c 🔊 **1.13** Focus on the task and go through the **Glossary** with the class.

Go through the jobs Emma mentions in the last paragraph of the article and elicit / explain what each one is.

Elicit from the class which jobs they think she liked the most and the least, and why. Tell Sts that this is an unscripted interview with Emma, and that she speaks quite fast, though very clearly.

Play **Part 1** of the audio for Sts to listen and check.

Check answers.

EXTRA SUPPORT Read through the script and decide if you need to pre-teach any new lexis before Sts listen.

She liked alpaca farming the most and publishing the least.

🔊 **1.13**

(script in Student's Book on *p.130*)

I = interviewer, E = Emma

Part 1

I So first of all, Emma, how did you actually manage to get the jobs?

E Well, I got the jobs through a mixture of networking and cold-calling. So, applying to different organizations, finding email addresses online, writing cover letters, explaining my project and attaching my CV. Networking was a big part of it, too. So, speaking to someone, aware that they themselves might not work in that area, but they might know someone who does.

I Was two weeks long enough to get a feel for what doing the jobs more long-term would be like?

E For me it was, yes, because it was just meant to be enough to get a sense of whether this is something I want to learn more about or whether it's something that's actually not for me. And I found I was very quickly able to decide whether I wanted to learn more or, or actually maybe not so much. It was just enough to get a flavour of it.

I Was it an issue that you had none of the qualifications for some of the jobs?

E Well, no, because I was doing work shadowing, which is more about following a professional around, shadowing their daily lives, rather than having my own set work and projects to do. I wasn't expected to have qualifications or to lead my own work. And this is the case quite often with young people, who go in and just do some work shadowing, and they just don't have the degree or several years' experience that you would need to do professional-level work. It's just to find out if that's the sort of job they would like to do before they then go and do the qualifications and get the experience.

I Which job did you enjoy most?

E One thing that I enjoyed most was alpaca farming in Cornwall, which is in southern England. And I enjoyed it most because it was one of the most – one of the jobs that challenged all of my assumptions about what being a farmer in the twenty-first century and earning a sustainable living was like. The first half of each day was traditional farming jobs, so feeding, looking after the animals. But the second half of the day, the farmer was an entrepreneur: she would take her alpacas, shear them, make the wool spun, make the, make the wool into high-end luxury children's clothes that she then sold to department stores across the country. And this was a placement that broke down all of my presumptions and preconceptions about what a job was like.

I Wow. Were there any jobs that you completely ruled out?

E So one that I didn't get on quite so well with was publishing, because I'm very dyslexic, and so for me, copy editing – so, spotting typos and grammar mistakes in long pieces of text – I find very challenging. It's not one of my strengths, which in publishing, as an editor, is one of the big things that you have to do.

d Focus on the task and the five points, making sure Sts understand number 4. Put Sts in pairs to see what they can remember about 1–5.

Play the audio again for Sts to listen and complete any missing information.

Get Sts to compare with their partner, and then check answers.

1 By networking and cold-calling – making applications, writing letters and emails, sending her CV, speaking to people

2 She got a flavour of the jobs; she found out whether she wanted to learn more about them or not.

3 Because she wasn't actually working, she was shadowing people.
4 Being a farmer, i.e. feeding, looking after, and shearing alpacas; also being an entrepreneur, making children's clothes from the wool and selling them to shops
5 Finding spelling and grammar mistakes in texts

EXTRA SUPPORT If there's time, you could get Sts to listen again with the script on *p.130*, so they can see exactly what they understood / didn't understand. Translate / Explain any new words or phrases.

e ◉ **1.14** Tell Sts they are now going to listen to **Part 2** of the interview and for questions 1–5, they must choose the best option, *a*, *b*, or *c*.

Give Sts time to read 1–5.

Now play **Part 2** of the audio for Sts to listen and complete the task.

Get Sts to compare with a partner, and then play again if necessary.

Check answers.

EXTRA SUPPORT Read through the script and decide if you need to pre-teach any new lexis before Sts listen.

1 c 2 b 3 a 4 c 5 b

◉ **1.14**
(script in Student's Book on *pp.130–131*)
Part 2
I What did you learn about yourself during this process?
E I learned that there's not just one job that is right for me. I went into the experience thinking I will do twenty-five and I will figure out which is my dream job, and that's what I'll go away and do. But what I found out was that that's not necessarily true at all. I discovered the concept of portfolio careers, which is the idea of having multiple, part-time, short-term, freelance contract jobs that make up the equivalent of one permanent role.
I Do you think young people nowadays have to be prepared to do many different jobs? That the whole idea of going into one career for life doesn't exist any more?
E Absolutely! I would completely agree with that: I think the idea of one permanent nine-to-five job is, if not dead yet, it will be in the next twenty years. Young people today will have, on average, five different career changes – not job changes, career changes – over the course of their lives, and to do that, they need to be able to continuously upskill and be able to get on with different people. So I think it's people skills, almost more so than technical skills, that will get us through the longevity of our careers. And bear in mind that people of our age are going to be working well into their seventies; our careers are likely to be ultra-marathons, so we have to like what it is that we're doing.
I And how do you think we can teach 'people skills'?
E So, personally, I think our education system, both in terms of secondary school, college, and, and university, needs to be much more focused on skills rather than technical subject-based learning. We need to be teaching young people how to network, for example, which is one of the absolute core skills to progress yourself in your career: it's learning how to walk into a room of people you don't know and to find people that are mutually beneficial that you can develop relationships with.
I So, what are you doing now?
E So what I came away with was several different jobs that I ended up doing. So, I now work as a public speaker, as a writer doing bits of journalism, and as a speech writer as well – so altogether they make up the equivalent of one full-time job.
I Do you think your future career might take off in a completely different direction?
E I very much expect it to. So, one of the main things that I also learnt from doing the project was that there are different

careers that are appropriate for different stages of your life. As you get older, you have different priorities, different financial commitments, different stages of your personal life, and that means that you have different jobs that are relevant at different stages of life. So whilst I adored farming and it was one of my favourite placements, I don't think it is right for me, in my twenties, living in a very urban city like London, but me in my forties perhaps with a family, I might love to move out to the countryside and start a small, a smallholding farm as part of several other elements of a career!
I Well, thank you, Emma, so much for talking to us today.

EXTRA SUPPORT If there's time, you could get Sts to listen again with the script on *pp.130–131*, so they can see exactly what they understood / didn't understand. Translate / Explain any new words or phrases.

f Focus on the task and give Sts time individually to write a list of five jobs they would like to try.

When Sts are ready, put them in pairs to compare their lists and explain why they chose each job.

Elicit some feedback from various pairs. Find out if any Sts had similar lists.

Now do the question as a whole-class activity.

3 PRONUNCIATION & SPEAKING the rhythm of English

Pronunciation notes

Encouraging Sts to improve their control of stress, both of syllables in individual words and of words in sentences, is still important at this level. Misplaced stress in an individual word can cause a breakdown in communication, and stressing the correct words in a sentence will help Sts speak English with a good rhythm and make them sound more fluent.

a ◉ **1.15** Focus on the **Fine-tuning your pronunciation: the rhythm of English** box and explain / elicit the meaning of *fine-tuning*. Now go through the box with the class.

Play the audio once the whole way through for Sts just to listen.

◉ **1.15**
See sentences in Student's Book on *p.11*

Now play the audio again, pausing after each sentence for Sts to try to copy Emma's rhythm and intonation as much as possible.

EXTRA IDEA After Sts have finished **a**, give them some more sentences for them to identify / underline stressed words.

b Focus on the task and give Sts time, individually, to think of their answers for the two people they know.

EXTRA SUPPORT Give Sts time to write some notes to help them with **c** next.

c Put Sts in small groups of four and get them to tell each other about the two people they thought about in **b**. Encourage them to use natural rhythm.

d Focus on the task. Tell Sts that they must think about all the jobs that have been mentioned in their group, and each choose one that they would like to try, or they might try if they needed the money, or definitely would never try. Encourage them to explain their choice.

Get some feedback from various groups. Find out if there were any jobs that everybody agreed / disagreed about.

4 READING

a Focus on the task and make sure Sts understand the meaning of the verb *reveal* /rɪˈviːl/ (= to make sth known to sb). Do the question as a whole-class activity, or put Sts in pairs and then get some feedback.

b Tell Sts to read all three articles to check their ideas in **a** and to answer questions 1–6.

Get Sts to compare with a partner, and then check answers to **a** and **b**.

EXTRA SUPPORT Before Sts read the articles the first time, check whether you need to pre-teach any vocabulary, but not the highlighted phrases.

b
1 A   2 C   3 C   4 A   5 B   6 B

c Tell Sts to read the articles again and find the six phrases or sentences. They should try to work out what the people mean.

Put Sts in pairs and tell them, when they are ready, to discuss 1–6.

Check answers.

1 It's the thing that gives my life a pattern, and it stops me going mad.
2 I make people think about their beliefs.
3 Night receptionist isn't a very impressive job.
4 It's great to be travelling in the opposite direction to most of the traffic.
5 Have unpredictable days off from Monday to Friday
6 With almost no chance to enjoy other hobbies or interests

d Focus on the task and give Sts time to first try to work out the meaning of the highlighted phrases from their context, and then to match them to their definitions. You might want to elicit / explain the meaning of *respite* (= a short break) in definition 5. Elicit or model its pronunciation /ˈrespaɪt/.

EXTRA SUPPORT Get Sts to work in pairs.

If Sts worked individually, get them to compare with a partner, and then check answers. You might want to tell Sts that a *grindstone* is a round stone that is turned like a wheel and is used to make knives and other tools sharp.

1 made it   2 missed the point   3 never think twice
4 hold my own   5 keep my nose to the grindstone
6 has long gone   7 fair enough

Deal with any other new vocabulary. Model and drill the pronunciation of any tricky words.

e Do this as a whole-class activity, or put Sts in pairs and then get some feedback. You could also tell the class which person's answers surprised you.

EXTRA IDEA Ask Sts if they know anyone who works in the sports, hospitality, or entertainment industries. If so, what would they say are the pros and cons of their jobs?

5 GRAMMAR   discourse markers (1): linkers

a Focus on the task and the jobs in the list, making sure Sts know what they all are. Elicit or model the pronunciation of any words you think your Sts might find tricky, e.g. *hygienist* /haɪˈdʒiːnɪst/.

Give Sts time, individually, to read the extracts, match a job to each one, and think about the point each person is trying to make.

Check answers, and for each one, elicit the point they are making.

1 999 operator – Some people call emergency services for trivial reasons.
2 university lecturer – Sometimes his / her students don't pay attention, which is frustrating, but sometimes they respond positively.
3 A&E doctor – There are too many patients and he / she's overworked.
4 fashion stylist – Some fashion models are very difficult to work with, and he / she had to stand up for him / herself.
5 political advisor – His / Her boss isn't properly qualified for the job.
6 dental hygienist – He / She understands that people don't like going to the dentist, and tries to help them to relax.

b Focus on the task and the headings in the four columns. Point out that the first one (*Although*) has been done for them.

Put Sts in pairs and get them to write the highlighted linkers in the extracts in **a** in the correct column.

Check answers.

result	consequently, so
reason	because
purpose	to, in order to
contrast	Yet, However, though, despite

EXTRA SUPPORT Before Sts do **b**, elicit that the most common linkers to introduce a reason, a purpose, and a contrast are *because*, *to*, and *but*. You could then do **b** as a whole-class activity, eliciting the linkers from the class.

c Tell Sts to go to **Grammar Bank 1B** on *p.143*.

Grammar notes

In this lesson, Sts revise discourse markers in these four areas (result, reason, purpose, and contrast), and learn some more sophisticated expressions, e.g. *due to / owing to*, *yet*, etc. There is also a strong focus on register to enable Sts to use these markers appropriately. Highlight that using a variety of discourse markers will make their English sound more advanced.

Reason

Highlight that we use *because* (not *as* or *since*) to answer a *Why…?* question.

Contrast

Point out that *though* and *mind you* can also be used in informal / spoken English to show a contrast, e.g. *He's very friendly – he's a bit mean, though. He's very friendly – mind you, he's a bit mean.*

Focus on the term *discourse markers*. Explain to Sts that discourse markers are words and expressions, often linkers, adverbs, or adverbial expressions, which help you to understand:

- the connection between what a speaker is saying and what has already been said.
- the connection between what a speaker has said and what he / she is now going to say.
- what the speaker thinks about what he / she is saying.

Tell Sts that here they are focusing on discourse markers which express connections (those which give information about a speaker's attitude are focused on in **3B**).

Focus on the example sentences for **result** and go through the rules with the class.

Repeat for **reason**, **purpose**, and **contrast**.

Focus on the exercises and get Sts to do them individually or in pairs. If they do them individually, get them to compare with a partner.

Check answers after each exercise, getting Sts to read the full sentences. When checking answers to **b**, ask Sts which sentences are formal.

a
1 as   2 so that   3 in spite of   4 seeing that   5 though
b
1 because of   2 consequently (formal)
3 Nevertheless (formal)   4 to   5 though   6 due to (formal)
c
1 We enjoyed the play in spite of our seats being a long way from the stage. / in spite of the fact that our seats were a long way from the stage. / in spite of having seats which were a long way from the stage.
2 It took us ages to get there because of the heavy traffic.
3 I took the price off the bag so (that) Becky wouldn't know how much it had cost.
4 Keep the receipt for the sweater, in case your dad doesn't like it.
5 Susanna isn't at all spoilt, even though she's an only child.
6 Prices have risen due to increased production costs. / the increase in production costs. / the fact that production costs have increased.

Tell Sts to go back to the main lesson **1B**.

EXTRA SUPPORT If you think Sts need more practice, you may want to give them the **Grammar** photocopiable activity at this point.

d 🔊 **1.16** Focus on the instructions and make sure Sts understand what they have to do.

Play the sentence halves one by one, pausing after each one to give Sts time to write.

Get Sts to compare with a partner, and play again as necessary.

Elicit the beginning of each sentence onto the board.

🔊 **1.16**
1 I want to find a job nearer home so that I don't…
2 I didn't tell my boss how bad I thought his idea was, so as not to…
3 Being a junior doctor is very demanding, partly because of…
4 Even though I was offered a good salary, I…
5 Our sales have gone up dramatically, and as a result, we…
6 Staff will be given a bonus payment in December due to the…
7 I wasn't offered the job, in spite of having…
8 The company has not been able to find a buyer, therefore it will…

Now put Sts in pairs and get them to predict how each sentence might end.

Elicit their ideas, and tell them if they are grammatically correct and make sense.

e 🔊 **1.17** Tell Sts they will now hear the whole sentences and they need to write the endings of the audio.

Play the audio sentence by sentence, pausing after each one to give Sts time to write.

Get Sts to compare with a partner, and play again as necessary.

Elicit the ending of each sentence onto the board. Find out if any Sts had predicted what was on the audio.

🔊 **1.17**
1 I want to find a job nearer home so that I don't **have to spend so much time commuting.**
2 I didn't tell my boss how bad I thought his idea was, so as not to **lose my job.**
3 Being a junior doctor is very demanding, partly because of **the long hours.**
4 Even though I was offered a good salary, I **decided not to accept the job.**
5 Our sales have gone up dramatically, and as a result, we **need to hire more staff.**
6 Staff will be given a bonus payment in December due to the **rise in annual profits.**
7 I wasn't offered the job, in spite of having **all the necessary qualifications.**
8 The company has not been able to find a buyer, therefore it will **be closing down in two months' time.**

Finally, put Sts in pairs and tell them to practise saying the sentences as naturally as possible.

6 WRITING a job application

This is the first of seven **Writing** tasks. In today's world of email communication, being able to write in English is an important skill for many Sts, and at this level many Sts are also preparing to take formal exams, which include a writing paper. We suggest that you go through the analysing and planning stages in class, but set the actual writing (the last stage) for homework.

In this lesson, the focus is on writing a job application. The writing skills focus on error correction, using appropriate register, and including relevant information.

Tell Sts to go to **Writing A job application** on *p.116*.

ANALYSING A MODEL TEXT

a Focus on the text type (*a job application*) and tell Sts that if you apply for a job in the UK, you normally send a CV (Curriculum Vitae) and a covering letter or email, which explains briefly what post you are applying for, who you are, and why you think you are suitable for the job. The same is true if you are applying for a grant or scholarship, or for a place on a course of study.

Focus on the **Key success factors** and go through them with the class.

Now focus on the job advert, and give Sts time to read it. Elicit / Explain the meaning of *core hours*, *shifts*, *can-do attitude*, and *liaising*. Elicit or model pronunciation of any words you think your Sts might find tricky.

Then ask Sts if they would be interested in applying, and elicit opinions.

b Focus on the instructions and the email. You might want to point out to Sts that the email has mistakes in it, but they shouldn't worry about it at this stage.

Tell Sts to read it quickly, and then elicit the contents of the three main paragraphs.

paragraph 1 Information about qualifications and skills (her studies and level of English)
paragraph 2 Information about her work experience
paragraph 3 Why she thinks she would be suitable for the job

c Focus on the **Improving your first draft** box and go through it with the class.

Now read **1** and then elicit why *My name is Agata Beck* has been crossed out, and elicit that it is inappropriate, as you give your name at the end. To include it here as well is unnecessary and repetitive.

Tell Sts to find the other three irrelevant or inappropriate sentences.

Get them to compare with a partner, and then check answers and elicit whether they are irrelevant or inappropriate.

Sts should have crossed out:
I made many American friends during this period, but we lost touch when I came home. (irrelevant)
He is, in fact, my uncle. (irrelevant)
I would definitely not panic when things got busy! (inappropriate, too informal)

Now focus on **2** and look at *Dear Miss Foster* in the email, which has been crossed out, and elicit that Agata doesn't know Irena Foster at Best Travel, so she doesn't know if she is married or not. *Ms* is appropriate for both married and unmarried women. (Nowadays most women prefer to use this title.) Then

Set a time limit for Sts to correct the ten highlighted mistakes

Get Sts to compare with a partner, and then check answers.

advertised **on** your website
a high level of spoken **E**nglish
in the United States **for** six months
an exchange programm**e**
marketing a**ss**istant and administrator
The director of **the** company
enthusiastic **about** travelling
apart **from** my work experience
calm and conscien**t**ious
(**any**) **further** information

d Ask the question to the class and elicit opinions. (In fact, she probably would be given an interview, as despite some mistakes, the email is well organized and gives all the necessary information.)

USEFUL LANGUAGE

e Focus on the task and get Sts to do it individually or in pairs.

EXTRA SUPPORT Do the first one as a class and elicit that although they both mean the same thing, the slightly more formal / professional-sounding style in *I am writing to apply...* is more appropriate.

Check answers. Take this opportunity to remind Sts that in this kind of letter, they should not use contractions.

EXTRA SUPPORT If you think your Sts will have problems remembering the expressions, get them to quickly re-read the email first.

1 I am writing to apply for the post of receptionist.
2 I have recently graduated from Humboldt University, where I completed a degree in Business Studies.
3 I have a high level of spoken English.
4 I have some relevant experience.
5 My tasks have included...dealing with clients by phone.
6 I...would welcome the chance to be part of such a high-profile and successful company.
7 I attach a full CV.
8 If you require any further information, I would be very happy to provide it.
9 I look forward to hearing from you.

Highlight that these phrases would be appropriate, with the relevant adjustments, in most letters of application (e.g. for a grant or course of study).

EXTRA IDEA Test Sts on the phrases by saying the informal phrase and getting them to say the more formal one.

PLANNING WHAT TO WRITE

a Focus on the task. Set a time limit for Sts to read the advertisement, underline what they need to respond to, and make notes.

b Put Sts in pairs and get them to compare their notes. Then get feedback from individual Sts.
Finally, go through the **Tips** with the class.

EXTRA SUPPORT If you think your Sts may have forgotten how to begin and end letters, elicit the rules from them and write them on the board.

1 If you know the name of the person you're writing to, begin *Dear* + title + surname. If not, begin *Dear Sir* or *Dear Madam*.
2 Finish your letter with *Yours sincerely* if you know the person's name, and *Yours faithfully* if you don't.
3 If you are writing a letter rather than an email, print your name underneath your signature.

WRITING

Go through the instructions and set the writing for homework.

Lesson plan

This is the first of five **Colloquial English** lessons featuring interviews and conversations commissioned and filmed specially for *English File*. In the first part, **The Interview**, there is an interview related to one or more of the topics in the preceding Files – for example, in the first interview, Eliza Carthy, a well-known member of a family of English folk musicians, talks about her family and her work, both topics covered in File 1. The interviewees (Eliza Carthy, Mary Beard, Jordan Friedman, Quentin Blake, and George McGavin) are all leading figures in their field and offer interesting perspectives on what they do, as well as giving Sts an opportunity to interact with authentic, unscripted speech.

In the second part of each **Colloquial English** lesson, **The Conversation**, there is an authentic unedited conversation between three people about an aspect of the same topic. It is often hard for Sts to follow a conversation on audio when three (or more) people are speaking amongst themselves, and having these conversations on video will enable Sts to follow more easily who is saying what, and to focus on aspects of language related to such conversations, e.g. responding, interrupting, etc. This section ends with Sts discussing further questions related to the topic, in groups of three.

At the end of each section of **The Interview**, and at the end of **The Conversation**, we suggest that Sts watch the video a final time with subtitles. This will let them see what they did / didn't understand, and help them to further develop their awareness of features of spoken English, such as elision, false starts, discourse markers, hesitation devices, etc.

In **The Interview**, the person interviewed is Eliza Carthy, an English folk musician known for both singing and playing the violin. In this three-part interview, she talks about her musical family and ancestors, her life as a musician, and the effect it has on her own children. This is followed by a language focus on discourse markers which Eliza Carthy uses. It both revises some which Sts should already know, and previews some which they will learn in **3B**.

In **The Conversation**, Sts watch three people discussing the advantages and disadvantages of working in a family business. Sts then discuss this question, as well as a couple of other questions related to the topic, focusing on responding to a speaker's points and encouraging them to speak.

These lessons can be used with *Class DVD* or *Classroom Presentation Tool*.

Sts can find all the video content in the *Online Practice*.

More materials

For teachers

Teacher's Resource Centre
Video Colloquial English 1
Quick Test 1
File 1 Test

For students

Workbook Colloquial English 1
　　　　　Can you remember? 1

Online Practice Colloquial English 1
　　　　　Check your progress

OPTIONAL LEAD-IN (BOOKS CLOSED)

Write the following questions on the board and get Sts to discuss them in small groups.

1 WHAT STYLES OF FOLK MUSIC OR TRADITIONAL MUSIC ARE THERE IN YOUR COUNTRY?

2 ARE THEY POPULAR? WHO WITH?

3 WHERE WOULD YOU GO TO SEE THEM LIVE?

4 DO THEY HAVE A FUTURE, OR ARE THEY DYING OUT?

5 ARE THEY BEING REINVENTED BY MODERN MUSICIANS?

Get some feedback from various groups.

Then tell Sts they are going to watch an interview with a well-known English folk musician.

If you have internet access in your classroom or Sts have it on their phones, give them a few minutes to google *Eliza Carthy* and find out a bit about her.

1 ▶ THE INTERVIEW Part 1

a Books open. Focus on the photos and the biographical information about Eliza Carthy. Give Sts time to read it.
   Do the question as a whole-class activity.

b Focus on the task and go through the **Glossary** with the class.
   Play the video (**Part 1**) once the whole way through for Sts to answer the question.
   Give Sts time to tell each other what they understood.
   Check the answer.

EXTRA SUPPORT Before playing the video, go through the listening scripts and decide if you need to pre-teach / check any lexis to help Sts when they listen.

Eliza's overwhelming memory of her childhood is of being with her family on the farm, surrounded by travelling musicians, listening to music, singing, and playing.

I = interviewer, E = Eliza Carthy
Part 1
I Eliza Carthy, could you tell us a bit about your family background, your parents, and grandparents?
E Um, I come from a musical family: my parents are folk singers; my father is a guitarist who is known for playing, for playing guitar, um, and inventing a particular style of English folk guitar. Um, he started playing when he was seventeen, back in the fifties, and, um, really was, was quite instrumental in his youth in sort of

building the, the sixties folk club scene in London. He was a friend of Bob Dylan and Paul Simon many, many years ago, and, um, is known for reconstructing old, traditional ballads – traditional English ballads. My mother comes from a folk-singing family called The Watersons, and they were from the north of England. They're from Hull, which is in the north of England, and they were also instrumental in the beginning of the sixties folk revival, the formation of the folk clubs, and the, the beginning of, basically, the professional music scene that I work on now.

I   And were your parents both from musical families?

E   Um, really both sides of my family are musical: my my mother's side of the family were all travellers and gypsies. My, er, her grandmother – she was brought up by her grandmother: both of her parents died when she was very young. She had an uncle that played the trumpet, you know, her father played the banjo – he used to listen to American radio during the Second World War and he used to learn the songs off the radio like that. Her grandmother was very into the sort of old romantic ballads like the *The Spinning Wheel* and things like that, and she used to, she used to sing when they were little. The whole family sang; the whole family danced. And I was brought up in that kind of a family: my mother and her, her brother and her sister were in a singing group, my dad joined that singing group, and then, when I was old enough, I joined the family as well.

I   So you had a very musical upbringing?

E   My upbringing was, I suppose some people might think it was quite a hippy upbringing. I was brought up on a farm, um, that had three houses in a row, with me and my mum and dad in the end house, my uncle – my mum's brother – and his wife and their four children in the middle house, and then my mum's sister and her husband and their two children on, on the other end house. And we grew up basically self-sufficient: we had animals and, um, we had chickens and goats and pigs and horses, and things like that, and we, we grew up singing together and living together in that environment in North Yorkshire in the nineteen seventies. Because my parents were professional musicians and touring musicians, we had a lot of touring musician friends who would come and stay at the farm, and they would sing and play all the time, and there was music all around when I was a child, and that really, that really formed the basis of, of, of how I live now.

c   Focus on the questions and give Sts time, in pairs, to see if they can remember any of the information.

Play the video again the whole way through.

Get Sts to compare with their partner, and then check answers.

When you play the video the second time, pause after each point has been mentioned and get Sts to compare what they have understood.

1   He started playing the guitar in the 50s. In the 60s he helped to create the folk music scene in London. He was friends with Bob Dylan and Paul Simon.

2   The Watersons are a folk group from her mother's side of the family. They are from Hull. They were important in the 60s folk revival and in the development of folk clubs in the north of England.

3   Her mother's grandmother brought her mother up, as her parents had died.

4   Her mother's uncle played the trumpet. Her mother's father played the banjo. He used to listen to music on the radio and learn the songs he heard.

5   Her grandmother used to sing *The Spinning Wheel* when Eliza was young.

6   The farm had three houses in a row – one for Eliza and her parents, one for her mother's brother and his family, and one for her mother's sister and her family. They kept a lot of animals. There was always singing and music being played at the farm.

7   Her parents' friends were touring musicians who often stayed on the farm.

If there's time, you could get Sts to watch again with subtitles, so they can see exactly what they understood / didn't understand. Translate / Explain any new words or phrases.

d   Do this as a whole-class activity, or put Sts in pairs and then get some feedback.

▶ Part 2

a   Focus on the task and go through the **Glossary** with the class.

Play the video (**Part 2**) once the whole way through for Sts to answer the two questions.

Give Sts time to discuss the questions and what they understood.

Then play the video again if necessary.

Elicit opinions.

Suggested answers
Eliza Carthy was probably quite an independent and confident child.
As a mother, she focuses on her children and organizes her work around them.

Part 2

I   Do you think it was inevitable that you'd become a professional musician?

E   Well, if you, if you were ever to ask any of us, were it – we would definitely have all said no. I wanted to be, I wanted to be a writer; my mum certainly didn't want me to go on the road. My mum retired in nineteen sixty-six – sixty-five / sixty-six – from professional touring to raise me. I mean, the road is a difficult place, whether you're travelling with your family, or with a band, or on your own, and she certainly didn't want that for me. My dad also probably never thought that I would do it, but I ended up following, exactly following, his footsteps and quitting school when I was seventeen and going on the road, and I've been on the road ever since.

I   Can you tell us about your first public performance?

E   My dad says that my first public performance was at the Fylde Folk Music Festival in Fleetwood, in Lancashire, when I was six, and we were at the Marine Hall and they were singing – The Watersons, the family, the family group were singing – and I asked if I could, I asked if I could go up on stage with them, and I was six. And Dad said, 'Well, you know, you probably don't know everything, so just stand next to me on stage and we'll start singing, and if you, if you know the song, just pull on my leg and I'll lift you up to the microphone and you can, you can join in.' God, I must have been awful! But yes, apparently, I just, the first song they started up singing, tugged on his leg, and he picked me up and he held me to the microphone and I sang that, and he was like, 'Did you enjoy that?''Yes, I did!' And he put me down again and they started singing the next one, tugged on his leg, same thing! And he just ended up doing the whole concert with me sitting on his hip! Which, er, now I have a six-year-old and I know how heavy she is, and it must have been quite difficult, God bless him!

I   Has having children yourself changed your approach to your career?

E   Er, yes, in a way. Yes, in a way it has. I've just reordered my working year because my eldest daughter has just started school, so I, you know, I'm, I'm not free to, to take the children with me on the road any more, and, and I'm now bound by the school terms. So, I try to work only on the weekends and in school holidays now, and I try to, to be Mummy from Monday to Friday, taking them to school, bringing them back again. I'm not getting a great deal of sleep, but then I don't know many mothers of, many mothers of six- and four-year-olds that are getting a great deal of sleep!

---

b Focus on the task and questions 1–6. Now give Sts time, in pairs, to see if they can remember any of the information.

Play the video again the whole way through.

Get Sts to compare with their partner, and then check answers.

When you play the video the second time, pause after each question has been answered and get Sts to compare what they have understood.

1 No, she wanted to be a writer.
2 To bring Eliza up, and because she didn't want her to grow up touring and travelling.
3 Six
4 She sang all the songs.
5 She now tries to only work at weekends and during school holidays, so that she can take care of her children during the week.
6 Sleep

If there's time, you could get Sts to watch again with subtitles, so they can see exactly what they understood / didn't understand. Translate / Explain any new words or phrases.

c Do this as a whole-class activity or put Sts in pairs, and then get some feedback.

▶ Part 3

a Focus on the task and point out the **Glossary**.

Play the video (**Part 3**) once the whole way through for Sts to answer the question.

Give Sts time to discuss the question and what they understood.

Then play the video again if necessary.

Get Sts to compare with a partner, and then check the answer.

When she was growing up, there were always a lot of musicians around, so now she doesn't like working alone.

Part 3

I You do a lot of collaborations with other musicians. What is it that appeals to you about working like that?
E I like working with other – I don't like working alone. I don't know if that's because I don't trust myself or I just don't like being alone; I like being surrounded by a big crowd of people. I suppose that's, that's partly to do with my upbringing: there was always so many people around that, um, I've, I'm at my best, I'm at my best in a, in a large event where loads of people are running around doing things, and we're all sort of collaborating with each other, and there's lots of ideas, and everyone's having, you know, a creative time. And that's how I feel – yeah, that's how I feel I, I work best, and that's why at the moment I have a thirteen-piece band and it's just heaven for me being with so many people and just feeling like a part of a big machine – I love that.
I Is there a difference between playing with your family and playing with other people?
E Um, yes, very much so. I'm not sure if I could tell you how different or why it's different. My dad is very eloquent on how and why it's different, and he, he knows that uniquely because he joined The Watersons, and The Watersons was a brother and two sisters. And he joined that, and of course he was married to my mum, but he wasn't related to her. And, there is this thing within family groups, this blood harmony thing, this intuition – you have similar sounding voices, you know where a relative is going to go, and that may be because you know each other so well, but it also may be whatever it is that binds a family together anyway.
I Would you like your children to follow in your footsteps?

E I get very, very excited when the children, um, when the children love music, I get very excited. My daughter Florence is very, very sharp: she listens and she can already – she plays *Twinkle Twinkle* on the violin, plucking like that, and on the guitar as well, and she's – yeah, she has a very, very good sense of rhythm. And she loves foreign languages as well – there's a real, um, there's a real sort of correlation there between, between language and singing. She has great pitch; she is able to learn songs and things very, very quickly, and I love that. And Isabella, my youngest, as well – she's really, she's really showing interest in it and I love it when they do that. As to whether or not I'd want them to be touring musicians, I think I would probably of the same opinion as my mother, which is, 'No, not really!' But, you know, I, I think the – I think the world is changing anyway, I don't know how many touring musicians there are going to be in the world in twenty years, when they're ready – I don't know.

b Focus on the task and give Sts time to read sentences 1–8. Remind them to correct the ones that are false.

Play the video again the whole way through.

Get Sts to compare with a partner, and then check answers.

When you play the video the second time, pause after each point has been mentioned and get Sts to compare what they have understood.

1 T
2 F (She has a 13-piece band.)
3 T
4 F (The Watersons were her mother's relatives.)
5 F (She plays two musical instruments – the violin and the guitar.)
6 T
7 F (She is showing an interest.)
8 T

Ask Sts if they like the music that Eliza plays and sings. Would they listen to more of it? Why (not)?

If there's time, you could get Sts to watch again with subtitles, so they can see exactly what they understood / didn't understand. Translate / Explain any new words or phrases.

c Do this as a whole-class activity, or put Sts in pairs and then get some feedback.

2 ▶ LOOKING AT LANGUAGE

a Focus on the **Discourse markers** box and go through it with the class.

Now focus on the task and give Sts time to read extracts 1–8.

Ask Sts if they can guess any of the gapped words or phrases before they listen to the extracts.

Play the video, pausing after each extract to give Sts time to write.

Get Sts to compare with a partner, and then check answers.

1 basically   2 really   3 I mean   4 apparently
5 in, way, in, way   6 of course   7 As to   8 anyway

---

1 …and they were also instrumental in the beginning of the sixties folk revival, the formation of the folk clubs, and the, the beginning of, basically, the professional music scene that I work on now.

2 I   And were your parents both from musical families?
   E   Um, really both sides of my family are musical…
3 My mum retired in nineteen sixty-six – sixty-five / sixty-six – from professional touring to raise me. I mean, the road is a difficult place…
4 But yes, apparently, I just – the first song they started up singing, tugged on his leg…
5 I   Has having children yourself changed your approach to your career?
   E   Er, yes, in a way. Yes, in a way it has.
6 …The Watersons was a brother and two sisters. And he joined that, and of course he was married to my mum, but he wasn't related to her.
7 And Isabella, my youngest, as well – she's really, she's really showing interest in it and I love it when they do that. As to whether or not I'd want them to be touring musicians,…
8 But, you know, I think the – I think the world is changing anyway, I don't know how many touring musicians there are going to be in the world in twenty years…

b Do this as a whole-class activity.

1 *basically* introduces an important or fundamental point
2 *really* introduces an interesting or unexpected fact
3 *I mean* introduces more details or clarification
4 *apparently* introduces something that she learnt from someone else (she doesn't remember it herself, but she's been told)
5 *in a way* shows that she is uncertain
6 *of course* introduces a clear fact
7 *As to* introduces a point she wants to address
8 *anyway* shows that she's introducing a new angle on the topic

3 ▶ THE CONVERSATION

a Focus on the photo and tell Sts they are going to watch these three people discuss a question. Focus on the task and play the video, pausing after the title screen to give Sts time to read the question.

Then play the video once the whole way through.

Check answers.

Before playing the video, go through the listening script and decide if you need to pre-teach / check any lexis to help Sts when they listen.

1 Joanne   2 Alice   3 Duncan

What do you think are the advantages and disadvantages of working in a family business?

Joanne   OK, so when I was a teenager my dad started a business which very quickly involved the whole family. That could have been stressful, I'm sure it was very stressful for my mother, often, but as a teenager, that was a ready-made job. Um, my parents offered that as an opportunity. At one point I went off and got a job somewhere else, but they were cool about that, um, so I think actually in that sense, that, at the time, for me, was very good. I could see it could cause a few stresses.

Duncan   Was there a, a time, through the day, that work stopped and family began, or did it all blur into one?

Joanne   Do you know, when we first started it was, the office was, um, our spare bedroom and the warehouse was our dining room. It was very hard to genuinely get away from it and I should imagine that's – I'm sure those lines could be blurred quite often if it's a whole family working together. I, I actually don't think I'd want to do that now.

Duncan   It's a bit of a buzzword, these days, 'work-life balance'. It must be quite hard to strike that balance if you're working as part of a family.

Joanne   I bet it is. I think I'd find that very difficult nowadays.

Alice   Yeah, I think, as well, I, I know of someone who grew up in a family business, um, and she was quite heavily exploited by her mum.

Joanne   Oh dear!

Alice   But, um, but I, I think that it does have advantages as well. I think the main one is you – growing up in a family business, you can see where your parents work and make their money, whereas in, you know, my parents would go off to work and I knew that was a place that they went off…

Joanne   Yes.

Alice   …to make money…but I didn't see it, so I –

Joanne   I think that's really important, to appreciate it. Yes, totally.

Alice   It makes you appreciate it, it more and you see the hard work and the stresses…

Joanne   Yes.

Alice   …of running a business.

Joanne   So it could be an opportunity…

Alice   Definitely.

Joanne   …one hopes, rather than an exploitative situation.

---

b Focus on the task and give Sts time to read statements 1–7.

Play the video again for Sts to watch and complete the task.

Check answers.

1 J   2 J   4 D   5 A   7 A

If there's time, you could get Sts to watch again with subtitles, so they can see exactly what they understood / didn't understand. Translate / Explain any new words or phrases.

c Do the question as a whole-class activity, or put Sts in pairs and then get some feedback.

d Focus on the extract and give Sts time to read it.

Play the video once the whole way through.

Elicit the missing words and check the answer to the question.

1 Yes   2 important   3 totally   4 Yes   5 opportunity
6 hopes

Joanne is responding to Alice's points and encouraging her to speak.

Alice   But, um, but I, I think that it does have advantages as well. I think the main one is you – growing up in a family business, you can see where your parents work and make their money, whereas in, you know, my parents would go off to work and I knew that was a place that they went off…

Joanne   Yes.

Alice   …to make money…but I didn't see it, so I –

Joanne   I think that's really important, to appreciate it. Yes, totally.

Alice   It makes you appreciate it, it more and you see the hard work and the stresses…

Joanne   Yes.

Alice   …of running a business.

Joanne   So it could be an opportunity…

Alice   Definitely.

Joanne   …one hopes, rather than an exploitative situation.

---

e Put Sts in small groups of three if possible. Focus on the questions and check Sts understand what they mean.

Give Sts time to discuss them.

Monitor and help, and encourage them to use the different strategies focused on in **d** to respond to their classmates and encourage them to speak.

Get feedback from various groups. You could also tell the class what you think.

G the past: habitual events and specific incidents
V word building: abstract nouns
P word stress with suffixes

Lesson plan

The topic of the lesson is childhood memories.

The theme is explored first through an extract from *Boy*, Roald Dahl's autobiography, where he explains how an experience at school inspired him to write *Charlie and the Chocolate Factory*. The grammar focus here is on past forms. Sts revise narrative tenses (past simple and continuous, and past perfect simple and continuous) for describing specific incidents in the past. This is combined with a revision of *used to* and *would* + infinitive to describe situations and repeated past actions. The first half of the lesson ends with speaking and writing activities about childhood, where Sts put the grammar into practice.

The second half of the lesson begins with a listening task. Sts first hear three people talking about childhood memories, and then listen to an interview about research that has been done into our earliest memories (what age we have them and what they usually consist of). Sts then talk about their own early memories. This is followed by a lexical and pronunciation focus on abstract nouns, e.g. *childhood*, *boredom*, *fear*, etc., and word stress with suffixes. Sts also study common collocations using abstract nouns. The lesson ends with a speaking activity where Sts bring together the grammar, vocabulary, and pronunciation from the lesson.

More materials
For teachers
Photocopiables
Grammar the past: habitual events and specific incidents *p.169*
Communicative Childhood questionnaire *p.195* (instructions *p.187*)
For students
Workbook 2A
Online Practice 2A

OPTIONAL LEAD-IN – THE QUOTE

Write the quote at the top of *p.16* on the board (books closed) and the name of the person who said it, or get Sts to open their books and read it.

Elicit / Explain that Ingrid Bergman (1915–1982) was a Swedish actress who starred in many of Alfred Hitchcock's films, but is probably best known for her role in *Casablanca* with Humphrey Bogart. She won many awards, including three Oscars. She had four children, including Isabella Rossellini.

Ask Sts what they think the quote means and if they agree with it.

1 READING expressing a response to a creative text / literature

a Focus on the task and make sure Sts know the meaning of an *incident* (= sth that happens, especially sth unusual or memorable) and do not confuse it with *accident*.

Do this as a whole-class activity, or put Sts in pairs and then get some feedback.

b Focus on the task and find out if Sts have heard of the author Roald Dahl (1916–1990). You could tell them that he was a British novelist, short-story writer, poet, fighter pilot, and screenwriter. Some of his best-loved children's stories include *Charlie and the Chocolate Factory*, *Matilda*, *James and the Giant Peach*, *The Witches*, *Fantastic Mr Fox*, and *The BFG* – a lot of these, and others, have been made into films.

Focus on questions 1–5 and make sure Sts understand all the lexis, especially *sampling the products* in question 5.

Before Sts start reading, you might want to explain what *House* means here (= many UK boarding schools are divided into 'Houses' and each student belongs to one; Houses compete with one another in sports and other activities) and the old-fashioned expression *with great gusto* (= with enthusiasm and energy). You could also tell Sts that the Milk Flake and Lemon Marshmallow were two Cadbury products, and that the Flake is still popular.

Now put Sts in pairs and tell them to read **Part 1** and then answer the questions with their partner.

Check answers.

EXTRA SUPPORT Before Sts read the extract, check whether you need to pre-teach any vocabulary.

1 So that the boys could give each chocolate bar a mark and write a comment.
2 To give the boys something they knew well, that they could compare the products against.
3 They had to taste each chocolate bar, mark it from 0 to 10, and comment on why they liked or didn't like it.
4 Because they knew a lot about all the chocolate bars that were available.
5 They were very enthusiastic and took it very seriously.

Deal with any vocabulary problems that arose.

c Focus on the questions for **Part 2**, making sure Sts know the meaning of *recurring* (= to happen again or a number of times). Elicit or model its pronunciation /rɪˈkɜːrɪŋ/.

Point out the **Glossary**, and tell Sts to now read **Part 2** and answer the questions with their partner.

Check answers.

EXTRA SUPPORT Before Sts read the extract, check whether you need to pre-teach any vocabulary, but not the verbs in **d**.

1 A long white room like a laboratory, full of pans of chocolate and other sweets cooking, with scientists working on their inventions
2 Working in the lab and suddenly creating something that tasted wonderful, and running to show it to the owner of the factory, Mr Cadbury

3 He imagined Mr Cadbury tasting his chocolate carefully and then congratulating Roald Dahl on his wonderful idea.

4 He used the experience in his book *Charlie and the Chocolate Factory*.

LANGUAGE IN CONTEXT

d 🔊 **2.1** Focus on the task, the verbs in the list, and synonyms for 1–7. Give Sts time to see if they can match any.

Now play the audio once the whole way through for Sts to read and listen at the same time.

Give Sts time to do the matching activity, and then get them to compare with a partner.

Check answers.

1 leap   **2** grab   **3** concocting   **4** bubble away   **5** rushing
6 slap   **7** picture

🔊 **2.1**
See **Part 2** in Student's Book on *p.17*

Deal with any other vocabulary problems that arose.

e Do this as a whole-class activity, or put Sts in pairs and then get some feedback. You could tell the class what you used to dream of doing as a child.

2 GRAMMAR the past: habitual events and specific incidents

a Focus on the task and give Sts a couple of minutes to answer the question with a partner, or do it as a whole-class activity.

If Sts worked in pairs, check answers. Clarify that the whole section beginning *I used to picture…* refers to something that he repeatedly imagined happening, not just on one occasion.

1 when I was looking for, I remembered, I began
2 I used to picture, I used to imagine, I would come up with, I would grab

b Do the question as a whole-class activity.

specific incidents in the past: the past perfect, the past perfect continuous
repeated or habitual actions in the past: past simple (often with an adverb of frequency)

If Sts don't know, tell them they will now look at this in the **Grammar Bank**.

c Tell Sts to go to **Grammar Bank 2A** on *p.144*.

Grammar notes

Although Sts should have met the majority of these forms and structures before, even at Advanced level they still tend to use mainly the past simple when talking about the past, and need to be encouraged to use a variety of tenses and forms.

Sts should be very familiar with narrative tenses, though they may still have problems with differentiating between past perfect simple and continuous and with using a variety of tenses in spoken English.

They should also be very familiar with *used to* for past habitual or repeated actions or states. The structure which they may be less familiar with is the use of *would* + infinitive for habitual past actions (but not states). It is important to stress to Sts that past simple, *used to*, and *would* are alternative structures to use when describing repeated past actions, and that varying structures will make their language sound more fluent and advanced.

Focus on the example sentences for **narrative tenses: describing specific incidents in the past** and go through the rules with the class.

Repeat for ***used to*** **and** ***would*****: describing habitual events and repeated actions in the past**.

Go through the ***used to*** **and** ***be / get used to*** box with the class to remind them of this different meaning.

Focus on the exercises and get Sts to do them individually or in pairs. If they do them individually, get them to compare with a partner.

Check answers after each exercise, getting Sts to read the full sentences.

a
1 was sitting, had been crying
2 ✓
3 used to live, bought
4 didn't use to look
5 ✓, ✓
6 had crashed, was pouring
b
1 spent / used to spend (not *would* because of the position of *often*)   **2** had died   **3** would cook / used to cook / cooked
4 would take / used to take / took   **5** invited / had invited
6 went   **7** tried   **8** got up   **9** decided   **10** was sleeping
11 wanted   **12** had told   **13** climbed   **14** saw
15 had been asking   **16** had refused   **17** heard   **18** realized
19 had got up   **20** was coming   **21** opened   **22** had caught
23 had forbidden

Tell Sts to go back to the main lesson **2A**.

EXTRA SUPPORT If you think Sts need more practice, you may want to give them the **Grammar** photocopiable activity at this point.

3 SPEAKING

a 🔊 **2.2** Focus on the task and play the first extract. Elicit the phrase the speaker uses to refer to her age (*From the age of about seven till I was 16…*).

Then play the rest of the audio for Sts to write the rest of the phrases. Play the audio again as necessary.

Check answers and highlight that:

• you can say *When I was small…* instead of *When I was little…*

• *kid* is more informal than *child*

• you can also say *As a child…* instead of *When I was a child…*

2 When I was little…
3 When I was a young child…
4 From the age of about nine…
5 When I was at primary school…
6 When I was a kid…

◆) 2.2

1 From the age of about seven till I was sixteen, I went to an all-girls school in North London…
2 When I was little, and actually still now, I was absolutely terrified of spiders…
3 When I was a young child, I used to have a lot of nightmares…
4 From the age of about nine, I was ill and I had, I had an overactive thyroid gland…
5 When I was at primary school, I used to hate school dinners…
6 When I was a kid, we always used to go on holiday down to Cardigan in West Wales…

b Focus on the task and the example. Make it clear to Sts that they have to talk about <u>habitual</u> actions and feelings. Demonstrate the activity by talking about some of the topics yourself. Then get Sts, in pairs, to take turns to talk about two of the topics. Highlight that they should be using past forms / *used to* and *would* + infinitive to describe their experiences.

Monitor and help.

c Focus on the instructions and highlight that this time, they should use narrative tenses to describe a specific incident they can remember from their childhood.

Give Sts some time to choose a topic and think of an incident.

While Sts exchange anecdotes, monitor and support, helping Sts with vocabulary and correcting any wrong use of tenses. Fast finishers could choose another topic and describe another incident from their childhood.

4 WRITING an article

Tell Sts to go to **Writing An article** on *p.118*. The writing skills focus is on choosing a good title, paragraphing, discourse markers, and on making your writing more interesting by using synonyms and a richer range of vocabulary.

ANALYSING A MODEL TEXT

a Focus on the text type (*an article*) and tell Sts that they may want to write an article for an English-language magazine or website, or they may be required to do this for an exam such as Cambridge English: Advanced (CAE). There are tips and strategies that Sts will learn in this lesson, which will help them to write good articles.

Focus on the **Key success factors** and go through them with the class.

Now focus on the task, and get Sts, in pairs, to discuss what information they might include if they were writing about their country, e.g. the way schools have changed.

Get feedback and write Sts' ideas on the board.

b Set a time limit for Sts to read the article to see what ideas were included and also to choose a title.

Put Sts in pairs and get them to discuss the three titles.

Get feedback about which title they prefer and why.

The lost joys of childhood fits the article best.

c Get Sts to read the article again and answer the questions with their partner.

Check answers. Elicit opinions for question 3. When checking answers to 4, elicit that the discourse markers are used either to introduce the main ideas (*First, Another major change*, etc.) or to express cause and result (*As a result, so*, etc.).

1 The effect is to get the readers' attention and make them want to read on and find the answer. It makes it clear that the article discusses the answer to that question. The question is answered in the conclusion, based on the writer's own opinion.
2 The writer's own childhood memories; examples are playing games, playing outside with other children
3 Families are smaller because fewer people have the time to bring up a large family.
Youngsters spend most of their free time at home, inside, because parents worry about letting them play outside.
4 *As a result, Another major change, so, Finally*

USEFUL LANGUAGE

d Focus on the **Using synonyms** box and go through it with the class. Stress that it isn't that you can't repeat a word or phrase (*children* is used six times), but that also using *youngsters, boys and girls*, etc. makes the vocabulary more varied. You may want to suggest that Sts could use a thesaurus, e.g. *The Oxford Learner's Thesaurus*.

Now give Sts time to find the synonyms in the article.

Get Sts to compare with a partner, and then check answers.

1 these days, today
2 boys and girls, youngsters, young people
3 by themselves, on their own

e Focus on the **Using richer vocabulary** box and go through it with the class.

Focus on the task and get Sts to try to do it without looking back at the article.

Check answers. You might want to elicit or model the pronunciation of *idyllic* /ɪˈdɪlɪk/.

1 neighbourhood children 2 racing around 3 hardly ever 4 hazardous 5 dramatically 6 It is common for 7 idyllic

EXTRA CHALLENGE You could elicit other synonyms that the writer could have used, e.g. 1 *hugely*, 2 *local children*, 3 *dashing / rushing*, 4 *scarcely*, etc.

PLANNING WHAT TO WRITE

a Focus on the task and article topics, and give Sts time to brainstorm ideas in pairs for each topic.

Get brief feedback from various pairs for the three topics.

Then tell Sts to individually choose which topic they want to write about and which two or three changes they will focus on in their article.

Get feedback, asking Sts why they have chosen these changes.

b Now get Sts to individually think of titles for their article, and compare / discuss them with a partner.

Get feedback and help Sts to improve their titles where appropriate.

Finally, go through the **Tips** with the class.

WRITING

Go through the instructions and set the writing for homework.

Tell Sts to go back to the main lesson **2A**.

5 LISTENING & SPEAKING using existing knowledge to make sense of information

a 🔊 **2.3** Focus on the task and the three questions. Before playing the audio, tell Sts that *nana* (used by Speaker 2) is a word some British people use (also *gran, nan, granny*) to refer to their grandmother.

Play **Part 1** of the audio once the whole way through for Sts to listen and answer the questions. You could pause between each speaker to give Sts more time.

Get Sts to compare with a partner, and then play the audio again if necessary.

Check answers.

EXTRA SUPPORT Read through the scripts and decide if you need to pre-teach any new lexis before Sts listen.

Speaker 1	**Age:** about three
	Memory: letting go of a balloon outside
	Emotion(s): devastated, heartbroken
Speaker 2	**Age:** three or four
	Memory: having a book read to her
	Emotion(s): annoyed
Speaker 3	**Age:** two and a half
	Memory: breaking a Christmas decoration
	Emotion(s): resentful

🔊 **2.3**
(script in Student's Book on *p.131*)
P = presenter, S = speaker
Part 1
P1 Good afternoon, and welcome to *Mind Over Matter*, our regular programme about psychology and mental health. Today we're going to be looking at childhood memories.
P2 Yes, and we'll be investigating where people's first memories come from, and hear a story about the famous Swiss psychologist Jean Piaget. But first, let's hear some early childhood memories sent in by our listeners.
S 1 My, my earliest memory – I must have been about three, I guess, possibly two – was when we'd been to, to a funfair – and I would have gone with my brother, who's a bit older than me, and my parents. And I'd been bought a, a helium balloon, and for some reason the balloon had a snowman inside it. It was only September; I don't why there was a snowman – but, but there was, and I took it out into the back garden, and because it was full of helium, obviously, it was pulling on the string. It wanted to, to fly away. And I let go – I didn't let go by accident; I remember letting go on purpose, to see what would happen, and of course what happened was the balloon flew up into the sky, over the neighbours' trees, and disappeared, and I was absolutely devastated – heartbroken – by the loss of the balloon, and stood there crying and crying. And my dad had to go back to the funfair and get me another identical balloon, which did nothing to console me; I kept crying and crying and crying. And that's my, my earliest memory – not a very happy one!
S 2 My earliest memory is probably from when I was about three or four years old and it was Christmas, and I was at my nana's house with all my family. And my uncle was reading to me: he was reading *The Little Mermaid*, except that he was making it up. He wasn't actually reading the words in the book; he was just saying things like, 'Ariel went to buy some fish and chips,' and things like that, and that made me quite annoyed because I was at an age where I couldn't really read myself, but I knew that he was reading it wrong. So I got quite annoyed at him and told him to read it properly, but yeah, that's my earliest memory.
S 3 So, my earliest memory, I think I was around two, or two and a half, anyway, something like that. I know that because we were living in a house that my parents lived in before we moved to the house that we lived in sort of for the rest of our lives. Anyway, it

was Christmastime because I remember there was a Christmas tree in the corner of the room, of the living room and I remember the carpet, it was a sort of, it was kind of like a dark green check and all the sort of glowing of the baubles on the Christmas tree, anyway I remember my mum putting up these Christmas decorations, new they were, onto the Christmas tree, these new baubles, and they were made out of glass, and then she had to go out of the room for something, and I remember taking one of these new glass baubles in my hand, and I remember putting my finger into the glass and breaking one of them – I don't really know why I did it – anyway, then my mum came back into the room and I remember her shouting at me and, and being really angry because I'd broken one of these new baubles, and I remember feeling actually quite resentful at the time because I didn't really think it was a bad thing to do.

EXTRA SUPPORT If there's time, you could get Sts to listen again with the script on *p.131*, so they can see exactly what they understood / didn't understand. Translate / Explain any new words or phrases.

b Put Sts in pairs and get them to discuss questions 1–4, making sure Sts know the adjective *unreliable* (= that cannot be trusted or depended on). Elicit or model its pronunciation /ˌʌnrɪˈlaɪəbl/.
Monitor and help.
Elicit some feedback from individual Sts.

c 🔊 **2.4** Play the audio for Sts to check their answers in **b**. Play the audio again if necessary.
Check answers.

EXTRA SUPPORT Pause the audio where indicated in the script (see ***) to give Sts time to note their answers.

1 Between the ages of two and four
2 Before that age, children don't have a clear sense of their own identity, they don't have the language skills, and the part of the brain needed for memories isn't fully formed.
3 Strong emotions, like happiness, unhappiness, pain, surprise, fear and events related to these things, like the birth of a brother or sister, a death, or a family visit, or a festive celebration
4 Because they tend to be family stories that children incorporate into their memory.

🔊 **2.4**
(script in Student's Book on *p.131*)
Part 2
P1 So, what age do most people's first memories come from? And are our first memories reliable, or are they sometimes based on something people have told us? John's been looking at some of the research into how our memories work. Let's start at the beginning, then, John. At what age do first memories generally occur?
P2 Well, according to research, eighty per cent of our first memories are of things which happened to us between the ages of two and four. In fact, a large study by Professor Martin Conway in twenty eighteen concluded that it's impossible to remember events from before the age of two.
***
P1 That's interesting, because a lot of people would say they do have earlier memories.
P2 Yes, in fact, the twenty-eighteen study asked six thousand people for their earliest memories, and around forty per cent of them said they remembered being in their pram or cot, or the first time they walked, or the first word they spoke. But according to research, that just isn't possible.
P1 Why is that?
P2 There seem to be two main reasons, according to Professor Draaisma. The first reason is that before the age of two, children

don't have a clear sense of themselves as individuals – they can't usually identify themselves in a photo. And you know how a very small child enjoys seeing himself in a mirror, but he doesn't actually realize that the person he can see is him. Children of this age also have problems with the pronouns *I* and *you*. And a memory without *I* is impossible. That's to say, we can't begin to have memories until we have an awareness of self.

P1 And the second reason?

P2 The second reason is related to language. According to research, first memories coincide with the development of linguistic skills, with a child learning to talk. And as far as memory is concerned, it's essential for a child to be able to use the past tense, so that he or she can talk about something that happened in the past, and then remember it. And finally, it seems that the part of the brain needed for memories to form doesn't function fully until a few years after birth.

***

P1 And what are first memories normally about? I mean, is it possible to generalize at all?

P2 Early memories seem to be related to strong emotions, such as happiness, unhappiness, pain, and surprise. Research suggests that three quarters of first memories are related to fear, to frightening experiences like being left alone, or a large dog, or having an accident – things like falling off a swing in a park. And of course, this makes sense, and bears out the evolutionary theory that the human memory is linked to self-preservation. You remember these things in order to be prepared if they happen again, so that you can protect yourself.

P1 So are first memories only related to emotions, or are there any specific events that tend to become first memories?

P2 The events that are most often remembered – and these are always related to one of the emotions I mentioned before – are the birth of a baby brother or sister, a death, or a family visit. Another interesting aspect is that first memories tend to be very visual. They're almost invariably described as pictures, not smells or sounds. For example, festive celebrations with bright lights are mentioned quite frequently.

***

P1 Is it true that first memories are often unreliable, in that sometimes they're not real memories, just things our families have told us about ourselves or that we've seen in photos?

P2 Absolutely! As I said, some people insist that their first memories are of learning to walk or sitting in a pram, but it's very unlikely that they would form such early memories, for all the reasons I've mentioned. But family stories can definitely be incorporated into our memory. So, if your mother tells you the first word you ever said, over the years that becomes your memory; you think you can remember it. A good example of that is the famous case of the Swiss psychologist Jean Piaget…

Finally, ask Sts if they think the memories they heard in **a** are reliable and why.

d Tell Sts they are going to listen to **Part 2** again and they must say why the presenter mentions items 1–6. Make sure Sts understand all the lexis.

Put Sts in pairs to see if they can remember any of the information.

Now play the audio again, pausing each time one of the items has been mentioned, to give Sts time to make notes.

Get Sts to compare with their partner, and then check answers.

1 Around 40% of people say they remember this.
2 A child seeing him- / herself in a mirror doesn't realize that the person is him / her.
3 A child can't have a memory of a past event before he / she has learned to use the past tense.
4 Evolutionary theory suggests that human memory is linked to emotions / feelings which are related to protecting yourself.

5 First memories tend to be visual, rather than smells or sounds.
6 If your mother tells you about the first word you ever said, that becomes something you think is a memory.

EXTRA SUPPORT If there's time, you could get Sts to listen again with the script on *p.131*, so they can see exactly what they understood / didn't understand. Translate / Explain any new words or phrases.

e Tell Sts that in **Part 3**, they are going to hear a short anecdote about the first memory of the famous Swiss psychologist Jean Piaget. Focus on the photo and the words, and elicit the meaning of any words Sts don't know.

Now put Sts in pairs and get them to predict what they think the memory is about.

Get some feedback from various pairs, but <u>don't</u> tell them if they are correct or not.

f 🔊 **2.5** Play the audio once the whole way through for Sts to listen and check their predictions in **e**.

Get Sts to compare with a partner and see if they can retell the story together.

Finally, elicit the story from the class and ask what happened years later. Find out if any Sts guessed correctly.

The story: He was sitting in his pram as a one-year-old baby. A man tried to kidnap him. He remembered his nanny fighting to save him. His parents gave her a reward (a watch).

Years later, Piaget's nanny confessed that she had made the story up.

🔊 **2.5**
(script in Student's Book on *p.131*)
Part 3

P2 A good example of that is the famous case of the Swiss psychologist Jean Piaget. In the eighteen nineties, when Piaget was a baby, his nanny used to take him for walks around Paris in his pram. Piaget had always thought that his first memory was of sitting in his pram as a two-year-old baby when a man tried to kidnap him. He remembered exactly where it happened, on the Champs-Elysées. He remembered his nanny fighting the kidnapper, and he could remember a policeman appearing, and the man running away. The nanny was then given a watch as a reward by Jean's parents. But many years later, when Piaget was fifteen, his parents received a letter from the nanny in which she returned the watch to them. The nanny confessed that she'd made up the whole story, and that was why she was returning the watch. Of course, Jean had heard the story told so many times that he was convinced that he'd remembered the whole incident.

P1 That's fascinating. Thank you very much, John.

EXTRA SUPPORT If there's time, you could get Sts to listen again with the script on *p.131*, so they can see exactly what they understood / didn't understand. Translate / Explain any new words or phrases.

g Focus on the task and tell Sts to answer the three questions in **a** to help them talk about their first memory. When they have finished, they should decide, on the basis of what they have heard in the listening, how reliable they think their first memory is.

EXTRA SUPPORT Demonstrate the activity by telling the class about your first memory and how reliable you think it is.

Get some feedback from various Sts.

6 VOCABULARY & PRONUNCIATION word building: abstract nouns; word stress with suffixes

Vocabulary and Pronunciation notes

At this level, Sts should be aware of the different possible noun endings, but will still need practice in using the correct ones, and to help them remember the nouns which do not add a suffix but change the word.

Here Sts also learn some common collocations with abstract nouns.

As with other multi-syllable words, they may still be stressing the wrong syllable, and it with help to remind them that:

- the endings -hood, -ship, -dom, -ment, and -ness never affect the stress of the word they are added to.
- multi-syllable nouns ending in -tion and -ity are always stressed on the syllable before the ending. This sometimes causes the stress to shift, e.g. celebrate – celebration, inform – information, curious – curiosity, possible – possibility.

a Focus on the **Abstract nouns** box and go through it with the class.

Now focus on the task and do the first two words, achieve and adult, with the whole class as examples (achievement, adulthood).

In pairs, give Sts time to complete the task.

b 🔊 **2.6** Play the audio for Sts to listen and check.

Check answers. Highlight the vowel change from wise /waɪz/ to wisdom /ˈwɪzdəm/.

🔊 2.6

1 adulthood, neighbourhood
2 friendship, membership, partnership, relationship
3 curiosity, generosity, possibility
4 awareness, happiness, illness, kindness, sadness
5 boredom, freedom, wisdom
6 celebration, frustration, imagination, temptation
7 achievement, amazement, disappointment, excitement, improvement

c 🔊 **2.7** Focus on the task and tell Sts to use their instinct to underline the stressed syllables in the words.

Then play the audio for them to listen and check.

Check answers and elicit which suffix ending(s) often cause the stress to change.

1 <u>a</u>dult – <u>a</u>dulthood
2 re<u>la</u>tion – re<u>la</u>tionship
3 free – <u>free</u>dom
4 <u>cu</u>rious – curi<u>o</u>sity
5 <u>happy</u> – <u>happiness</u>
6 <u>celebrate</u> – cele<u>bra</u>tion
7 disa<u>ppoint</u> – disa<u>ppoint</u>ment

The two endings which often cause a change are -(a)tion and -ity.

🔊 2.7
See words in Student's Book on p.19

Now get Sts to go back to the chart in **a** and practise saying the words correctly.

EXTRA SUPPORT You could play the audio again, pausing after each word or group of words, for Sts to listen and repeat.

d Focus on the task and the two sections, 1–4 and 5–8.

Give Sts time to complete the Adjective and Verb columns. Tell Sts the adjective or verb will be a different word.

e 🔊 **2.8** Play the audio for Sts to listen and check.

Check answers. There are sometimes other possible adjectives or verbs which you might want to mention: 2 shameful / shameless, 3 deadly, 4 endangered, 8 memorize.

🔊 2.8

1	anger	angry
2	shame	ashamed
3	death	dead
4	danger	dangerous
5	belief	believe
6	hatred	hate
7	loss	lose
8	memory	remember

EXTRA SUPPORT Play the audio again, pausing for Sts to listen and repeat.

Finally, tell Sts to cover the abstract nouns, look at the Adjective and Verb columns, and see if they can remember the nouns.

EXTRA SUPPORT You could get Sts to close their books. You call out one of the nouns for them to tell you the adjective or verb, or vice versa, e.g.:

T death
Sts dead

EXTRA SUPPORT Get Sts to test themselves or a partner. In **a**, Sts can cover the chart, look at the words in the list and try to remember the abstract nouns. In **c** and **d**, they can cover the left-hand or right-hand column and remember the words.

f Focus on the **Collocations** box and go through it with the class to remind them of the meaning.

Now focus on the task and make sure Sts know they must use abstract nouns from **a** and **d**.

Check answers.

1 loss 2 amazement 3 relationship 4 possibility
5 danger 6 disappointment 7 belief 8 imagination

7 SPEAKING

a 🔊 **2.9** Focus on the task and then play the audio for Sts to listen and answer the questions.

Get Sts to compare with a partner, and then check answers.

He was moving house, and they arrived at the new flat in the dark. He ran around the rooms with a torch.
He felt excited about the idea of living in a flat in the dark; he was disappointed when the power came on the next day and he realized what he'd imagined wouldn't happen.

🔊 2.9
(script in Student's Book on p.131)
My earliest memory is from when I must have been nearly three and we were moving house. We moved to a block of flats, and I remember arriving and it was, it was dark. And we'd had quite a long journey, and we arrived and we went in the door and we turned the lights on, and nothing happened and the whole flat was completely black and dark – no power, no electricity, no lights –

and I thought this was fantastic. And we had a torch, and I was just running around, running around the, the hall and the rooms, finding all these new rooms, all with a torch, and I imagined that it was always going to be like that – that we'd, we'd arrived in a house that wasn't going to have light, so I was always going to have to use a torch. And I thought that was going to be brilliant. My mother was in tears – obviously, she, she was very stressed from the journey and arriving somewhere and having no power. But I, I was really, really excited by it, and the next day when the power came on, I was really disappointed.

b Focus on the task and go through the feelings and events.

Give Sts time to think about and write key words for one of the feelings and one of the events, where they have a clear memory and are happy to recount it.

c Focus on the **Talking about memories** box and go through it with the class, and then focus on the example.

If you have a good early memory story to tell, contribute it at this point.

Put Sts in small groups of three or four. Tell them to take turns to talk about their memories.

If you have time, you could find out whether anyone has a funny / surprising / dramatic memory to retell to the whole class.

On the tip of my tongue

G pronouns
V lexical areas
P sound–spelling relationships

Lesson plan

The main topic of the lesson is the English language.

The first half of the lesson begins with a look at some commonly misspelt English words. Sts then read about the origin of the English language from a website called The English Spelling Society, which wants to simplify English spelling in the hope of improving literacy. This leads to a discussion about how important (or not) spelling is in English as well as in other languages. This is followed by a pronunciation focus on common sound–spelling relationships in English. The grammar focus is on pronouns, revising what Sts should already know and introducing advanced points such as the use of *they* to refer to a singular subject when the gender of the person is not specified or known. There is then a listening with a focus on understanding different speakers' English accents, an interesting challenge for advanced Sts.

The second half starts with a lexical focus on terminology used to describe aspects of language, e.g. *collocation*, *phrasal verbs*, *synonyms*, *register*, and *idioms* – terms which will be used throughout the course – and this is consolidated through a language quiz, where Sts learn words and phrases under these headings, related to language learning. Sts then read extracts from a *Guardian* article by the author of *The Accidental Dictionary: The Remarkable Twists and Turns of English Words* about some words which have changed meanings over time. The lesson ends with a documentary about the history of English from Roman times to today.

More materials

For teachers

Photocopiables
Grammar pronouns *p.170*
Communicative All about English *p.196*
(instructions *p.188*)

For students
Workbook 2B
Online Practice 2B

OPTIONAL LEAD-IN – THE QUOTE

Write the quote at the top of *p.20* on the board (books closed) and the name of the person who said it, or get Sts to open their books and read it.

Elicit / Explain that Burt Bacharach is an American composer, songwriter, record producer, pianist, and singer. He has won many awards over the years.

Ask Sts if they agree with the quote, and to think of examples if they can.

1 READING & SPEAKING

a 🔊 **2.10** Focus on the instructions and make sure Sts understand the task.

Give Sts time to read sentences 1–8.

EXTRA CHALLENGE Put Sts in pairs and get them to predict what the missing words are. Then play the audio for Sts to listen and write the words.

Play the audio, pausing after each sentence to give Sts time to write.

Elicit the words onto the board, either getting individual Sts to write the words, or getting Sts to spell them for you.

1 accommodate **2** Which **3** received **4** until
5 occurred **6** separate **7** government **8** definitely

🔊 **2.10**
1 The hotel can accommodate two hundred and fifty guests.
2 Which do you prefer, coffee or tea?
3 We received a very warm welcome.
4 I won't leave until she gets here.
5 Something unexpected occurred on their journey.
6 I saw her on three separate occasions.
7 The government is planning to raise taxes.
8 We'll definitely be there by seven.

Find out, with a show of hands, how many words Sts spelled correctly.

Ask the class what they think makes the words difficult to spell.

A lot of the words have double consonants, silent consonants, or vowel sounds that can be spelt in many different ways.

EXTRA IDEA Get Sts to test each other on English words that are difficult to spell. Ask Sts to write five words each that they think are hard to spell (they should use a dictionary to make sure they're spelling them correctly themselves). Then, in pairs, they read the words for their partner to spell. Finally, they compare with the correct spellings and see who got most words correct.

b Focus on the instructions and then put Sts in pairs to answer questions 1–5.

Elicit some ideas, but <u>don't</u> tell Sts if they are correct or not.

EXTRA SUPPORT Do this as a whole-class activity.

c Tell Sts to read the information from a website called The English Spelling Society. They must check their answers to **b** and answer questions 1–4. You might want to check Sts understand the meaning of the expression *knock-on effect* (= causing other events to happen one after another in a series).

Get Sts to compare with a partner, and then check answers.

EXTRA SUPPORT Before Sts read the website the first time, check whether you need to pre-teach any vocabulary.

b

1 (old) German and (Norman) French **2** 26 **3** 46
4 Pronunciation **5** More slowly

c

1 It's looking for alternatives to English spellings that will make it easier to write correct English.
2 They have less time available to learn other subjects.
3 There is no agreed way.
4 It makes it more likely that they will re-offend.

Deal with any new vocabulary. Model and drill the pronunciation of any tricky words.

d Focus on the task and give Sts time to complete it individually. You might want to elicit / explain what *fiend* means (= a very cruel or unpleasant person). Elicit or model its pronunciation /fiːnd/.

Whilst Sts are completing the task, you could write the paragraph on the board for Sts to then underline the words, or elicit from Sts which words they underlined.

Then elicit the correct spelling of the underlined words, and for some instances, ask Sts why the simplified spelling is easier.

If u hav a por memory, yor chances of becumming a good speller ar lo. But wors stil, yor chances of lerning to read ar not good either, because of nonsens like 'cow–crow, dream–dreamt, friend–fiend' and hundreds mor like them.

EXTRA IDEA You could get a strong student to read the text aloud.

e Do this as a whole-class activity, or put Sts in pairs and then get some feedback.

2 PRONUNCIATION sound–spelling relationships

Pronunciation notes

According to research, when a non-native speaker is talking to another person in English, the main reason for a breakdown in communication is incorrect pronunciation, often the mispronunciation of individual sounds.

a and **b** help remind Sts of common sound–spelling 'rules' in English and, in some cases, exceptions to those rules.

a Focus on the **Learning spelling rules or patterns** box and go through it with the class, highlighting that English pronunciation is a lot less irregular than many people may think.

Now focus on the task and give Sts, in pairs, time to say the words in each group. If there is an odd one out according to the sound of the pink letters, they should circle it.

EXTRA SUPPORT You may want to elicit the sound-picture words for each phonetic symbol, e.g. *house, phone, bike, witch, jazz, chess, snake, horse,* and *bird* (see **Sound Bank** *pp.174–175*).

b 🔊 **2.11** Play the audio for Sts to listen and check.

Check answers, eliciting the pronunciation rule in each case and any more exceptions that Sts can think of.

1 dishonest /dɪsˈɒnɪst/
Rule: the letter *h* is nearly always pronounced /h/.
Common exceptions: *heir, honest, honour, hour, exhausted*
2 allow /əˈlaʊ/
Rule: the letters *ow* are often pronounced /əʊ/, as in *blow, window, below*, but are also often pronounced /aʊ/, as in *frown, towel, now*. At the end of a word, the letters are usually pronounced /əʊ/. Occasionally, the same letters have different pronunciations according to the meaning, e.g. *row* /raʊ/ (= argument) but *row* /rəʊ/ (= a line of seats). These are called *homographs*.
3 river /ˈrɪvə/
Rule: the letter *i* + consonant + *e* is usually /aɪ/.
Common exceptions: *river, give, live* (the verb), *since*
4 whose /huːz/
Rule: the letters *wh* are nearly always /w/, but occasionally /h/, e.g. *whose, who, whole*.
5 All the same pronunciation
Rule: the letter *j* is always pronounced /dʒ/.
6 chorus /ˈkɔːrəs/
Rule: the letters *ch* are usually pronounced /tʃ/, but occasionally /ʃ/, e.g. *machine, chef, cliché*, when the words are of French origin, or /k/, e.g. *chemist, architect*, when the word comes from Greek.
7 sure /ʃɔː/
Rule: the letter *s* at the beginning of a word is nearly always /s/.
The only two exceptions are *sugar* and *sure*, where the *s* is pronounced /ʃ/.
8 All the same pronunciation
Rule: the letters *aw* are always /ɔː/ when they come at the end of a word, or when *aw* is followed by another consonant.
9 reporter /rɪˈpɔːtə/
Rule: the letters *or* are usually pronounced /ɔː/, but are usually /ɜː/ after a *w*, e.g. *work, word, world*.
10 All the same pronunciation
Rule: the letters *ir* are always /ɜː/ when they are followed by a consonant, but are pronounced /aɪə/ when followed by an *e*, e.g. *require*.

🔊 **2.11**
See words in Student's Book on *p.21*

---

c This exercise shows how Sts can use their instinct to predict pronunciation from spelling. Focus on the task and encourage Sts, in pairs, to predict the pronunciation of the words. If Sts have dictionaries, get them to check both the meaning and pronunciation.

Check answers, eliciting how to pronounce each word, and making sure Sts know the meaning.

chime /tʃaɪm/: verb; (of a bell or clock) to ring
howl /haʊl/: verb; (of a dog, wolf, etc.) to make a long, loud cry
jaw /dʒɔː/: noun; either of the two bones at the bottom of the face that contain the teeth
whirl /wɜːl/: verb; to move around quickly in a circle
worm /wɜːm/: noun; a long, thin creature with no bones or legs, which lives in soil

3 GRAMMAR pronouns

a 🔊 **2.12** This exercise focuses on why spellcheckers don't always correct the word *there* when it isn't correct in the context of a sentence.

Focus on the task and then play the audio once the whole way through for Sts just to listen.

Now play it again, pausing after each sentence to give Sts time to write.

Now put Sts in pairs to compare sentences and answer the question.

Check answers.

> they're, their, there

🔊 **2.12**
1 My students have great imaginations, but they're not very good at spelling.
2 I often have to correct their mistakes, some of which are pretty basic.
3 They now have notebooks and write down problem words there.

b Tell Sts to go to **Grammar Bank 2B** on *p.145*.

Grammar notes

Advanced Sts may be familiar with most of these uses of pronouns; however, the majority have never been overtly focused on, e.g. *one*, *one another*, the use of *they* / *their* to mean *he* and *she*, and the emphatic use of reflexive pronouns.

Reflexive pronouns

You may want to point out that nowadays in restaurants and other places waiters often simply say *Enjoy!* when they give you your food. This is short for *Enjoy it* / *Enjoy your meal*.

Focus on the example sentences for **generic pronouns** and go through the rules with the class.

Repeat for **reflexive and reciprocal pronouns**, and *it* and *there*.

Focus on the exercises and get Sts to do them individually or in pairs. If they do them individually, get them to compare with a partner.

Check answers after each exercise, getting Sts to read the full sentences.

> **a**
> 1 ✓ 2 you 3 ✓ 4 himself 5 their 6 them 7 They
> **b**
> 1 If anyone has not yet paid **their** course fees, **they** should go to registration immediately.
> 2 She finds it very hard to control **herself**.
> 3 I wouldn't stay in that hotel – **they** say the rooms are tiny and the service is awful.
> 4 They just don't like **each other** / **one another** at all.
> 5 Did they enjoy **themselves** at the festival?
> 6 Are you going to have the flat repainted, or will you and Jo do it **yourselves**?
> 7 **You** can never find one when **you** need one!
> **c**
> 1 Look. **There**'s a spelling mistake in this word. **It** should be *j*, not *g*.
> 2 **It**'s illegal to use a handheld mobile while you're driving. **There** used to be a lot of accidents caused by this.
> 3 How many miles is **it** to Manchester from here?

> 4 **It**'s scorching today. **It** must be at least 35 degrees.
> 5 **There**'s no need to hurry. The train doesn't leave for ages.
> 6 **It**'s not worth reading the paper today. **There**'s absolutely nothing interesting in it.

Tell Sts to go back to the main lesson **2B**.

EXTRA SUPPORT If you think Sts need more practice, you may want to give them the **Grammar** photocopiable activity at this point.

4 LISTENING understanding accents

a 🔊 **2.13** Focus on the **Understanding accents** box and go through it with the class. RP is the pronunciation most Sts of British English will be familiar with, probably due to the fact that they are likely to have heard it frequently in coursebook audio or in the media. However, if Sts are going to be able to communicate successfully with native speakers, given the small percentage of people who speak RP (only 2% of the UK population), it is essential that they are frequently exposed to different accents, even though this may be harder for them than listening to RP speakers. Sts at this level should be able to recognize US accents, but may well have problems identifying the others. It is probably worth pointing out that many native speakers also sometimes confuse different accents, especially regional ones they are not familiar with.

Now focus on the instructions and make sure Sts understand that each speaker is a native speaker from one of the countries in the list. Sts need to match the speakers to their country of origin. We have 'beeped out' the names of their hometowns and countries in 🔊 **2.13**, but Sts hear them in 🔊 **2.14**.

Focus on questions 1–3. Play the audio once the whole way through. Sts may notice that Anita, although very fluent, makes a few grammatical errors, e.g. *there is lots of students*, *there is always people*.

Encourage Sts to discuss the answers to 1 and 2, before listening again and trying to match any speakers they can to a country.

EXTRA SUPPORT Read through the script and decide if you need to pre-teach any new lexis before Sts listen.

🔊 **2.13**
See script 2.14

b 🔊 **2.14** Go through questions A–H, making sure Sts understand all the lexis, e.g. *inward-looking*, etc.

Now play the audio again, pausing after each speaker for Sts to listen and check their answers to **a** and answer questions A–H.

EXTRA SUPPORT You could pause the audio after the speaker says where he / she is from and elicit the answer from the class.

Get Sts to compare with a partner, and then check answers to **a**.

> **a**
> 1 **Mairi:** Scotland 2 **Diarmuid:** Ireland 3 **Laura:** Lithuania
> 4 **Jerry:** England (RP) 5 **Andrea:** Australia 6 **Anita:** Spain
> 7 **Lily:** the USA 8 **Paul:** South Africa

Now ask Sts which accents they are familiar with and why.

Check answers to **b**.

🔊 **2.14**
(script in Student's Book on *p.132*)
1 Mairi
I'm from a small village on the south-east coast of Scotland. It's a very small place – not very many people live there. I liked growing up there, but I think it's a better place to visit than it is to actually live because there isn't very much for young people to do there. The people are quite nice and friendly, but most people have spent their whole lives there and their families have been there for several generations, so sometimes it can seem a bit insular.

2 Diarmuid
I'm from Tipperary, which is in the middle of Ireland. It's quite a rural place. The town I'm from has a population of around two thousand, so it's quite small, but that means that most people know each other. So, I'd say the people there are friendly and quite welcoming.

3 Laura
So, I was born in Kaunas, which is the second-largest city in Lithuania. It is very modern. It has a lot of art galleries, and we even have seven universities in the city, which is quite a lot considering the size of it. It is super green, it has a lot of lakes and within the country it's considered to be a centre for cultural, academic, and economic activities. I would say as well that it's a home to various nationalities, and once you get to know people, they're really friendly, and really welcoming.

4 Jerry
I'm from Oxford, in the south-east of England. I, I was born here and I've, I've lived here my whole life. Difficult to say what the people are like because it's, in a way, it's a city of two halves, famous for its university, but also – which obviously has people from all over the world – but also it's a city in its own right. It has a very large BMW factory where they make Minis, so, but it's a nice place – I like it. I've lived here my whole life pretty much, so, so there we are.

5 Andrea
So I'm from Melbourne, which is on the south-east coast of Australia, just in, in the state of Victoria. This is a really cultural city – very European. You've got everything from beaches to art galleries, lots of shopping, and bars and restaurants, so it's a fantastic city to be in. The people are really laid-back and, and quite friendly there. We've got a very big mixture of cultures there, so a very multicultural city. So, it's quite diverse and a really interesting place to be.

6 Anita
I'm from Salamanca in Spain. It's a really beautiful city. It's got an old town with lots of monuments, and people are really nice, because there is a big university as well, there is lots of students, and that means there is always something going on. Students like organizing theatre or music events, lots of different things. And people like going out a lot, so there is always people out in the street, full families, from grandparents to parents to, to children. And there is also lots of tourists throughout the year, so you can always go somewhere and there is something happening.

7 Lily
I'm from New Jersey, and it's a nice mix between rural and city life, because it, it has a lot of nature and nice kind of mountain landscapes where you can go hiking or walking, but it also has nice access to the city and lots of nice little shops and restaurants as well.

8 Paul
OK, I was born in Johannesburg in the late fifties. I moved to Cape Town when I went to university, and of course it's a very beautiful old colonial centre, with lovely buildings, and the aspect of Table Bay with the beautiful backdrop of Table Mountain, wonderful vegetation, and a wonderful, friendly community of people. It's very vibrant and exciting – people like bright colours in the strong sunlight; it's a very creative environment.

EXTRA IDEA You may want to highlight some aspects of the different accents, e.g.:
Scottish – She pronounces *er* and *um* as /er/ and /em/ rather than /ə/ and /əm/.
American – She pronounces some *ts* like *ds*, e.g. she says /sɪdi/ for *city*.
South African – He often makes an /ɪ/ sound where English would make an /e/ sound, e.g. /wɪnt/, /frɪdli/.

EXTRA SUPPORT If there's time, you could get Sts to listen again with the script on *p.132*, so they can see exactly what they understood / didn't understand. Translate / Explain any new words or phrases.

c Do this as a whole-class activity, or put Sts in pairs and then get some feedback.

5 VOCABULARY lexical areas

a This exercise recycles language terminology and words and expressions from the first three lessons of the Student's Book. Set a time limit and get Sts, in pairs, to say what the four headings mean.
Check answers.

1 **a collocation** = a common combination of words
2 **a phrasal verb** = a verb combined with an adverb and / or a preposition to give a new meaning
3 **a synonym** = a word or expression that has the same meaning
   register = the level or style of language that is appropriate for the situation in which it is being used
4 **an idiom** = a group of words whose meaning is different from the meanings of the individual words

EXTRA SUPPORT Do this as a whole-class activity.

b Now put Sts in pairs and give them time to complete all four sections.
Check answers. Model or elicit pronunciation where necessary.

1 Collocations
1 sought   2 complete   3 quick   4 couple   5 distant
6 career   7 hurt   8 a rough   9 strongly   10 under
2 Phrasal verbs
1 go   2 put   3 get   4 came   5 carry   6 makes
7 dressing   8 turned   9 laid   10 carry
3 Synonyms and register
1 G (*ill-fated* is more formal)
2 D (*siblings* is more formal)
3 I (*conversation* is more formal)
4 A (*task* is more formal)
5 B (*benefit* is more formal)
6 J (*opposed to* is more formal)
7 C (*resign* is more formal)
8 E (*man* is more formal)
9 F (*resemble* is more formal)
10 H (*require* is more formal)
4 Idioms
1 white lie   2 catch, eye   3 dead, night   4 down, earth
5 pain, neck   6 How, earth   7 letter   8 big(ger) picture
9 nose, grindstone   10 gut feeling

EXTRA SUPPORT Make the *Word Challenge* into a team competition. Divide the class into small groups and set a time limit. They then calculate their score out of 40, to find the winner.

Find out how many answers Sts got correct.

Deal with any vocabulary problems that arose.

6 READING reading notes and expanding them into a spoken explanation

a Tell Sts they are now going to read about the origin of five different words. When they have finished, they should decide which words they think have changed their meaning the most.

Get Sts to discuss their answer, and then elicit answers from the class. You could ask Sts which extract they found the most interesting, and tell them what you think.

EXTRA SUPPORT Before Sts read the extracts the first time, check whether you need to pre-teach any vocabulary, but not the highlighted words.

b Tell Sts to read the extracts again and this time to answer questions 1–5.

Get them to compare with a partner, and then check answers.

1 alcohol **2** a treadmill **3** a girl **4** a blockbuster
5 a cupboard

LANGUAGE IN CONTEXT

c Focus on the task and make sure Sts understand the meaning of *used metaphorically* /metəˈfɒrɪkli/ (= used in a non-literal way, not being used with its basic meaning, e.g. *flew* in the sentence *When the doorbell rang, she flew to answer it*. She didn't literally fly; *flew* is being used metaphorically to mean she ran very fast. The literal meaning is to move through the air.)

Now do this as a whole-class activity, or put Sts in pairs and then get some feedback. Model or elicit the pronunciation of *pounce* /paʊns/ and *resurrect* /rezəˈrekt/.

pounce on = move suddenly forward in order to catch sth
borrow = take and use sth that belongs to sb else
pick up = take hold of sth and lift it up
resurrect = bring a dead person back to life

d Write the following words on the board: DEER, NAUGHTY, AWFUL, DISMANTLE. Elicit / Explain what they mean.

Now tell Sts to go to **Communication Changing meanings**, **A** on *p.107* and **B** on *p.112*. Here they each read about how two of the above words have changed their meanings, and then tell each other.

Go through the instructions and make sure Sts understand what they have to do.

Monitor and help where necessary.

Check answers by getting Sts to tell the class about the meanings of the four words.

Tell Sts to go back to the main lesson **2B**.

7 ▶ VIDEO LISTENING

This is the first of five **Video Listenings** which are incorporated into the Student's Book. If you are unable to show the video in class, remind Sts that they can find the video on *Online Practice*, and ask them to watch the video and do the activities for homework.

a Tell Sts they are going to watch a documentary on the history of the English language. Focus on the list of influences, and make sure Sts understand all the lexis, e.g. *Anglo-Saxons, colonies*, etc.

Now put Sts in pairs and tell them to try to number the influences in the order in which they think they happened. Point out that the first one (*the Romans*) has been done for them.

b Play the video once the whole way through for Sts to watch and check.

Check answers.

EXTRA SUPPORT Read through the script and decide if you need to pre-teach any new lexis before Sts watch the video.

2 the Anglo-Saxons **3** Christian monks **4** the Vikings
5 the French **6** Shakespeare **7** British colonies **8** America
9 technology

The history of English

Hello, I'm Chris, and welcome to London. But before we move from Big Ben to the London Eye, I need to send a tweet.

Only a few years ago a *tweet* was something only birds did; now everybody's *tweeting*…often using *textspeak* or *emoticons*. But the inventiveness of the English language is nothing new. It has been evolving for over one thousand six hundred years.

In AD forty-three, the Romans invaded Britain, conquering the indigenous Celts and taking over most of the country.

In AD four hundred and nine, they left, and around fifty years later several tribes from around northern Germany – including the Angles, the Saxons, and the Jutes, better known as the Anglo-Saxons – started to move in.

They settled in the east, but unlike the Romans, the Anglo-Saxons didn't set out to conquer. They shared many things with the Celts, including language.

Unlike Latin – which had never really caught on with the locals – people started using Anglo-Saxon terms for lots of everyday things, like *man*, *woman*, and *friend*.

But then Latin made a comeback! This time, it didn't arrive with Roman soldiers; it arrived with Christian monks. Christianity became very popular with the locals, and introduced a whole new alphabet and religious vocabulary.

Then the Vikings arrived in around eight hundred AD. Their warrior spirit was reflected in their language. They *raced* through the country, *ransacking* towns and villages, armed with *knives* and *clubs*.

They *took* land, goods, and slaves, but they *gave* English around two thousand words.

The Vikings and the Anglo-Saxons battled for almost three hundred years, until the English King Harold won the Battle of Stamford Bridge.

But only three weeks later, the unlucky Harold was killed by William the Conqueror – a Norman from France – at the Battle of Hastings.

William became the King of England and started building castles all over the country.

French became the language of the wealthy elite. It was the native tongue of all *princes*, *dukes*, *barons*, and *dames*.

But English remained the language of the peasants. Farmers herded *cows* and *sheep*, which were Anglo-Saxon words…but the nobility ate *beef* and *mutton*, which were French words.

Over the next three hundred years, the two languages mixed, until English eventually won out, albeit with ten thousand new words from the French.

This richer language was the perfect plaything for poets and playwrights, and one literary genius contributed more than most.

William Shakespeare wrote thirty-eight plays and one hundred and fifty poems. He also coined around two thousand new words, and his turn of phrase transformed the entire language.

The sixteenth century was also the Age of Discovery, and for Britain this meant the birth of an Empire that stretched across the globe.

The British colonialists often used native words, and soon words like *safari* from the African language Swahili, *pyjamas* from the Urdu language in India, and *boomerang* from the native Australian language Dharuk, had entered the language.

But the country that had the most impact on English was America.

The newly independent America needed a new type of English – American English. American English kept many of the old English words, so today English *curtains* are still American *drapes*, English *wardrobes* are American *closets*, and English *trousers* are American *pants*.

But the language changed a lot, too. The father of American English was Noah Webster. He created a new dictionary which simplified the spelling of lots of complicated English words. He also introduced uniquely American words, like *squash*, *chowder*, and *skunk*.

By the twentieth century, there were two main types of English – British English and American English. But throughout the twentieth century, both continued to change and borrow from one another, especially with the invention of 'computers' and the 'internet'. Suddenly we needed new words to describe our 'blogs', 'posts' and, of course, 'tweets'.

Today English is truly global. There are around three hundred and seventy-five million native speakers, and about one point five billion people learn it as a foreign language. But it is always changing and shifting to suit our needs. Today the English vocabulary has over one hundred and seventy thousand words…and counting. We are inventing new words every day and if we don't know them we just *google* them on our *smartphones* or…send a *tweet*.

c Focus on the task and give Sts time to read sentences 1–7.
Play the video again, pausing if necessary to give Sts time to mark each statement *T* (true) or *F* (false), and to correct the false ones.
Check answers.

1 F (It's been changing for over 1,600 years.)
2 F (The monks invented the alphabet.)
3 T
4 T
5 T
6 F (They borrowed from each other.)
7 F (There are 375 million native speakers and 1.5 billion learners.)

EXTRA SUPPORT You could get Sts to watch again with subtitles, so they can see exactly what they understood / didn't understand. Translate / Explain any new words or phrases.

d Do this as a whole-class activity if your Sts come from the same country. If not, put Sts in pairs and then get some feedback.

Revise and Check

There are two pages of revision and consolidation after every two Files. These exercises can be done individually or in pairs, in class or at home, depending on the needs of your Sts and the class time available.

The first section revises the **grammar** and **vocabulary** of the two Files. The exercises add up to 50 (grammar = 20, vocabulary = 30), so you can use the first page as a mini-test on Files 1 and 2.

The second section presents Sts with a series of skills-based challenges. First, there is a **reading** text which is of a slightly higher level than those in the File, but which revises grammar and vocabulary Sts have already learned. The **listening** is some unscripted street interviews, where people are asked questions related to the topics in the Files. Sts can either watch the interviews on video or listen to them on audio. You can find these on the *Teacher's Resource Centre*, *Classroom Presentation Tool*, *Class DVD*, and *Class Audio CDs* (audio only). Alternatively, you could set this section / activity as homework. Sts can find the video on *Online Practice*.

More materials
For teachers
Teacher's Resource Centre
Video Can you understand these people? 1&2
Quick Test 2
File 2 Test
For students
Online Practice Check your progress

GRAMMAR

a
1 We need to **have** the broken window fixed soon, before it starts getting cold.
2 The Chinese economy is growing and **as** a result, the standard of living is rising.
3 We were very late **because** of an accident on the motorway.
4 Everybody seemed to enjoy the barbecue even **though** the weather wasn't very good.
5 She wants to take six months' unpaid leave **so** she can travel round the world.
6 When I was young, my family **would** spend every summer holiday at the seaside.
7 Didn't **there** use to be a sweet shop on the corner?
8 Will the person who left **their** boarding pass at security please go back and collect it?
9 If we lived closer to **one** another, we'd probably spend more time together.
10 Joe is quite reserved – he never talks about **himself**.

b
1 I **have got to pick my mum up from the station.**
2 If we buy a dishwasher, **we won't have to do the washing-up.**
3 I **haven't seen him since** 2010.
4 They managed to get here **despite the heavy traffic. / despite the traffic being heavy. / despite the fact that the traffic was heavy.**
5 The train was cancelled **due to snow / due to the snow.**
6 She wore dark glasses **so as not to be recognized.**

7 My aunt **was always baking biscuits** for us.
8 **If one learns a bit of the language,** the local people…
9 Jane and Martha **see each other** once a month.
10 The children wrapped the present **by themselves.**

VOCABULARY

a
1 comes across 2 spontaneous 3 self-sufficient 4 resourceful 5 sympathetic 6 determined 7 straightforward 8 deep down

b
1 pain 2 temper 3 heart 4 earth 5 letter 6 earth 7 picture

c
1 off 2 qualifications 3 sack 4 promoted 5 rewarding 6 Job-hunting 7 monotonous 8 staff

d
1 neighbourhood 2 generosity 3 friendship 4 loss 5 Freedom 6 excitement 7 memory

CAN YOU understand this text?

a
1 early 2 fast 3 same 4 good 5 what

b
1 T
2 F (They can only recognize that a sentence in their own language sounds different from a sentence in a different language.)
3 F (They learn objects first.)
4 T
5 F (They can often use simple words to say how they feel or what they want.)
6 F (Some produce larger chunks.)
7 T
8 T
9 T

▶ CAN YOU understand these people?

1 c 2 b 3 c 4 a

◉ 2.15
1
I = interviewer, A = Alison
I Who are you closest to in your family?
A I would say I'm closest to my brother. He's my twin brother, so obviously I've known him forever. Er, we're quite different people on the outside, but on the inside we're quite similar, so he understands me and we've always been there for each other.

2
I = interviewer, R = Roslinn
I Have you always done the same job?
R No. So, er, I've done a variety of jobs. Different sectors and different job roles.
I What have you done?
R So I've worked in a biomedical charity, um, helping to issue grants to scientific researchers. Um, I've worked in customer services, and I've done some staff training to train people on how to use their different systems at work.

3

I = interviewer, R = Rabia

I   Can you remember your first day at school?

R   Um, I don't remember the first name, but, er, the first day, but, um, the first year, I have, um, a few, um, memories from the first year.

I   Was it good or bad?

R   Um, it was good, um, I didn't understand the language very well because, er, I was born in the French part of Switzerland and my parents originally come from Turkey, so I couldn't speak French, um, the first year, so it was interesting. I was looking at the teacher, but couldn't understand, but yeah, later on it, it went better.

4

I = interviewer, M = Margaret

I   Do you think you're a good speller?

M   I'm a terrible speller, which is why I studied engineering.

I   Are there any words in particular that you find difficult to spell?

M   Um, I have, so I grew up in Quebec which is half English and half French, so I have a very hard time spelling, um, a lot of words and, so the, like 'precious' is hard for me to remember how to spell. Um, anything that has, anything that you don't use all the time. I love spellcheck now, um, in the phones and that.

Revise and Check

3A A love-hate relationship

G *get*
V phrases with *get*
P identifying attitudes

Lesson plan

This lesson deals with the topic of relationships, and contrasts dating apps with meeting people in real life, which is now coming back into fashion!

First, Sts discuss what they think is important for people to have in common for relationships to work, and then they read two articles about a dating app called Hater, which links people up according to what they hate. Language in context focuses on using synonyms to improve your vocabulary range. Then in Pronunciation, Sts focus on pitch and intonation to identify enthusiasm and sarcasm.

In the second half of the lesson, Sts listen to a journalist describe how, after years of online dating, she decided to try meeting people in real life. A second Language in context focuses on the three different possible structures after the verb *suggest*. There is then a grammar focus on different uses of *get*. The lexical focus is on verbs and idioms related to the verb *get*, probably the most versatile verb in English. The lesson ends with a questionnaire which recycles both lexical and grammatical examples of this verb.

More materials

For teachers

Photocopiables
Grammar get p.171
Communicative Reconciliation? p.197 (instructions p.188)
Vocabulary Phrases with get p.220 (instructions p.214)

For students
Workbook 3A
Online Practice 3A

OPTIONAL LEAD-IN – THE QUOTE

Write the quote at the top of *p.26* on the board (books closed) and the name of the person who said it, or get Sts to open their books and read it.

Elicit / Explain that Rashida Jones is an American actress, writer, and producer. Her mother, Peggy Lipton, was also an actress, and her father is Quincy Jones, a musician and record producer.

Get Sts to discuss what they think the quote means (that it's become a game, to see how many people match you, going on dates, etc., but not really looking for a life-partner) and whether they agree with it.

1 READING & SPEAKING inferring general meaning / skimming

a Focus on the task and then give Sts time, individually, to tick three things in the list that they think are the most important to make a relationship work. If they think any of the items are not important, then they should put a cross by them.

b Put Sts in pairs to compare their lists and to discuss if there is anything missing from the list in **a** that they think is important.

Get some feedback from various pairs about their answers in **a**. You could find out if there were any disagreements within the pairs.

Finally, elicit from the class any other things they think are important for a relationship to work.

c Focus on the task and give Sts time to read the paragraph about the app Hater.

EXTRA SUPPORT Ask Sts some comprehension questions to make sure they have understood the app, e.g. *What is the difference between swiping left and right? (You swipe left if you love something and right if you don't)*, etc. Or read the paragraph with the class, to make sure they understand all the lexis, e.g. *chew, guacamole, swipe*, etc.

Elicit opinions from the class about the app. You could also ask Sts what they think of the three topics suggested (*loud chewing, cargo shorts, guacamole*).

d Focus on the task and the name of the two people who wrote articles about the app. Point out that Giles Coren and Victoria Coren Mitchell are brother and sister (Giles is a food critic and journalist, and Victoria presents a TV quiz show).

Tell Sts to quickly skim-read the two articles and try to match the original title of the article to each one, and decide who liked the idea of the app.

Get Sts to compare with a partner, and then check answers. You could ask Sts which phrases or sentences helped them to work out the answers.

EXTRA SUPPORT Before Sts read the articles the first time, check whether you need to pre-teach any vocabulary, but not the highlighted words.

1 If you want to be a good lover, be a great hater
2 Share the hate, ruin the date
Giles Coren likes the idea of the app; Victoria Coren Mitchell doesn't.

Deal with any other vocabulary problems that arose.

e Focus on the task and give Sts time to read the articles again and tick all the reasons Giles and Victoria give for their opinion of the app.

Get Sts to compare with a partner, and then check answers.

Giles 1 and 4
Victoria 6 and 7

f Focus on the task and make sure Sts know what *tone* means here (= the general mood).

Now focus on questions 1–6 and make sure Sts understand all the lexis, e.g. *mixed feelings*, *provocative*.

Give Sts time to answer the questions and find examples to explain their answers.

Get Sts to compare with a partner, and then check answers.

1 V: *One of the key dangers of the internet is that it encourages us to give everything an immediate verdict…*
2 G: *Just as I knew from the first kiss that this was a woman who had no time for sandals on men…*
3 V: *Nevertheless, like most apps, it would pass the time happily enough at a bus stop.*
4 V: *More openly expressed hatred in the world – just what we need!*
5 G: *My wife and I have absolutely no interests in common. None.*
6 G: *The idea that a romantic life together is about sharing your stupid hobbies is deluded and childish.*

LANGUAGE IN CONTEXT

g This highlights the advantage of using a wide range of vocabulary, especially in writing. Focus on the task and get Sts to match the highlighted words to 1–6.

Get Sts to compare with a partner, and then check answers. You might want to point out that both *hey* and *boy* are informal exclamations, and *boy* is more common in American English. Elicit or model pronunciation of the words.

1 eager   2 Boy   3 aversions   4 loathe   5 bond
6 singletons

h Tell Sts to cover 1–6 in **g** and read the first paragraph of Victoria Coren Mitchell's article, replacing the highlighted words with the synonyms in 1–6.

EXTRA SUPPORT Write the words in 1–6 in **g** in random order on the board for Sts to refer to if necessary.

Finally, deal with any other new vocabulary. Elicit or model the pronunciation of any tricky words.

i Do this as a whole-class activity, or put Sts in pairs and then get some feedback. You could tell Sts who you agree with more and why.

2 PRONUNCIATION identifying attitudes

Pronunciation notes

British English speakers frequently use intonation to show their attitude, e.g. to show that they are being sarcastic rather than sincere. This use of intonation often confuses not only foreign speakers, but also American or Australian speakers, who may not use intonation in this way.

The focus here is more on receptive pronunciation, and helping Sts to distinguish between different intonation patterns, but they are encouraged to practise the enthusiastic intonation themselves, as sometimes Sts can unwittingly sound sarcastic or negative because of their intonation when this is not intentional.

a 🔊 3.1 Focus on the task and then play the audio once the whole way through for Sts to listen to the two sentences.

Check answers.

1 genuinely enthusiastic   2 sarcastic

🔊 **3.1**
See sentences in Student's Book on *p.27*

b 🔊 3.2 Focus on the **Fine-tuning your pronunciation: identifying enthusiasm and sarcasm** box and go through it with the class.

Tell Sts they are going to listen to eight mini-conversations twice. Each time, they need to pay attention to the final speaker's response: once the response will be genuinely enthusiastic, and once it will be sarcastic. Their task is to identify which is which.

Play conversation 1 a and b, pausing at the end for Sts to make a note of their answers. Check the answers (*a* E, *b* S) to make sure Sts have understood what they have to do.

Now play the rest of the audio, pausing after each mini conversation.

Check answers.

2 a S b E   3 a S b E   4 a E b S   5 a E b S   6 a S b E
7 a S b E   8 a E b S

🔊 **3.2**
1
a
A My parents have invited us over next Sunday.
B (*Enthusiastically*) Oh great! Your mum's such a wonderful cook.
b
A My parents have invited us over next Sunday.
B (*Sarcastically*) Oh great! Your mum's such a wonderful cook.
2
a
A I don't believe it – the car won't start.
B Why don't we walk instead?
A (*Sarcastically*) Good idea – it's only two miles.
b
A I don't believe it – the car won't start.
B Why don't we walk instead?
A (*Enthusiastically*) Good idea – it's only two miles.
3
a
A Do you want me to lend you five pounds?
B (*Sarcastically*) Five pounds? Yes, thanks, that'll really help!
b
A Do you want me to lend you five pounds?
B (*Enthusiastically*) Five pounds? Yes, thanks, that'll really help!
4
a
A I've booked that new vegetarian restaurant for dinner tomorrow.
B (*Enthusiastically*) Oh good, I love vegetarian food.
b
A I've booked that new vegetarian restaurant for dinner tomorrow.
B (*Sarcastically*) Oh good, I love vegetarian food.
5
a
A Gary and Melanie have put pictures of their baby on Facebook.
B (*Enthusiastically*) Cool. I was dying to see some!
b
A Gary and Melanie have put pictures of their baby on Facebook.
B (*Sarcastically*) Cool. I was dying to see some!
6
a
A Happy Birthday, darling! It's a scarf.
B (*Sarcastically*) Thanks, that's just what I needed.

b
A Happy Birthday, darling! It's a scarf.
B (*Enthusiastically*) Thanks, that's just what I needed.

7
a
A I've done the washing-up.
B (*Sarcastically*) Oh great, well done.

b
A I've done the washing-up.
B (*Enthusiastically*) Oh great, well done.

8
a
A The family are all going to spend Christmas with us.
B (*Enthusiastically*) That'll be fun!

b
A The family are all going to spend Christmas with us.
B (*Sarcastically*) That'll be fun!

c 🔊 **3.3** Focus on the task and point out that Sts are only responding enthusiastically with the lines in **b**.

Play the audio, pausing after each mini-conversation for Sts to listen and respond with enthusiasm.

🔊 **3.3**
See sentences in **b** in Student's Book on *p.27* said with enthusiasm

Now play the audio again, pausing after each mini-conversation to elicit individual responses.

EXTRA CHALLENGE Tell Sts to try to read the sentences in both a sarcastic and an enthusiastic way. Then put Sts in pairs, **A** and **B**. Sts **A** say a sentence and Sts **B** decide if they sound enthusiastic or sarcastic. They then swap roles.

3 LISTENING & SPEAKING

a Focus on the question and the four alternatives, and make sure Sts know what a *blind date* is.

Put Sts in pairs or small groups, or do this as a whole-class activity.

If Sts worked in pairs or small groups, get some feedback.

b Focus on the task and the title of the article, and elicit the meaning of *IRL* (= in real life).

Now give Sts time to read the beginning of the article and answer the questions.

Get Sts to compare with a partner, and then check answers.

She feels (felt) very nervous.
Because she has been using dating apps unsuccessfully for years.

c 🔊 **3.4** Focus on the task, photos, and questions.

Play the audio, pausing after each challenge to give Sts time to answer the questions.

Get Sts to compare with a partner, and then check answers.

EXTRA SUPPORT Read through the script and decide if you need to pre-teach any new lexis before Sts listen.

Challenge 1
1 In a bookshop
2 No because it didn't feel natural.
3 She thinks it might work for some people, but not for her, and gave it 2/5.

Challenge 2
1 In a club that had minigolf
2 Yes, with someone called Rob
3 She recommends trying something new outside your comfort zone, and gave it 5/5.

Challenge 3
1 At a singles' event
2 No because there was an awkward / embarrassing atmosphere and the three men she approached weren't interested in her.
3 She didn't think singles events worked, and gave it 1/5.

Challenge 4
1 In a restaurant
2 Yes, with her blind date, Tom
3 She thought it was a good experience, and gave it 4/5.

🔊 **3.4**
(script in Student's Book on *p.132*)
Challenge one: Approach a stranger
James suggested that I talk to guys in bookshops, mainly because I love books, but also because, as he pointed out, bookshops are a nice, calm space to start a conversation – much better than a packed Tube train. So I had a go, but it was absolutely terrifying. I tried smiling and saying, 'Ooh, that one's very good', but it just didn't feel natural at all, and even though a couple of guys responded positively, I just couldn't move from 'that one's very good' to natural conversation. So, in the end, I left the shop with zero phone numbers and more books to gather dust on my shelves.
I can sort of see how this method might work for some people, but I'd still rather use my thumb and my phone. I'd give this challenge two out of five.
Challenge two: Try a new activity
OK, so my next challenge was to try something new, and I thought I'd take my housemate, Charlie, to a club that had minigolf. This challenge was Hayley's idea, and she suggested I shouldn't use conventional chat-up lines like, I don't know, 'Do you come here often?' and that I should try and be as natural as possible.
Anyway, so after our game of minigolf, I managed to catch the eye of a guy who was sipping a pint of beer across the bar. He was tall and had dark hair – my typical type, in fact. I remembered Hayley's advice, and I walked over to him, with Charlie to help me feel more confident, and I told him that Charlie and I had a bet to guess his name. Of course, our guesses were all wrong and we ended up laughing hysterically. He turned out to be called Rob – our idea was Harold – and though I was nervous talking to him at first, it quite quickly felt as easy as talking to a friend at a party. And guess what? We exchanged numbers and have been chatting online ever since. So, I'd definitely recommend trying something new, outside of your comfort zone. Five out of five.
Challenge three: Go to an event for singles
I decided to go to a singles' event because I thought that before dating apps existed, these must have worked. I sort of imagined there'd be professional people who live in London, a bit like me – people who'd signed up because they were too busy to go looking for dates, or perhaps who were also fed up of apps.
So, as soon as I got there, I had two glasses of wine and that meant I was happy to chat with pretty much anyone, but the awkward atmosphere was painful and sort of embarrassing. No one was talking – they were just standing in small groups of either men or women, and sort of looking round at the others in the room. Anyway, I plucked up the courage and went up to a couple of guys, but they both made it clear that they weren't interested in me. And then I tried chatting to another guy eating a burrito, but he seemed more interested in the burrito than me. So I felt like a bit of a failure, and to be honest, I'd only give singles events one out of five.
Challenge four: Ask a friend to set up a blind date
A blind date is one of the most classic dating techniques I could think of, so I texted a few friends and asked them to set me up. They took ages, but after a while I finally managed to get a friend to organize a date for me. She gave me his first name, which was

Tom, and a photo, and told me to head to a restaurant that night at seven thirty. Of course, I really wanted to look him up on every social media site in order to prepare, but then I reminded myself that this was supposed to be real life. But because I knew nothing about him, I got way more nervous than before any other first date I'd been on. Tom was a bit late, but we immediately got chatting about American politics, and I think I was probably more 'myself' than I'd ever been on a date from a dating app. The fact that we didn't know anything about each other meant we discovered things on equal terms, and that was a nice change. And he was funny, and asked interesting questions, and all that showed me that dating in real life can be fun. And I'd only just left the restaurant when he texted me to say that he'd had a great time. So that was a good experience – four out of five.

Finally, elicit if Anna agrees with Sts' opinions from **a**.

d Focus on the task and Anna's feelings in A–D.

Put Sts in pairs to see if they can remember how Anna felt.

Play the audio again, pausing after each challenge to give Sts time to choose the correct answer.

Get Sts to compare with their partner and explain why she felt that way.

Check answers.

A challenge 3   **B** challenge 1   **C** challenge 4   **D** challenge 2

EXTRA SUPPORT   If there's time, you could get Sts to listen again with the script on *p.132*, so they can see exactly what they understood / didn't understand. Translate / Explain any new words or phrases.

LANGUAGE IN CONTEXT

e 🔊 **3.5** Focus on the task and give Sts time to read 1–3.

Play the audio for Sts to listen and complete the phrases.

Check answers.

1 trying   **2** that I talk   **3** I shouldn't use

🔊 **3.5**
1 The dating coaches suggested trying four ways of meeting someone new.
2 James suggested that I talk to guys in bookshops.
3 Hayley suggested I shouldn't use conventional chat-up lines.

---

f Focus on the *suggest* box and go through it with the class. You may want to point out that in 2, with *he*, *she*, and *it* we can say *I suggest (that) she talk / talks to her boss*. *Talk* here is the subjunctive form. You could tell Sts if *suggest* is in the present, then we use the present after it, e.g. *I suggest (that) you talk to your boss*. If *suggest* is in the past, we can use the present or the past after it, e.g. *He suggested (that) I talk / talked to my boss*. You could also point out in 3 that this structure is not common after *you*, e.g. *I suggest (that) you get a new job* is more natural than *I suggest (that) you should get a new job*.

Now give Sts time, individually or in pairs, to say how sentences 1–3 could be said in three different ways with *suggest*.

EXTRA SUPPORT   Give Sts time to write their sentences.

Check answers.

1 She suggested going to the doctor.
    She suggested (that) I go / went to the doctor.
    She suggested (that) I should go to the doctor.

2 I suggested visiting the museum.
    I suggested (that) they visit / visited the museum.
    I suggested (that) they should visit the museum.

3 He suggested talking to her.
    He suggested (that) I talk / talked to her.
    He suggested (that) I should talk to her.

g 🔊 **3.6** Focus on the task and questions 1–3.

Play the audio for Sts to listen and answer the questions.

Get Sts to compare with a partner, and then play again if necessary.

Check answers.

EXTRA SUPPORT   Read through the script and decide if you need to pre-teach any new lexis before Sts listen.

1 She learned that there are many opportunities to meet people in real life.
2 The advantage of real-life dating was that it gave her a buzz and boosted her confidence, but apps have the advantage that you know beforehand whether people are single or not, and whether you have things in common.
3 She is not going to rule out real-life dating in the future, but will continue to use her apps.

🔊 **3.6**
(script in Student's Book on *p.132*)
The verdict
Well, after the four challenges, I think the main thing I learnt was that pushing myself out of my comfort zone, and actually looking at men outside of a screen, showed me just how many opportunities there are to meet people in real life. Catching a stranger's eye started off as terrifying, but it also gave me a real buzz, and I really surprised myself that I was able to chat someone up for the first time in my life. Obviously, I didn't find love, and sadly the texting with Rob and Tom has dried up – but those positive experiences taught me a lot, and I won't rule out real-life flirting in the future. But although I found the experience confidence-boosting, I'm not sure I'm completely converted. I found that approaching guys with no idea even whether they're single or not was more stressful than fun. If I get a match on an app, we already have things in common, and I know they're looking for a match, too. So I'm not giving up my apps just yet.

EXTRA SUPPORT   If there's time, you could get Sts to listen again with the script on *p.132*, so they can see exactly what they understood / didn't understand. Translate / Explain any new words or phrases.

h Put Sts in pairs or small groups to discuss the question.

Get some feedback from various pairs or groups. You could also tell the class what you think.

EXTRA IDEA   Ask Sts which of Anna's challenges they would consider trying.

4 GRAMMAR & VOCABULARY *get*

a Focus on the task and give Sts time to match the meanings of the **bold** phrases to the verbs in the list.

Check answers.

1 obtain   **2** became   **3** arrived   **4** persuade

b Tell Sts to go to **Grammar Bank 3A** on *p.146*.

Grammar notes

Apart from the many phrases and idioms involving *get*, *get* is also frequently used as a main verb, often as a more informal alternative to another verb, e.g. *obtain*, *receive*, *understand*. In spoken English, *get* is also often used in certain grammatical structures, e.g. as an alternative to *be* in the passive, or instead of *have* in the structure *get sth done*. Here all these different uses are pulled together.

- **Rule 1: *get* + noun / pronoun**

***get to* + a place** = *arrive at / in*.

Remind Sts that with *home* or *here / there* it's without *to*, e.g. NOT ~~What time did you get to home?~~

- **Rule 5: *get* + object + infinitive**

Have someone send you the details is more formal than *get someone to send you the details* in British English.

Focus on the example sentences for ***get*** and go through the rules with the class.

Focus on the exercises and get Sts to do them individually or in pairs. If Sts do them individually, get them to compare with a partner.

Check answers after each exercise, getting Sts to read the full sentences. Remind Sts that if we substitute *make* for *get* in 3 and 10 in **a**, we need to cut *to*.

a

1 is becoming   2 buy / have   3 persuade / tell (*make* is also possible, but without *to*)   4 have   5 received   6 catch / take   7 arrive at   8 fetch / bring   9 be   10 persuade (*make* is also possible, but without *to*)

b

1 I only just **got my work permit renewed** in time.
2 My husband has only been in the UK for two months and he just can't **get used to driving** on the left.
3 Monica's fiancé **nearly got killed** in a car crash.
4 I can **get my sister to babysit** tomorrow night, so we can go out.
5 If you can't find your keys, we'll have to **get all the locks changed**.
6 We **got stopped** by the police today.
7 I went to the optician's yesterday to **get my eyes tested**.
8 We could drive there if you could **get your parents to lend us** their car.
9 My job has **got / been getting more stressful** over the last few years.
10 We really want to **get the kitchen replaced** soon.

Tell Sts to go back to the main lesson **3A**.

EXTRA SUPPORT   If you think Sts need more practice, you may want to give them the **Grammar** photocopiable activity at this point.

c Put Sts in pairs and give them time to complete the *get* phrases.

Check answers.

1 on   2 together   3 to know   4 me down

d Tell Sts to go to **Vocabulary Bank** Phrases with ***get*** on p.164.

Vocabulary notes

Phrasal verbs with *get*

Highlight that:

- you *get over* a broken relationship, death, illness, or other trauma.
- *get by* can also be used to mean *manage* in the context of speaking languages, e.g. *I know enough French to get by when I go on holiday there*. Sts saw this use in **2A**.

Remind Sts that phrasal verbs with *get* will be found in the dictionary under *get*, but that as *get* is such a common verb, expressions and idioms will probably come under the other word, e.g. *get rid of* will come under *rid*.

Focus on **1 Expressions with *get*** and get Sts to do **a** individually or in pairs.

🔊 **3.7** Now focus on **b**. Play the audio for Sts to listen and check.

Check answers and elicit the meaning of each phrase from Sts.

1 **get the impression** = think, have an idea or opinion
2 **get the wrong end of the stick** = to understand sth in the wrong way
3 **get the chance** = have the opportunity
4 **get the joke** = understand a joke
5 **get to know** = discover what sb or sth is really like
6 **get hold of** = make contact with
7 **get rid of** = throw away, make yourself free of sb / sth
8 **get my own back on** = take revenge on sb
9 **get into trouble with** = find yourself in a situation in which you can be criticized or punished
10 **get out of the way** = move to one side to allow sb or sth to pass

---

🔊 **3.7**
Phrases with *get*
1 Expressions with *get*
1 I get the impression you're a bit annoyed with me.
2 When I told him to meet us at the station, he got **the wrong end of the stick** and went to the bus station, not the train station.
3 Since we stopped working together, we hardly ever get **the chance** to see each other.
4 Everyone else laughed, but I didn't get **the joke**.
5 When you get **to know** him, I think you'll really like him.
6 I need to speak to Martina urgently, but I just can't get **hold of** her.
7 I want to get **rid of** that awful painting, but I can't because it was a wedding present from my mother-in-law.
8 I'm going to get **my own back on** my brother for telling our parents I got home late. Now I won't lend him my bike.
9 He's going to get **into trouble with** his boss if he's late again.
10 I tried to walk past him, but he wouldn't get **out of the way**.

Focus on **2 Idioms with *get*** and get Sts to do **a** individually or in pairs.

🔊 **3.8** Now focus on **b**. Play the audio for Sts to listen and check.

Check answers and elicit the meaning of each idiom from Sts.

1 **I Get real** = see things as they really are, don't act in a stupid / unreasonable way
2 **J Get a life** = used to tell sb to do sth more exciting with their life

3 A get nowhere (not get anywhere) = to make no progress or have no success

4 F get on sb's nerves = to annoy sb

5 D get your act together = to organize yourself more effectively in order to be able to achieve sth

6 C get on like a house on fire = to get on very well with sb

7 E get a move on = you tell sb to get a move on when you want them to hurry

8 B to be getting on (always in the continuous form) = to be getting old

9 H get the message = understand what sb is trying to tell you

10 G get your own way = get or do what you want, especially when sb has tried to stop you

---

🔊 **3.8**

2 Idioms with *get*

1 I
Get real! There's no way you can afford that car!

2 J
Get a life! You're forty and you're still living with your parents!

3 A
I'm not getting anywhere with this crossword. It's just too difficult for me.

4 F
She really gets on my nerves. Everything about her irritates me: her voice, her smile – everything!

5 D
She really needs to get her act together. Her exam is in two weeks and she hasn't even started studying.

6 C
They get on like a house on fire. They have exactly the same tastes and interests.

7 E
You should get a move on. If you don't leave soon, you'll miss the train.

8 B
Your grandfather must be getting on a bit. Is he in his eighties now?

9 H
My boss just never gets the message. I keep dropping hints about a pay rise, but he takes no notice.

10 G
She always gets her own way. Everyone just does whatever she tells them to.

Finally, highlight that all these idioms are informal.

EXTRA SUPPORT Tell Sts to write four personal sentences – two with expressions from **1** and two with idioms from **2**.

When they are ready, put them in pairs and get them to tell each other their sentences.

Get some Sts to read their sentences to the class.

Focus on **3 Phrasal verbs with *get*** and get Sts to do **a** individually or in pairs.

🔊 **3.9** Now focus on **b**. Play the audio for Sts to listen and check.

Check answers. Highlight that the meaning of some of the phrasal verbs given is correct for the context here, for example *get together* here means *start a relationship*, but it can also mean *meet up with*.

🔊 **3.9**

3 Phrasal verbs with *get*

1 J
Get together means start a relationship.

2 A
Get over something means recover from it.

3 K
Get on with something means continue doing it.

4 D
Get through to somebody means make them understand.

5 B
Get into means start a career or profession.

6 C
Get around means move from place to place.

7 L
Get away with something means do something wrong without getting caught.

8 E
Get by means manage with what you have.

9 F
Get behind means fail to make enough progress.

10 G
Get somebody down means make them feel depressed.

11 I
Get out of something means avoid a responsibility or obligation.

12 H
Get back to somebody means respond to them by speaking or writing.

Focus on **Activation** and get Sts to cover sentences 1–12, look at phrases A–L, and see if they can remember the phrasal verbs.

EXTRA SUPPORT Put Sts in pairs, **A** and **B**. Sts **A** cover sentences 1–12 and look only at phrases A–L. Sts **B** read some sentences from 1–12 in random order and Sts **A** have to say the phrase. They then swap roles.

Tell Sts to go back to the main lesson **3A**.

EXTRA SUPPORT If you think Sts need more practice, you may want to give them the **Vocabulary** photocopiable activity at this point.

5 SPEAKING

This exercise activates both the lexical and grammatical uses of *get* in the lesson.

Put Sts in pairs. Then get them to read the questionnaire and tick eight questions they would like to ask their partner.

Sts take turns to ask each other their questions.

Get feedback from various pairs.

EXTRA IDEA Finally, you could tell Sts to cover the questionnaire and get them to ask you some of the questions from memory.

G discourse markers (2): adverbs and adverbial expressions
V conflict and warfare
P stress in word families

Lesson plan

In this lesson, the topic is history, as seen through the cinema, in historical films, and TV series.

The lesson begins by introducing the vocabulary of conflict and warfare through a quiz. The pronunciation focus is on shifting word stress in some of the word 'families' Sts have just learned. Sts then read the descriptions of memorable scenes from two historical films, and in Language in context, focus on how the same word can change meaning and parts of speech depending on the context. They go on to describe memorable scenes of their own to each other and they then write a paragraph describing the film or series and the scene. You may want to ask Sts to research a historical film or TV series in advance.

In the second part of the lesson, the topic shifts to historical accuracy in films. Sts listen to an interview with a scriptwriter who has worked on historical films and series. There is then a grammar focus on discourse markers, and the lesson ends with a communication activity, *Historical inaccuracies*, where Sts predict and then tell each other about factual errors in recent historical films.

More materials

For teachers

Photocopiables

Grammar discourse markers (2): adverbs and adverbial expressions *p.172*
Communicative Classic historical films *p.198* (instructions *p.188*)
Vocabulary Conflict and warfare *p.221* (instructions *p.214*)

For students

Workbook 3B

Online Practice 3B

OPTIONAL LEAD-IN – THE QUOTE

Write the quote at the top of *p.30* on the board (books closed) and the name of the person who said it, or get Sts to open their books and read it.

Elicit / Explain that Eduardo Galeano (1940–2015) was a Uruguayan journalist, writer, and novelist, best known as the author of *Las venas abiertas de América Latina* (*Open Veins of Latin America*, 1971) and *Memoria del fuego* (*Memory of Fire Trilogy*, 1982–6).

Get Sts to discuss what they think the quote means and whether they agree with him.

1 VOCABULARY conflict and warfare

EXTRA IDEA Before beginning **a**, you may want to focus on the lesson title and explain that it is an expression which means 'the freedom of artists or writers to change facts in order to make a story, film, play, or painting, etc. more interesting or beautiful'.

a Focus on the heading and explain / elicit the meaning of *conflict* (= a situation in which people, groups, or countries are involved in a serious disagreement or argument) and *warfare* (= the activity of fighting a war or competing in an aggressive way with another group, company, etc.).

Now focus on the quiz and tell Sts, in pairs, to look at the highlighted words in questions 1–8 of the quiz and try to work out their meaning.

Check the meaning of the highlighted words. Elicit or model pronunciation of any tricky words.

1 **executed** /ˈeksɪkjuːtɪd/ = killed, especially as a legal punishment
   blow up /bləʊ ʌp/ = explode
2 **Civil War** /ˈsɪvl wɔː/ = a war between groups of people in the same country
3 **Revolution** /revəˈluːʃn/ = an attempt by a large number of people in a country to change their government
4 **troops** /truːps/ = soldiers in large groups
5 **captured** /ˈkæptʃəd/ = caught a person and kept them as a prisoner or in a confined space
   looted /ˈluːtɪd/ = stole things from shops or buildings after a riot, fire, etc.
6 **treaty** /ˈtriːti/ = a formal agreement between two or more countries
7 **casualties** /ˈkæʒuəltiːz/ = people who have been killed or injured in war
8 **overthrown** /əʊvəˈθrəʊn/ = removed a leader or a government from a position of power by force
   coup /kuː/ = a sudden change of government that is illegal and often violent

Now tell Sts to do the quiz by circling the correct option in each question.

Check answers.

1 Guy Fawkes   2 Abraham Lincoln   3 Czechoslovakia
4 China   5 the Visigoths   6 Versailles   7 World War II
8 Chile

b Tell Sts to go to **Vocabulary Bank Conflict and warfare** on *p.165*.

Vocabulary notes

People and events

Highlight that *wounded* is also an adjective (*He couldn't fight because he was wounded*) and that (*the*) *wounded* can only be used for deaths / injuries caused in wartime. For accidents in daily life, use *injured* (adj.) or *the injured*, e.g. *The injured were taken to hospital*.

Highlight the collocations in the definitions, e.g. *heavy casualties*, *armed forces*, etc. Remind Sts that the *p* is silent in *coup* /kuː/ because it is a French word.

Highlight the difference between:
- *rebellion* (an attempt by some of the people in a country to change their government, using violence)
- *revolution* (= an attempt, by a large number of people, to change the government of a country, especially by violent action)
- *coup* (= a sudden change of government that is illegal and often violent)

You may also want to teach *uprising*, *revolt*, and *insurgency* as synonyms for *rebellion*.

Conflict verbs

You may want to point out to Sts that the verbs *capture*, *defeat*, *loot*, *overthrow*, *retreat*, *shell*, and *surrender* can also be used as nouns. You could also point out that *outbreak* is the noun from the verb *break out*.

Now focus on **1 People and events** and get Sts to do **a** and **b** individually or in pairs.

🔊 **3.10** Now focus on **c**. Play the audio for Sts to listen and check **a** and **b.**

Check answers.

🔊 **3.10**
Conflict and warfare
1 People and events
a
1 casualties
2 refugees
3 forces
4 troops
5 commander
6 the wounded
7 civilians
8 snipers
9 survivors
10 ally
b
1 rebellion
2 coup
3 ceasefire
4 siege
5 civil war
6 treaty
7 revolution

Now either use the audio to drill the pronunciation of the words, or model and drill them yourself. Give further practice of any words your Sts find difficult to pronounce.

EXTRA CHALLENGE You may want to teach some collocations for **People and events**, e.g. *suffer heavy casualties*, *evacuate the wounded*, *sign a peace treaty*.

Now focus on **2 Conflict verbs** and get Sts to do **a** individually or in pairs.

🔊 **3.11** Now focus on **b**. Play the audio for Sts to listen and check.

Check answers.

🔊 **3.11**
2 Conflict verbs
1 The rebels **overthrew** the government.
2 Fighting **broke out** between the rebels and the army.
3 The army **shelled** the rebel positions.
4 The rebels **retreated**.
5 Some of the rebels **surrendered**.
6 The rebels **blew up** the airport runway.

7 The government **declared** war on the rebels.
8 Some rebels **looted** the city.
9 The army **captured** over three hundred rebels.
10 They finally **defeated** the rebels.
11 The army **released** most of the rebel prisoners.
12 They **executed** the rebel leader.

Highlight any words your Sts may have problems pronouncing correctly, e.g. *overthrew* /əʊvə'θruː/.

Now focus on **3 Metaphorical uses of 'conflict verbs'** and check Sts can remember the meaning of *metaphorical*, which they saw in **2B**.

Get Sts to do **a** individually or in pairs.

🔊 **3.12** Now focus on **b**. Play the audio for Sts to listen and check.

Check answers.

🔊 **3.12**
3 Metaphorical uses of 'conflict verbs'
1 The fire broke out at three o'clock in the morning.
2 The police have **released** details of the accident.
3 The new princess has **captured** the imagination of the public.
4 I read the instructions three times, but they completely **defeated** me.
5 The minister was arrested and forced to **surrender** his passport.
6 A crisis has **blown up** over the new education policy.
7 He **declared** that he was in love with her.
8 The flood water took a long time to **retreat** from the streets.

Highlight any words your Sts may have problems pronouncing correctly, e.g. *captured* /'kæptʃəd/.

EXTRA IDEA If appropriate in your teaching situation, you could put Sts in pairs and get them to tell their partner about any current stories related to conflict or warfare, or do this as a whole-class activity.

Tell Sts to go back to the main lesson **3B**.

EXTRA SUPPORT If you think Sts need more practice, you may want to give them the **Vocabulary** photocopiable activity at this point.

2 PRONUNCIATION stress in word families

Pronunciation notes

Sts sometimes make mistakes with shifting word stress in word 'families' (e.g. *history*, *historical*) because they tend to stress the same syllable as in the base word. It is important to point out that in many such 'families' the stress changes, and Sts need to check and underline the stress when they come across these words.

a Focus on the **Changing stress in word families** box and go through it with the class.

Then focus on the chart. Give Sts a few minutes to complete it individually or in pairs, and to underline the stressed syllable in all multi-syllable words.

EXTRA SUPPORT Elicit the answers from the class and write them on the board.

b 🔊 **3.13** Play the audio once or twice for Sts to check they have the correct syllables underlined.

Check answers and elicit that the 'families' where the stress changes are *execution*, *history*, *rebellion*, *revolution*, and *victory*.

capture, <u>cap</u>tive / <u>cap</u>tor, <u>cap</u>tive, **capture**
com<u>mand</u>, **com<u>mand</u>er**, com<u>mand</u>ing, com<u>mand</u>
exe<u>cu</u>tion, **exe<u>cu</u>tioner**, **<u>exe</u>cute**
<u>his</u>tory, his<u>to</u>rian, his<u>to</u>ric / **his<u>to</u>rical**
<u>loot</u>ing, <u>loot</u>er, **loot**
re<u>bel</u>lion, **<u>re</u>bel**, re<u>bel</u>lious, re**bel**
revo<u>lu</u>tion, **revo<u>lu</u>tionary**, revo<u>lu</u>tionary, re<u>volt</u>
siege, be<u>sieged</u>, **be<u>siege</u>**
sur<u>vi</u>val, **sur<u>vi</u>vor**, sur<u>vi</u>ving, **sur<u>vive</u>**
<u>vic</u>tory, **<u>vic</u>tor**, vic<u>to</u>rious

Elicit / Explain the difference between:
- *captive* (= person who has been captured) and *captor* (= person who captures sb).
- *historical* (= connected with the past, e.g. *historical documents*) and *historic* (= important in history, e.g. *a historic occasion*).

EXTRA SUPPORT Play the audio again, pausing after each group of words for Sts to listen and repeat.

EXTRA IDEA Dictate some or all of these sentences for Sts to write down:

1 *The rebels were captured and executed.*
2 *All the captives survived the siege.*
3 *It was a historic victory.*
4 *In the end, the revolutionaries were victorious.*
5 *The troops rebelled against the commander.*
6 *Historians disagree on the causes of the rebellion.*

Check answers, eliciting the sentences onto the board.
Then get Sts, in pairs, to practise saying the sentences.

3 READING scanning for specific information

a Focus on the two photos from the films and ask Sts if they have seen either of them and what historical period they are set in (*the Roman empire in the 2nd century AD*, and *the Second World War*). If they have seen the films, elicit who the main characters in the stills are (*Maximus Decimus Meridius* and *Winston Churchill*) and elicit / explain that whereas Churchill was a historical figure, Maximus is fictional. You could also ask Sts if they recognize the scene in the still and what is happening.

b Focus on the task and set a time limit for Sts to read the descriptions and decide what information is given about each.
   Get Sts to compare with a partner, and then check answers.

   1 A,B 2 A,B 3 A 4 B 5 A 6 B 7 A

LANGUAGE IN CONTEXT

c Give Sts time to go through the highlighted words in sentences 1–5 with a partner and check they know what they mean.
   Check answers, eliciting what part of speech each word is.

succeed /sək'siːd/ (verb) = achieve sth that you have been trying to do
engineering /ˌendʒɪ'nɪərɪŋ/ (noun) = the study of how to apply scientific knowledge to the design and building of machines, roads, bridges, etc.

gripping /'grɪpɪŋ/ (verb) = hold on tightly to sth
stirring /'stɜːrɪŋ/ (verb) = move sth round and round with a spoon in order to mix it thoroughly
servant /'sɜːvənt/ (noun) = a person who works in another person's house and cooks and cleans, etc. for them

d Now tell Sts, in their pairs, to find the highlighted words in 1–5 in **c** in text A, and decide if they are the same part of speech and what they mean in the context of the text.
   Check answers. Model and drill pronunciation.

succeed (verb) = come next after sb and take their place / position
engineering (verb) = arrange for sth to happen, especially when this is done secretly to give you an advantage
gripping (adj) = exciting or interesting in a way that holds your attention
stirring (adj) = causing strong feelings
servant (noun) = a person who works for another person, company, or organization (e.g. a public servant, a civil servant)

   Deal with any other vocabulary problems that arose from the texts.

e Do this as a whole-class activity, or put Sts in pairs and then get some feedback.

EXTRA IDEA If you have access to the videos of either film, you could show Sts the scenes and ask them which they thought was more dramatic, or ask Sts to find them and watch them at home.

4 SPEAKING & WRITING

a Focus on the **Describing a scene from a film** box and go through it with the class.
   Focus on the instructions. Remind Sts that a historical film or TV series is one set in a historical period or based on a real event, so the term covers a wide range of films. Try to have the titles of a few well-known historical films or series to suggest for Sts who are having problems thinking of one.
   Give Sts time to look at the prompts. Monitor and help with any vocabulary they may need.

EXTRA SUPPORT Give Sts time to write or make notes.

b Put Sts in small groups of three or four and tell them to describe their film or TV series and the scene. If the others in the group have seen it, they should say whether they agree or not.
   Monitor and help.
   Get a few Sts to tell the class about a memorable scene.

EXTRA CHALLENGE Tell Sts not to mention the title of the film or name the characters, but to refer to them as, e.g. *a man, a woman, a soldier, a slave*, etc., and see if the others in the group can name the title of the film.

c Set a time limit, e.g. 20 minutes, for Sts to write their paragraphs, or set this for homework. Tell them to use the two descriptions in **3** as models.

5 LISTENING

a 🔊 **3.14** Focus on the photo of Adrian Hodges and the instructions.

Now focus on the task and give Sts time to read the three possible options. Make sure they know the meaning of the expression *as long as*.

Focus on the **Glossary** and go through it with the class.

Play **Part 1** of the audio once the whole way through for Sts to listen and choose the best option.

Check the answer.

EXTRA SUPPORT Read through the script and decide if you need to pre-teach any new lexis before Sts listen.

2

🔊 **3.14**
(script in Student's Book on *pp.132–133*)
I = interviewer, A = Adrian Hodges
Part 1

I How important is historical accuracy in a historical film?

A The notion of accuracy in history is a really difficult one in drama because, you know, it's like saying, well, 'Was Macbeth accurate?', 'Was – is – Shakespearean drama accurate?' The iro– the thing is, it's not about historical accuracy, it's about whether you can make a drama work from history that means something to an audience now. So I tend to take the view that, in a way, accuracy isn't the issue when it comes to the drama. If you're writing a drama, you, you have the right as a writer to create the drama that works for you, so you can certainly change details. The truth is nobody really knows how people spoke in Rome or how people spoke in the courts of Charles the Second or William the Conqueror or Victoria, or whoever. You have an idea from writing – from books, and plays, and so on. We know when certain things happened, what sort of dates happened. I think it's really a question of judgement. If you make history ridiculous, if you change detail to the point where history is an absurdity, then obviously things become more difficult. The truth is, the, the more recent history is, the more difficult it is not to be authentic to it. In a way, it's much easier to play fast and loose with the details of what happened in Rome than it is to play fast and loose with the details of what happened in the Iraq War, say, you know. So, it, it, it's all a matter of perspective in some ways. It, it, it's something that you have to be aware of and which you try to be faithful to, but you can't ultimately say a drama has to be bound by the rules of history, because that's not what drama is.

I Do you think that the writer has a responsibility to represent any kind of historical truth?

A Not unless that's his intention. If it's your intention to be truthful to history and you, and you put a piece out saying, 'This is the true story of, say, the murder of Julius Caesar exactly as the historical record has it,' then of course, you do have an obligation, because if you then deliberately tell lies about it, you are, you know, you're deceiving your audience. If, however, you say you're writing a drama about the assassination of Julius Caesar purely from your own perspective and entirely in a fictional context, then you have the right to tell the story however you like. I don't think you have any obligation except to the, to the story that you're telling. What you can't be is deliberately dishonest; you can't say, 'This is true,' when you know full well it isn't.

---

b Focus on the task and give Sts time to read points 1–8.

Play the audio again the whole way through.

Get Sts to compare with a partner, and then check answers.

Sts should have ticked:
1, 2, 4, and 6.

EXTRA SUPPORT If there's time, you could get Sts to listen again with the script on *pp.132–133*, so they can see exactly what they understood / didn't understand. Translate / Explain any new words or phrases.

c 🔊 **3.15** Focus on the **Glossary** and go through it with the class. Find out if any Sts have seen the films. If they have, find out what they thought of them. Don't worry if they haven't.

Focus on the task and play **Part 2** of the audio once the whole way through for Sts to listen and answer the question.

Check the answer.

EXTRA SUPPORT Read through the script and decide if you need to pre-teach any new lexis before Sts listen.

Adrian is positive.

🔊 **3.15**
(script in Student's Book on *p.133*)
Part 2

I Can you think of any examples where you feel the facts have been twisted too far?

A Well, I think the notion of whether a film, a historical film, has gone too far in presenting a dramatized fictional version of the truth is really a matter of personal taste. The danger is – with any historical film – that if that becomes the only thing that the audience sees on that subject, if it becomes the received version of the truth, as it were, because people don't always make the distinction between movies and reality and history, then obviously if that film is grossly irresponsible or grossly fantastic in its, in its presentation of the truth, that could, I suppose, become controversial. I mean, if you – you know, I think that the only thing anybody is ever likely to know about *Spartacus*, for example, the movie, is Kirk Douglas and all his friends standing up and saying, 'I am Spartacus, I am Spartacus', which is a wonderful moment and it stands for the notion of freedom of individual choice and so on. So, *Spartacus* the film, made in nineteen sixty-two, I think, if memory serves, bec– has become, I think, for nearly everybody who knows anything about Spartacus, the only version of the truth. Now in fact, we don't know if any of that is true, really. There are some accounts of the historical Spartacus, but very, very few and what – virtually the only thing that's known about it is that there was a man called Spartacus and there was a rebellion, and many people were, you know, were crucified at the end of it, as in, as in the film. Whether that's irresponsible I don't know. I, I can't say that I think it is. I think in a way it's, it's, it's…*Spartacus* is a film that had a resonance in the modern era.

There are other examples, you know: a lot of people felt that the version of William Wallace that was presented in *Braveheart* was really pushing the limits of what history could stand. The whole, in effect, his whole career was invented in the film, or at least, yeah, built on to such a degree that some people felt that perhaps it was more about the notion of Scotland as an independent country than it was about history as an authentic spectacle. But you know, again, these things are a matter of purely personal taste – I mean, I enjoyed *Braveheart* immensely.

---

d Before Sts listen again, focus on questions 1–5.

Play the audio again once the whole way through.

Get Sts to compare with a partner, and then play the audio again as necessary.

Check answers.

1 That if there is a film that is the only thing people ever see or know about a historical event, then it becomes accepted as the truth.

2 The scene when Kirk Douglas and all his friends stand up and say, 'I am Spartacus.'

3 Very few. That he was a man who led a rebellion and many people died (were crucified) at the end.
4 It was completely invented in the film.
5 That *Braveheart* was about the idea of Scotland as an independent country.

EXTRA SUPPORT If there's time, you could get Sts to listen again with the script on *p.133*, so they can see exactly what they understood / didn't understand. Translate / Explain any new words or phrases.

e Put Sts in pairs or small groups to discuss the two questions.
  Elicit opinions and ideas.

EXTRA SUPPORT Do this as a whole-class activity and elicit opinions from the class.

6 GRAMMAR discourse markers (2): adverbs and adverbial expressions

a 🔊 **3.16** Focus on the instructions, sentences 1–4, and uses A–D.
  Play the audio, pausing after each item to give Sts time to complete the task.
  Get Sts to compare with a partner, and then check answers.

1 C 2 A 3 D 4 B

🔊 **3.16**
See sentences in Student's Book on *p.33*

b Tell Sts to go to **Grammar Bank 3B** on *p.147*.

Grammar notes

Recognizing discourse markers is an essential part of understanding both written and spoken English. Using them correctly is also an important aspect of communication that enables the reader or listener to follow your ideas.

Sts have already worked on discourse markers (commonly called *linkers*) which introduce a result, a purpose, a contrast, and a reason in **1B**. Here they focus on a more diverse group. Sts should now be familiar with the term *discourse marker*, so when others come up, refer to them that way for Sts to add to their knowledge.

Focus on the example sentences for **discourse markers (2): adverbs and adverbial expressions** and go through the rules with the class.
Focus on the exercises and get Sts to do them individually or in pairs. If Sts do them individually, get them to compare with a partner.
Check answers after each exercise, getting Sts to read the full sentences.

a
1 Basically   2 In any case   3 Obviously   4 I mean
5 at least   6 All in all   7 By the way   8 Otherwise
9 In fact   10 Talking of
b
1 And **anyway / in any case / besides**, I decided that I didn't really like them that much.
2 **After all / I mean**, you've got nothing to lose.

3 **Talking of / Speaking of** Simon, did you know he's moving?
4 **By the way / Incidentally**, did you remember to get a birthday present for Mum?
5 **As regards / Regarding** salary, you will be paid on the last day of each month, with a bonus in December.
6 It was a very overcast day, but **at least / on the other hand** it didn't rain.
7 **On the one hand**, buying our own place would mean not paying rent, but **on the other hand**, I'm not sure we can afford a mortgage.
8 They've employed me as a troubleshooter – **in other words / that's to say**, somebody who sorts out any problems.
9 **All in all**, the meal was a great success.
10 **Actually / In fact / As a matter of fact**, they live in the flat below us.
11 You'd better hurry up with your homework, **otherwise** you won't be able to watch TV tonight.

EXTRA SUPPORT If you think Sts need more practice, you may want to give them the **Grammar** photocopiable activity at this point.

c Focus on sentence prompts 1–8 and tell Sts to complete them in their own words.
  When Sts have finished, put them in pairs to compare sentences.
  Find out if any pairs completed any sentences in exactly the same way.

EXTRA SUPPORT Get Sts to complete the sentences in pairs, and then put two pairs together in small groups of four to compare sentences.

7 SPEAKING

a Focus on the task and find out if any Sts have seen any of the films or the TV series. Now get them to match the images to the time periods.

EXTRA SUPPORT Do this as a whole-class activity.

  Check answers.

A *The Favourite* – 18th century
B *Victoria and Abdul* – 19th century
C *Mary Queen of Scots* – 16th century
D *The Crown* – 20th century

b Focus on the task and give Sts time, in pairs, to guess which two are fact and which are fiction.
  Elicit some ideas, but <u>don't</u> tell Sts if they are correct or not.

c Put Sts in pairs, **A** and **B**, and tell them to go to **Communication Historical inaccuracies**, **A** on *p.107*, **B** on *p.113*.
  Sts **A** read about *The Favourite* and *Victoria and Abdul*, and Sts **B** read about *Mary Queen of Scots* and *The Crown*.
  When Sts have finished telling each other what is fact and what is fiction, find out how many Sts had guessed correctly.
  Tell Sts to go back to the main lesson **3B**.

d Put Sts in pairs to discuss the three questions.
  Get some feedback from various pairs.

EXTRA IDEA If you think some Sts may not have much to say here, you could put two pairs together in groups of four, or ask the questions to the whole class.

Lesson plan

In The Interview, the interviewee is Mary Beard, a professor of Classics at the University of Cambridge, who frequently appears on TV and in the media talking about history. In this three-part interview, she talks about how to get people interested in ancient history and what we can learn from it, about the importance of considering ordinary people's lives when studying history, and her view on historical films. The interview is followed by a language focus on typical collocations which Mary Beard uses in the interview.

In The Conversation, Sts watch three people discussing if there's a period in history they would like to go back to, and if so, what kind of people they would like to meet. Sts then discuss these questions, as well as two other questions related to the topic, focusing on ways to respond to keep a conversation going.

More materials
For teachers
Teacher's Resource Centre
Video Colloquial English 2&3
Quick Test 3
File 3 Test
For students
Workbook Colloquial English 2&3
Can you remember? 2&3
Online Practice Colloquial English 2&3
Check your progress

OPTIONAL LEAD-IN (BOOKS CLOSED)

Write on the board ANCIENT HISTORY and elicit the pronunciation of *ancient* /ˈeɪnʃənt/.

Ask Sts what nationalities they associate with the expression, and elicit, e.g. *the Greeks, the Romans, the Egyptians, the Persians*, etc.

Then ask Sts if they studied any of these at school, and what they remember about them.

Finally, tell Sts they are going to watch an interview with a well-known historian.

If you have internet access in your classroom or Sts have it on their phones, give them a few minutes to google *Mary Beard* and find out a bit about her.

1 ▶ THE INTERVIEW Part 1

a Books open. Focus on the photo and the biographical information about Mary Beard. Give Sts time to read it as well as the **Glossary**. You might want to tell Sts that the title *Dame* in Britain is given to a woman as a special honour because of the work she has done.

Do the question as a whole-class activity.

Classics refers to the study of ancient Greek and Roman culture, especially their languages and literature.

A *classicist* is an expert in ancient Greek and Roman language, literature, art, architecture, or culture.

b Focus on the task and go through the **Glossary** with the class.

Play the video (**Part 1**) once the whole way through for Sts to answer the questions.

Give Sts time to tell each other, in pairs, what they understood.

Check answers.

EXTRA SUPPORT Before playing the video, go through the listening scripts and decide if you need to pre-teach / check any lexis to help Sts when they listen.

> Professor Beard thinks the right way is to ask people questions about their contemporary culture and geography. The wrong way is to look at obscure and complicated ancient literature. She thinks we can learn how to deal with a lot of political issues we have nowadays.

I = interviewer, M = Mary Beard
Part 1
I Professor Beard, what's the secret to getting people interested in the Romans, in ancient history?
M Well, you have to go about it in the right way, really. Um, ah, you know, I think that, you know, it's, perhaps starting from rather arcane and difficult bits of literature isn't the right way. But, you know, one thing that you see in Britain, you know, is one thing that we know is that an awful lot of our culture and our geography and our place names, and so on, are actually formed by the Romans, you know. You ask somebody, um, 'Why do you think so many English place names end in -*chester* or -*caster*, you know, *Manchester, Doncaster*?' And they'll often say, 'Oh, I don't know'. And then you say, 'That's because that bit – -*caster* – is from the Latin for 'military camp', and every place that ends -*caster* or -*chester* once had a Roman fort on it.' And I've got a pretty ninety-nine per cent success record with getting people interested after that, 'cause suddenly it is a question, not of these, um, uh, remote people who wrote some literature that you probably suspect would be boring; it's the people who formed the geography of our country and much of Europe. Why is London the capital of, of Britain? It's because the Romans made it so.
I What do you think we can learn from Roman history?
M In political terms, many of the issues and questions and dilemmas that we face now, uh, were faced by the Romans. And in many ways, we're still thinking about and using their answers. I mean, one classic example of that is a famous incident in Roman history in sixty-three BC, where there's a terrorist plot in, in the city of Rome to, to assassinate the political leaders – to torch the city, um, and to take over – revolution. Um, and that plot is discovered by, uh, one of the most famous Romans of all, Marcus Tullius Cicero – you know, the great orator and wit of Roman culture. And he discovers the plot. He lays it before the Senate. He then decides to execute the leading conspirators without trial – summary execution. Um, and a couple of years later, he's exiled. Now, in many ways that's the kind of problem we're still facing, uh, with modern responses to terrorism. I mean, what, how far does, how far should homeland security be more important than civil rights, you know? Uh, you know, what about those people in Guantanamo Bay without trial? Um, you know, where, where does the boundary come between the safety of the state and the liberty of the citizen? Now, the Romans were debating that in the sixties BC. And in many ways, we're debating it, uh, along the same terms. And in part, we've learnt from how they debate those rights and wrongs.

c Focus on the task and give Sts time, in pairs, to see if they can complete any of the sentences.

Play the video again the whole way through.

Get Sts to compare with their partner, and then check answers.

EXTRA SUPPORT You could pause the video after each point has been mentioned and, in pairs, get Sts to compare orally what they have understood.

1 …once had a Roman fort or military camp there.
2 …the Romans made it the capital.
3 …assassinate leaders and take over.
4 …tell the Senate about it and then execute the leading conspirators without trial.
5 …responses to modern-day terrorism.

EXTRA SUPPORT If there's time, you could get Sts to watch again with subtitles, so they can see exactly what they understood / didn't understand. Translate / Explain any new words or phrases.

d Do this as a whole-class activity, or put Sts in pairs and then get some feedback. You could also tell Sts if you enjoyed history as a subject at school.

▶ Part 2

a Focus on the task and give Sts time to read sentences 1–7. Tell them the first time they watch, they just need to mark each sentence *T* (true) or *F* (false).

Play the video (**Part 2**) once the whole way through for Sts to do the task.

Get Sts to compare with a partner.

EXTRA SUPPORT You could check answers now, so when Sts are listening again in **b**, they only need to correct the *F* sentences.

Part 2

I   If you could go back in time, is there one particular historical period that you'd like to go back to?

M   I think it would be a terrible kind of, er, punishment to be made to go back in history, you know, particularly if you're a woman, you know. There's, um, you know, there is not a single historical period in world history where women had halfway as decent a time as they do now. So, deciding to go back there, uh, you know, that would, that would be a self-inflicted punishment. I think I'd rather go in the future. Um, and there's also, I mean, even for men there's considerable disadvantages about the past – you know, like, you know, no antibiotics and no aspirin.

I   Today, we live in a celebrity culture, but in *Meet the Romans* you focus on the lives of the ordinary people in Rome. Was that a conscious decision, to try to get people away from celebrity culture?

M   I was rather pleased that people did actually find, you know, the non-celebrity, um, version of the Romans interesting. Um, and in some ways, if it, if it was a small antidote to modern celebrity culture, I'm extremely pleased.
Um, I think that that wasn't quite what was driving me, though, because, uh, I think the celebrities of the ancient world are so remote from us in some ways. Um, and one of the things that puts people off ancient history is that, you know, you know, the big narrative books, the kind of the history of 'the big men', you know, never seem to answer all those questions that we know we all want to know about the ancient world, you know, or any period in the past, you know: where did they go to the loo, you know. Um, and actually I think people are often short-changed, uh, about, um, the, in, in terms of the, providing an answer to questions which are really good ones, you know. Um, you know, in the end, most of us, most women – don't know about men – most women, you know, do really want to know what having a baby was like, um, uh, before the advent of modern obstetrics, you know. That's

a big question. It's not a, it's, it's not, simply because it's, uh, intimate and female doesn't mean it's a less important question than why Julius Caesar was assassinated.
And actually, world history contains a lot more people like me and my family, and women, and slaves, and people who, you know, want to do many of the things that we want to do, you know. But they can't clean their teeth 'cause there's no such thing as an ancient toothbrush. Now, how does that feel? And I'm not saying in that I guess that those big bloke-ish issues aren't important, you know. The assassination of Julius Caesar, you know, is an event in world history that has formed how we look at every other assassination since, you know. When Kennedy's assassinated, we see that partly in relationship to that, that formative, defining bit of political assassination in Rome. But it's not the only way that Rome's important.

---

b Tell Sts that they are going to watch again, and that this time, they need to correct the false sentences.

Play the video again the whole way through.

Get Sts to compare with a partner, and then check answers.

EXTRA SUPPORT You could pause the video after each point has been mentioned and, in pairs, get Sts to compare orally what they have understood.

1 T
2 T
3 F (She says, '…for men there's considerable disadvantages about the past…')
4 F (She focused on ordinary people.)
5 T
6 T
7 F (She says it 'has formed how we look at every other assassination since…')

EXTRA SUPPORT If there's time, you could get Sts to watch again with subtitles, so they can see exactly what they understood / didn't understand. Translate / Explain any new words or phrases.

c Do this as a whole-class activity, or put Sts in pairs and then get some feedback.

▶ Part 3

a Focus on the task and the **Glossary** on *p.35*.

Play the video (**Part 3**) once the whole way through for Sts to do the task.

Give Sts time to discuss the questions and what they understood, then play the video again if necessary.

Get Sts to compare with a partner, and then check answers.

1 Not particularly important
2 *Gladiator* because she thought it was a good re-creation of ancient Rome and because it showed a realistic image of Roman combat.
3 She is very pleased about it because it brings history into the popular consciousness and it shows that it can be enjoyable.

Part 3

I   As a historian, how important do you think it is that historical films should be accurate?

M   Um, I'm not sure quite how keen I am on accuracy above everything else. The most important thing, if I was going to make a historical movie, I'd really want to get people interested. And I think that, that, um, film and television, um, programme makers can be a bit, can be a bit sort of nerdish about accuracy.

I remember a friend of mine once told me that, uh, he'd acted as advisor for some Roman film and the, the crew were always ringing up when they were on location, um, saying things like, 'Now, what kind of dog should we have?' You know, 'Should it, you know, if we're going to have a dog in the film, should it be an Alsatian or, you know, a Dachshund, or whatever?' And, you know, to start with, he said he'd go to the library and he'd kind of look up and he'd find a breed. And eventually, after question after question, he'd think, 'Look, these guys are getting the whole of Roman history in, in the big picture utterly wrong, and yet there they are worrying about the damned dogs,' you know.

I   Can you think of any historical films that you've really enjoyed?

M   I absolutely loved *Gladiator*. Um, you know, I, never mind its horribly schmaltzy plot, you know; I thought in all kinds of ways, it was just a wonderful, uh, brilliant, and I don't know if it was accurate, but a justifiable re-creation of ancient Rome. The beginning scenes of *Gladiator* which show, you know, Roman combat, um, just in a sense punctured the kind of slightly sanitized version of, you know, legionaries standing, you know, with their, all their shields, you know, face to, you know, facing the enemy, um, you know, all looking ever so kind of neat and tidy. I mean, it was messy, and it was bloody, and it was horrible. And it was such a different kind of image of, uh, Roman combat that I remember we set it in Cambridge as an exam question, you know, um, you know: how, how would, how would students judge that kind of representation of Roman warfare?

I   It's very interesting that there seem to be more and more historical films recently, and many have won Oscars. Is that because history has all the best stories?

M   Yes, there's no such good story as a true story – and that's what history's got going for it, you know, actually. Um, you know, non-fiction in a, in a kind of way is always a better yarn than fiction is. Um, and I think it's, you know, I feel very pleased because, uh, and I think, you know, for one thing, it gets, it gets some of the best stories from history into the popular, into, into popular attention, popular consciousness. But I think also, I mean, it shows that you don't always have to be deadly serious about history. I mean, you know, history, like classics, you know, is often treated as something which is good for you, but isn't actually going to be much fun, you know. You'll be improved by knowing about it, but it probably will be a bit tedious in the process.
And I think that, you know, showing that history can be larky, it can be funny, it can be surprising, um, it can be something that you can sit down and have a good two and a half hours at the cinema enjoying, is really all to the good.

b Focus on the task and give Sts time to read sentences 1–6.

Put Sts in pairs and get them to try and work out what the highlighted words and phrases mean.

Now play the video again the whole way through.

Get Sts to compare with their partner, and then check answers.

You could pause the video after each point has been mentioned and, in pairs, get Sts to compare orally what they have understood.

1 boring in an unfashionable way
2 or something of a similar type
3 people
4 too sentimental
5 its advantage or strength
6 a long story, especially one that is exaggerated or invented

If there's time, you could get Sts to watch again with subtitles, so they can see exactly what they understood / didn't understand. Translate / Explain any new words or phrases.

c Do this as a whole-class activity, or put Sts in pairs and then get some feedback.

2 ▶ LOOKING AT LANGUAGE

Focus on the **Collocations** box and go through it with the class.

Focus on the task and give Sts time to read extracts 1–8.

Play the video, pausing after each extract to give Sts time to write.

Get Sts to compare with a partner, and then check answers. You could remind Sts that they saw the idiom *the big picture* in **2B**, in the lexical quiz.

Ask Sts if they can guess any of the missing highlighted words before they watch the extracts.

1 awful   2 classic, plot   3 facing   4 civil   5 wrongs
6 celebrity   7 picture   8 serious

1 …an awful lot of our culture and our geography and our place names, and so on, are actually formed by the Romans…
2 …one classic example of that is a famous incident in Roman history in sixty-three BC, where there's a terrorist plot in, in the city of Rome…
3 Now, in many ways, that's the kind of problem we're still facing…
4 I mean, what – how far does, how far should homeland security be more important than civil rights…?
5 And in part, we've learnt from how they debated those rights and wrongs.
6 …if it was a small antidote to modern celebrity culture, I'm extremely pleased.
7 …look, these guys are getting the whole of Roman history in, in the big picture utterly wrong…
8 But I think also, I mean, it shows that you don't always have to be deadly serious about history.

3 ▶ THE CONVERSATION

a Focus on the photo and tell Sts they are going to watch these three people discuss two questions. Focus on the task and **Glossary**. Then play the video, pausing after the title screen to give Sts time to read the questions.

Now play the video once the whole way through.

Check answers.

Before playing the video, go through the listening script and decide if you need to pre-teach / check any lexis to help Sts when they listen.

1 B   2 C   3 A

Is there a period of history that you would like to go back to? What kind of people would you be interested to meet?

Joanne   Do you know, I think I'd probably want to go back to the nineteen twenties. Probably more so because it was a time when my grandmother, my late grandmother was a child…

Emma   Mhmm.

Joanne   …and in, you know, in those days she grew up not having plastic anything. They would just go to the grocer's and they'd buy fresh food regularly. Um, electricity wasn't normal in the way that it is now, equally nor was having running water, frankly, so I think I'd find that really interesting to see how that shaped the woman that she became and maybe how that shaped who we are now. Maybe we could learn something from it.

Emma   Yeah, I think it'd be great to learn more about your ancestors and where you came from.

Joanne   Yes. Yeah, definitely.

Sean   I grew up in the nineteen eighties, and, um…

Joanne Yeah, me too.

Sean I, I felt, why on earth am I stuck here, and I became really obsessed with the nineteen sixties.

Joanne Oh gosh.

Sean You know, why can't I be living there instead of here? So, I think if I had the chance, to travel back in time, that's where I'd go, I think, to experience some of the, some of the culture, and um –

Joanne Go and hang out at the Cavern Club with The Beatles.

Sean I think particularly the music and the writing and things like that –

Joanne I bet it was – I bet that would have been awesome.

Sean Yeah.

Emma I think it's interesting because those are both, sort, of changing periods, aren't they, in time?

Joanne True, yes.

Emma But I think I'd go even further back. Um, I used to really, really be interested in the Tudors when I was at school, um, and I think there was a lot going on politically with women being in power and Elizabeth the First not getting married, and I think all the dramas in the books that you read about that period, there was a lot of intrigue and plots and things, and to find out if it was really like that. But I don't think you'd want to go, you know, too close to it with the uncleanliness…

Sean Mmm.

Emma and disease and things that was around, so maybe, kind of, viewing from a safe platform.

Sean Who would you like to speak to?

Emma I think Elizabeth the First, I did a dissertation on her, and I think she's just so interesting.

Joanne I think that would be fascinating. To me, they're all periods of change, particularly for women, as well, weren't they?

Emma Mmm, yeah.

Joanne But I quite like your point about not getting too close.

Sean Absolutely.

Joanne Maybe just observe history from a safe-ish distance and not have to live there for very long.

Emma Mmm.

---

b Focus on the task and give Sts time to read the questions.

Play the video again the whole way through, pausing if necessary to give Sts time to write.

Check answers.

1 Having no plastic, buying fresh food, having limited electricity and running water
She'd see how these things influenced what her grandmother was like.

2 The music and the writing of the 1960s

3 Elizabeth I
She'd like to avoid the dirt and disease.

EXTRA SUPPORT If there's time, you could get Sts to watch again with subtitles, so they can see exactly what they understood / didn't understand. Translate / Explain any new words or phrases.

c Do the questions as a whole-class activity, or put Sts in pairs and then get some feedback.

EXTRA SUPPORT You could demonstrate the activity by answering the questions yourself.

d This exercise focuses on how the speakers respond to the others in order to keep the conversation going. Focus on the phrases and give Sts time to read them.

Play the video, pausing after the first extract and replaying it as necessary. Repeat for the other five extracts.

A 2 **B** 5 **C** 1,3 **D** 6 **E** 4

1

Joanne …Um, electricity wasn't normal in the way that it is now, equally nor was having running water, frankly, so I think I'd find that really interesting to see how that shaped the woman that she became and maybe how that shaped who we are now. Maybe we could learn something from it.

Emma Yeah, I think it'd be great to learn more about your ancestors and where you came from.

2

Sean You know, why can't I be living there instead of here? So, I think if I had the chance, to travel back in time, that's where I'd go, I think, to experience some of the, some of the culture, and um –

Joanne Go and hang out at the Cavern Club with The Beatles.

3

Sean I think particularly the music and the writing and things like that –

Joanne I bet it was – I bet that would have been awesome.

Sean Yeah.

4

Emma I think it's interesting because those are both, sort, of changing periods, aren't they, in time?

Joanne True, yes.

Emma But I think I'd go even further back. Um, I used to really, really be interested in the Tudors when I was at school…

5

Emma But I don't think you'd want to go, you know, too close to it with the uncleanliness…

Sean Mmm.

Emma …and disease and things that was around, so maybe, kind of, viewing from a safe platform.

Sean Who would you like to speak to?

Emma I think Elizabeth the First, I did a dissertation on her, and I think she's just so interesting.

6

Joanne I think that would be fascinating. To me, they're all periods of change, particularly for women, as well, weren't they?

Emma Mmm, yeah.

Joanne But I quite like your point about not getting too close.

---

e Put Sts in small groups of three if possible. Focus on the questions and then give Sts time to discuss them.

Monitor and help, and encourage them to use the different strategies focused on in **d** to keep the discussion going.

Get feedback from various groups. You could also tell the class what you think.

G adding emphasis (1): inversion
V describing books and films
P foreign words

Lesson plan

The two main contexts of this lesson are books and translation. However, the angles also apply to films and TV series, so if your Sts don't read, open the topic out to include them.

The first half of the lesson begins with Sts listening to six people talking about books which they started but didn't finish, think would make a good film, couldn't put down, etc. Sts then talk about their reading habits past and present, which provides a good opportunity for you to find out how much Sts read in English, and for Sts themselves to exchange information and advice about suitable books / authors to read. Then Sts read an article about spoilers and whether knowing how a book or film ends really affects our enjoyment. Sts then discuss the topic. This leads to a vocabulary focus on adjectives commonly used to describe books or films. The first half ends with a grammar focus on inversion for dramatic effect after adverbs or adverbial phrases.

In the second half of the lesson, the topic shifts to the role of the translator. Sts listen to an interview with a translator talking about the pros and cons of the job and some of the trickier aspects. Sts then read a couple of extracts about foreign words which don't have an English translation, and tell you a little about the culture of their country. Sts then focus on some more words from around the world that don't exist in English and try to think of any English words that cannot be translated into their own language. The pronunciation focus is on how to say foreign words, such as *coup* and *angst*, in English. The lesson concludes with writing a review, which includes a focus on using participle clauses.

More materials
For teachers
Photocopiables
Grammar adding emphasis (1): inversion *p.173*
Communicative First or last? *p.199* (instructions *p.188*)
For students
Workbook 4A
Online Practice 4A

OPTIONAL LEAD-IN – THE QUOTE

Write the quote at the top of *p.36* on the board (books closed) and the name of the person who said it, or get Sts to open their books and read it.

Elicit / Explain that Stephen King is an American author of horror, supernatural fiction, suspense, science fiction, and fantasy. His books have sold more than 350 million copies, many of which have been adapted into feature films, television series, and comic books.

Ask Sts whether they agree with the quote.

1 LISTENING & SPEAKING

EXTRA IDEA Before beginning **a**, you may want to focus on the lesson title and ask Sts what they think *an open book* means when you use it to describe somebody (= that you can easily understand them and know everything about them).

a Do this as a whole-class activity, or put Sts in pairs and then get some feedback. Don't worry if they haven't heard of or read any of the books.

b ◉ **4.1** Focus on the task and give Sts time to read topics 1–6.

Play the audio, pausing after each speaker to give Sts time to match them to the topic they are talking about.

Check answers.

EXTRA SUPPORT Read through the script and decide if you need to pre-teach any new lexis before Sts listen.

1 D **2** B **3** F **4** C **5** A **6** E

◉ **4.1**
(script in Student's Book on *p.133*)
Speaker A
Well, I, I remember reading *Catch Twenty-Two* by I think it's Joseph Heller. And I actually started it one night – it was, we'd gone to, to France, to this campsite and they'd all gone to bed, so I went ahead and started it that night. And when I woke up the next morning, I just sat under a tree in the shade and read the whole thing from start to finish. Yeah, I think it's the only book I've ever done that with, didn't do it before or since, yeah.

Speaker B
Yeah, yes, so there is a book that, well, it's a, a book from my childhood and it's called *Carbonel*, by Barbara Sleigh. And I always really feel that, well, you know, it's got everything, it's got…what's in it? It's got a, a talking cat, a curse, there's a witch, there's loads of children. And I really just don't understand why this hasn't been made into a children's film or even an animated film really, to be honest. It's, it's just such a good story, and it's got really great characters, and it's, it's a very visual book. So a lot of the things that it describes, you can, you can just sort of see it, and I think it's a missed opportunity. I really think someone in Hollywood should definitely pick this one up.

Speaker C
Well, there's been a couple of things recently that I've seen on television and then read the book afterwards, and one of those was *Big Little Lies*. So, that was turned into a TV series on HBO, I think. And another was on, it was a film on Netflix and it was called *To all the boys I've loved before*, which is a young adult book that I then went on to read afterwards, it wouldn't usually be my thing, but I read the whole series of three books, it was fantastic.

Speaker D
So, there's a book I've started a couple of times, it's called *The Silmarillion* by Tolkien, and like, it's sort of more information about the world that *The Lord of the Rings* saga happens in. But I just find the beginning so boring and I cannot finish it, and I know that a friend of mine has told me about some really interesting bits that come up later on, but I cannot get to them. I just keep reading about someone, son of someone and it gets really, really boring, really, really soon. So I think I'll have to try again, but I still have not managed to get to the end of it.

Speaker E

I remember we had to read *The War of the Worlds*, by H. G. Wells, when I was at school. I was about ten at the time, and I remember thinking oh, this looks, you know, really exciting, 'cause I really, I really was into science fiction as a kid, and, and, and, the cover looked, you know, like, really exciting. So I thought this is going to be fantastic; we're going to be, you know, doing something really this exciting, it's, you know, we're really lucky, but…I started it and oh, it was, it was just too hard for somebody, well I think if ten years old. The, the vocabulary was difficult; the sentences went on forever, it was really hard to follow them. And it was just frustrating, because I was just sort of looking at the words and I sort of knew when to turn the page, but I hadn't really remembered what I'd just read. So yeah, I didn't get to understand the story at all, and I – the thing is, it sort of put me off H.G. Wells, because I've not really read any since.

Speaker F

Well I've got to say, I've hardly read any classics at all, or any of those ones that win prizes, and, and stuff, that get reviewed in, in papers. So, like, I've never read *To Kill a Mockingbird*, for example, um, yeah, you know, all those, those classics. Think I've read one Jane Austen book. And I, I feel as if I should address this, maybe read some Charles Dickens or…and I just can't concentrate on it, to be honest. It's just…, and for me, reading is a way of switching off, so I don't really want to read anything that's quite a struggle.

c Focus on the task and give Sts time to read 1–6.

Play the audio again, pausing after each speaker to give Sts time to match them to what they said.

Get Sts to compare with a partner, and then check answers.

1 B 2 A 3 E 4 F 5 C 6 D

d 🔊 **4.2** Tell Sts they are now going to listen to six extracts from the audio and they need to complete sentences 1–6.

Play the audio, pausing after each extract to give Sts time to write the missing words.

Get Sts to compare with a partner, and then check answers. Make sure Sts understand the words and expressions.

1 start, finish   2 missed opportunity   3 turned into   4 saga
5 into, cover   6 switching, struggle

🔊 **4.2**

1 …I just sat under a tree in the shade and read the whole thing from start to finish.
2 …I think it's a missed opportunity.
3 So, that was turned into a TV series on HBO, I think.
4 …it's sort of more information about the world that *The Lord of the Rings* saga happens in.
5 …I really was into science fiction as a kid, and, and, and, the cover looked, you know, like, really exciting.
6 …for me, reading is a way of switching off, so I don't really want to read anything that's quite a struggle.

EXTRA SUPPORT   If there's time, you could get Sts to listen again with script 4.1 on *p.133*, so they can see exactly what they understood / didn't understand. Translate / Explain any new words or phrases.

e Give Sts time to look at topics 1–6 in **b** and choose three they want to talk about.

Put Sts in pairs and get them to tell each other about their three books.

Get some feedback from various pairs.

EXTRA IDEA   You could do this as a class activity, getting Sts to mingle. When you think Sts have told each other about their topic, say *Change* and Sts find a new partner and repeat the process.

2 READING   understanding the plot of a novel / reading for pleasure

a Do this as a whole-class activity.

b Focus on the two titles and authors. Ask Sts what they know about Arthur Conan Doyle (1859–1930). You could tell them that he was the British writer who created the character Sherlock Holmes. He was a prolific Scottish writer of novels, short stories, plays, and poems. Elicit / Explain the meaning of *speckled* (= covered with small marks or spots). Elicit or model its pronunciation /ˈspekld/. Then elicit / explain the meaning of *band* here (= a thin flat strip of material that is put around things, for example to hold them together, e.g. a hair band). Now ask Sts what they can remember about Roald Dahl (1916–1990), whom they read about in **2A**. Elicit / Explain the meaning of *slaughter* (= the killing of animals for their meat). Elicit or model its pronunciation /ˈslɔːtə/.

Give Sts time to read both texts and decide which book they would most like to read.

Get Sts to tell a partner, explaining their choice.

Get some feedback from various Sts. You could have a class vote, with a show of hands, to see which book is more popular. You could also tell Sts which book you would choose.

❗ If any Sts have already read one or both books, ask them which one they would most like to re-read. Also tell them that, if they can remember the ending, not to give it away.

c Put Sts in pairs, **A** and **B**, and tell them to go to **Communication What happens in the end?**, **A** on *p.108*, **B** on *p.112*.

Sts **A** read about *The Adventure of the Speckled Band* and Sts **B** read about *Lamb to the Slaughter*.

EXTRA SUPPORT   Put two **A**s and two **B**s together first to work out the stories, then put Sts in **A/B** pairs.

When they are ready, Sts tell each other what happens at the end of their book.

They then discuss what they thought of the endings and whether they would still like to read the books. If any Sts had already read the book, ask them if they would want to re-read it despite knowing how it ended.

Finally, elicit each ending from the class, and find out what Sts think of it and whether they would like to read the books. If your Sts complain that the two books are now spoiled for them, tell them to wait until they've read the next text in the Student's Book, and then to see what they think.

Tell Sts to go back to the main lesson **4A**.

d Give Sts time to read the title of the article, *Spoilers actually enhance your enjoyment*, and the first paragraph.

Elicit what a *spoiler* is.

A *spoiler* is information that you are given about what is going to happen in a book, film, TV series, sports match, etc. before you have read it or seen it.

Now ask Sts what *enhance* means (= to increase or further improve the good quality of sth). Elicit or model its pronunciation /ɪnˈhɑːns/.

EXTRA CHALLENGE Get Sts to discuss why / how spoilers could enhance the enjoyment of a book. Then get them to read the rest of the article to see if their ideas are mentioned.

e Focus on items 1–4 and make sure Sts know what they have to do.

Get Sts to compare with a partner, and then check answers.

EXTRA SUPPORT Before Sts read the article the first time, check whether you need to pre-teach any vocabulary.

1 …knowing in advance in an Agatha Christie story that Poirot will discover that the 'victim' of the attempted murder is, in fact, the real murderer…
2 …I need to check the hero or heroine is still alive at the end of the book.
…to make sure who is going to end up with whom.
3 …once you know how the story turns out, you're more comfortable processing the information and can focus on a deeper understanding of the story.
4 …that the sad ending will turn into a happy one!

Deal with any other new vocabulary. Model and drill the pronunciation of any tricky words.

f Put Sts in pairs and get them to discuss the questions.
Get some feedback from various pairs.

3 VOCABULARY describing books and films

Vocabulary notes

It's important at this level for Sts to expand their vocabulary and to use near-synonyms accurately, e.g. *intriguing* has a more specific meaning than *interesting*, and *heavy going* doesn't mean exactly the same as *boring*.

You might want to highlight:

- *creepy* = causing an unpleasant feeling of fear or slight horror
- *gripping* = exciting or interesting in a way that keeps your attention
- *haunting* = literally, what a ghost does. Figuratively, it means to keep coming into your mind.
- *heavy going* = difficult to follow or understand, and so becoming tiring / boring
- *implausible* = not seeming likely to be true
- *intriguing* = interesting because it's unusual and with an element of mystery
- *thought-provoking* = making people think seriously about a particular subject or issue.

You might also want to tell Sts that *moving* is often negative, linked to crying, whilst *heart-warming* is happy.

a Focus on the task and highlight that the reviews about the books and films explain the meaning of the adjectives.

Give Sts time, in pairs or individually, to complete the sentences, telling them to try to guess the meaning of adjectives they haven't seen before. Point out that the first one (*haunting*) has been done for them.

b 🔊 **4.3** Play the audio for Sts to listen and check.

Check answers, and get Sts to tell you which syllable is stressed. Then elicit from the context of the sentences the exact meaning of each adjective.

🔊 **4.3**
1 <u>haun</u>ting
2 <u>mo</u>ving
3 <u>grip</u>ping
4 <u>heart</u>-<u>warm</u>ing
5 <u>fast</u>-<u>mo</u>ving
6 in<u>trig</u>uing
7 <u>thought</u>-pro<u>vok</u>ing
8 <u>cree</u>py
9 <u>hea</u>vy <u>go</u>ing
10 im<u>plau</u>sible

EXTRA CHALLENGE You could get Sts to add some synonyms to some of the adjectives in the list, e.g. *gripping – riveting*, *moving – heartbreaking*, etc.

EXTRA IDEA Put Sts in pairs and tell them to take turns to choose an adjective from the list in **a** and name a book or film that could be described with one of the adjectives. They should also say why. You could demonstrate the activity by giving a few examples yourself of books or films you think your Sts might know and that could be described with one or more of these adjectives.

4 GRAMMAR adding emphasis (1): inversion

a Focus on the instructions and give Sts time to complete the matching task.

Get Sts to compare with a partner, and then check answers.

1 D 2 B 3 A 4 C 5 E

Now ask Sts how the word order changes when the sentence starts with an adverbial expression.

The verb and subject are inverted.

b Tell Sts to go to **Grammar Bank 4A** on *p.148*.

Grammar notes

Inverting the subject and verb after some (mainly negative) adverbial expressions is commonly used for dramatic effect, especially, but not exclusively, in written English. Sts should be encouraged to use inversions where appropriate, but not to overuse them, as this would make their English sound unnatural.

Highlight that after *No sooner…*, we use *than*, but after *Hardly / Scarcely*, we use *when* or *before*.

Focus on the example sentences for **adding emphasis (1): inversion** and go through the rules with the class.

Go through the **Overuse of inversion** box with the class.

Focus on the exercise and get Sts to do it individually or in pairs. If Sts do it individually, get them to compare with a partner.

Check answers, getting Sts to read the full sentences.

1 Not until **years later did I realize my mistake**.
2 Never **had we seen such magnificent scenery**.
3 Not only **did they dislike her, but they also hated her family**.

4 Only when **we read his autobiography did we understand what he had really suffered**.
5 Hardly **had we started to eat when we heard someone knocking at the door**.
6 Rarely **have I read such a badly written novel**.
7 Not until **you've tried to write a novel yourself do you realize how hard it is**.
8 Not only **was the hotel room depressing, (but) it was cold as well**.
9 Only when **it is unusually cold do we light the fire**.
10 No sooner **had he gone to sleep than the phone rang**.
11 Only then **did I realize the full scale of the disaster**.
12 Never **has he regretted the decision he took on that day**.
13 Only when **I spoke to the manager was the problem taken seriously**.
14 Scarcely **had he had time to destroy the evidence before / when the police arrived**.
15 Never again **would he see his homeland**.

Tell Sts to go back to the main lesson **4A**.

EXTRA SUPPORT If you think Sts need more practice, you may want to give them the **Grammar** photocopiable activity at this point.

c Focus on the task and give Sts time to think of how they want to complete the sentences. They could do this in pairs, or individually and then compare with a partner.

Go round monitoring and correcting.

Elicit sentences from the class, writing some good ones on the board.

5 LISTENING understanding opinions and explanations

a Focus on the four questions and make sure Sts know the meaning and pronunciation of *dubbed* /dʌbd/ in 4.

Put Sts in small groups of three or four and get them to discuss the questions.

Get some feedback from various groups. If dubbed films are common in your Sts' country, you could do question 4 as a class and have a class vote for watching films dubbed vs with subtitles. Then you could elicit advantages and disadvantages of both from the class.

b 🔊 **4.4** Focus on the task and then play **Part 1** of the audio once the whole way through for Sts to see how Beverly Johnson describes her job.

EXTRA SUPPORT Ask Sts what they think are the pros and cons of working as a translator. Write their ideas on the board, and then play the audio for Sts to see if Beverly mentions any of their ideas.

Now ask Sts if they would enjoy working as a translator, based on what Beverly said, and to give reasons.

EXTRA SUPPORT Read through both parts of the script and decide if you need to pre-teach any new lexis before Sts listen.

🔊 **4.4**
(script in Student's Book on *p.133*)
I = interviewer, B = Beverly Johnson
Part 1
I What made you want to be a translator?
B It was something that I'd done when I was at university, and when I moved to Spain, it was difficult to get a job that wasn't teaching English, so I went back to England and I did a postgraduate

course in translation. After doing the course, I swore that I would never be a translator – I thought it would be too boring – but I kept doing the odd translation, and eventually I, I came round to the idea because I liked the idea of working for myself, and it didn't require too much investment to get started. And, and actually, I enjoy working with words, and it's, it's very satisfying when you feel that you've produced a reasonable translation of the original text.
I What are the pros and cons of being a translator?
B Well, um, it's a lonely job, I suppose – you know, you're on your own most of the time. It's hard work – you're sitting there and, you know, you're working long hours, and you can't programme things because you don't know when more work is going to come in, and people have always got tight deadlines. You know, it's really rare that somebody'll, 'll ring you up and say, 'I want this translation in three months' time.' You know, that, that just doesn't really happen.
I And the pros?
B Well, the pros are that it, it gives you freedom because you can do it anywhere if you've got an internet connection and electricity, and I suppose you can organize your time, 'cause you're freelance – you know, you're your own boss, which is good. I, I like that.
I What advice would you give someone who's thinking of going into translation?
B I'd say that, I'd say, in addition to the language, get a speciality. Do another course in anything that interests you, like economics, law, history, art, because you really need to know about the subjects that you're translating into.

c Give Sts time to read the four questions and their options. You might want to point out *drawbacks* in 2 (in **a** Sts saw *disadvantages* and on the audio they heard *cons*) and the adjective *would-be* in 4 (= used to describe sb who is hoping to become the type of person mentioned).

Put Sts in pairs to see if they can remember any of the information. Highlight that in questions 2 and 3, they must circle two answers.

Play **Part 1** again for Sts to listen and choose the best option, *a*, *b*, or *c*.

EXTRA SUPPORT You could pause the audio after Beverly has answered each question.

Check answers.

1 c   2 a and c   3 b and c   4 a

EXTRA SUPPORT If there's time, you could get Sts to listen again with the script on *p.133*, so they can see exactly what they understood / didn't understand. Translate / Explain any new words or phrases.

d Do this as a whole-class activity, or put Sts in pairs and then get some feedback.

e 🔊 **4.5** Play **Part 2** of the audio for Sts to listen and tick the kinds of text in **d** that Beverly mentions.
Check answers.

Sts should have ticked: novels, poetry, advertising slogans, film titles, and film dialogue (for subtitles).

🔊 **4.5**
(script in Student's Book on *pp.133–134*)
Part 2
I What do you think is the most difficult kind of text to translate?
B Literary texts, like novels, poetry, or drama because you've got to give a lot of consideration to the author, and to the way it's been written in the original language.
I In order to translate a novel well, do you think you need to be a novelist yourself?
B I think that's true, ideally, yes.

I And is that the case? I mean, are most of the well-known translators of novels, generally speaking, novelists in their own right?

B Yes, I think in English, anyway. People who translate into English tend to be published authors, and they tend to specialize in a particular author in the other language. And of course, if it's a living author, then it's so much easier because you can actually communicate with the author and say, you know, like, 'What did you really mean here?'

I Another thing I've heard that is very hard to translate is advertising, for example slogans.

B Yeah, well, with advertising, the problem is that it's got to be something punchy, and, and it's very difficult to translate that. For example, one of the Coca-Cola adverts, the slogan in English was 'the real thing', but you just couldn't translate that literally into Spanish – it, it just wouldn't have had the same power. In fact, it became *Sensación de vivir*, which is 'sensation of living', which sounds, sounds really good in Spanish, but it, it would sound weird in English.

I What about film titles?

B Ah, they're horrific, too. People always complain that they've not been translated accurately, but of course it's impossible because sometimes a literal translation just doesn't work.

I For example?

B OK, well, think of, you know, the Julie Andrews film *The Sound of Music*. Well, that works in English because it's a phrase that you know – you know, like, 'I can hear the sound of music'. But it doesn't work at all in other languages, and in Spanish it was called *Sonrisas y Lágrimas*, which means 'Smiles and Tears'. Now, let me – in German it was called *Meine Lieder, Meine Träume*, which means 'My Songs, My Dreams', and in Italian it was *Tutti insieme appassionatamente*, which means, I think, 'All Together Passionately', or, I don't know, something like that. In fact, I think it was translated differently all over the world.

I Do you think there are special problems translating film scripts, for the subtitles?

B Yes, a lot. There are special constraints, for example the translation has to fit on the screen as the actor is speaking, and so sometimes the translation is a paraphrase rather than a direct translation, and of course, well, going back to untranslatable things, really, the big problems are cultural and humour, because they're, they're just not the same. You can get across the idea, but you might need pages to explain it, and, you know, by that time the film's moved on. I also sometimes think that the translators are given the film on DVD – I mean, you know, rather than a written script – and that sometimes they've simply misheard or they didn't understand what the people said. And that's the only explanation I can come up with for some of the mistranslations that I've seen. Although sometimes it might be that some things, like, like humour and jokes, especially ones which depend on wordplay, are just, you know, they're, they're simply untranslatable. And often it's very difficult to get the right register, for example with, with slang and swear words, because if you literally translate taboo words or swear words, even if they exist in the other language, they may well be far more offensive.

f Give Sts time to read the questions, making sure they know the meaning of *slang and swear words* in 7.

Put Sts in pairs to see if they can remember any of the information.

Play **Part 2** again for Sts to listen and answer the questions.

Get Sts to compare with their partner, and then play the audio again if necessary.

Check answers.

1 A novelist / author yourself
2 You can communicate with them and ask them, e.g. what they mean by something.
3 The English translation of the Spanish Coca-Cola slogan
4 It's often impossible to translate it literally because the phrase only works in English.

5 The translation has to fit on the screen as the actor is speaking.
6 Humour is not the same in other languages, and some jokes are untranslatable.
7 It's difficult to get the right register.

EXTRA SUPPORT If there's time, you could get Sts to listen again with the script on *pp.133–134*, so they can see exactly what they understood / didn't understand. Translate / Explain any new words or phrases.

g Do this as a whole-class activity, or put Sts in pairs and then get some feedback.

6 READING & SPEAKING

a Do this as a whole-class activity, and elicit opinions from the class. Don't tell Sts if they are correct or not.

b Tell Sts to read the extracts to check their ideas in **a** and to answer the question.

Check the meaning of both words and then elicit what they tell us about each culture. You could tell Sts that *sobremesa* can occasionally refer to after dinner in the evening, but normally it's lunch. Point out also that *Persian*, which is also called *Farsi*, is the language of Iran.

EXTRA SUPPORT Before Sts read the extracts the first time, check whether you need to pre-teach any vocabulary.

Possible answer

sobremesa that the Spanish are convivial and like spending a long time at the table with friends. They value food and friendship.

ta'arof that politeness and hospitality are very highly valued in Iran

Deal with any vocabulary problems that arose.

c Focus on the task and give Sts time to read the words and their definitions.

Do the question as a whole-class activity if your Sts are from the same country. If not, put Sts in pairs and get some feedback.

EXTRA IDEA Elicit what the words suggest about the culture of that country.

EXTRA IDEA If your Sts are enjoying these words, here are a few more you could give them:

l'esprit d'escalier (French) a witty response which occurs to you too late

barcode men (Japanese) for men with thin black careful combovers

uitwaaien (Dutch) to take a bracing walk in the wind

isbiltur (Icelandic) going for a drive and ending up with an ice cream

mambo (Swedish) an adult who still lives with their parents

Neidbau (German) a building constructed for the sole purpose of annoying your neighbour

Backpfeifengesicht (German) a face that needs hitting

d Do this as a whole-class activity, or put Sts pairs and then get some feedback.

EXTRA IDEA You could also ask *Are there any (more) words in your language which you think are 'untranslatable' into English? How could you explain them?*

7 PRONUNCIATION foreign words

Pronunciation notes

Throughout the centuries, a feature of English has been that it has always borrowed words from other languages (called *loan words*), typically where there is not an English word available to describe, e.g. a custom, a type of food, or a technology which has been imported from another country. Common examples of loan words are *sauna* (from Finnish), *pasta* (from Italian), and *robot* (from Czech). The pronunciation of these words is usually anglicized. However, there is quite a large group of loan words and phrases (especially from French) which are pronounced in a similar way to the way a native speaker of that country would say them, e.g. *nouveau riche* /ˌnuːvəʊ ˈriːʃ/ (= an expression to describe a person who has recently become rich and likes to show it off in a very obvious way). An advanced dictionary will give these words and phrases, and their pronunciation.

a Focus on the **Saying foreign words in English** box and go through it with the class.

Give Sts time to underline the foreign word or phrase in each sentence. Tell them to guess if they don't know.

Put Sts in pairs and get them to discuss the meaning of the words and phrases they underlined, and their origin.

Check answers. For 6, *pasta* is also a possible answer, although it is now a very common word in English. At this stage, <u>don't</u> worry about pronunciation.

1 *faux pas* (from French) = an action or remark that causes embarrassment because it is not socially correct
2 *déjà vu* (from French) = the feeling that you have experienced sth before
3 *cliché* (from French) = a phrase or an idea that has been used so often that it no longer has meaning and is not interesting
4 *debacle* (from French) = an event or situation that is a complete failure and causes embarrassment
5 *aficionado* (from Spanish) = sb who likes a particular sport, activity, or subject very much and knows a lot about it
6 *al dente* (from Italian) = not too soft, still with a perfect bite
7 *schadenfreude* (from German) = a feeling of pleasure at the bad things which happen to other people
8 *tsunami* (from Japanese) = an extremely large wave often cause by an earthquake

Find out if any of the words or expressions are used in your Sts' L1.

b 🔊 **4.6** Play the audio, pausing after each sentence, to elicit how the foreign words or phrases are pronounced.

EXTRA CHALLENGE Elicit the pronunciation and then play the audio for Sts to listen and check.

Elicit the pronunciation of the foreign words or phrases.

1 faux pas /ˌfəʊ ˈpɑː/
2 déjà vu /ˌdeɪʒɑː ˈvuː/
3 cliché /ˈkliːʃeɪ/
4 debacle /dɪˈbɑːkl/
5 aficionado /əˌfɪʃəˈnɑːdəʊ/
6 al dente /ˌæl ˈdenteɪ/
7 schadenfreude /ˈʃɑːdnfrɔɪdə/
8 tsunami /tsuːˈnɑːmi/

🔊 **4.6**
See sentences in Student's Book on *p.39*

EXTRA SUPPORT Play the audio again, pausing after each sentence for Sts to listen and repeat.

Give Sts time to practise saying the sentences, in pairs or individually.

Finally, get individual Sts to say the sentences.

c Do this as a whole-class activity if your Sts come from the same country. If not, put Sts in pairs and then get some feedback.

8 WRITING a review

In this lesson, the focus is on writing a review. The model text is a book review, but all the information could equally apply to writing a review of a film, play, or even a concert. The writing skills focus is using participle clauses and using a variety of adverbs of degree.

Tell Sts to go to **Writing A review** on *p.120*.

ANALYSING A MODEL TEXT

a Focus on the text type (*a review*) and highlight that nowadays many people write reviews of books, films, etc., and post them on the internet. Sts may also be asked to write a review in an international or final-year school exam. The structure of reviews tends to be broadly similar, and you would normally include factual information, your opinion, and a recommendation.

Focus on the **Key success factors** and go through them with the class.

Now focus on the task, and get Sts, in pairs, to discuss what factors influence them to choose a book to read, or do this as a whole-class activity.

b Focus on the task and the book review, and find out if any Sts have read the book or seen the film. You might want to explain / elicit the meaning of *appeal to* in the last point.

Set a time limit for Sts to read the review and do the task individually.

Get them to compare with a partner, and then check answers. Also elicit whether Sts now want to read the book.

the strong points of the book	3
the basic outline of the plot	2
what happens in the end	DS
where and when the story is set	1
the weakness(es) of the book	3
whether the reviewer recommends the book or not	4
who the author is	1
who the main characters are	2
who the book is published by	DS
who the book will appeal to	4

EXTRA IDEA Ask Sts what else would be included if this were a film review, e.g. who the actors were in paragraph 2, what their performances were like in paragraph 3, and maybe some mention of the soundtrack or the special effects.

Elicit that despite what they have just read about spoilers, reviews normally never give away what happens in the end, in case this puts some people off reading the book.

Tell Sts that when writing a book or film review, they should give the reader a brief idea of the plot. Now tell them that they are going to look at a specific way of making the description of a plot more concise.

c Focus on the task and get Sts to read the extracts and the **Participle clauses** box. You might want to point out to Sts that there is always a comma after a participle clause.

Check answers.

> **1** which is **2** who are **3** which was

Highlight that participle clauses are very common in written English, but very rarely used in spoken English.

d Focus on the task and give Sts time to rewrite the highlighted phrases.

Check answers.

> **1** Believing him to be the murderer,…
> **2** Armelle, forced to marry a man she did not love,…
> **3** Simon, realizing that the police are after him,…
> **4** First published in 1903,…
> **5** Hearing the shot,…
> **6** Based on his wartime diaries,…

USEFUL LANGUAGE

e Focus on the task and do it as a whole-class activity.

> *Totally* increases the strength of the adjective and *slightly* reduces the strength of the verb.

f Get Sts to work in pairs. Explain / Elicit the meaning of *denouement* (= the end of a book, in which everything is explained or settled).

Check answers.

> **1** ✓
> **2** *Very* should be crossed out. It can't be used with strong adjectives like *fascinating*, *amazing*, etc., which already mean 'very interesting', 'very surprising', etc.
> **3** ✓
> **4** *Incredibly* and *extremely* should be crossed out. Like *very*, they can't be used with strong adjectives. They are used with 'normal' adjectives, as stronger intensifiers than *very*.

PLANNING WHAT TO WRITE

a Focus on the task. Tell Sts to choose either a book or film they have read or seen recently, or one that they have read or seen several times and know well. Tell them not to worry if they can't remember, e.g. the names of actors or characters, as they can research this on the internet when they come to write their full review.

Set a time limit of about ten minutes for Sts to write their list, using paragraph 2 in the review for ideas. Monitor and help with vocabulary.

EXTRA SUPPORT Get Sts, in pairs, to choose a book or film that they have both read or seen and do the task together.

b Get Sts to swap lists with other Sts and identify each other's books / films.

Finally, go through the **Tips** with Sts.

WRITING

Go through the instructions and set the writing for homework.

4B The sound of silence

G speculation and deduction
V sounds and the human voice
P consonant clusters

Lesson plan

This lesson has two main contexts, noise and silence.

The first half of the lesson focuses on sounds. It starts with a vocabulary focus on verbs and nouns to describe sounds and the human voice, and there is a pronunciation focus on consonant clusters which occur in many of these words, e.g. *screech*, *splash*, etc. Sts then look at a list of sounds and try to guess whether people like or dislike the sounds. They then listen to eight people talking about sounds they love or noises they hate, and Sts then talk about this themselves. The first half of the lesson ends with the grammar focus, which is on speculation and deduction.

In the second half of the lesson, the focus is on silence. Sts read an article about the growing popularity of 'silent events', such as silent speed-dating. Then Sts look at noise regulations from different countries and discuss whether they are a good idea and how they would adapt them for their own country. The lesson ends with Sts watching a documentary about the percussionist Evelyn Glennie, who has been profoundly deaf since the age of 12.

More materials

For teachers

Photocopiables
Grammar speculation and deduction *p.174*
Communicative Sound or noise? *p.200*
(instructions *p.189*)
Vocabulary Sounds and the human voice *p222*
(instructions *p.215*)

For students
Workbook 4B
Online Practice 4B

OPTIONAL LEAD-IN – THE QUOTE

Write the quote at the top of *p.40* on the board (books closed) and the name of the person who said it, or get Sts to open their books and read it.

Point out that Publilius Syrus (1st century BC) was a writer who went to Rome as a slave from Syria. His wit and talent won the favour of his master, who freed and educated him.

Get Sts to discuss what they think the quote means and whether they agree with it or not, and why.

1 VOCABULARY sounds and the human voice

a Focus on the task and then get the class to sit for one minute in silence.

Get Sts to compare their lists with a partner.

Elicit what noises Sts heard in their classroom, e.g. traffic noise, noise from adjoining classrooms, etc., and find out which noises, if any, affect their concentration. If some of your Sts work, ask them what noises annoy or distract them in their workplace.

You may want to elicit from Sts the difference in meaning between a *sound* and a *noise*. Although they are similar in meaning, there is a clear difference (a *sound* is something you can hear and has a neutral or positive meaning, e.g. *I love the sound of the sea*. A *noise* is a sound which is often loud or unpleasant, e.g. *The noise of the traffic was deafening*).

b Tell Sts to go to **Vocabulary Bank Sounds and the human voice** on *p.166*.

Vocabulary notes

Sounds

Point out to Sts that when you are talking about sounds, you can use these expressions:

* *the* + noun + *of*, e.g. *the roar of an engine*, *the crash of waves*
* *the noise / sound of* + noun (phrase), e.g. *the sound of birds singing*
* *the* + adjective + *noise / sound of…*, e.g. *the popping noise of…*, *the scraping sound of…*
* *someone / people* + *-ing* form, e.g. *someone sniffing*, *people partying*

When the sound words are used as adjectives, it is usually the *-ing* form of the verb, e.g. *That hooting sound nearly gave me a heart attack*. However, a few of the words become adjectives by adding *-y*, but apart from the meaning related to the sound, they can also have a different meaning, e.g.:

* *creaky* = old and not in good condition
* *crunchy* = firm and crisp and making a sharp sound when you bite or crush it
* *drippy* = boring, stupid, and weak or sentimental
* *splashy* = bright and very easy to notice
* *sniffy* (about something) = not approving about sth / sb because you think they are not good enough for you
* *hissy* only exists in the expression *a hissy fit* = a state of being bad-tempered and unreasonable, e.g. *She had a hissy fit because someone else was wearing a dress just like hers*.

🔊 **4.7** Focus on **1 Sounds** and read the task for **a**. Play the audio for Sts to hear the sounds, and point out how the words are often onomatopoeic.

◀)) 4.7
Sounds and the human voice
1 Sounds, a
Sound effects and words in Student's Book on *p.166*

Now either use the audio to drill the pronunciation of the words, or model and drill them yourself. Give further practice of any words your Sts find difficult to pronounce.

Now focus on **b** and get Sts to complete the *Sounds* column with the words in the list in **a**. They can do it individually or in pairs.

◀)) 4.8 Now focus on **c**. Play the audio for Sts to listen and check.

Check answers. You could tell Sts that 15 could also be *whistle*.

◀)) 4.8
1 Sounds, b
1 tick
2 sniff
3 click
4 splash
5 bang
6 creak
7 buzz
8 hoot
9 tap
10 slurp
11 hiss
12 drip
13 roar
14 whistle
15 hum
16 slam
17 crunch
18 snore
19 rattle
20 screech, crash

EXTRA CHALLENGE Play audio **◀)) 4.7** again, pausing after each sound, and elicit the word from the class before they hear it.

Now focus on **2 The human voice** and get Sts to do **a** individually or in pairs.

◀)) 4.9 Now focus on **b**. Play the audio for Sts to listen and check.

Check answers.

◀)) 4.9
2 The human voice
1 scream
2 yell
3 giggle
4 whisper
5 mumble
6 groan
7 stammer
8 sob
9 sigh

Now either use the audio to drill the pronunciation of the words, or model and drill them yourself. Give further practice of any words your Sts find difficult to pronounce.

Focus on **c** and get Sts to do it in pairs.

Check answers.

Suggested answers
nervous – stammer / giggle
terrified – scream
lose their temper – yell
not supposed to be making any noise – whisper
amused or embarrassed – giggle
speak without opening their mouth enough – mumble
relieved – sigh
team misses a penalty – groan
very unhappy – sob

Focus on **Activation** and make sure Sts understand what they have to do.

Put Sts in pairs and get them to make the sounds for their partner to guess.

Tell Sts to go back to the main lesson **4B**.

EXTRA SUPPORT If you think Sts need more practice, you may want to give them the **Vocabulary** photocopiable activity at this point.

c ◀)) 4.10 Focus on the task and play the first sound to elicit *crash* from the class.

Now play the rest of the audio, pausing after each sound to elicit the word from the class.

◀)) 4.10
(sound effects of the following:)
1 *crash*
2 *crunch*
3 *giggle*
4 *groan*
5 *hum*
6 *mumble*
7 *roar*
8 *sigh*
9 *slurp*
10 *sniff*
11 *tap*
12 *whisper*

2 PRONUNCIATION consonant clusters

Pronunciation notes
Consonant clusters are groups of consonants with no vowel in between, e.g. *spring*. Pronouncing them may be a problem for Sts, depending on their first language. The typical error is to insert a vowel sound before, after, or in the middle of the cluster.

a ◀)) 4.11 Focus on the **Fine-tuning your pronunciation: consonant clusters** box and go through it with the class.

Play the audio once the whole way through for Sts just to listen.

◀)) 4.11
See words in the chart in Student's Book on *p.40*

Now get Sts to practise saying them.

EXTRA SUPPORT If these sounds are a problem for your Sts, play the words one by one and pause, getting Sts to repeat them.

b ◖)) **4.12** Play the audio for Sts to listen and repeat the sentences one by one.

◖)) **4.12**
See sentences in Student's Book on *p.40*

Get Sts to practise saying them quietly to themselves.

Finally, get individual Sts to say the sentences out loud.

c Give Sts time to invent their sentences while you monitor and help.

Put Sts in pairs and get them to exchange sentences and say them.

You could get some Sts to say their sentences to the class.

3 LISTENING & SPEAKING

a Focus on the task and give Sts time to read the list. There might be some new lexis, but Sts should be able to work out the meaning of unknown words from the context and the photos.

Monitor and help if necessary whilst Sts tick the items they think are 'best sounds' and put a cross next to those that they think are 'worst sounds'.

You could let Sts compare lists, and then find out if there were any disagreements.

b ◖)) **4.13** Tell Sts they will first hear a list of all the items that are 'best sounds' (not in any particular order) and then those that are 'worst sounds'.

Play the audio once the whole way through for Sts to listen and check their ideas in **a**.

Check answers. Now ask Sts if they agree.

◖)) **4.13**
The best sounds in the world, in no particular order, are…
the crunch of walking on a fresh layer of snow
the patter of rain on the roof while you're in bed
the crackling noise of an open fire
the sound of a golf ball dropping into the hole
the popping noise when you squeeze bubble wrap
people laughing at one of your jokes
the 'ding' sound when a plane has landed and switched off the
    engines
the crashing of waves on a beach
birds singing very early in the morning
The worst sounds in the world, in no particular order, are…
the tap of the keys on a mobile phone when someone hasn't turned
    off the keyboard sound
the roar of a revving motorbike
the whine of a dentist's drill
the strange hum in your house that you can't locate
someone eating popcorn at the cinema
the sound of someone filing their nails
someone sniffing
people slurping their food
someone else's child crying

c ◖)) **4.14** Focus on the task and play the audio, pausing after each speaker for Sts to answer the two questions.

Check answers.

Speaker 1	**1** Neighbour's dog barking	**2** He hates it.
Speaker 2	**1** Daughter eating popcorn in the cinema	
	2 She hates it.	
Speaker 3	**1** Children breathing when they're asleep	
	2 She loves it.	
Speaker 4	**1** The sea	**2** He loves it.
Speaker 5	**1** The beep of kitchen appliances when they've	
	finished a programme	
	2 She hates it.	
Speaker 6	**1** A baby laughing	**2** She loves it.
Speaker 7	**1** Very quiet music	**2** He hates it.
Speaker 8	**1** Sound of a train	**2** She loves it.

◖)) **4.14**
(script in Student's Book on *p.134*)

1 My next-door neighbours have just got a dog. I've always really liked dogs, but this one just absolutely drives me mad. It barks at everything. It barks at the rain, it barks at traffic, barks at the wind. And it's got a really high-pitched, yappy bark. And, yeah, it barks all day, all night, it drives me mad.

2 A sound that I really can't stand, I actually detest this sound, is the sound of my daughter eating popcorn whenever we go to the cinema together. I always make her buy a small box because otherwise it takes her forever to finish and get to the bottom. But it's the, the crunch, the sound of the little kernels in her mouth, the, the, the chew, the, the, all the sounds inside her mouth. It's just so irritating.

3 I do this quite funny thing, so when my kids are in bed, I often go in and I just listen to them breathing when they're asleep. And it's – really calms me down, this sort of, steady breathing. And it makes me feel really happy and calm, and reassured that they're healthy, and they're at home, and well actually, also the fact that they're fast asleep! So I can get some time to myself, you know, some peace and quiet.

4 I find the sound of the sea just, just makes me feel relaxed, it makes me at peace. Doesn't matter if it's a gentle sea against a beach, or ocean crashing against rocks, I just, it just calms me down. I love it. I've even got an app on my phone of sea sounds which helps me if I'm travelling and I can't get to sleep somewhere. I always put that on, helps me relax.

5 I think it's when I hear the constant beeping of all my different kitchen appliances, you know, the washing machine, or the dishwasher. And…when you think they've, they've finished, and, but you don't know and then it goes beep, and then a minute later, beep, beep, beep and it gets louder, just so you know it's really finished what it's doing, you know, it's talking to you. I just find it so annoying. It really annoys my husband too, you know, you're sitting there, trying to have a nice relaxing evening watching the TV and then, you know, one of you has to get up and go and attend to it, go and turn it off .

6 Well, the sound of a baby laughing – or like, giggling, I love that. I was watching something on YouTube the other day, and, with like, young babies and pets, and the babies were just giggling all over the place, they were roaring with laughter, and I thought it was one of the happiest, like, sweetest sounds I'd ever heard.

7 Listening to music played very quietly so that you can't actually hear it. Music should be something that you want to hear properly and more loudly, not just there, playing quietly, irritating you. And the other thing is background music, like lift music, that you don't want to hear at all. I don't like hearing any music 'unwillingly'!

8 Well, the sound of the train – I, I find it really relaxing because the sound fits perfectly along with the movement of the train, moving along and the jolting backwards and forwards, and… Oh, but I do need to be sitting facing forwards rather than backwards because otherwise I feel train-sick.

d Give Sts time to read the eight questions.

Play the audio again, pausing after each speaker to give Sts time to answer the relevant question.

Get Sts to compare with a partner, and then check answers.

1 Everything – the rain, the traffic, and the wind
2 Because otherwise it takes her daughter a very long time to eat it
3 Because it makes her feel happy and relaxed, as she knows she can have some time to herself. Also because her children are at home and healthy.
4 An app with sea sounds
5 When she's relaxing and watching TV
6 On YouTube
7 Background music, lift music
8 Facing forwards

EXTRA SUPPORT If there's time, you could get Sts to listen again with the script on *p.134*, so they can see exactly what they understood / didn't understand. Translate / Explain any new words or phrases.

e Put Sts in small groups of three or four and give them time to answer all the questions.

Get some feedback from various groups. Find out if there were any surprising sounds that people loved or hated.

4 GRAMMAR speculation and deduction

a ◑ 4.15 Focus on the instructions and make sure Sts understand what they have to do. For each story, they must listen to the sounds and then write three sentences, using the phrases in the order given.

Play the first group of sounds, then pause the audio for Sts to write their sentences. Play again if necessary.

Repeat the same process with the two other groups of sounds.

EXTRA SUPPORT Get Sts to work in pairs. Play **Story 1** and elicit what the sounds were, and possible sentences for the three verb phrases. Then play **Story 2** and get Sts to write their sentences together. Then in **b**, put two pairs together to compare sentences.

◑ **4.15**
(sound effects of the following:)
1
Clock ticking, man snoring, mosquito buzzing, man groans, sounds of spraying insecticide, sounds of whacking with newspaper, man grunts with satisfaction, man snoring again, mosquito starts buzzing again, more grunts from man, more spraying and whacking
2
Street noise, man yelling 'Hey', running feet, moped revving, screech of brakes, moped driving off
3
Car arrives, couple walk to door and put key in, bumping noises coming from inside
Woman   What's that noise?
Man   What noise?
Woman   There's someone inside.
Man and woman whispering, 'You open it,' 'I'm too scared. You do it,' 'All right, here we go. OK, ready?' *opening creaking door, noise of something being knocked over, both screaming,* 'Arghhh!'

b ◑ **4.16** Put Sts in pairs and get them to compare sentences.

Elicit what the sounds were, and some possible sentences for each story.

Possible answers
1 It must be a mosquito; the man might be trying to kill it; he can't have killed it, as it's still buzzing.
2 The man could have been robbed; someone might have stolen his phone; it's unlikely that the police will catch the thief.
3 The couple are probably arriving home; the noise could be a burglar; they must have left the cat inside / the window open.

Now play the audio for Sts to hear what really happened. Check answers.

1 The man is asleep, is woken up by a mosquito, sprays the room, then whacks it with newspaper and thinks he's killed it. He goes back to sleep, the mosquito appears again; this time he gets it.
2 Someone grabs the man's bag in the street and runs off, gets onto a scooter / motorbike, drives off but crashes, the police arrive and give the man his phone back.
3 A man and a woman arrive home late at night and hear a noise as if someone is in the house; they open the door and find it's the cat

◑ **4.16**
(As 4.15 but with additional endings)
1
Sound effects +
Wife   What are you doing? Is it a mosquito?
Husband Got it! At last! Go back to sleep!
2
Sound effects +
Horns hooting, sound of motorbike crashing, a police siren
Policeman Are you OK, sir? Is this your phone?
Man   That's my phone! He's pinched it!
3
Sound effects +
Cat miaowing / yowling, sighs of relief,
Woman   It's only the cat.

c Tell Sts to go to **Grammar Bank 4B** on *p.149*.

Grammar notes

Sts should be familiar with the use of modal verbs *may / might*, *must*, and *can't* for speculation; however, it is a structure which most Sts do not use with any fluency until advanced level. Here the structure is revised, and other expressions for speculation or deduction using adjectives or adverbs are also presented and practised.

Remind Sts that *have* after *must, could,* etc. is pronounced /əv/.

Focus on the example sentences for **modal verbs: must, may, might, can't, could, should, ought** and go through the rules with the class.

Go through the **Infinitive or continuous infinitive after modals?** box with the class.

Then focus on **adjectives and adverbs for speculation** and go through the rules with the class.

Focus on the exercises and get Sts to do them individually or in pairs. If Sts do them individually, get them to compare with a partner.

Check answers after each exercise, getting Sts to read the full sentences.

a

1 ✗ Someone must have moved them.
2 ✓
3 ✗ I think it could / might / may be
4 ✓
5 ✗ She definitely won't like
6 ✗ Julian is bound to be late
7 ✓
8 ✗ I think she must still be studying.
9 ✓

b

1 He **probably won't have time to call in and see us**.
2 She **may never get over** the break-up.
3 They **ought to have heard the news by** now.
4 I **can't have left my credit card in the restaurant**.
5 Your sister **is bound to like the scarf**.
6 The company director **is unlikely to resign**, despite the disastrous sales figures.
7 He **must have been in love with her**, otherwise he wouldn't have married her.
8 Did **you definitely** lock the back door?
9 According to press reports, it's **likely that the couple will get divorced** soon.

Tell Sts to go back to the main lesson **4B**.

EXTRA SUPPORT If you think Sts need more practice, you may want to give them the **Grammar** photocopiable activity at this point.

d Put Sts in pairs and get them to talk about the photo using language for speculations and deductions.
Elicit some ideas from the class. Then tell them what had really happened.

This photo was taken in Sendai, Japan. Chacha, a 24-year-old male chimpanzee, had escaped from the zoo. After two hours, he was found near some houses, climbing on power lines. Eventually, he was captured and returned safely to the zoo.

EXTRA SUPPORT Do this as a whole-class activity.

e Put Sts in pairs, **A** and **B**, and tell them to go to **Communication What's going on?**, **A** on *p.108*, **B** on *p.113*.
Go through the instructions and make sure Sts understand what they have to do.
When they have finished, find out if any Sts guessed correctly.
Tell Sts to go back to the main lesson **4B**.

5 READING identifying benefits

a Focus on the task. You may want to teach *piped music / lift music / muzak* as expressions for the kind of recorded music that is played continuously in shops, restaurants, etc. 'Muzak' was the name of the US company that first developed special background music for shops and restaurants – it started using the name Muzak in 1934.
Now give Sts time to read the list and think of their answers for each question.
Put Sts in pairs and get them to compare answers.
Elicit some feedback from the class. You could have a class vote to see if Sts prefer silence or background / piped music in general.

b Give Sts time to read the introduction to *How being quiet can change your life* and answer the question.

Check the answer.

It involves enjoying spending silent time with strangers rather than family or friends.

c Focus on the task and tell Sts to read the rest of the article and match each **bold** event (1–4) to summaries A–D.
Check answers.

EXTRA SUPPORT Before Sts read the article the first time, check whether you need to pre-teach any vocabulary.

A 2 **B** 4 **C** 3 **D** 1

d Give Sts time to find phrases 1–10 in the article with a partner and check they know what they mean.
Check answers. Give further practice of any words your Sts find difficult to pronounce, e.g. *hubbub* /ˈhʌbʌb/.

Possible answers

1 **something quite radical** = sth new, different, and likely to have a great effect
2 **show up, shut up, and read** = come along, don't speak, and read
3 **escape the hubbub** = get away from a situation in which there is a lot of noise, excitement, and activity
4 **break the ice** = to say or do sth that makes people feel more relaxed, especially at the beginning of a meeting, party, etc.
5 **uninterrupted eye contact** = to look, without stopping, at sb at the same time as they look at you
6 **the age-old connections** = links that have existed for a long time
7 **strips away** = takes away
8 **hadn't been able to deal with** = hadn't been able to cope with
9 **cherish rare moments of peace and quiet** = to love silence very much and want to protect those moments
10 **muster up the self-restraint** = find the ability to stop yourself doing or saying sth that you want to because you know it is better not to

Deal with any vocabulary problems that arose.

e Do this as a whole-class activity, or put Sts in pairs and then get some feedback. You could tell Sts which silent activity you would choose and why. You could also have a vote with a show of hands for each activity to see which would be the most popular.

6 SPEAKING

a Do this as a whole-class activity.

b Focus on the task and make sure Sts know what an *online thread* is (= a series of comments posted online, e.g. on Twitter).
Give Sts time to read the comments and answer the question.
Check the answer.

Two (3 and 6)

c ◀)) **4.17** Get Sts to focus on the highlighted phrases used for emphasizing your opinion and underline the words they think are stressed.
Get Sts to compare with a partner.
Play the audio for Sts to listen and check.
Check answers.

4.17
1 As far as I'm concerned, the sign is completely pointless.
2 My feeling is that it's best to live and let live.
3 In my view, that's their job.
4 If you ask me, they're never going to work.
5 Personally, I think that normal conversation is acceptable.
6 I'd say the only way round it is to buy yourself a set of noise-cancelling headphones.

d Focus on the task and make sure Sts understand all the lexis.

Put Sts in small groups to discuss each noise regulation. Encourage them to use the useful phrases in **b**.

Monitor and help.

Get some feedback from various groups.

EXTRA IDEA Get Sts to decide on at least three more noise regulations that they would like to have in the town / region where they live.

7 ▶ VIDEO LISTENING

a Focus on the task and make sure Sts know what a *percussionist* is (= a person who plays musical instruments that are hit with your hand or with a stick, e.g. drums). Elicit or model its pronunciation /pəˈkʌʃənɪst/. Now go through the 12 items mentioned and make sure Sts understand all the lexis, e.g. *repertoire*.

Play the video once the whole way through for Sts to watch and tick the items mentioned.

Check answers.

EXTRA SUPPORT Read through the script and decide if you need to pre-teach any new lexis before Sts watch the video.

N = narrator, E = Evelyn Glennie
A world of sounds
N *Evelyn Glennie is a British musician and composer. Evelyn was born in Aberdeen in Scotland. From the age of eight, she started to lose her hearing and she's been profoundly deaf since the age of twelve. Evelyn was learning the piano, but, at twelve, she decided she wanted to take up percussion, the first step in her journey to becoming the world's premier solo percussionist.*

E Well, to be a solo percussionist, of course you need repertoire to play and there was very little repertoire for solo percussion. So my main focus had to be targeting the composers and asking them to write pieces of music, otherwise there was not enough repertoire to sustain the career of a solo percussionist and, er, so that really was my main task. But I think a lot of people couldn't quite visualize what a solo percussionist could be, so to bring percussion from the back of the orchestra to the front of the orchestra, that took a little while for people to really think about and to visualize but for me, it was very, very clear in my mind, but getting the repertoire was absolutely key.

N *With this in mind, Evelyn has commissioned over two hundred new works for solo percussion. She performs these and other older works across the world, either solo or with other musicians and orchestras. She often performs barefoot in order to feel the music better.*

E I love the diversity of the types of performances I give, so sometimes they're by myself and sometimes they're with other people. I'm collaborating with different, different types of artists so not necessarily musicians, they can be dancers, they can be visual artists, they can be storytellers, they can be sound designers and so on. So, and I love that combination, you know, I love the fact that when I'm performing by myself, I have absolute control over the sound that I'm creating at that time, I have control over how I want something to be interpreted. When with, when you're with other people, of course, there's got to be this give and take, that's what makes it special too, it's almost like having a conversation and you can learn an awful lot when you're collaborating with other people.

N *Although her training was in classical music, Evelyn has also collaborated with a diverse range of other musicians, including the Icelandic singer, Bjork, and the British rock guitarist, Mark Knopfler. Throughout her career, Evelyn has collected percussion instruments from various countries and cultures, and some from closer to home, like this thundersheet that Evelyn picked up from a nearby building site. In fact, she has so many that she can't store them all in her home studio.*

E Well, my collection of percussion instruments is around two thousand, bearing in mind that many of those instruments are quite small, so they can be hand-held and then of course, we have much larger instruments such as the marimba, the vibraphone, timpani, drum kit, gamelan, lots of different things like that. And each instrument is unique, it's almost like asking, 'What is your favourite child?', and that's impossible, you know?! So, each instrument has a story, you know, each instrument just has its own unique sound world and really, again, whichever instrument is in front of me, that's my favourite.

N *These instruments are not for show. Evelyn plays all the instruments in her collection and has recorded over thirty albums. She also composes music for percussion herself, both for classical performance and for the theatre, for film and TV, and for advertising.*

E I do compose music and most of my compositions are related to media purposes, so for films, for radio, television and so on and that aspect I really love because I can use a lot of the more unusual instruments in my collection. And the thing about writing to what is mainly a picture, so it could be that you're writing for a, a detective drama series, or a car advert, or a milk advert or something, is that you have that visual aid and it can just be a sound, a mood that you're creating that will make the difference in what you see and ultimately, how engaged you become with that drama or advert or product. So, it's a really different type of, of composition, as opposed to writing for the concert platform, so I very much enjoy that with the, the types of tools that I have at my disposal.

N *Given the number of instruments she owns and the variety of instruments and things she plays, what instrument would she recommend to a beginner?*

E To advise someone as to which instrument would be good to start with, I think it depends on many aspects, the space they have, whether they're close to neighbours and so on and obviously I'm referring to percussion. But I think it's important to find an instrument b- whereby all four limbs, your two arms, two legs can participate in so that the body is completely balanced.

N *In two thousand and twelve, Evelyn performed in the opening ceremony of the Olympic Games in London, a highpoint for any performer. She has also been made a dame and a Companion of Honour by the Queen. Although these are proud moments, she says she has many other career highlights.*

E You know, I remember playing to a group of five-year olds and giving my first workshop, it was a fantastic feeling, you know. I remember seeing my first ever solo recording and just handling that, having it in my hand, it was an amazing feeling, or having the first copy of my autobiography, it was an amazing feeling and it goes on and on like that. So, all of those things are building blocks really, but it's important to see the big picture and ultimately, a career is about hard work as well, it's about redefining yourself, it's about focus, visualizing and that has to come from within.

N *Throughout her career, Evelyn has been the focus of attention due to the virtuosity of her playing, but she's also attracted attention because of her profound deafness. Her need to teach herself to listen again after she became deaf, and her experience as a musician and performer, have prompted her to advocate listening as central to how humans interact, through an initiative called 'Teach the World to Listen'.*

E Well to 'Teach the World to Listen' really is realizing that listening is the glue, it's the glue that binds us together and we often find that many of the challenges we might have in the home environment or in the work environment, socially and so on, they often break down and it's often because of our listening skills. We, we just somehow don't know often how to listen and listening isn't always about sound or reacting to sound, it's being present at that moment, it's being aware of our environment. So, for example, if I'm sitting with someone who might have dementia and there is no spoken word, there is no sound, but there's the presence there, that's an incredible thing, it's an incredible feeling and that is a form of listening that binds two people together.

b Focus on the task and give Sts time to read 1–9, making sure they understand all the lexis.

Play the video again, pausing if necessary to give Sts time to write.

Get Sts to compare with a partner, and then play again if necessary.

Check answers.

1 She had to target composers because there was very little repertoire for solo percussion, and she needed them to write music for her.
2 She wanted to move percussion from the back of the orchestra, where percussionists usually are, to the front of the orchestra – to make it a solo instrument, and to give it greater importance.
3 These are some of the different kinds of artists that she's worked with.
4 She compares choosing a favourite instrument to choosing a favourite child – it's impossible.
5 Most of the music that she writes is for films, radio, and television.
6 How close you are to your neighbours is something to consider if you're thinking of taking up a percussion instrument.
7 This was the first workshop she gave, and it gave her an amazing feeling.
8 She says that listening is 'the glue that binds us together' – it helps us to live with and understand each other.
9 If someone has dementia and doesn't speak, it's still possible to listen to them by being with them.

EXTRA SUPPORT You could get Sts to watch again with subtitles, so they can see exactly what they understood / didn't understand. Translate / Explain any new words or phrases.

c Do this as a whole-class activity.

For instructions on how to use these pages, see *p.43*.

More materials
For teachers
Teacher's Resource Centre
Video Can you understand these people? 3&4
Quick Test 4
File 4 Test
For students
Online Practice Check your progress

GRAMMAR

a
1 It's 2.30 now – what time do you think we'll get **to** London?
2 Unfortunately, Allie got **caught** cheating in her final exam.
3 Shall we get someone **to clean** them?
4 I don't think Keith will ever get **used** to doing his own laundry – his parents always did it for him.
5 My visa expires quite soon, so I really need to get it **renewed**.

b
1 ✗ Basically
2 ✗ all in all
3 ✗ Not only did we see the sights
4 ✓
5 ✗ he might have got lost
6 ✗ The waiter probably didn't notice
7 ✓
8 ✗ Somebody must be baking / Somebody must have baked
9 ✓
10 ✓

c
1 No sooner **had they got** married than James lost his job.
2 Never **had (have) I seen** such a wonderful view.
3 The traffic is quite bad – she's unlikely **to arrive** before 7.00.
4 Maria is bound **to have heard** the news…
5 My neighbour can't **work** very long hours.

VOCABULARY

a
1 know   2 together   3 hold   4 nerves   5 over   6 way
7 by   8 chance

b
1 declared   2 ceasefire   3 siege   4 refugees   5 casualties
6 blew up   7 surrender   8 release

c
1 slammed   2 whispered   3 whistled   4 sighed   5 rattled
6 screeched   7 buzzed   8 creaked

d
1 thought-provoking   2 heart-warming   3 intriguing
4 gripping   5 moving   6 implausible

CAN YOU understand this text?

a He couldn't speak any English when they first met. Now he understands a lot, but is not fluent.

b
1 b   2 d   3 a   4 a   5 c   6 d   7 a   8 b   9 d   10 c

▶ CAN YOU understand these people?

1 c   **2** a   **3** c   **4** b

◀)) 4.18

1
I = interviewer, S = Sophie
I Do you think nowadays it's better to meet people online or in real life?
S I think, nowadays, it's probably easier to meet people online. I've got a lot of friends who've met their partners online, er, and I think it's a really good way to meet people because you can talk about your interests, um, before you even meet.
I If you have a partner, how did you meet them?
S So I met my husband, er, when we were at school. Um, but then we kind of went our separate ways and didn't see each other for many, many years and he got back in contact with me on Facebook, so a little bit face to face, a little bit online.

2
I = interviewer, S = Sarah
I What was the last historical film you saw? How accurate did you think it was? Do you think you learned anything about the people and the period from the film?
S Um, well, it wasn't a film, but I did watch the TV drama *Victoria* about Queen Victoria. Um, and I don't think it was entirely accurate because she had about eight children and didn't seem to age at all, er, and also, um, there, there was a storyline about a, a Duke and his wife who had an affair with, um, um, a butler, er, and I did actually google that to see if it was a true story, but the, the Duchess, er, didn't actually exist so I think they obviously, um, just write things in to, to keep people's interest and make it a bit more exciting. Um, but, I did actually learn a lot, I think the Victorian era is the one that we, we hear about a lot because, um, so much like the train line was, was developed around then, but I didn't actually know that much about her and her relationship with her husband and, and her family, so I think I learnt a lot about that.

3
I = interviewer, J = James
I Do you prefer fiction or non-fiction?
J Um, I really enjoy both of them actually. I read a lot of fiction, er, and I read quite a lot of non-fiction as well depending on, you know, what, what mood I'm in.
I What kind of books do you like reading?
J Um, well, fiction, um, I really enjoy fantasy and science fiction books especially. Um, and in non-fiction, um, historical, historical books about pretty much any country, any period really.
I What are you reading at the moment?
J Er, I'm reading, er, a fantasy novel by a, a guy called Adrian Tchaikovsky, um, who, I've read a lot of his novels and they're, they're fantastic.

4
I = interviewer, A = Amy
I Can you think of a sound you really love and one you hate, and why?
A A sound I love is autumn leaves because, um, I love the crunch and the fact it immediately makes me think of autumn, which is my favourite season. A sound I'd hate is like someone tapping a pen because I find that it's always done when you want to focus and concentrate and it can be quite irritating.

5A No time for anything

G distancing
V expressions with *time*
P linking in short phrases

Lesson plan

The topic of this lesson is time: the pros and cons of being busy and how we feel about having to wait for things.

In the first half of the lesson, Sts begin by doing a quiz to see how busy they are, and whether they are, in fact, too busy. They then read two articles about busyness, one positive and one negative. The focus in Language in context is verb phrases. One technique that busy people use to reduce stress is mindfulness, and Sts then listen to a well-known meditation exercise called *The Chocolate Meditation*, which gives them a practical experience of mindfulness. This listening will be even more enjoyable if you are able to bring in some small wrapped bars of chocolate to distribute to Sts before doing the listening, or ask them to bring in their own. This leads into the grammar focus of the lesson, which is on distancing, i.e. using certain language (e.g. *apparently*, *it seems*, etc.) to 'distance' ourselves from information we are giving to others.

In the second half of the lesson, Sts listen to a survey by Timex watch manufacturer about how long we are prepared to wait in certain situations before getting impatient and reacting angrily. This survey is in American English, so Sts then look at some equivalent British English expressions. Sts also talk about how long they would wait in the situations presented in the survey. They then learn expressions related to time, and there is a pronunciation focus on short phrases where words are normally linked together. The lesson ends with Sts answering questions in a time questionnaire, which recycles all the lexis.

More materials

For teachers

Photocopiables
Grammar distancing *p.175*
Communicative Managing time *p.201* (instructions *p.189*)
Vocabulary Expressions with *time p.223*
(instructions *p.215*)

For students

Workbook 5A

Online Practice 5A

OPTIONAL LEAD-IN – THE QUOTE
Write the quote at the top of *p.46* on the board (books closed) and the name of the person who said it, or get Sts to open their books and read it.

Point out that Henry David Thoreau (1817–1862) was an American poet and philosopher. He is best known for his book *Walden*, which is about leading a simple life in natural surroundings.

Ask Sts whether they agree with the quote.

1 SPEAKING

a Do this as a whole-class activity, or put Sts in pairs and then get some feedback. You could tell the class what you did, too.

b Focus on the ten statements in the quiz, making sure Sts understand them all, especially number 9. You might want to point out how *schedule* is used as a verb in 9 and a noun in 10. You might also want to highlight the different pronunciation in British English (/ˈʃedjuːl/) and American English (/ˈskedʒuːl/).
  Give Sts time to do the quiz individually.

c Tell Sts to go to **Communication Am I too busy?** on *p.111* to find out what their score means.
  Give them time to read the information.
  Tell Sts to go back to the main lesson **5A**.

d Put Sts in pairs to compare their answers and scores, and find out if they are similarly busy.
  Get some feedback from various pairs.

2 READING understanding contrasting points of view

a Do this as a whole-class activity, getting Sts to say both words out loud.

business /ˈbɪznəs/ = the activity of making, buying, selling, or supplying goods or services for money; a company
busyness /ˈbɪziːnəs/ = the state or condition of having a lot to do

b Focus on the task and put Sts in pairs.
  When they have finished reading the first paragraphs, they should complete each title and decide which article is positive and which is negative about being busy.
  Check answers.

EXTRA SUPPORT Before Sts read the articles the first time, check whether you need to pre-teach any vocabulary, but not the verb phrases in **d**.

1 Are you a**ddicted** to being busy? – negative
2 What keeps you h**ealthy** is being busy, busy, busy! – positive

c Now tell Sts to read the rest of the two articles and answer questions 1–8. Tell them that the acronym *FOMO* in 1 is explained in the article.
  Get Sts to compare with a partner, and then check answers.

1 Because other people often post about exciting things that they're doing, which makes busy people worry that they are missing out.
2 To keep their minds occupied, so they don't think about their break-up
3 Because society is obsessed with achievement and being busy creates a sense of importance and value.
4 Because they feel that they shouldn't be relaxing and doing nothing.
5 Because people are working for longer, and because smartphones and social media don't allow us to disconnect.

6 Because they have lots of reasons for getting up in the morning, and they have an active day.
7 Because people who retire early risk losing muscle strength and getting ill, and they may develop cognitive problems.
8 Because being active helps to prevent dementia.

LANGUAGE IN CONTEXT

d Focus on the instructions and elicit / explain what a *particle* is (= a preposition or adverb that goes after, e.g. a verb).

Give Sts time to complete each gap with a particle.

Get them to compare with a partner, and then decide what the verb phrase means.

Check answers. You might want to tell Sts that 1, 3, and 6 are phrasal verbs, and 2, 4, and 5 are idioms. 5 (*keep sth at bay*) is quite similar in meaning to 6 (*ward off*).

1 get **back** to sb = to speak or write to sb again later, especially in order to give a reply
2 be **on** the go = to be very active and busy
3 stand **for** sth = to be an abbreviation or symbol of sth
4 keep your mind **off** sth = stop thinking about sth
5 keep sth **at** bay = to prevent an enemy from coming close or a problem from having a bad effect
6 ward **off** sth = to protect or defend yourself against danger, illness, attack, etc.

Finally, deal with any vocabulary problems that arose in either of the two articles.

e Put Sts in pairs to discuss the five questions.

Get some feedback from various pairs. You could tell the class your opinion of being busy.

3 LISTENING

a This is an authentic piece of audio of a real 'meditation'. Your Sts may notice that the speaker uses *-ing* forms where they might expect imperatives (e.g. *At a certain point, bringing it up to your mouth, noticing how the hand knows where to position it, and popping it in the mouth…*). This shouldn't interfere with your Sts' understanding, but it is unusual, and they may be curious about it – it is part of a deliberate approach to mindfulness and meditation, to focus on the process of experiencing an activity more intensely.

Focus on the instructions and go through them with the class, making sure Sts understand what *mindfulness* is. Ask Sts what they think *The Chocolate Meditation* might be.

Put Sts in pairs and get them to say what they think the verbs mean.

Check answers.

unwrap = to take off the paper, etc. that covers or protects sth
inhale = to take in air through your nose or mouth
pop (sth) into = (inf) to put sth somewhere quickly, suddenly, or for a short time
melt = to become (or make sth become) liquid as a result of heating
chew = to bite food into small pieces in your mouth to make it easier to swallow
swallow = to make food, drink, etc. go down your throat into your stomach

b 🔊 **5.1** Tell Sts to close their eyes, listen, and imagine they are doing all the stages mentioned on the audio. If you or your Sts have brought in chocolate bars, tell them not to close their eyes, as they will hear instructions to look at the chocolate.

Play the audio once the whole way through.

If your Sts actually ate the chocolate, ask them if it tasted in any way different. If they imagined it, ask them how they felt during the listening.

EXTRA SUPPORT Read through the script and decide if you need to pre-teach any new lexis before Sts listen.

🔊 **5.1**
(script in Student's Book on *p.134*)
The Chocolate Meditation
Again and again, people tell us that mindfulness greatly enhances the joys of daily life. In practice, even the smallest of things can suddenly become captivating again. For this reason, one of our favourite practices is the chocolate meditation. In this, you ask yourself to bring all your attention to some chocolate as you're eating it. So, if you want to do this right now, choosing some chocolate, not unwrapping it yet. Choosing a type that you've never tried before, or one that you've not eaten recently. It might be dark and flavoursome, organic, or Fairtrade, or whatever you choose. Perhaps choosing a type you wouldn't normally eat, or that you consume only rarely.
***

Before you unwrap the chocolate, look at the whole bar or packet – its colour, its shape, what it feels like in your hand – as if you were seeing it for the very first time.
***

Now very slowly unwrapping the chocolate, noticing how the wrapping feels as you unfold it, seeing the chocolate itself. What colours do you notice? What shapes? Inhaling the aroma of the chocolate, letting it sweep over you.
***

And taking or breaking off a piece and looking at it as it rests on your hand, really letting your eyes drink in what it looks like. Examining every nook and cranny. At a certain point, bringing it up to your mouth, noticing how the hand knows where to position it, and popping it in the mouth, noticing what the tongue does to receive it. See if it's possible to hold it on your tongue and let it melt, noticing any tendency to chew it, seeing if you can sense some of the different flavours, really noticing these.
***

If you notice your mind wandering while you do this, simply noticing where it went, then gently escorting it back to the present moment. And then, when the chocolate has completely melted, swallowing it very slowly and deliberately, letting it trickle down your throat.
***

What did you notice? If the chocolate tasted better than if you'd just eaten it at a normal pace, what do you make of that? Often, we taste the first piece and perhaps the last, but the rest goes down unnoticed. We're so often on autopilot, we can miss much of our day-to-day lives. Mindfulness is about bringing awareness to the usual routine things in life, things that we normally take for granted. Perhaps you could try this with any routine activity, seeing what you notice? It could change your whole day.

---

c Focus on the six questions and give Sts time to read them. You could point out that *Fairtrade* is a system which supports small-scale farmers and workers, giving them better prices, decent working conditions, and fair terms of trade.

Play the audio again, pausing where you see *** in the script to give Sts time to answer the questions. Play again as necessary.

Get Sts to compare with a partner, and then check answers.

1 Choose a type that you've never tried before, or one that you haven't eaten recently.
2 Look at it – its colour and shape, what it feels like – as if you were seeing it for the very first time.
3 Notice how the wrapping feels, see the chocolate itself; look at it and smell it.
4 Look at it in great detail as you hold it in your hand.
5 Notice how your hand knows where to put the chocolate. Put it on your tongue and let it melt. Notice if you chew and notice the different flavours.
6 Swallow the chocolate when it has completely melted.

EXTRA SUPPORT If there's time, you could get Sts to listen again with the script on *p.134*, so they can see exactly what they understood / didn't understand. Translate / Explain any new words or phrases, e.g. *every nook and cranny* (= every single part).

d Do the questions as a whole-class activity and elicit opinions and ideas.

Suggested answer
The main message of the meditation is that by slowing down and paying attention to the small things we do in our daily lives, we can appreciate them more.

EXTRA IDEA You could also ask Sts if they can think of any other everyday activities they could try the approach from *The Chocolate Meditation* with.

4 GRAMMAR distancing

a Go through the instructions and give Sts time to read the sentences.
Check the answer.

The highlighted expressions all distance the writer from the information, i.e. they imply that it might not be a definite fact. If they were left out, the information in each sentence would be presented as a definite fact.

b Tell Sts to go to **Grammar Bank 5A** on *p.150*.

Grammar notes
Distancing expressions are often used, particularly in journalism where a speaker or writer wants to stress that the information is second-hand and comes from a specific source or sources, rather than being their own knowledge or opinion. Expressions like *It is said that…* are also often used where a writer is not sure of the sources, and by using these expressions they can avoid the possibility of libel.

Sts should have come across most of these expressions before, but will probably never have focused on their exact function, and may well not be familiar with the two possible ways of using *seem* and *appear*. You may want to point out that *appear* is slightly more formal than *seem*.

Focus on the example sentences for **seem** / **appear** and go through the rules with the class.
Repeat for **the passive with verbs of saying and reporting** and **other distancing expressions:** *apparently, according to, may / might, claim*.

Focus on the exercises and get Sts to do them individually or in pairs. If they do them individually, get them to compare with a partner.
Check answers after each exercise, getting Sts to read the full sentences.

a
1 It **seems** / **appears** that the less children sleep, the more likely they are to behave badly.
2 It **would** appear that someone has been stealing personal items from the changing rooms.
3 Matt **seems** / **appears** to have aged a lot over the last year.
4 He may not look it, but he is **said** / **thought** / **believed** to be one of the wealthiest people in the country.
5 **According** to some sources, the latest research is seriously flawed.
6 Despite the fact that there will be an autopsy, his death is **said** / **thought** / **believed** / **understood** to have been from natural causes.
7 **There** are thought to be several reasons why the experiment failed.
8 The troubled celebrity is believed **to** have had financial difficulties.
9 It is understood **that** the minister will be resigning in the near future.

b
1 It would **seem** / **appear that people who work night shifts die younger.**
2 The prisoners may **have escaped** to France.
3 The Prime Minister is **expected to make a statement** this afternoon.
4 It **has been announced (by the company) that the new drug** will go on sale shortly.
5 Stress **is believed to be responsible** for many common skin complaints.
6 According **to the instructions, the battery lasts** for at least 12 hours.
7 The government **appears** / **seems to be intending to lower** the top rate of income tax.
8 It **has been suggested that birth order has** a strong influence on children's personalities.
9 There **seem** / **appear to be more cyclists on the roads** than there used to be.

Tell Sts to go back to the main lesson **5A**.

EXTRA SUPPORT If you think Sts need more practice, you may want to give them the **Grammar** photocopiable activity at this point.

c Focus on the task. Tell Sts that they should write two or three sentences for each headline and invent the details; they should distance themselves from the information they give.
Monitor and help.

EXTRA SUPPORT Sts could do this in pairs or small groups. You could also help to start them off by eliciting the first sentence for one of the headlines.

Finally, get Sts to read each other's stories before collecting them in to check for accuracy.

5 LISTENING understanding comparison

a Focus on the task and the title of the survey, *How long are we prepared to wait before we freak out?*, and elicit the meaning of *freak out*. If Sts don't know, or guess incorrectly, get them to read the introduction, and then ask them again (= get annoyed, react very strongly).

Now tell Sts to look at the survey and choose the two situations which would make them the most impatient.

Get Sts to tell a partner what they chose, and then elicit some answers from individual Sts. You could tell the class the two you would choose.

b Put Sts in pairs and tell them to try to complete the survey with the times in the list.

Elicit some ideas, e.g. for the shortest time (50 seconds) and the longest (32 minutes).

c **5.2** Tell Sts they are going to listen to an American journalist talking about the survey. You might want to remind them that Americans call (mobile) phones *cell phones*.

Play the audio once the whole way through for Sts to listen and check their answers to **b**.

Check answers. Find out if any Sts guessed all the answers correctly and whether they found any answers surprising.

EXTRA SUPPORT Read through the script and decide if you need to pre-teach any new lexis before Sts listen.

1 50 seconds	**2** 1 minute 52 seconds		
3 2 minutes 41 seconds	**4** 32 minutes	**5** 21 minutes	
6 7 minutes	**7** 26 minutes	**8** 2 minutes 25 seconds	

5.2

(script in Student's Book on *p.134*)

How long is it before we get frustrated at people talking during a movie, or waiting for a date who hasn't shown up? I veer wildly between patience and impatience. It's probably good to know whether you're more or less patient than the average person, so I was interested to read the results of a survey by the watch company Timex, asking people how long they were willing to wait in various situations before losing patience. Some of the results seem about right. However, some seem wildly unlikely, based on my experience of how people tend to behave.

First, a car in front of you at a green light – average time before getting annoyed: fifty seconds. This is the one result that seems least believable to me. Fifty seconds waiting behind someone at a green light? From what I've observed, it's more like five seconds – maybe even less.

Then, waiting for people to stop talking in a movie theater – average wait: one minute fifty-two seconds. This also seems a long time. For me, it depends – if it's a really sad or emotional story, and they're ruining the atmosphere, I shush them after five seconds, but if it's a full-blown action movie, then it doesn't really bug me.

Next, crying babies. Apparently, it takes almost three minutes (two minutes forty-one seconds, to be precise) before someone gives parents a dirty look because their baby is screaming. That sounds quite a long time to me, and what they didn't ask was how long people would wait to ask a flight attendant if they can switch seats when they realize they're sitting right next to a screaming baby. That would have to be in the thirty-second range, right?

Waiting to see the doctor is something everyone expects to take a while. Thirty-two minutes on average before people get mad doesn't seem unreasonable. I suppose there are always magazines to read, even though they're usually several years out of date.

Now, what about waiting for your partner to get ready? Average wait, twenty-one minutes. I assume that means twenty-one minutes after you're ready yourself. I think that's too long to wait. I can get ready to go out in approximately ten minutes – shower, change, coat on, ready! My wife, on the other hand…

The next one also seems pretty long. Maybe from entering the coffee shop to actually drinking your coffee could take seven minutes. But just waiting in line? Presumably not during rush hour, when customers just want a takeout and the baristas generally know what they're doing?

What about if your blind date is late? The survey says that the average time before people get angry and leave is twenty-six minutes. That seems like the right amount of time for you to experience that scene from romantic comedies where the main character is sitting at a table, checking his or her phone, and finally decides to leave when the server offers them 'More bread?' for the fourth time.

Finally, the average wait before angrily asking some over-confident business-type next to you talking loudly on a cell phone to quiet down – two minutes twenty-five seconds. Well, everyone in the world must be more patient than me. But my tip here is: just make facial expressions to let them know you're annoyed. Really exaggerated facial expressions. Works every time.

You might want to highlight the American English phrase *quiet down* (i.e. *the average wait before angrily asking some over-confident business-type next to you talking loudly on a cell phone to quiet down*), which in British English is *quieten down*. Tell Sts they will be looking at more of the American English language Sam used later in **e**.

d Give Sts time to read the two questions.

Play the audio again, pausing it after Sam has discussed each situation.

Get Sts to compare with a partner, and then check answers.

1 (strongly) disagrees	**2** disagrees	**3** disagrees	**4** agrees
5 disagrees	**6** disagrees	**7** agrees	**8** disagrees

Sam is less patient than the average person – he thinks five of the times are too long.

LANGUAGE IN CONTEXT

e Put Sts in pairs and get them to try to work out the British English equivalent of 1–6.

Check answers.

1 a cinema	**2** it doesn't really annoy me	**3** get annoyed / angry
4 queuing	**5** a takeaway	**6** a waiter

EXTRA SUPPORT If there's time, you could get Sts to listen again with the script on *p.134*, so they can see exactly what they understood / didn't understand. Translate / Explain any new words or phrases.

f In pairs, Sts now say how long they would wait in each situation, and in what other situations they hate having to wait. If Sts are having trouble thinking of other situations, give them some suggestions, e.g. for a bus or train to arrive, to be given a table in a restaurant, etc., but <u>not</u> the things mentioned by the speakers in audio ◖ **5.3**.

Get feedback from various pairs.

EXTRA SUPPORT You could do this as a whole-class activity.

6 VOCABULARY expressions with *time*

a 🔊 **5.3** Focus on the task and then play the audio, pausing after each speaker for Sts to listen and answer the question.

Check what each speaker hates waiting for, and then ask the class if anyone feels the same.

1 Waiting at home for a delivery
2 Waiting for films or TV programmes to download
3 Waiting for an appointment with, e.g. a hairdresser / dentist / doctor

🔊 **5.3**
(script in Student's Book on *p.134*)
1
One thing I really, really hate is waiting at home for a delivery, 'cause sometimes they'll give you a, a delivery slot of, of, of two hours and that's fine you know when it's coming, but more often they'll say it could be any time from 7 a.m. to 7 p.m., and then you're just stuck in the house – you don't even dare go out in case you miss them – and of course it always ends up coming at two minutes to seven, and you've just spent the whole day waiting, wasting your time at home.
2
So, what annoys me is, oh, you know when you have to wait for ages for like, films and TV programmes to download? It doesn't really happen so much nowadays, but from time to time, I'll be somewhere where there's like, really bad internet connection and it really irritates me. I'll be sort of sitting there, watching that little download icon moving at at an absolute snail's pace.
3
I really hate waiting for anything where I've been given an appointment time for a specific hour – you know, a specific time – and then having to wait for ages before I actually have it, so, well, you know, for example a hairdresser or a dentist, or a doctor. I mean, I'm very punctual, so I always turn up on time – in fact, usually at least five minutes early – and it really, really annoys me if I have to wait for a long time. Anything more than fifteen minutes over the appointment time drives me completely insane.

b Play the audio again, pausing after each speaker for Sts to listen and complete the extracts.

Check answers and elicit what the phrases mean.

1 **could be any time** = at a time that is not fixed
2 **from time to time** = occasionally
3 **turn up on time** = arrive at exactly the correct time

c Tell Sts to go to **Vocabulary Bank Expressions with** *time* on *p.167*.

Vocabulary notes

1 Verbs

You may want to highlight that:

- *kill time* suggests that you want to make time pass quickly because you are bored
- *make up for lost time* = try to compensate for time or opportunities missed in the past
- *give sb a hard time* = to deliberately make a situation difficult and unpleasant for sb
- *can't spare the time* = you don't have enough time to devote any of it to another activity
- *take up (time)* = fill your time

- *have the time of your life* (inf) = enjoy yourself very much. You could also teach the synonym *have a whale of a time*.
- *play for time* = to deliberately delay doing sth, or to do it more slowly than usual, so that you have more time to decide what to do

2 Prepositional phrases

You may need to elicit / explain:

- the difference between *on time* (= punctually, at the agreed time) and *in time* (= arriving early enough to do sth, e.g. catch a train). You could also teach the expression *in the nick of time* (= at the very last moment).
- *before my time* = before I was old enough to be aware of / remember this
- *by the time* = all the time up to a certain point, e.g. *By the time we got to the top of the mountain, we were exhausted* = We had been getting progressively more exhausted during the climb.
- *behind the times* = old-fashioned in your ideas, methods, etc. (the opposite is *ahead of your time*)
- *in no time* = very quickly

3 Expressions

You may need to elicit / explain:

- *time left* = time remaining
- *short of time* = synonym of *pushed for time*, but *pushed for time* is less formal
- *for the time being* = for the moment
- *it's a matter of time* = it's inevitable that sth will happen
- *time on my hands* = more free time than I actually want
- *time's up* = the allotted time for sth has expired
- *time to spare* = with more than enough time
- *me time* = an informal expression meaning time when a person who is normally very busy relaxes or does sth they enjoy
- *time-consuming* = taking or needing a lot of time
- *about time* = used to say that sth should have happened before now

Focus on **1 Verbs** and get Sts to do **a** individually or in pairs.

🔊 **5.4** Now focus on **b**. Play the audio for Sts to listen and check.

Check answers, and make sure Sts understand the meaning of each phrase.

🔊 **5.4**
Expressions with *time*
1 Verbs
1 I waste a lot of time playing games and messaging on my computer instead of studying.
2 If you take the motorway, you'll **save** time – it's much quicker than the local roads.
3 I had three hours to wait for my flight, so I sat there doing sudoku puzzles to **kill** time.
4 There's no hurry, so **take** your time.
5 When my mother was young, she never had the chance to travel. Now she's retired and wants to **make up for** lost time, so she's booked a trip around the world.
6 The novel is seven hundred pages long and I'm a slow reader. It's going to **take** me a long time to finish it.

7 I'd better go home now. If I'm late again, Dad will **give** me a hard time.
8 I would like to go camping this weekend, but my final exams are next week, so I can't **spare** the time.
9 My children **take up** all my time – I never seem to get to read a book or watch a film!
10 New York's such a fantastic city! You're going to **have** the time of your life there.
11 Let's not **spend** too long at the museum or we'll **run out of** time.
12 They want us to sign the contract today, but I'm not sure about it. I think we should **play for** time.

Focus on **2 Prepositional phrases** and get Sts to do **a** individually or in pairs. Remind them to write their answers in the *Prepositions* column and <u>not</u> in the sentences.

🔊 **5.5** Now focus on **b**. Play the audio for Sts to listen and check.

Check answers, and check Sts understand the meaning of each **bold** phrase.

🔊 **5.5**
2 Prepositional phrases
1 I'm really punctual, so I hate it when other people aren't on time.
2 I've never heard of that singer. He must have been **before** my time.
3 **By** the time we got to our hotel, it was nearly midnight.
4 I missed the birth of my first child. I was on a plane **at** the time.
5 She's been working too hard recently. She needs some time **off**.
6 If we don't take a taxi, we won't get to the airport **in** time for the flight.
7 I don't eat out very often, but I do get a takeaway **from** time **to** time.
8 He suffers from back pain and it makes him a little irritable **at** times.
9 You can come any time **from** ten **to** two.
10 My dad's a bit **behind** the times – he still thinks men should wear a suit and tie at work.
11 Don't try to multitask. Just do one thing **at** a time.
12 I thought it would take ages, but in fact I finished it **in** no time.

Focus on **3 Expressions** and get Sts to do **a** individually or in pairs.

🔊 **5.6** Now focus on **b**. Play the audio for Sts to listen and check.

Check answers, and check Sts understand the meaning of each **bold** sentence or phrase.

🔊 **5.6**
3 Expressions
1 I
The referee's looking at his watch. There isn't much time left.
2 B
He hardly spoke to me at lunch. He spent the whole time talking on his phone.
3 J
I'm really looking forward to my holiday. This time next week I'll be lying on the beach.
4 D
I'm sorry, I can't help you this week. I'm a little short of time.
5 F
I can't afford a new car. I'll have to carry on with this one for the time being.
6 G
She's sure to find a job eventually. It's only a matter of time.
7 E
I think I need to take up a hobby. I've got time on my hands since I retired.
8 C
Stop writing, please. Time's up. The exam is over.

9 A
I really thought I was going to be late. But in the end, I got to the airport with time to spare.
10 H
Why not spend a morning at our spa? It's very popular with people who want a bit of me time.
11 L
I hate having to fill in my tax return. It's incredibly tedious and time-consuming.
12 K
You've had that computer for ages. It's about time you got a new one.

Finally, focus on **Activation** and give Sts time to choose six time expressions and write a synonym or synonymous phrase for each one.

You could put Sts in pairs and get them to show each other their choice of time expressions.

Get individual Sts to read some of their synonyms or phrases to the class.

Tell Sts to go back to the main lesson **5A**.

EXTRA SUPPORT If you think Sts need more practice, you may want to give them the **Vocabulary** photocopiable activity at this point.

d Focus on the task and give Sts time to complete the sentences with their own ideas.

Get Sts to compare with a partner and say whether their partner's sentences are true for them as well, or reflect what they think.

Get some feedback from different Sts.

7 PRONUNCIATION linking in short phrases

Pronunciation notes

The focus here is on three specific areas where words are commonly linked, i.e. when a word ends with a consonant sound and the next word begins with a vowel sound (e.g. *She went out at eleven o'clock*), when one word ends and the next word begins with the same consonant sound (e.g. *We should get together*), and the added /r/ sound when a word ending in a silent *r* is followed by one beginning with a vowel sound (e.g. *the father of the bride*). Focusing on linking and getting Sts to practise doing it themselves, apart from making Sts' speech sound more natural, will help them to decipher linked speech when they are listening.

a 🔊 **5.7** Focus on the instructions and the ten sentences.

Play the audio once the whole way through for Sts just to listen.

Ask the question to the class to see if Sts have worked out why the words are linked.

Focus on the **Linking in fast speech** box and go through it with the class.

Now go back to sentences 1–10 and elicit why each pair of words is linked, e.g. 1 *need to* = rule 2, *make up* = rule 1, and *lost time* = rule 2.

Check answers.

2 hard time = rule 2
3 run out = rule 1, out of = rule 1
4 Could I = rule 1, time off = rule 1

5 At times = rule 2, times I = rule 1, feel like = rule 2,
giving up = rule 1
6 Time's up = rule 1, Please stop = rule 2
7 waste time = rule 2, time on = rule 1
8 It's only = rule 1, matter of = rule 3, break up = rule 1
9 have a = rule 1, good time = rule 2
10 It's about = rule 1, about time = rule 2, learned to = rule 2

🔊 **5.7**
See sentences in Student's Book on *p.49*

---

b 🔊 **5.8** Tell Sts that the focus here is on deciphering
phrases when the speaker runs two or more words
together. Make sure they understand that they only need
to write the phrase, not the whole sentence.

Play the audio, pausing after each sentence or mini
conversation for Sts to write the phrase. Play again as
necessary.

Check answers, getting feedback from Sts as to which
phrases they found most difficult to understand and why.

1 Not at all   **2** First of all   **3** Pick it up   **4** In an hour
5 on our own

🔊 **5.8**
1 Not at all. (*pause*) **A** Thanks very much. **B** Not at all.
2 First of all,… (*pause*) First of all, we're going to revise the
vocabulary from yesterday.
3 Pick it up. (*pause*) That's your towel on the floor. Pick it up.
4 In an hour… (*pause*) **A** When'll you be back? **B** In an hour or so.
5 on our own (*pause*) Don't worry. We'll find it on our own.

---

c Get Sts to practise saying the sentences in **a** and **b**, linking
the words. They can do this quietly by themselves or with
their partner.

Now get some individual Sts to say the sentences.

EXTRA SUPPORT You could use the audio (🔊 **5.7** and **5.8**) to
model the sentences, with Sts repeating after each sentence.

8 SPEAKING

a Focus on the questionnaire and give Sts time to complete
the questions. They could do this individually or in pairs.

Check answers by eliciting the time phrase in each
question.

1 save you time   **2** time **left**, **run out** of time   **3 give** you a
hard time   **4 short** of time   **5 kill** time   **6 take** your time
7 taking up a **lot** of your time   **8 on** time   **9 with** time to
spare   **10 me** time

b Tell Sts to give examples when they answer the questions.

Put Sts in small groups of three or four and get them to
work through the questionnaire, answering the questions
together.

Monitor while Sts are doing this, correcting any slips in the
time phrases, and noting any other problems to deal with
later.

Finally, get feedback from various groups.

G unreal uses of past tenses
V money
P silent consonants

Lesson plan

The topic of this lesson is money, ways of spending less and leading a less capitalist life, and setting up a small business.

The first half of the lesson starts with a lexical focus on words, phrases, and idioms related to money. Pronunciation looks at silent consonants. Sts then read an article about small ways in which people can fight capitalism in their daily lives. They then discuss the suggestions in the article, and whether small changes in our own lifestyles are effective.

In the second half of the lesson, the grammar focus is on special uses of the past tense after expressions like *I wish*, *I would rather*, etc., and Sts ask and answer some questions on past, present, and future wishes. This leads to an interview with Alessandro Savelli, one of the co-founders of a business called Pasta Evangelists, who explains how and why he set up his business. Sts then work in groups and make a business proposal for a new, small business of their own. Finally, the lesson ends with a writing focus on analysing and writing a proposal.

More materials
For teachers
Photocopiables
Grammar unreal uses of past tenses *p.176*
Communicative Money *p.202* (instructions *p.189*)
Vocabulary Money *p.224* (instructions *p.215*)
For students
Workbook 5B
Online Practice 5B

OPTIONAL LEAD-IN – THE QUOTE

Write the quote at the top of *p.50* on the board (books closed) and the name of the person who said it, or get Sts to open their books and read it.

Point out that Brunello Cucinelli is an Italian fashion designer who has been described as a 'philosopher-designer' and 'part businessman, part philosopher, and part monk'.

Make sure Sts understand the lexis in the quote, and then ask them what they think of it.

1 VOCABULARY money

a Focus on the task and put Sts in pairs to complete it.

Check answers and elicit if Sts have similar expressions in their own language.

1 Money isn't easy to get (so don't spend it carelessly).
2 He doesn't like spending or giving away money.
3 It must have cost a lot of money. (Also *It must have cost a fortune*.)
4 I'm not earning enough money to be able to pay for the things I need.
5 We owe money to the bank because we've spent more than we have in our account. (Also *We're overdrawn*.)
6 It's far too expensive for what it is.
7 We're going to have to spend less because we have less available.
8 She's spending more than she can afford.

b Tell Sts to go to **Vocabulary Bank Money** on *p.168*.

Vocabulary notes

Nouns

Sts may ask about the difference between a *grant* and a *scholarship*. Explain that a grant can be for other things apart from education, and is not associated with having got particularly good marks or grades, as scholarships often are.

Adjectives

Another synonym of *rich* you may want to teach is *prosperous*.

Colloquial language

Highlight that *bucks* is American English slang for *dollars*.

Focus on **1 Nouns** and get Sts to do **a** individually or in pairs.

🔊 **5.9** Now focus on **b**. Play the audio for Sts to listen and check.

Check answers.

🔊 **5.9**
Money
1 Nouns
1 budget
2 grant
3 loan
4 fee
5 fare
6 quote
7 donation
8 fine
9 instalment
10 deposit
11 will
12 lump sum

Now either use the audio to drill the pronunciation of the words, or model and drill them yourself. Give further practice of any words your Sts find difficult to pronounce.

Focus on **2 Money in today's society** and put Sts in pairs to do **a**.

🔊 **5.10** Play the audio, pausing after each sentence to give Sts time to read the sentence and discuss what the **bold** phrases mean.

Check answers sentence by sentence.

1 **consumer society** = a society where buying and selling material goods is considered very important
2 **standard of living** = the amount of money and level of comfort that a particular person or group has
3 **income** = the money sb earns from work, from investing money, or from business
   inflation = the rise in the prices of goods and services in a particular country which results in a fall in the value of money
   cost of living = the amount of money people need to pay for food, clothing, and somewhere to live
4 **can't afford** = not have enough money to be able to buy or do sth
5 **manage their accounts** = deal with their money in the bank
   balance = the amount of money that sb has in their bank account at a particular time
   make transfers = move money from one place to another
   make payments = pay a sum of money
6 **interest rates** = the percentage of extra money that you pay back when you borrow money
7 **in debt** = the situation of owing money, especially when you cannot pay
   mortgage = a legal agreement by which a bank or similar organization lends you money to buy a house, etc., and you pay the money back over a particular number of years
8 **shares** = any of the units of equal value into which a company is divided and sold to raise money. People who own shares receive part of the company's profits.
   stock market = the business of buying and selling shares in companies and the place where this happens (also called the **stock exchange**)
9 **currency** = the system of money that a country uses
   exchange rates = the amount of money you get when you change one currency into another
10 **went bankrupt** = to be without money to pay what you owe
   the recession = a difficult time for the economy of a country, when there is less trade and industrial activity than usual and more people are unemployed

🔊 **5.10**
2 Money in today's society
See sentences in Student's Book on *p.168*

Highlight any words your Sts may have problems pronouncing correctly, e.g. *mortgage* /ˈmɔːɡɪdʒ/.

Now focus on **b** and do this in pairs, small groups, or as a whole-class activity.

If Sts worked in pairs or small groups, get some feedback.

Focus on **3 Adjectives** and elicit that a *thesaurus* is a kind of dictionary which gives you synonyms for words.

Get Sts to do **a** individually or in pairs.

🔊 **5.11** Now focus on **b**. Play the audio for Sts to listen and check.

Check answers.

🔊 **5.11**
3 Adjectives
1 rich / wealthy
2 affluent
3 well-off
4 loaded
5 poor
6 penniless
7 hard up
8 broke

Now either use the audio to drill the pronunciation of the words, or model and drill them yourself. Give further practice of any words your Sts find difficult to pronounce.

🔊 **5.12** Focus on **4 Colloquial language** and make sure Sts know the meaning of both *colloquial* (= used in conversation, but not in formal speech or writing) and *slang* (= very informal words and expressions that are more common in spoken language, especially used by a particular group of people, e.g. teenagers, etc.).

Play the audio, pausing after each conversation to elicit the meaning of the words in **bold**.

1 Five thousand pounds   2 five dollars   3 five pounds
4 fifty thousand (pounds)   5 five pounds (or ten pounds)

🔊 **5.12**
4 Colloquial language
See conversations in Student's Book on *p.168*

Focus on **Activation** and get Sts to write six sentences about their country, or people from their country, using two words or expressions from sections **1**, **2**, and **3**.

Get as many Sts as possible to then read out one of their sentences to the class.

Tell Sts to go back to the main lesson **5B**.

EXTRA SUPPORT If you think Sts need more practice, you may want to give them the **Vocabulary** photocopiable activity at this point.

c Focus on the task and give Sts time to circle the correct words and to compare answers with a partner.

Check answers.

1 broke (*penniless* too formal)
2 loan (*mortgage* is for a house / flat)
3 in the red (*in the black* = you do not owe the bank money)
4 lump sum
5 loaded (*affluent* too formal)
6 exchange rate
7 standard
8 pounds (*quid* too informal)

d Focus on the task and give Sts time to choose two or three questions to tell their partner about.

Put Sts in pairs and tell them to take turns to talk about people they know for the categories they chose.

Get some feedback from various pairs.

EXTRA IDEA Tell Sts about some people you know first.

2 PRONUNCIATION silent consonants

Pronunciation notes

Sts at this level are aware of the fact that some consonants (and vowels, or even syllables) are not pronounced. However, these continue to cause problems, especially in less familiar words like *debt* and *mortgage*.

a Do this as a whole-class activity, or put Sts in pairs and then check answers. (The consonants that are not pronounced are marked in colour in the key.)

de**b**t   mor**t**gage   dis**h**onest

b ◀)) **5.13** Focus on the instructions and make sure Sts don't write the whole sentence, just the last word.

Play the audio, pausing after each sentence to give Sts time to write the last word and cross out the silent consonant.

Get Sts to compare with a partner, and then check answers by eliciting the words onto the board and getting Sts to tell you which consonant they crossed out.

1 **k**nowledge   **2** **p**sychologist   **3** s**c**ientific   **4** receip**t**
5 overw**h**elming   **6** bom**b**   **7** **w**hispered   **8** colum**n**
9 resi**g**n   **10** **w**reck

◀)) **5.13**
1   I'm afraid I don't have any expert knowledge.
2   Did you know that James was a psychologist?
3   It's an interesting theory, but it's not very scientific.
4   I'm afraid you can't change it if you don't have the receipt.
5   I found the whole experience a bit overwhelming.
6   When I heard the explosion, I thought it was a bomb.
7   'Don't make a noise,' she whispered.
8   The National Gallery was great, but I was a bit disappointed by Nelson's Column.
9   Do you think the prime minister is going to resign?
10 It was quite a bad accident and the car was a complete wreck.

---

3 READING & SPEAKING categorizing information

a Focus on the task and make sure Sts understand all the lexis.

Put Sts in pairs to choose the correct definition. You could remind them of the quote they saw at the beginning of the lesson.

Check the answer.

1

b Focus on the instructions. First, give Sts time to read the introduction, and tell them not to worry about the highlighted words. Second, go through the ten headings with the class, making sure they understand what they mean, e.g. *Freecycle* (= to give away used objects to people who want them, or to obtain such items for free), *an allotment* (= a small plot of land which people can rent to grow fruit and vegetables), etc.

Now put Sts in pairs and get them to discuss whether they already do any of these things.

Elicit some answers from the class.

c Focus on the task and then give Sts time to read the article and put each activity in at least one category.

Get Sts to compare with a partner, and then check answers. Your Sts may argue for other answers, too, so feel free to accept them if you agree.

EXTRA SUPPORT Before Sts read the article the first time, check whether you need to pre-teach any vocabulary, but not the highlighted words and phrases.

Doing things that are free   3, 4, 7
Giving things away   1, 2, 8
Creating or producing things   3, 5, 6, 8
Doing sth that doesn't pollute   3, 5, 6, 8, 9
Doing sth to avoid spending   1, 3, 5, 6, 7, 10

d Get Sts to read the article again.

In pairs or individually, Sts match the highlighted words and phrases to meanings A–H.

Check answers. Highlight any words your Sts may have problems pronouncing correctly, e.g. *deluge* /ˈdeljuːdʒ/.

A 3   **B** 4   **C** 7   **D** 1   **E** 8   **F** 5   **G** 2   **H** 6

Deal with any other vocabulary problems that arose.

e Put Sts in small groups to discuss the questions. You could do question 2 as a whole-class activity.

Get some feedback from various groups.

EXTRA IDEA Put Sts in small groups and get them to come up with another idea to help people in their country to lead an anti-capitalist life. Then get the groups to present their ideas to the class, and have a class vote on the best idea.

4 GRAMMAR unreal uses of past tenses

a Focus on the photo and give Sts time to read the people's thoughts.

Ask the question to the class and elicit the answer.

The woman (Sarah)

b Put Sts in pairs to answer the questions about the highlighted verbs in **a**.

Check answers.

1 (*got married*, *were*) and 6 (*didn't accept*) refer to things that really happened in the past.
The others are all hypothetical situations.

c Tell Sts to go to **Grammar Bank 5B** on *p.151*.

Grammar notes

Sts at this level should be aware that past tenses are not only used to refer to past time, but also to hypothetical present / future time (the past simple or continuous) and hypothetical past time (the past perfect), as in second and third conditionals. Here they focus on various structures which involve this use of past tenses, e.g. after *wish*, *if only*, *would rather*, and *it's time*.

Focus on the example sentences for **unreal uses of past tenses** and go through the rules with the class.

Focus on the exercises and get Sts to do them individually or in pairs. If they do them individually, get them to compare with a partner.

Check answers after each exercise, getting Sts to read the full sentences.

a

1 It's high time the government **realized** that most people disagree with their education policy.
2 My wife would rather we **bought** a flat nearer the city centre, but we can't afford it.
3 I wish you**'d / had been able** to stay a bit longer last night – we were having such a good time!
4 Would you rather we **didn't discuss** the subject now?
5 I think it's time the company **stopped** expecting us to do overtime for no extra pay.
6 If only I**'d / had saved** a bit more when I was earning a salary, I wouldn't be so hard up now.
7 I'd rather you **paid** me in cash, please.
8 If only we **knew** the name of the shop, we could google it and see where it is.
9 Do you wish you **had gone / had been** to university or are you glad you left school and started work?

b

1 **I'd rather you didn't wear shoes in the living room** if you don't mind.
2 **I wish I could afford to** travel more.
3 **If only we hadn't painted the room blue** – it looks awful!
4 Don't you think **it's (high) time you started to look / looking** for your own flat?
5 **If only he wasn't / weren't so rude**, he'd be easier to work with.
6 **Would you rather we came** another day?
7 **I wish I had bought the tickets** last week.
8 **If only he would let us know** before he turns up.

Tell Sts to go back to the main lesson **5B**.

EXTRA SUPPORT If you think Sts need more practice, you may want to give them the **Grammar** photocopiable activity at this point.

d Put Sts in small groups, focus on the question prompts, and highlight that Sts have to ask all the questions with *Do you ever wish…?*

Give Sts time to decide which question stems refer to the past and which refer to the present / future.

Now give them time to ask and answer the questions, giving as much information as possible.

Elicit some answers from individual Sts.

5 LISTENING understanding how a business works

a Focus on the instructions and point out to Sts that the small business can be physical or online.

Give them time to read the extract, and then either do the questions as a whole-class activity, or put Sts in pairs and then get some feedback.

Ask Sts if they can think of any more reasons to shop from small businesses.

b Focus on the task and name of the website, Pasta Evangelists. Elicit / Explain that the word *evangelist* was originally to do with religion, but is now used to describe a person who tries to persuade people to accept views or opinions that they strongly believe are correct, so *pasta evangelists* means people who strongly believe in good, fresh pasta and want to convince other people to buy it. Elicit or model its pronunciation /ɪˈvændʒəlɪst/.

After Sts have read the extract, either do the questions as a whole-class activity, or put Sts in pairs and then get some feedback.

c 🔊 **5.14** Tell Sts they are going to listen to an interview with Alessandro Savelli, and make sure they know what a *co-founder* is. Point out that he is half Italian, so speaks English with a slight Italian accent.

Give Sts time to read the information, making sure they know what *price structure* means (= an approach in business which defines various prices, discounts, and offers consistent with the organization goals and strategy) and what *USP* stands for and means (= *Unique Selling Point* – a feature of a product or service that makes it different from all the others that are available and is a reason for people to choose it).

Before Sts listen, you might want to tell them that Farringdon is an area in central London, a *concession* here is a shop in a larger building or store, and the Isle of Man is an island in the Irish Sea, between Great Britain and Ireland.

Point out that the first one (*spotting a new business opportunity*) has been done for them.

Go through the **Glossary** with the class.

Now play the audio once the whole way through for Sts to listen and number the information in the order he talks about it.

Get Sts to compare with a partner, and play again as necessary.

Check answers.

EXTRA SUPPORT Read through the script and decide if you need to pre-teach any new lexis before Sts listen.

2 the location of the business
3 the cooking team
4 their suppliers
5 how much money was originally invested in the business
6 an opportunity to promote the business
7 their USP
8 the competition
9 their price structure
10 the profile of their customers
11 where they deliver to
12 their plans for the future

🔊 **5.14**
(script in Student's Book on *pp.134–135*)
I = interviewer, A = Alessandro

I So, Alessandro, how did the idea of Pasta Evangelists come about?
A Well, I'm half Italian, half English; and I've always been interested in, in the sector of food and beverages; and I'd been thinking about creating a new brand in the food and beverage sector for quite a while. And I saw an opportunity of creating potentially the first premium, artisanal fresh pasta brand in the UK, even internationally, and so two and a half years ago we started by selling gnocchi to my friends.
I Where are you based?
A Our business is based in London; however, our product is distributed and sold everywhere in the UK. We have an office in Farringdon, our kitchen is in East London, and we also have a concession – a Pasta Evangelist concession – in Harrods.
I Who actually makes the pasta?
A So, so yeah, we have a whole team of *sfoglini* – Maria Rosaria, Olivia, Michelangelo, Federica, Francisca – who make fresh pasta every day. So, *sfoglini* is an Italian word which means 'pasta artisans', and it derives from the word *sfoglia*, which is the pasta sheet. All our *sfoglini* are Italians. Having said that, we are also training non-Italians to, to make pasta, such as Dorina, Semeya, Veronica – so people from Poland, Russia, Bangladesh – why not?

I Where do you get your ingredients from?

A We have a quite an extensive number of different suppliers for our ingredients because we make hundreds of different recipes. So we're always, always working with new suppliers, veg, meat, fish, eggs, flours, and I would say that we, we, we work with a mix of both Italian suppliers for some ingredients, but also British suppliers, and I think I would say that the quality and the freshness of the produce is what we're most after, as well as the authenticity, whether it's the pistachios from Sicily or hazelnuts from Piemonte. It really depends.

I Approximately how much money did you need to raise to get the project off the ground?

A So, whilst it was relatively inexpensive to get the business started – i.e. I invested two thousand pounds – and even the second step was relatively, well, was not colossal – i.e. sixty thousand pounds – once we were keen to increase growth, we had to raise larger amounts of money, i.e. we raised half a million, and then one point seven million pounds.

I One of the ways in which you tried to get more investment was appearing on *Dragons' Den*. What happened when you went on the programme?

A The *Dragons' Den* was really an amazing, an amazing experience. We, we really enjoyed it. It gave immediate visibility to the brand to approximately two million individuals across the UK. It was free. And the brand was shown in a very positive light and we were able to showcase our products, our craftsmanship, and our story. Having said that, we didn't raise the capital from the Dragons.

I What would you say is the unique selling point, the USP, of Pasta Evangelists?

A The USP is probably the quality, the quality of the product, which is reflected, which is a reflection of the artisanality, the freshness, the originality, the ingredients themselves, the craftsmanship of the product, the fact that it's made by hand. So, yeah, a hand-made fresh product probably is our USP.

I Who are your main competitors?

A I don't think there is direct competition, i.e. at the moment, to our knowledge, there aren't companies doing what we're doing, exactly what we're doing. Having said that, the food industry itself is massively competitive and therefore we're fighting for the same share of wallets as thousands of other companies. Especially in the UK, in London, people are bombarded with different offers, different companies, new brands, existing brands, restaurants, takeaway, Deliveroo, recipe boxes – so it is very competitive overall.

I How do your prices compare with having an Italian pasta dish in a restaurant?

A I'm glad you, you suggested that our competition is Italian restaurants, rather than supermarket pasta or takeaway pasta, or other recipe boxes, because indeed we see ourselves as 'restaurant quality' delivered to your home. Having said that, our dishes are on average twenty, thirty, in some cases forty per cent less expensive than a equivalent dish sold in a restaurant in London, an Italian restaurant. And our pricing varies depending on what dish it is. We've done more than two hundred different pasta recipes to date, and the pricing varies from six pounds for perhaps a more, let's say, simple dish, to twelve pounds for a more luxurious pasta dish.

I How would you describe a typical customer?

A It's hard to say because we do have, our product is…we, we define it as quite democratic, in that it's a product which appeals to several different types of customers – we have families, we have younger couples, we have people who buy it as a special occasion for dinner parties.

I Where do you sell your products?

A So, roughly a third of our sales are in London; two thirds are outside of London. So every day we ship hundreds of boxes from Cornwall, to Scotland, to Wales, to the Isle of Man, everywhere, everywhere, we find - and we actually find that most locations where we ship to, apart from London, are small villages we've never heard of, where there is less availability of high, you know, high-quality convenience food, where, where it's more difficult to find a product like ours.

I Are you hoping to expand your business?

A So yeah, we, we think that the market for our products in the UK is, is fairly vast. We think we've just scratched the surface. There's much more we can do. And we just started only two years ago, and so our plan is certainly to grow. Hopefully we can grow four-fold this year.

I Yes, well thank you very much Alessandro, it's been lovely talking to you.

---

d Give Sts time to read 1–10 and see if they can remember any of the information. You might want to point out that 3 is in italics because it is an Italian word. It is pronounced /ˈsfɒliːni/. You could tell Sts that Piemonte is a region in northwest Italy.

Play the audio again, pausing after Alessandro answers each question.

Get Sts to compare with a partner, and then play the audio again if necessary.

Check answers.

1 Their first product was gnocchi, which they sold to his friends.
2 There's a Pasta Evangelist concession in Harrods.
3 *Sfoglini* is the Italian word for the chefs who make the pasta. It means 'pasta artisans'.
4 Sicily and Piemonte are two places where they get ingredients from – pistachios from Sicily and hazelnuts from Piemonte.
5 £2,000 was the amount that Alessandro first invested in the business.
6 Two million individuals saw Pasta Evangelists on the TV programme *Dragons' Den*.
7 These are two of the types of business that compete with Pasta Evangelists for people's money.
8 This is the price of one of their more luxurious dishes.
9 Most of their deliveries outside London go to people living in small villages.
10 They think they've only just started to reach the vast potential market for their products.

EXTRA SUPPORT If there's time, you could get Sts to listen again with the script on *pp.134–135*, so they can see exactly what they understood / didn't understand. Translate / Explain any new words or phrases.

e Do this as a whole-class activity.

6 SPEAKING

a Tell Sts that having learned about Pasta Evangelists, they're now going to come up with an idea for a food-related business of their own. Give Sts time to read about the scheme.

EXTRA SUPPORT Ask some comprehension questions to check Sts understand the scheme, e.g. *Who is running the scheme?* (The local council / government) *How will they help people with a small business?* (They will offer a them a loan), etc.

b Focus on the task, making sure Sts understand all the lexis.

Put Sts in small groups and give them time to work out their business proposal.

Monitor and help as necessary.

c Give each group time to present their proposal to the class.

When everyone has presented their proposal, have a class vote to see which proposal will get the loan. Tell Sts they can't vote for their own proposal. If there is a tie, you could vote for the one you think is better.

7 WRITING a proposal

In this lesson, the focus is on writing a proposal. The model text is a proposal for the expansion of a language school, but all the information could equally apply to writing a proposal for a new business, improvements to an existing business, etc. The writing skills focus is using common expressions for generalizing and making recommendations.

Tell Sts to go to **Writing A proposal** on *p.122*.

ANALYSING A MODEL TEXT

a Focus on the text type (*a proposal*) and highlight that the structure of all proposals tends to be broadly similar. If Sts have written a report in a previous level, elicit the structure from the class. If not, you could tell them that the structure is similar to that of a proposal:

* state the purpose in an introduction
* explain where the information you are reporting came from (e.g. research, statistics, etc.)
* organize the information under headings
* present both positive and negative points
* summarize the general findings in a conclusion, and include your opinion
* use an impersonal, formal style.

Focus on the **Key success factors** and go through them with the class.

Focus on the task, and get Sts to read the proposal and find the recommendations.

Check answers.

The classes
* maximum of 12 students per class
* students who arrive more than five minutes late for a class have to wait for a break to enter

The self-study centre
* buying more computers
* extending opening hours to 9.00 p.m.

The cafeteria
* reopening the cafeteria
* offering healthy snacks and hot meals

b Give Sts time to read the highlighted phrases in 1–8 and then find their more formal equivalent in the proposal.

EXTRA SUPPORT Get Sts to do this in pairs.

Get Sts to compare with a partner, and then check answers.

1 The **aim of this proposal** is…
2 …is to **suggest a range of improvements to** the classes and facilities…
3 In general, students **rate the quality of teaching very highly**.
4 **As regards class size**, we suggest that there should never be more than 12 students in a class.
5 **Regarding class duration**, lessons officially last an hour…
6 …we suggest, **firstly, purchasing** more computers…
7 …**the majority of students currently attending courses at King James** are positive…
8 …that **if the suggested changes are implemented**, student numbers could be increased by as much as 10%.

USEFUL LANGUAGE

c Focus on the task and give Sts time to complete the missing words.

Get Sts to compare with a partner, and then check answers.

1 In general   2 Generally speaking   3 It is generally considered   4 The general view   5 Overall

d Get Sts, in pairs or individually, to complete the sentences to make them more formal.

Check answers.

1 We propose (**that**) **you make / making the classes smaller**.
2 It would be far preferable for classes **to last an hour**.
3 We suggest (**that**) **you buy / buying new computers**.
4 It would be advisable to **extend / for you to extend the opening hours until 9 p.m.**
5 We strongly recommend **opening / (that) you (should) open the cafeteria again**.

PLANNING WHAT TO WRITE

a Focus on the task and make sure Sts understand all the lexis in the information, e.g. *halls of residence*.

Set a time limit of about ten minutes for Sts, in pairs, to decide on their ideas for points 1–2. Monitor and help with vocabulary.

b Get Sts to think of improvements for the three areas of the study trip in the feedback they read. Tell them to try to use different expressions from **Useful Language c** and **d**.

Finally, go through the **Tips** with Sts.

WRITING

Go through the instructions and set the writing for homework.

Lesson plan

In The Interview, the person interviewed is Jordan Friedman, an American specialist in the field of stress and stress reduction. In this three-part interview, he talks about what causes stress, the effect it can have on the mind and body, and different ways of managing stress. This is followed by a language focus on compound nouns, which Jordan Friedman frequently uses in the interview.

In The Conversation, Sts watch three people discussing whether they think life today is more stressful than it used to be. Sts then discuss this question as well as two other questions related to the topic, focusing on how people in a conversation refer back to something that was mentioned earlier.

More materials
For teachers
Teacher's Resource Centre
Video Colloquial English 4&5
Quick Test 5
File 5 Test
Progress Test Files 1–5
For students
Workbook Colloquial English 4&5
Can you remember? 4&5
Online Practice Colloquial English 4&5
Check your progress

OPTIONAL LEAD-IN (BOOKS CLOSED)

Write on the board the word STRESS. Then elicit from Sts the two adjectives *stressed* and *stressful*, and make sure they know the difference in meaning.

Now write the following definitions on the board:

A PHRASAL VERB WHICH MEANS 'MAKE SB FEEL VERY STRESSED'

STRESS SB _____

A TECHNICAL WORD FOR STH THAT CREATES STRESS, MORE COMMON IN AMERICAN ENGLISH

STRESS _____

Elicit the expressions *stress sb out* and *stressor*. You could also point out that *stressed out* is often used as an adjective meaning the same as *stressed*.

Then tell Sts they are going to watch an interview with a successful American stress expert.

If you have internet access in your classroom or Sts have it on their phones, give them a few minutes to google Jordan Friedman and find out a bit about him.

1 ▶ THE INTERVIEW Part 1

a Books open. Focus on the photo and the biographical information about Jordan Friedman. Give Sts time to read it.

Do the question as a whole-class activity.

b Focus on the task and go through the **Glossary** with the class.

Play the video (**Part 1**) once the whole way through for Sts to answer the question.

Give Sts time to tell each other what they understood.

Check the answer.

EXTRA SUPPORT Before playing the video, go through the listening scripts and decide if you need to pre-teach / check any lexis to help Sts when they listen.

Because it has a negative impact on the body and makes people ill.

I = interviewer, J = Jordan Friedman

Part 1

I In your experience, what are the main causes of stress?

J My clients and audiences tell me that their big stressors are, er, too much to do, too little time, er, money stressors, commuting is a big stressor. I think that the opportunities to be stressed are everywhere.

I Do you think life is more stressful now than it was, say, twenty years ago?

J I think that today there are many more opportunities to be stressed; there are many more distractions, especially ones that are technology-driven. And I'm a big fan of technology – we can use technology to help us reduce stress – but when you have emails coming in, and text messages left and right, and Twitter feeds, and Facebook messages, and, TV, and the kids, and a job, and maybe school, it really divides our attention and it produces a stress response that is often ongoing – continuous – within us. And all of that stuff can take away the time to just relax, er, take a walk, not think about who's trying to communicate with us, and not needing to be on all of the time. So, er, so I think there are just more chances to be stressed today, er, and therefore we need to really pay more attention to reducing stress.

I Can you tell us something about the effects of stress on the body and mind?

J Stress impacts the body because it produces wear and tear, and when we are constantly stressed, our organs, our immune system, become the punching bags of our stress response. Stress is really important, and, in fact, it can be a lifesaver, but when it kicks into action all the time, it, er, has a corrosive effect on us. So, for example, our immune systems are weakened when we are under a lot of stress, and especially for a long period of time. When our immune systems are weaker, it opens us up to be more susceptible to illnesses in the environment. Er, stress contributes to high blood pressure, which contributes to heart problems and stroke. Stress impacts our sleep, so when we get stressed during the day, it often makes it more difficult for us to fall asleep at night, or to stay asleep, or to have a quality night's sleep. And if we don't get a good night's sleep, then we are tired the next day, which makes us more stressed in many cases, so it becomes a stress-poor sleep cycle that is stressful and tiring. So, these are all reasons to really pay attention to our stress levels and to take action to reduce the stress.

c Focus on the sentences and give Sts time, in pairs, to see if they can complete them in their own words.

Play the video again the whole way through for Sts to do the task.

Get Sts to compare with their partner, and then check answers.

EXTRA SUPPORT You could pause the video after each point has been mentioned and, in pairs, get Sts to compare orally what they have understood.

1 …having too much to do, too little time, money problems, and commuting.
2 …there are more opportunities to be stressed / there are many more distractions, especially related to technology.
3 …just relax / switch off.
4 …we are more likely to become ill.
5 …then we are tired the next day, which makes us more stressed.

EXTRA SUPPORT If there's time, you could get Sts to watch again with subtitles, so they can see exactly what they understood / didn't understand. Translate / Explain any new words or phrases.

d Do this as a whole-class activity, or put Sts in pairs and then get some feedback.

▶ Part 2

a Focus on the task and go through the **Glossary** with the class.

Give Sts time to read sentences 1–6. Tell them the first time they listen, they just need to mark each sentence *T* (true) or *F* (false).

Play the video (**Part 2**) once the whole way through for Sts to do the task.

Get Sts to compare with a partner.

EXTRA SUPPORT You could check answers now, so when Sts are watching again in **b**, they only need to correct the *F* sentences.

Part 2

I How can you help people deal with stress, and how long does it take to find a solution?
J The great thing about stress management is that it's like a salad bar. There are thirty different choices on a salad bar, and some of us like most of the things that are offered, but some of us don't like everything, but we get to choose what works for us and what we enjoy. Same thing with stress management: there are more than thirty different ways you can manage stress – there are probably, er, thirty million and counting – and we should pick the techniques, many of them easy and simple and fun, that we like, and therefore we'll be more likely to use them on an ongoing basis. So, stress management can take as little as ten seconds. You can look at a beautiful picture that you took on your last vacation – you can put it on your computer screen; you can put it next to your bed; you can put it on your desk – and just focusing on that photo of the ocean or a mountain or a beach can alleviate stressed feelings immediately. We can do one-minute breathing exercises; we can, er, exercise; we can take a ten-minute walk around the block; we can meditate each day. So, there are many different ways to prevent and reduce the stress that we're experiencing; the key is to do it on a regular basis.
I Are the solutions to stress physical, mental, or both?
J Stress management involves both the mind and the body; they make great partners when we're trying to feel better and to cut down on the stress that we're experiencing. I once worked in a school where a student identified his stressor as riding on the subway. He felt very stressed going to school every day and very stressed when it was time to go home because the subway made him feel very closed-in and like he wanted to escape; he couldn't

stand the, the crowds. And then we opened up to the rest of the group and we asked them for different ways that this student might think about this stressor and different ways that he might act to try and reduce it. And the group came up with all sorts of great possibilities, including that he ride in a different car – in the first car or the last car because it's often less crowded compared to the centre car, which is where he always used to ride. And he liked that idea, and I heard from the principal of the school a few weeks later that he in fact had started riding in the first car, and for the first time in his subway-taking life, he didn't feel stressed, he didn't feel anxious because the car was less crowded and he felt so much better. And you might think, 'Well, that's such an easy answer, why didn't he think of, of that himself?' The truth is – and I think we all identify with this – we get into very fixed ways, habits almost, of thinking and acting, because we, we deal with our stressors and have dealt with them in similar ways for a long, long time, so we lose the perspective; we don't take as much time to think about how we could deal with our stressors in different ways. So, this is an example of how the mind and body and actions and thoughts can work together to really make a big difference in the way we feel.

---

b Tell Sts that they will watch again and that this time, they need to correct the false sentences.

Play the video again the whole way through.

Get Sts to compare with a partner, and then check answers.

EXTRA SUPPORT You could pause the video after each point has been mentioned and, in pairs, get Sts to compare orally what they have understood.

1 T
2 F (He mentions exercising, walking for ten minutes, and meditating.)
3 T
4 F (He felt very stressed about going on the subway / underground.)
5 F (They suggested he should travel in the first or last car of the train as it is less crowded.)
6 T

EXTRA SUPPORT If there's time, you could get Sts to watch again with subtitles, so they can see exactly what they understood / didn't understand. Translate / Explain any new words or phrases.

c Do this as a whole-class activity, or put Sts in pairs and then get some feedback. You could tell the class what makes you stressed and what you do to reduce the stress.

▶ Part 3

a Focus on the task and go through the **Glossary** on *p.55* with the class.

Play the video (**Part 3**) once the whole way through for Sts to answer the question.

Give Sts time to tell each other what they understood. Elicit opinions.

Part 3

I Are some age groups more susceptible to stress than others?
J Stress is a very democratic occurrence, so older people are stressed, college students are stressed, babies get stressed, thirty-somethings get stressed, men are stressed, women are stressed, so, er, it's hard to say if one group is more stressed than another.
I What makes students stressed? How does stress affect their lives or their studies, and what are the most stressful times in a typical student's life?

J   College and being a student can be really fun and exciting and rewarding. There are also a lot of stressors associated with it: there's the studying, there's the pressure to do well on exams so that you can get a better job and perhaps make more money. You are in a different environment that doesn't have the same support that you used to have, especially if you were back home. Er, there is the social stress of needing to meet new people, and also for a lot of young people, especially those in their teens and twenties, we see a lot of mental, er, health issues arise, and there's a greater need to get help for, er, them while in school, but if you're not with your usual support network, it's even more challenging sometimes to do so. Stress makes it difficult to study, to focus, to concentrate. When you're sitting down to take an exam and you studied really hard for the exam, and then all of a sudden, you're having trouble remembering what you studied, stress can play a big role in making it more difficult for us to recall information. If you're doing a presentation – public speaking – that can be very stressful for a lot of students as well as professionals. In fact, still, public speaking is feared more than death by most people. Then there's the financial stress of being in school, not only, er, not having a lot of money to spend on things that you want to do – fun activities – but what awaits you when you graduate, which for many, er, students is a lot of financial, er, stress and loans to repay. So being a student – great fun, and also can provide a lot of – great stress.

I   You set up Stressbusters as an anti-stress programme for students. Can you tell us something about it and how it works?

J   We train teams of students to provide five-minute free back rubs at events all over campus, all year long, and people on campus come to the events, and not only do they get an amazing stress-relieving back rub, but they also learn about other stress reduction and wellness resources on campus that we train our students to provide. And we have seen incredible reductions in feelings of stress, tension, anxiety, lowering of feelings of being overwhelmed, from before someone has the Stressbusters experience to after. We also find students telling us that they're better able to cope with their stressors and they're better able to complete the tasks that they have at hand after they have one of our Stressbusters experiences.

b   Focus on the task and give Sts time to read questions 1–5.

Play the video again the whole way through for Sts to answer the questions.

Get Sts to compare with a partner, and then check answers.

EXTRA SUPPORT You could pause the video after each point has been mentioned and, in pairs, get Sts to compare orally what they have understood.

1   There is no particular age at which people are most stressed.
2   Studying, feeling pressure to do well in exams so you can get a good job, being in a different environment so you don't have the same support as at home, socializing, financial stress
3   Stress can make it very difficult to focus and remember information. Stressed students might be unable to remember information in an exam.
4   It teaches students how to give (five-minute free) back rubs and about other stress reduction and wellness resources.
5   Students have said that they feel less stressed and they are able to cope with their stressors and complete their tasks.

EXTRA SUPPORT If there's time, you could get Sts to watch again with subtitles, so they can see exactly what they understood / didn't understand. Translate / Explain any new words or phrases.

c   Do this as a whole-class activity. You too could answer the questions.

2 ▶ LOOKING AT LANGUAGE

a   Focus on the **Compound nouns** box and go through it with the class.

Now focus on the task and give Sts time to read extracts 1–8.

In pairs, get Sts to try to complete the compound nouns.

b   Play the video, pausing after each extract to give Sts time to write.

Get Sts to compare with a partner, and then check answers.

EXTRA CHALLENGE Ask Sts if they can guess any of the missing highlighted words before they listen to the extracts.

1 text   2 lifesaver   3 blood, heart   4 stress   5 management
6 breathing   7 college   8 support

1   …when you have emails coming in, and text messages left and right…
2   Stress is really important, and, in fact, it can be a lifesaver…
3   Er, stress contributes to high blood pressure, which contributes to heart problems and stroke.
4   So these are all reasons to really pay attention to our stress levels and to take action to reduce the stress.
5   The great thing about stress management is that it's like a salad bar.
6   We can do one-minute breathing exercises, we can, er, exercise, we can take a ten-minute walk around the block…
7   Stress is a very democratic occurrence, so older people are stressed, college students are stressed, babies get stressed…
8   …there's a greater need to get help for, er, them while in school, but if you're not with your usual support network, it's even more challenging sometimes to do so.

3 ▶ THE CONVERSATION

a   Focus on the photo and tell Sts they are going to watch these three people discuss a question. Focus on the task and play the video, pausing after the title screen to give Sts time to read the question.

Then play the video once the whole way through.

Check answers.

EXTRA SUPPORT Before playing the video, go through the listening script and decide if you need to pre-teach / check any lexis to help Sts when they listen.

Josie: frustrating   Ida: a different   John: patience

Do you think life today is more stressful than it used to be?

Josie   I definitely think it's more stressful than it used to be, and I think a big part of that is, sort of, online culture and social media. So, everything you do is online, everyone can comment on what you're doing. You're, sort of, seeing yourself against – you're pitted against everyone else in your career field, doing everything, the same things as you and, and you never, sort of, get satisfaction anymore, because you'll do something and think you've done really well, and then you'll go online, share it, look at what other people have done and then suddenly everyone else seems to be doing so much more than you.

Ida   I think it's – using that phrase 'pitted against other people' is really interesting, because it, it sort of highlights the fact that life at the moment is more about being in competition with other people rather than achieving things for yourself. And I think you're absolutely right, it's all about comparing yourself, this constant comparing, whether consciously or unconsciously, with other people. I mean, I remember a time – I imagine you do as well – where things were slower, as well. The pace of life and the things that you did were slower so that was a different kind of stress. So, you know if you'd write a letter to achieve something, you'd have to wait for that response and there was nothing you could do in between, whereas now you send an email, you're expected to do a million things before you get a response and you're expected to be reachable at all times, whereas before it was more about doing things because of need, rather than want, I think.

John   Sure, sure. There's no hiding place nowadays, that's the problem, and you are so easily exposed to everybody around you and there's reality shows and all sorts of things. People want to succeed so quickly, whereas many, many times, years ago, you, you would never succeed that quickly, you would begin to build a career for yourself, or, um, meet people and, and then open yourself out to the outside world. But nowadays it's like 'Now. I want it now.'

Ida   Yeah.

John   And it's a need, rather than a want.

Ida   And I think the definition of success has changed as well.

John   Absolutely.

---

b Focus on the task and give Sts time to read 1–5.

Play the video once the whole way through, pausing every so often to give Sts time to write.

Get Sts to compare with a partner, and then play again if necessary.

Check answers.

1 You're competing with everyone around you in your area of work.
2 Doing things more slowly, as in the past, was also stressful.
3 You couldn't achieve anything until you received a reply to your letter.
4 People expect you to be available all the time.
5 Everyone can see what everyone else is doing.
6 People want to be immediately successful.

EXTRA SUPPORT If there's time, you could get Sts to watch again with subtitles, so they can see exactly what they understood / didn't understand. Translate / Explain any new words or phrases.

c Do the questions as a whole-class activity, or put Sts in pairs and then get some feedback.

d This exercise focuses on how the speakers refer back to something that has been mentioned earlier. Focus on the phrases and give Sts time to read them.

Play the video, pausing after the first extract and replaying it as necessary. Elicit what the **bold** word refers to. Repeat for the other four extracts.

1 'that' refers back to 'the fact that life is more stressful than it used to be'
2 'it' refers back to the phrase 'pitted against other people'
3 'you're absolutely right' refers back to 'life at the moment is more about being in competition with other people'
4 'you do as well' refers back to 'I remember a time'
5 'that' refers back to 'there's no hiding place'

1

Josie   I definitely think it's more stressful than it used to be, and I think a big part of that is, sort of, online culture and social media.

2

Ida   I think it's – using that phrase 'pitted against other people' is really interesting, because it, it sort of highlights the fact that life at the moment is more about being in competition with other people…

3

Ida   And I think you're absolutely right, it's all about comparing yourself, this constant comparing, whether consciously or unconsciously, with other people.

4

Ida   I mean, I remember a time – I imagine you do as well – where things were slower, as well.

5

John   There's no hiding place nowadays, that's the problem, and you are so easily exposed to everybody around you and there's reality shows and all sorts of things. People want to succeed so quickly…

---

e Put Sts in small groups of three if possible. Focus on the questions and then give Sts time to discuss them.

Monitor and help.

Get feedback from various groups. You could also tell the class what you think.

Help, I need somebody!

G verb + object + infinitive or gerund
V compound adjectives
P main and secondary stress

Lesson plan

The topic of this lesson is self-help: how to survive stressful life situations and how to change your life for the better by focusing on small pleasures.

Sts begin by reading some advice about long-distance relationships on an online forum. Then they do a jigsaw reading – two texts (from *The Guardian*) which give advice, one for a young adult living with their parents and the other for parents with an adult child still living at home. Sts tell their partner about the tips suggested in their text, and together they assess the usefulness of the tips. The grammar focus is on the pattern of verb + object + infinitive or gerund. This leads to Sts writing some tips for a survival situation which they have some experience of.

In the second half of the lesson, Sts listen to a talk about the significance of small pleasures in life from an educational company called The School of Life. They then choose a related topic to talk about, study tips on giving a presentation, and present their topic in small groups. In Vocabulary and Pronunciation, Sts extend their knowledge of compound adjectives and how they are stressed, and focus on some high-frequency collocations.

More materials
For teachers
Photocopiables
Grammar verb + object + infinitive or gerund *p.177*
Communicative Ask me a question *p.203*
(instructions *p.189*)
For students
Workbook 6A
Online Practice 6A

OPTIONAL LEAD-IN – THE QUOTE

Write the quote at the top of *p.56* on the board (books closed) and the name of the person who said it, or get Sts to open their books and read it.

Point out that John Steinbeck (1902–1968) was one of the greatest American authors of the 20th century. His books include *The Grapes of Wrath* and *East of Eden*. He won the Nobel Prize for Literature in 1962.

Ask Sts what point he is making about the value of advice, and whether they agree with him.

1 READING & SPEAKING understanding advice

a Focus on the instructions and go through problems 1–5.

Put Sts in pairs and get them to discuss where they would get advice for each problem.

Get some feedback from individual Sts.

b Focus on the title of the online forum and elicit / explain what a *long-distance relationship* is.

Now focus on the instructions and give Sts time to read all the advice. Tell them not to worry about the gaps.

Put Sts in pairs to discuss their three choices.

Get some feedback from the class.

EXTRA SUPPORT Before Sts read the forum posts the first time, check whether you need to pre-teach any vocabulary.

c Tell Sts to read the tips again and this time complete the gaps with the best words or phrases in options a–c in 1–10.

Check answers. Make sure that Sts understand all three options, and point out that *chill* in 3 is informal.

1 b   2 c   3 b   4 a   5 a   6 c   7 b   8 c   9 a   10 a

Deal with any other vocabulary problems that arose.

d Do this as a whole-class activity, or put Sts in pairs and then get some feedback.

e Focus on the task and make sure Sts understand from whose perspective each article is written.

Give Sts time to think of one piece of advice for each situation, one for young adults who are living with their parents, and one for parents whose adult children are living at home.

Monitor and help if necessary.

Elicit some advice from the class for each situation.

EXTRA SUPPORT Get Sts to work in pairs.

f Put Sts in pairs, **A** and **B**, and tell them to go to **Communication I need some help**, **A** on *p.109*, **B** on *p.114*.

Sts **A** read *How to survive living with your parents* and Sts **B** read *The secret to living with adult children*.

Give them time to read their article and tell their partner about the advice.

When Sts have finished, elicit which tips from the two articles are similar.

Doing housework – parents should get children to do some housework, and children should offer.
Get to know each other, and focus on the positive.

Now ask Sts which tips they strongly agree / disagree with.

EXTRA IDEA You could do **d** as a whole-class activity.

Tell Sts to go back to the main lesson **6A**.

g Do this as a whole-class activity, or put Sts in pairs and then get some feedback.

2 GRAMMAR verb + object + infinitive or gerund

a Focus on the sentences and make sure Sts know the meaning of *load the dishwasher* in 4.

Put Sts in pairs and give them time to decide whether the highlighted phrases 1–9 are correct or incorrect, and to correct the mistakes. Encourage them to use their instinct because although they may not have studied these structures before, they will have come across them frequently.

Check answers.

> 1 ✓   2 ✗ I want my boyfriend to come   3 ✓
> 4 ✗ I was always made to load   5 ✗ I hate my parents talking to me   6 ✓   7 ✗ I don't mind you not tidying   8 ✓   9 ✓

b Tell Sts to go to **Grammar Bank 6A** on *p.152*.

Grammar notes

Sts will be aware that when one verb follows another, the second verb is in either the infinitive (with or without *to*) or the gerund. Sts will have been passively exposed to many of these structures, and have also studied verb + object + infinitive in reported requests, e.g. *I told him to be here at 7.00.* However, for many Sts, these structures may be problematic – especially where in their L1 they would tend to follow some verbs with a *that*-clause, where in English a gerund or infinitive is used.

Remind Sts that structures with *suggest* are covered in Lesson **3A**.

Focus on the example sentences for **verb + object + to + infinitive** and go through the rules with the class.

Go through the **Other patterns** box with the class.

Repeat for **verb + object + infinitive without *to*** and the **Passive form of *make sb do sth*** box.

Finally, repeat for **verb + object + gerund**.

Focus on the exercise and get Sts to do it individually or in pairs. If they do it individually, get them to compare with a partner.

Check answers, getting Sts to read the full sentences.

> 1 You sit down. Let **me make** the coffee.
> 2 The situation at work made **me feel uncomfortable**.
> 3 We have arranged **for you to stay** with a British family.
> 4 I don't mind **Sarah coming**, but I'd rather her boyfriend didn't.
> 5 I would hate **you to think** that I didn't enjoy myself, because I did!
> 6 I didn't expect **you to pay** for everything.
> 7 I would love **you to visit** for a few days.
> 8 Living at home again will involve **your younger sisters having** to share a bedroom.
> 9 I reminded **Hannah to do** her homework.
> 10 I can't imagine **you being** shy!
> 11 The money my uncle left me enabled **us to buy** a bigger flat.
> 12 The guards prevented **us from crossing** the border.
> 13 Would you prefer **me to call back** later?
> 14 We don't want to risk **the car breaking down** while we're on holiday.
> 15 I dislike people **answering their phones** in restaurants.
> 16 When I was an intern, I **was made to do** all the photocopying.

Tell Sts to go back to the main lesson **6A**.

If you think Sts need more practice, you may want to give them the **Grammar** photocopiable activity at this point.

c Focus on the questions and make sure Sts understand them.

Put Sts in pairs and get them to ask and answer the questions, giving as much information as possible.

Get some feedback from various pairs.

Get Sts to write some more questions using other verbs from the **Grammar Bank**.

3 WRITING

a Focus on the four situations and give Sts time to think of a piece of advice for each one.

Get Sts to write their advice, or get them to work in pairs. Then in **b**, put two pairs together to compare their advice.

b Put Sts in pairs and get them to compare their advice for each situation.

Then focus on the instructions and make sure Sts understand that they are not writing a full text – they just need to choose one topic and think of four headings for tips (like the headings in the **Communication** texts), and then write some notes under each heading, giving the reasons.

Give Sts time to think of their tips and to make a note of their reasons and examples.

You could give Sts more ideas for *How to survive…* topics, such as *a driving test, a long flight, moving house, a job interview, a heatwave.*

c Put two pairs together in groups of four (ideally in pairs that have chosen different topics) and get them to tell each other their tips and share ideas.

d Back in their pairs, Sts now use their notes to write a paragraph for each tip, using the **Communication** texts as a model. If you don't have enough time, you could set this writing for homework.

4 LISTENING understanding a lecture or talk

a Give Sts time to read the paragraph about The School of Life.

Now ask them the questions.

b 🔊 6.1 Focus on the instructions and explain / elicit the meaning of *a big deal* (= sth very important).

Give Sts time to look at all the slides.

Focus on the **Glossary** and go through it with the class.

Now play the audio once the whole way through for Sts to listen and number the slides.

Check answers. Now ask Sts which things in the slides the presenter suggested were 'small pleasures'.

Read through the script and decide if you need to pre-teach any new lexis before Sts listen.

> A 6   B 4   C 2   D 8   E 3   F 7   G 9   H 5   I 1
> The small pleasures he mentions are: a cheese sandwich, a fig, and old photos.

�))) 6.1
(script in Student's Book on *p.135*)

Nowadays we're surrounded by some powerful ideas about the sort of things that will make us happy. The first of these is that we tend to think that really to deliver satisfaction, the pleasures we should aim for need to be rare. We've become suspicious of the ordinary, which we assume is mediocre, dull, and uninspiring, and likewise we assume that things that are unique, hard to find, exotic, or unfamiliar are naturally going to give us more pleasure.

Then, we want things to be expensive. If something is expensive, we value it more, whereas if something is cheap or free, it's a little harder to appreciate. The pineapple, for instance, dropped off a lot of people's wish list of fruit when its price fell from exorbitant – they used to cost the equivalent of hundreds of pounds – to unremarkable. Caviar continues to sound somehow more interesting than eggs.

Then, we want things to be famous. In a fascinating experiment, a well-known violinist once donned scruffy clothes and busked on a street corner and was largely ignored, though people would flock to the world's greatest concert halls to hear just the same man play just the same pieces.

Lastly, we want things to be large-scale. We're mostly focused on big schemes that we hope will deliver big kinds of enjoyment: marriage, career, travel, getting a new house.

These approaches aren't entirely wrong, but they unintentionally create an unhelpful bias against the cheap, the easily available, the ordinary, the familiar, and the small-scale. As a result, if someone says they've been on a trip to a Caribbean island by private jet, we automatically assume they had a better time than someone who went to the local park by bike. We imagine that visiting the Uffizi Gallery in Florence is always going to be nicer than reading a paperback novel in the back garden. A restaurant dinner at which lobster thermidor is served sounds a good deal more impressive than a supper of a cheese sandwich at home. The highlight of a weekend seems more likely to be a hang-gliding lesson rather than a few minutes spent looking at the cloudy sky. It feels odd to suggest that a modest vase of lily of the valley – the cheapest flower at many florists – might give us more satisfaction than a Van Gogh original. And yet the paradoxical and cheering aspect of pleasure is how unpredictable it can prove to be. Fancy holidays are not always one hundred per cent pleasurable. Our enjoyment of them is remarkably vulnerable to emotional trouble and casual bad moods. A fight that began with a small disagreement can end up destroying every benefit of a five-star holiday resort. Real pleasures often seem insignificant – eating a fig, having a bath, whispering in bed in the dark, talking to a grandparent, or scanning through old photos of when you were a child – and yet these small-scale pleasures can be anything but small. If we actually take the opportunity to enjoy them fully, these sort of activities may be among the most moving and satisfying we can have.

Fundamentally, this isn't really about how much small pleasures have to offer us. It's about how many good things there are in life that we unfairly neglect. We can't wait for everything that's lovely and charming to be approved by others before we allow ourselves to be delighted. We need to follow our own instincts about what is really important to us.

c Focus on the task and give Sts time to read questions 1–6.

Play the audio again, pausing if necessary after each point to give Sts time to write.

Get Sts to compare with a partner, and then check answers.

1 Pineapples used to be valued because they were so expensive, but are now cheap and unexciting. Caviar sounds more interesting than eggs.

2 In an experiment, almost nobody stopped to listen to the violinist when he played in the street, though if he'd played the same music in a concert hall, large numbers of people would have gone.

3 Marriage, career, and travel are examples of large-scale things that we hope will be very enjoyable.

4 A Caribbean island, the Uffizi Gallery, and a hang-gliding lesson are examples of things that we assume will be more enjoyable than small things like cycling to a local park, reading a book, or looking at the clouds.

5 Fancy holidays aren't always enjoyable – they can be ruined by fights or bad moods.

6 Having a bath and talking to a grandparent are examples of small pleasures which can seem insignificant, but actually are not.

EXTRA SUPPORT If there's time, you could get Sts to listen again with the script on *p.135*, so they can see exactly what they understood / didn't understand. Translate / Explain any new words or phrases.

d Focus on the task and put Sts in pairs to complete the summary of the central message of the presentation on the audio. Tell them it must only be two sentences.

Put two pairs together to compare sentences.

Find out if any pairs wrote the same or similar messages, and if any wrote completely different ones.

Suggested answer
We expect to get most pleasure from things which are **rare, expensive, famous, or large-scale**.
However, **small pleasures can be just as significant and enjoyable as large ones.**

5 SPEAKING

a Focus on the task and the four statements.

Give Sts time to choose one of the statements and to make notes about it.

EXTRA SUPPORT Get Sts to work in pairs.

b Elicit any ideas or techniques Sts already know or have heard for how to give a good presentation, e.g. writing key points on small cards to refer to as you speak, etc.

Then focus on the *Presentation tips* and go through them with the class.

Put Sts in small groups and tell them to take turns to give a short presentation to their group about the statement they chose in **a**. When each speaker has finished, the others should ask questions.

Get individual Sts to give their presentation to the class.

6 VOCABULARY & PRONUNCIATION
compound adjectives; main and secondary stress

Vocabulary and pronunciation notes

Compound adjectives are adjectives made up of two words. The meaning of these adjectives is usually clear (e.g. *home-made* = made at home), but Sts may not be confident with the form and use of compound adjectives, possibly because they're less common, have other translations, or are expressed in a different way in their language. Highlight that the second word in compound adjectives is often a past participle or an *-ing* form.

Unlike compound nouns, compound adjectives are almost always hyphenated when they come before a noun (*home-made cakes*, *a well-known film director*), but some needn't be hyphenated after a verb (*the cakes are home made*, *his films aren't very well known*). There are no rules for this, and it's best to check in a dictionary – though using a hyphen would rarely be considered wrong. Occasionally compound adjectives are one word, e.g. *groundbreaking*.

Sts at this level will all be aware that in multi-syllable words, one syllable is stressed more strongly. However, they may not be aware of secondary stress (another syllable less emphatic than the main stressed syllable, but carrying more stress than the other syllables in the word).

Secondary stress is common in many words with prefixes, e.g. *disobedient* /ˌdɪsə'biːdiənt/, and also in compound nouns and adjectives. Sts also learn here that unlike compound nouns, where the main stress is normally on the first word, e.g. *tin opener* /'tɪn əʊpənə/, with compound adjectives the main stress is usually on the second word, e.g. *second-hand* /ˌsekənd 'hænd/.

However, if the first word in the compound adjective is a noun, e.g. *air*, the first word is usually stressed, e.g. *air-conditioned* /'eə kəndɪʃnd/.

a Focus on the **Compound adjectives** box and go through it with the class.

Focus on question 1 and elicit the compound adjective formed by a word from each list (*second-hand*).

Now get Sts to continue individually or in pairs.

b ◑ **6.2** Play the audio for Sts to listen and check.

Check answers. You may want to point out that *worn out* in 5 and *well behaved* in 10 would often not be hyphenated in this position.

◑ **6.2**
1 second-hand
2 old-fashioned
3 last-minute
4 self-conscious
5 worn-out
6 home-made
7 air-conditioned
8 high-risk
9 narrow-minded
10 well-behaved

---

c Focus on the **Fine-tuning your pronunciation: main and secondary stress** box and go through it with the class. You may want to point out that it's more important to get the main stress correct, but that secondary stress is something Sts should be aware of.

Focus on the question and then play the audio again.

Check the answer, and then ask Sts what the exception to the rule is here, to elicit *air-conditioned*. You could point out here that when the first word in the compound adjective is a noun, e.g. *air*, the first word is usually stressed.

The second word in a compound adjective usually has the main stress.

Now put Sts in pairs and get them to ask and answer questions 1–10 in **a**, giving examples.

Monitor and help where necessary.
Get some feedback.

d Focus on the task and remind Sts of the meaning of *collocations*, i.e. words that often go together. Set a time limit for Sts to match the adjectives to the nouns.

e ◑ **6.3** Play the audio for Sts to listen and check.

Check answers, making sure Sts know the meaning of all the collocations. Elicit that *feel-good*, *groundbreaking*, *labour-saving*, and *life-changing* have the main stress on the first word, and the others on the second word. You may want to remind Sts that when the first word in a compound adjective is a noun, e.g. *labour-saving*, then the main stress is usually on the first word.

◑ **6.3**
1 **low-cost** airline
2 **extra-curricular** activity
3 **dead-end** job
4 **feel-good** movie
5 **groundbreaking** research
6 **high-pitched** voice
7 **labour-saving** device
8 **high-heeled** shoes
9 **eco-friendly** detergent
10 **life-changing** experience

---

f Give Sts time to write three questions, using a compound adjective from **a** or **d** in each. Tell them that if they're using a compound adjective from **d**, they should use it with its collocation.

EXTRA SUPPORT Give Sts a few suggestions to help them get going, e.g. *Do you ever buy second-hand or vintage clothes? Did you do any extra-curricular activities when you were at primary school?*

Monitor and help.

Get Sts to first ask you some of their questions, and then put them in pairs to ask each other.

Can't give it up

G conditional sentences
V phones and technology, adjectives + prepositions
P /æ/ and /ʌ/

Lesson plan

The topic of this lesson is behavioural addictions and obsessions, such as being addicted to our phones. Alcohol or substance addiction have not been included, as these may be sensitive or even taboo subjects in some teaching situations.

Sts begin by revising and expanding vocabulary related to phones and technology. This is followed by a pronunciation focus on the minimal pairs /æ/ and /ʌ/. Sts then read an article by a digital detox specialist about ways of reducing our screen time on our phones, with rules and challenges for a digital detox. They then read a continuation of the article, about someone who followed the detox, and listen to another person who also did it. There is then a writing stage where Sts focus on presenting a balanced argument in a discursive essay.

The second half of the lesson begins with a grammar focus which revises conditional sentences and introduces mixed conditionals and alternatives to *if*, such as *supposing* and *provided that*, etc. Sts then listen to five people talking about people they know with an obsession, and then talk about people they know who have an obsession or behavioural addiction. This leads to Sts doing some work on dependent prepositions after adjectives, e.g. *addicted to, hooked on*. The lesson ends with a video documentary about treating young people who are addicted to technology and gaming.

More materials
For teachers
Photocopiables
Grammar conditional sentences *p.178*
Communicative Case studies *p.204* (instructions *p.190*)
For students
Workbook 6B
Online Practice 6B

OPTIONAL LEAD-IN – THE QUOTE

Write the quote at the top of *p.60* on the board (books closed) and the name of the person who said it, or get Sts to open their books and read it.

Elicit / Explain that Gretchen Rubin is an American author who says she 'explores human nature to understand how we can make our lives better'.

Ask Sts what they think the quote means and if they agree with it.

1 VOCABULARY phones and technology

Vocabulary notes

The language of phones and technology may well be familiar to Sts, but it makes a worthwhile focus for two reasons: one is to make sure that Sts are clear about the exact differences between the meanings of similar words and concepts, and the other is to give valuable practice in paraphrasing and explaining.

Put Sts in pairs and give them time to discuss the difference between each item in 1–12. To get the most out of the activity, try to encourage Sts to be as clear and detailed as they can when explaining the differences between the words – they shouldn't just mime *to unplug*, but explain that it's when you pull a plug out of a socket or disconnect sth from a charger, etc.

Check answers. Sts may know more than you do, so get them to explain the words. You may want to model and drill the pronunciation of some of these words, e.g. *wi-fi*.

1 A **screen** is the flat surface of your phone, computer, or TV; a **touch screen** is a screen which allows you to give instructions by touching it rather than using a keypad, mouse, or keyboard.
2 A **keypad** is a (small) set of buttons with numbers or letters used to operate any electronic device, e.g. a phone, a remote control; a **keyboard** is the set of keys (digital or physical) for entering text on a phone, computer, or tablet.
3 A **password** is a secret word, or combination of letters + numbers, that you need to type into a computer or phone in order to use it; a **passcode** is a secret set of numbers (usually four or six digits, like a PIN) that you need to type into some electronic devices, e.g. phones, in order to use them.
4 Your **contacts** are the stored names, addresses, phone numbers, etc. of people who you know; your **settings** are the choices you make on a computer or other device to decide the way things look and work, e.g. sound level, brightness, etc.
5 **Broadband** is high-speed access to the internet; **wi-fi** is a way of connecting to the internet using radio waves.
6 An **update** is a recent change to a computer program that is sent to the user; a **pop-up** is a window that appears on the screen, especially one containing an advert, that you have not requested.
7 **Coverage** is the quality of the connection in a particular place (e.g. *The coverage isn't good in this area*); **signal** is the electrical waves that carry data to a mobile phone or other device (e.g. *I can't get a good signal in my house*).
8 To **download** is to get and store a file of data from the internet; to **stream** is to play video or sound files while they download (these are deleted after they're played).
9 To **scroll** is to move content on a screen up or down so that you can see different parts of it; to **swipe** is to move your finger quickly across the screen in order to give commands.
10 To **hang up** is to end a call; to **top up** (your phone) is to pay more money, so you can make calls or have more data.
11 To **put sb through** is to connect sb by phone to the person they want to speak to; to **get through to sb** is to manage to speak on the phone to the person you want to speak to.
12 To **switch off** (a device) is to turn it off; to **unplug** (a device) is to disconnect it from the power supply or from another device.

2 PRONUNCIATION /æ/ and /ʌ/

Pronunciation notes

This exercise gives Sts the opportunity to fine-tune their pronunciation of two vowel sounds which may still cause problems even at an advanced level.

The /æ/ sound can only be spelt by the letter *a*, usually between consonants, e.g. *bag*, *clap* – the only exception is *plait*. However, the /ʌ/ sound can be spelt in different ways, most commonly by the letter *u* between consonants, e.g. *bus*, but also by *o*, e.g. *son*; the letters *ou*, e.g. *touch*; or *oo*, e.g. *blood*. Many Sts find it hard to hear the difference between these sounds, and this can cause communication problems, as there are several common words or verb forms where the only difference is these vowel sounds. Getting Sts to focus on your mouth position (wider for the /æ/ sound) may also help.

a 🔊 **6.4** Focus on the **Fine-tuning your pronunciation: /æ/ and /ʌ/** box and go through it with the class.

Focus on the instructions and give Sts time to look at the pairs of words. You could encourage them to say the words out loud to themselves as they read them.

Play the audio once the whole way through for Sts just to listen.

🔊 **6.4**
See words in Student's Book on *p.60*

b 🔊 **6.5** Focus on the instructions and make it clear that this time, Sts are going to hear one of the words or phrases in a sentence.

Play the audio once the whole way through.
Check answers.

1 b   **2** b   **3** a   **4** b   **5** a

🔊 **6.5**
1   A What did she say?
    B She didn't say anything. She just hung up.
2   A Oh no. I don't believe it!
    B What's up?
3   A My computer's just crashed and I hadn't saved.
    B Oh no, how annoying.
4   A Can you print out this letter for me?
    B Sorry, the printer's run out of paper. We'll need to get some more.
5   A Is there still no news from the plumber?
    B Yes, he rang this morning to say he was coming.

c Get Sts to practise saying the sentences with a partner. Encourage them to try to say them quite fast, linking words where appropriate and concentrating on the two highlighted vowel sounds.

EXTRA SUPPORT Say each sentence first and get Sts to repeat after you. Then put Sts in pairs and get them to practise saying the sentences.

3 READING & LISTENING distinguishing between positive and negative effects

a Do this as whole-class activity. You could tell Sts how many hours a day you spend using your phone and whether you are happy with this.

b Focus on the task and the beginning of the article, as far as the end of the *Challenges* section. You might want to pre-teach the word *detox* (= the process of removing harmful substances from your body by only eating and drinking particular things) and then getting Sts to guess what a *digital detox* is.

EXTRA IDEA Focus on the title of the article and get Sts to guess what it is about.

Set a time limit for Sts to read the article and complete verbs 1–11.

Get Sts to compare with a partner, and then check answers.

EXTRA SUPPORT Before Sts read the article the first time, check whether you need to pre-teach any vocabulary.

1 Delete   **2** Turn   **3** Leave   **4** Keep   **5** take   **6** turn
7 check   **8** Take   **9** leave   **10** Keep   **11** switch

Deal with any vocabulary problems that arose.

c Focus on the task and get Sts to read the information about Anisah and Clive.

EXTRA SUPPORT Go through the information as a class, making sure Sts understand all the lexis, e.g. *coding*, *screen time* (= the amount of time you spend looking at your phone), *pick-ups* (= the number of times you pick up your phone), etc.

Now put Sts in pairs and get them to discuss who they think might have found it harder to do the detox.

Get some feedback from various pairs.

d Tell Sts they are now going to read about Anisah's experience. They need to underline all the positive aspects she mentions and circle the negative ones.

Get Sts to compare with a partner, and then check answers.

EXTRA SUPPORT Before Sts read the article the first time, check whether you need to pre-teach any vocabulary, but <u>not</u> the highlighted expressions.

Positive: reading more books, sleeping better, not having work emails
Negative: being left out of family WhatsApp communications, too quiet, not being able to listen to music, not communicating with anybody, not being able to take photos

e Put Sts in pairs and get them to look at the highlighted expressions in the article and match the **bold** words or phrases to their exact meaning in 1–5.

Check answers.

1 b   **2** c   **3** a   **4** b   **5** c

Deal with any vocabulary problems that arose.

f 🔊 **6.6** Focus on the task and elicit who Clive is (*a BBC news presenter and foreign correspondent*) and whether he uses his phone a lot (*Much less than Anisah. His daily screen time is 45 minutes and number of pick-ups is 11*).

Give Sts time to read questions 1–3.

Play the audio once the whole way through for Sts to listen and answer the questions.

Get Sts to compare with a partner, and then check answers.

EXTRA SUPPORT Read through the script and decide if you need to pre-teach any new lexis before Sts listen.

1 Generally less stressful because he doesn't rely on his phone as much – he doesn't use many apps and he's happy to put his phone away.
2 He uses his phone and Twitter more than he thought.
3 Because his phone screen time and pick-ups had gone up.

🔊 **6.6**

(script in Student's Book on *pp.135–136*)

I = interviewer, C = Clive

I How much do you depend on your phone in daily life?
C I'm a journalist, and when you're a journalist, it's very difficult to turn your phone off. My job can be unpredictable – for example, being sent to Las Vegas to cover the worst shooting in American history. You know, I get a phone call and I'm on the next flight out.
I Would you describe yourself as a techie?
C Not really. I only really use WhatsApp and Twitter. I know there's a whole world of apps out there, but I don't feel as if I'm missing out. I mean, I don't sit on the Tube frantically playing games on my phone.
I So deleting apps wasn't a problem for you?
C Well, I missed the two I normally use. But my phone's mainly for reading newspapers and getting information for stories.
I How did you find the challenges?
C Days one to four weren't a problem at all. In the evening, it feels absolutely fine to put my phone away. When I go out for dinner with my wife and leave my phone behind, it makes no difference, because it would never, ever be on the table. In fact, I get a little irritated if I'm in a group and someone is scrolling through a phone. I don't say anything; I just quietly get wound up.
I So there was nothing you missed?
C Not really. My only real guilty pleasure is checking the football, but the bottom line is: if I wasn't at work, I could live without my phone.
I What about the last three days?
C Days six and seven were more difficult. At the weekend, I normally work from one p.m. until after my programme ends, *News at Ten*, about eleven p.m., and without a phone it's tricky to get a heads-up on the stories before work. I considered going out and buying the papers, but part of the attraction of the phone is you don't have to go out in the cold, so I broke the rule and turned my phone on to go through the papers. I was also panicking that if the Queen dropped down dead, or some other big news story, they wouldn't be able to get hold of me, and I'd quite like to keep my job, so I decided to keep my phone on, but just not to look at it.
I What did you learn from the challenges?
C What I learned is that I use my phone more than I thought. By the end of the week, I was actually using it more than when I started. I still like to think I prefer talking face-to-face, but I missed not being able to pick up the phone when I wanted to use it. And I use Twitter more than I thought.
I What did you decide you couldn't cope with?
C I couldn't cope with not being kept in the loop with friends on WhatsApp. There were group messages I couldn't read or respond to.
I And what can you do without?
C I still think I can do without social media, but as a journalist, I have to play along with it up to a point because this is how the world works.
I Clive's results were surprising. His daily phone screen time had actually gone up from forty-five to fifty minutes, and his number of pick-ups a day from eleven to sixteen. So maybe he just didn't need to divorce his phone in the first place!

---

g Tell Sts they are going to listen to the interview again and this time, they need to make notes on what Clive says about items 1–8. Go through them with Sts to make sure they understand all the lexis, e.g. *a techie, be kept in the loop*.

Play the audio again, pausing after Clive mentions each thing to give Sts time to write.

Get Sts to compare with a partner, and then play the audio again if necessary.

Check answers.

1 He isn't really a techie – he only uses WhatsApp and Twitter, and he doesn't play games on his phone.
2 He missed the two he normally uses, but otherwise, it wasn't a problem.
3 He never has his phone at the table, and he doesn't like it when other people do.
4 Checking the football is his guilty pleasure – something he enjoys but knows he shouldn't do.
5 He works for *News at Ten*, and without a phone it was difficult to find out about the news stories they would be covering.
6 If the Queen died suddenly and he didn't have his phone, people wouldn't be able to let him know and he wouldn't be able to do his job.
7 It was the thing he couldn't cope with.
8 He can do without social media, but as a journalist, he has to use it because it's part of the job.

EXTRA SUPPORT If there's time, you could get Sts to listen again with the script on *pp.135–136*, so they can see exactly what they understood / didn't understand. Translate / Explain any new words or phrases.

h Put Sts in pairs and get them to answer the questions. Get some feedback from various pairs.

4 WRITING a discursive essay (1): a balanced argument

In this lesson, the focus is on writing a discursive essay. These are generally of two types: either a 'balanced argument' essay, where Sts are expected to give both sides of an argument and draw a conclusion, or an 'opinion' essay, where Sts decide whether they agree with a statement or not and give their reasons. The 'opinion' essay is focused on in Lesson **8B**. The writing skills focus here is on the content of introductory and concluding paragraphs, and there is a **Useful language** focus on expressing the main points in an argument, adding supporting information, describing cause and effect, and weighing up arguments.

Tell Sts to go to **Writing A discursive essay (1): A balanced argument** on *p.124*.

ANALYSING A MODEL TEXT

a Focus on the text type (*a discursive essay: a balanced argument*). Tell Sts that when they are asked to write an essay, it is normally one of two types, either giving a balanced argument, i.e. showing the pros and cons of something, or giving their own opinion clearly in favour of or against a particular statement. Point out that the latter kind of discursive essay will be focused on in **File 8**.

You should highlight that although some essay titles make it clear which type of essay is required, some titles allow Sts to decide for themselves which type they wish to write.

Focus on the **Key success factors** and go through them with the class.

Focus on the task and get Sts, in pairs, to discuss arguments for and against smartphones. They should then choose three arguments for smartphones and three against, and put them in order of importance.

Get feedback and write the arguments up on the board in FOR and AGAINST columns.

b Focus on the task and main sections of the essay.

Get Sts to read it quickly and check the arguments against the ones on the board.

Then ask the class where the writer put the main argument in each paragraph.

At the beginning for the 'in favour' paragraph, and at the end for the 'against' paragraph

c Focus on the task and the three possible introductions and conclusions.

Get Sts to read the **Introductions and conclusions** box, then choose individually which introduction they think is the best, and then compare with a partner.

Finally, get Sts to do the same with the conclusions.

Check answers, getting Sts to explain why.

Introduction 1 is the best – it describes the present situation (*Smartphones dominate the field of personal communications*) and refers to the question in the title of the essay.
Conclusion 3 is the best – it refers to both the pros and cons discussed in the essay (*a wonderful tool / they have both pros and cons*), and it provides a logical summary of the arguments in the form of a personal opinion (*they have to be used wisely / It is very important that we control them and not the other way round*).

USEFUL LANGUAGE

d Focus on the task and give Sts time to complete the phrases individually or in pairs. Stress that not all the phrases are in the model essay.

Check answers.

1 benefit **2** importantly **3** drawback **4** downside
5 addition **6** more **7** only **8** favour
9 whole **10** balance **11** All, all **12** considered

Remind Sts that these phrases are all useful for writing this kind of essay.

PLANNING WHAT TO WRITE

a Focus on the task. Tell Sts, in pairs, to read the title and brainstorm the pros and cons.

Then they should choose the three most important arguments in favour and against.

Elicit from the class which they think are the most important arguments on each side (they don't have to agree).

b Set a time limit of about ten minutes for Sts to write their introductory paragraphs.

c Tell Sts to compare their introduction with the partner they worked with in **a** and to write a final version together.

Finally, go through the **Tips** with the class.

WRITING

Go through the instructions and set the writing for homework.

Tell Sts to go back to the main lesson **6B**.

5 GRAMMAR conditional sentences

a Focus on the task and give Sts time to match the sentence halves.

Check answers.

1 c **2** f **3** d **4** b **5** e **6** a

b Focus on the questions and give Sts time, in pairs, to answer them.

Check answers. Elicit that in 2, the *if*-clause is like a second conditional (because it refers to the present) and the other clause is like a third conditional (because it refers to the past), but that mixed conditionals can also work the other way round, e.g. *If I hadn't passed all my exams* (third conditional, a hypothesis about the past), *I wouldn't be feeling so relaxed* (the consequence in the present).

Refer to present or future situations: 3 and 4 (second conditionals), 5 (first conditional)
Refer to past situations: 1 and 6 (third conditionals)
Sentence 2 is a mixed conditional (a combination of a second and a third conditional). It refers to a hypothetical situation in the present (*If my laptop wasn't so new…*) and the consequence it had in the past (*…I wouldn't have bothered to get it repaired*).

c Tell Sts to go to **Grammar Bank 6B** on *p.153*.

Grammar notes

Sts should be familiar by now with the two standard forms of unreal conditions, i.e. second and third conditionals, even though they may still make mistakes with the forms when speaking. It is worth reminding them that continuous forms (past continuous or past perfect continuous) can also be used in the *if*-clause, e.g. *If it was snowing now, I would leave work early*.

Mixed conditionals are much less common than standard conditionals, but Sts still need some practice in this area.

The use of *had* in inverted third conditionals is covered here, e.g. *Had I known about the meeting, I would have come*. Other types of inversion in conditionals, e.g. *Should you wish to…*, *Were I to…* are covered in *English File* Advanced Plus.

Focus on the example sentences for **real and unreal conditionals** and go through the rules with the class. Remind Sts that *unless* means *if…not* – you could ask them to rephrase the first example sentence using *if* (= *You won't get a phone upgrade if you haven't got a contract*). You could also point out that *would have* can be contracted as *'d have* or *would've*, e.g. *I'd have / I would've told you if I'd known*.

Go through **was or were in the *if*-clause?** with the class.

Repeat for **mixed conditionals** and **alternatives to *if* in conditional sentences**.

Focus on the exercises and get Sts to do them individually or in pairs. If they do them individually, get them to compare with a partner.

Check answers after each exercise, getting Sts to read the full sentences.

Tell Sts to go back to the main lesson **6B**.

EXTRA SUPPORT If you think Sts need more practice, you may want to give them the **Grammar** photocopiable activity at this point.

d Focus on the task and give Sts time to finish the sentences so they are true for them.

Monitor and correct any errors with conditional sentences.

Put Sts in pairs and get them to compare sentences.

Elicit some sentences from the class and find out if any Sts finished the sentences in a similar way.

6 LISTENING & SPEAKING

a Focus on the task and explain / elicit the meaning of the verb *to shortlist* (= to choose a small number of people, books, photos, etc., from all those that applied for a job, entered a competition, etc.). Remind Sts that they came across *millennial* in Lesson **1B** (= the generation of people who became adults in the early 21st century).

Give Sts time to look at the photo and think about why it illustrates an obsession with technology so well.

Elicit some ideas from the class, and then ask them if they know anyone who is obsessed with technology, or if they themselves are.

b ◑ 6.7 Tell Sts they are going to listen to five people talking about people they know with an obsession (not related to technology). First, they will just hear an extract and they need to guess what the obsession is.

Play the audio once the whole way through for Sts to listen and make a note of what they think the obsession is.

Get Sts to compare with a partner, but don't tell them the answers yet.

EXTRA SUPPORT Read through the script and decide if you need to pre-teach any new lexis before Sts listen.

◑ 6.7
A
I've never seen a kid quite so obsessed, and for such a long time, with one particular toy.
B
…the weird thing is, as far as I'm concerned, is that she doesn't really like eating what she makes. In fact, I don't think she has a sweet tooth.

C
I wouldn't exactly say he was a hypochondriac because he doesn't often go to the doctor, but I do think it's an obsession…
D
She also has two or three that live in her flat, and she even used to have one that lived in her office, but I think it died.
E
She collects the films themselves, and as much merchandising as she can. She has dolls from the films, small toys, and anything she can find.

c ◑ 6.8 Now tell Sts they are going to hear the full version and they must listen and check their ideas in **b**.

Check answers. Tell Sts that *Santa* is another term for *Father Christmas*.

A Lego B baking C his health D cats E Disney films

◑ 6.8
(script in Student's Book on *p.136*)
A
My nephew Sacha is absolutely obsessed with Lego. He's nine years old now, but he's been crazy about Lego since he was, well, since he was about three or four, years old, and he is so good at assembling the things he makes – he never asks for help, he never has done, what he does is he just reads the instructions and then he does it himself. When he wrote his letter to Santa this year, he just put Lego, Lego, and more Lego. Then a couple of days after Christmas, his parents, that's my brother and my sister-in-law, had a lunch party and a load of people came with kids, kids who were friends of his, and he just refused to come out of his room and he wouldn't play with them because all he wanted to do was carry on making one of the Lego sets he got for Christmas. I've never seen a kid quite so obsessed, and for such a long time, with one particular toy.
B
My sister-in-law, Miriam, she's really into baking. She has a very demanding job: she's a surgeon, but she spends loads of her time baking. I think she's got every single cookery book, baking book, that's in print, and in her kitchen she has a million and one different cake tins and equipment. I have to say she's incredibly good – makes the most amazing cakes, biscuits, whatever – but the weird thing is, as far as I'm concerned, is that she doesn't really like eating what she makes. In fact, I don't think she has a sweet tooth. Very weird.
C
So, my partner, Miguel, is totally obsessed with his health, you know, absolutely obsessed, and it drives me up the wall. He's always talking about how he feels, and taking his blood pressure on this wee machine he's got for it and how everything he's eaten has affected his body, and, like, he talks about how many times he's been to the loo, I mean, seriously. And he also takes all these, you know, like vitamins, you know, supplements and stuff, like the fridge is full of them. I wouldn't exactly say he was a hypochondriac, because he doesn't often go to the doctor, but I do think it's an obsession, and nothing makes him happier than sitting down with a lovely herbal tea and a mate and going on and on about his health problems. And of course, you know, at the end of the day there's actually nothing wrong with him, he's like the healthiest person you've ever met, so it's quite a joke really.
D
I've got a Polish friend called Dagmara who has a bit of an obsession with cats. She's got this small plot of land with like, a shed near where she lives, and she's got about forty cats there which she goes and feeds every day and they've all got names. And she's always rescuing new cats she finds all over the place and taking them there. She also has two or three that live in her flat, and she even used to have one that lived in her office, but I think it died. And everything in her house, like mugs, towels, crockery, all of it has got something to do with cats. And like, she's very normal in about every other way, but she does have a thing about cats. It's kind of weird.

E

A mate of mine, well, his girlfriend Silvia, really likes, actually, I think it's fair to say she's obsessed with Disney. Anything Disney, the films, she collects the films themselves and as much merchandising as she can. She has dolls from the films, small toys, and anything she can find. She even wears clothes, and the clothes have pictures of Disney characters all over them. Right now it's getting a bit out of hand, because she doesn't have a very big flat and there's Disney stuff everywhere and it takes up all the room, there's toys all over her bed. Her boyfriend's getting a bit fed up with the whole thing and I can't say I blame him.

d Focus on statements 1–5 and give Sts time to read them.

Play the audio again, pausing after each speaker to give Sts time to answer the questions.

Check answers. You might want to point out that Speaker C uses the adjective *wee* ('on this wee machine'), which is common in Scotland and means *little*.

1 Speaker B **2** Speaker C **3** Speaker E **4** Speaker A
5 Speaker D

Now ask Sts whose obsession they think is the most unusual.

LANGUAGE IN CONTEXT

e 🔊 **6.9** Focus on the instructions and give Sts time to read extracts 1–7.

Play the audio, pausing after each extract for Sts to listen and complete the highlighted phrases.

Get Sts to compare with a partner, and then check answers.

1 into **2** single **3** always **4** on, on **5** bit **6** thing
7 hand

🔊 **6.9**
1 …she's really into baking.
2 I think she's got every single cookery book, baking book, that's in print…
3 He's always talking about how he feels…
4 …and going on and on about his health problems.
5 …has a bit of an obsession with cats.
6 …she does have a thing about cats.
7 Right now, it's getting a bit out of hand because she doesn't have a very big flat…

EXTRA CHALLENGE Put Sts in pairs and get them to try to complete the gaps before they listen to the audio.

EXTRA SUPPORT If there's time, you could get Sts to listen again to audio 🔊 6.8 with the script on *p.136*, so they can see exactly what they understood / didn't understand. Translate / Explain any new words or phrases.

f Focus on the task and give Sts time to think about people they know before they start. Stress that it can be a mild obsession.

Demonstrate the activity by talking about a person you know.

Divide Sts into small groups and get them to talk about people they know. Remind them to try to use some of the phrases from **e**.

Monitor and help if necessary.

Get some feedback by asking the groups about any unusual obsessions that came up.

7 VOCABULARY adjectives + prepositions

Vocabulary notes

Sts will have met common adjective + preposition combinations before (e.g. *good at*, *tired of*) and should know the importance of learning prepositions with new adjectives when they meet them. Here the focus is on revising and expanding these combinations. Remind Sts that there are no rules for these combinations, and it is simply a question of learning the correct preposition with each adjective.

a Focus on the **Adjectives + prepositions** box and go through it with the class.

Give Sts time to complete the *Prepositions* column. Make sure they do not write the prepositions in the sentences. Point out that the first one (*with*) has been done for them.

b 🔊 **6.10** Play the audio for Sts to listen and check.

Check answers. You could remind Sts that if an adjective + preposition is followed by a verb, it is always the *-ing* form, as in sentence 10, e.g. *obsessed with playing video games*, *fed up with waiting*.

2 to **3** on **4** about **5** on **6** with **7** to **8** of
9 of **10** on **11** for **12** of **13** with **14** to **15** to

🔊 **6.10**
1 Nowadays, a lot of people are obsessed with celebrities and their lifestyles.
2 A lot of young people are addicted to social media.
3 Many young people are hooked on video games.
4 Lots of teenage boys are mad about football.
5 Many thirty-year-olds are still dependent on their parents.
6 Some people are fed up with the amount of sport on TV.
7 Older people aren't always as open to new ideas as younger people are.
8 People are sick of being bombarded with depressing news.
9 Most parents nowadays are aware of the negative effect of too much screen time.
10 Couples are not as keen on getting married as they used to be.
11 If TV programmes are unsuitable for children, they have to be shown after nine p.m.
12 People are becoming more suspicious of technology companies.
13 Far too many people are dissatisfied with their mobile phone network.
14 People are getting so accustomed to fake news that they can't tell what's true and what isn't.
15 It's going to be difficult to reduce emissions as long as people are so attached to their cars.

c Get Sts to test themselves by covering the *Prepositions* column and saying the sentences with the prepositions.

d Focus on the first sentence in **a** and ask Sts if they think it is true for their country, and elicit examples.

Then put Sts in pairs and get them to continue with the other sentences.

Get some feedback from the class.

Tell Sts that they can find a list of dependent prepositions on *p.173* of the Student's Book. This includes adjective + preposition, verb + preposition, and noun + preposition.

8 ▶ VIDEO LISTENING

a Tell Sts they are going to watch a documentary about addiction to technology. Focus on sentences 1–6, and give Sts time to read them. Now put Sts in pairs and tell them to discuss which sentences they think are true.

Get some feedback from various pairs, but <u>don't</u> tell them if they are correct.

b Play the video once the whole way through for Sts to watch and check their answers in **a**.

Check answers.

The sentences that are true are:
1, 2, and 5

The age of addiction
N = narrator, D = Dr Richard Graham

N *There are many forms of addiction, to substances like drugs, alcohol, nicotine and even chocolate and coffee. There are also behavioural addictions like work, gambling and shopping. A recent addition to these is an addiction to technology.*
The statistics surrounding technology and its use are staggering. The world population is currently around seven point seven billion. Four point four billion of us use the internet. Three point five billion of us use social media, and over five billion of us have a mobile phone. And there are huge profits to be made, too. According to recent reports, the video game industry is worth around one hundred and forty billion dollars worldwide and that figure is rising.
There are estimated to be over two point five billion video gamers globally, with the highest number in the Asia Pacific area. In the UK, there are an estimated thirty-seven point three million players. With those numbers, it is no surprise that both social media platforms and video games have the potential for addiction.

D I think social media and games have built into them what is sometimes called mechanics or games mechanics, that provide you with rewards and they're very carefully orchestrated to be sort of random and not predictable, to keep you interested and for social media, it might be likes or followers…or someone sharing something that you find rewarding, that you can then share and sort of be ahead of the curve. In games, there are all sorts of rewards from obviously getting up to the top levels of a game, equipment that you could win and now of course, even buy within games, they're all very rewarding and increase your, your status in those worlds.

N *Many of these carefully orchestrated rewards will work on any user, regardless of their age or background, but it is younger users who are particularly susceptible to them.*

D I think the youngest person I've treated in terms of face to face work is someone of nine years old, who was getting up at five o'clock in the morning, hiding under his bed at night to play *Fortnite*, running up enormous bills through purchasing equipment that the parents were oblivious to, but I've taken calls about younger children and sometimes it is very small children who get into fits of rage or distress when they can't access an iPad or other games platform to, to continue playing.

N *This alarming rise in addictive behaviour, combined with the increased accessibility of technology, games and social media, has led many people to ask what the difference is between a keen technology user and an addict.*

D One of the first things I would suggest a parent does if they're concerned about their child's use, is actually talk to other parents about what their children are doing. I think one of the things that often marks an addiction out from somebody who's an enthusiastic user, is the fact that the enthusiastic user will know when it's time to stop but somebody with addiction will keep going and keep going even though they know it might be getting them into sort of difficulty, may even be as basic as tiredness or it may be that it starts to then impact on other areas of their life, they're late for things or not doing homework or whatever it is.

N *So, in cases of genuine addiction, what kinds of treatment are available?*

D When I started out in the early days, the main focus of treatment was something that we called a digital detox, which was about helping the young person have a break from technology so they could kind of almost wake up to the extent of their use, and start to then look at their life in a wider sense, at what other priorities they had.

N *But with the advent of the smartphone and the enormous growth in social media, use of technology became something people couldn't really take a break from, and the approach to treatment had to change.*

D So then we had to take a step back and think, 'Well, what are we really needing to prioritize here?' and at that point I guess the impact on the person's health and well-being came to the fore. And we focused on sleep because one of the first things to be disrupted would be sleep by someone gaming excessively or late into the night on, on social media and we would then sort of work out a programme for how much sleep they needed for that age and work backwards, giving them an hour of no screen time before they should be asleep, working out what time they needed to be up for school. And very quickly, you could kind of establish a programme and, and work towards getting a good sleep habit and with that, of course, came better use of technology.

N *There are very few things we can be certain of in the future, but it is reasonable to assume that the phones in our pockets and the computers in our homes are going to get more and more powerful. So how does Doctor Graham see our relationship with technology developing in the future?*

D I think what we're going to see in the next few years is a growing recognition of just how frustrating technology is, I think we've been promised a great deal and often when we engage with it, we're hopeful of getting a deeper connection with others, but actually, we're wired in a way that means that being in a room with others will often afford us much more contact, much more interaction in a way that screens and voice channels as yet just can't match. And so whatever happens next, I think we will strike this balance between recognizing what technology can do for us and the fact that we still have bodies and we still have minds and they need certain things.

---

c Focus on the task and give Sts time to read questions 1–8. Play the video again, pausing if necessary to give Sts time to answer the questions.

Check answers.

1 Work, gambling, shopping, technology
2 3.5 billion
3 Around $140 billion
4 Getting to the top levels of a game, equipment you can win or buy within a game
5 A nine-year-old boy who got up early and stayed up late to play *Fortnite*, and who spent his parents' money on the game
6 A technology addict keeps going even if they know it's causing problems, and an enthusiastic user knows when to stop.
7 Because in the modern world people can't realistically take a break from technology
8 It can't give us a deep connection with other people, it can't replace face to face contact.

d Do this as a whole-class activity, or put Sts in pairs and then get some feedback.

For instructions on how to use these pages, see *p.43*.

More materials
For teachers
Teacher's Resource Centre
Video Can you understand these people? 5&6
Quick Test 6
File 6 Test
For students
Online Practice Check your progress

GRAMMAR

a
1 c 2 b 3 a 4 b 5 b 6 a 7 b 8 c 9 a 10 c

b
1 The president is believed **to be spending** his holiday in the Caribbean this week.
2 It's time you **started** to think about what subjects you want to study next year.
3 My parents always encouraged me **to learn** foreign languages.
4 My new job involves me **travelling** to Canada two or three times a year.
5 They're incredibly generous people and they wouldn't let me **pay** for anything.
6 Daniel can stay the night as long as he doesn't mind **sleeping** on the sofa.
7 Supposing Ajax lost their last two matches, **would** they still **win** the league?
8 Marcus might have hurt his head if he **hadn't been wearing** a helmet when he fell off his bike.
9 If you **had told** me earlier that you were coming, I would have taken the day off.
10 If I hadn't inherited a lot of money, we **wouldn't / couldn't live / wouldn't be living** in a house like this now.

VOCABULARY

a
1 with 2 behind 3 out 4 for 5 by 6 on 7 at
8 about
b
1 cost 2 loaded 3 Fares 4 bucks 5 a mortgage
6 income 7 budget 8 donation
c
1 minded 2 self 3 hand 4 worn 5 behaved 6 life
7 friendly
d
1 unplug 2 get 3 scroll 4 fed 5 hooked 6 addicted
7 keen

CAN YOU understand this text?

b
1 E 2 H 3 A 4 C 5 I 6 B 7 D 8 G

▶ CAN YOU understand these people?

1 c 2 b 3 c 4 a

◀) 6.11
1
I = interviewer, A = Adina
I Would you say you're patient or impatient?
A Oh, I'm rather impatient as, as you can tell, right? So, I would definitely, er, not last long, um, in a, in a queue or on a meeting. Yes, I tend to, um, er, change position, look out the window, er, find something to do with my hands, reach for the water, things like that.
2
I = interviewer, G = Guy
I Do you do any small things that you think make a difference to the planet?
G I do, we do as a family, yes, er, recycling all sorts of things, trying not to let the water run when brushing my teeth. Er, er, not using the car all of the time, but taking the bicycle, all things like that. Yes, we pay attention to those things.
3
I = interviewer, V = Vicky
I Can you tell us about the simple things that make you happy?
V Um, yeah, most of them are free. Um, waking up after a good night's sleep, having nice blue skies with pretty clouds, and the sound of my cat purring or my niece calling my name. Just generally those, those sort of things that make you happy.
4
I = interviewer, H = Hywel
I How difficult would you find it to live without your phone?
H Well, what did we do before we had mobile phones? I guess we actually called people on the landline or we consulted books or read newspapers a bit more. I think I probably would find it quite difficult if everybody else had them and I didn't. Um, so yeah I guess we've become pretty dependent on them, but they're fantastic machines, so like all things they can be a master or a slave.

As a matter of fact...

G permission, obligation, and necessity
V word formation: prefixes
P intonation and linking in exclamations

Lesson plan

The topic of this lesson is control and rules.

In the first half, the angle of the topic is about control in education, which Sts explore through a listening about the *QI* phenomenon, a TV quiz programme and series of books based on principles which the authors think should be applied to education, e.g. giving children control over their learning. This is followed by a pronunciation focus on intonation and linking in exclamations such as *How awful!* Then there is a vocabulary focus on word formation by adding prefixes to change the meaning of a word, e.g. *bilingual*, *anti-smoking*, etc., presented through more *QI* facts.

The second half of the lesson focuses on the absurdity of some health and safety rules. Sts read three extracts from a book, *In the Interests of Safety*, which exposes the truth and myths behind some of the rules which govern our lives. Sts then go into the grammar, which is on modal verbs and other expressions used to talk about permission, obligation, and necessity. Finally, they put the grammar into practice discussing the advantages or disadvantages of possible laws.

More materials
For teachers
Photocopiables
Grammar permission, obligation, and necessity *p.179*
Communicative Let's change the rules *p.205*
(instructions *p.190*)
Vocabulary Prefixes *p.225* (instructions *p.215*)
For students
Workbook 7A
Online Practice 7A

OPTIONAL LEAD-IN – THE QUOTE

Write the quote at the top of *p.66* on the board (books closed) and the name of the person who said it, or get Sts to open their books and read it.

Point out that Katharine Hepburn (1907–2003) was an American stage and film actress. She won many awards, including four Oscars.

Get Sts to discuss the quote in pairs, or do it as a whole-class activity.

1 LISTENING & SPEAKING

a Focus on the task and the *QI* quiz. Set a time limit for Sts to answer the questions in pairs. Elicit / Explain the meaning of the last category, *miscellaneous* (= consisting of many different kinds of things that are not connected and do not easily form a group). Elicit or model its pronunciation /ˌmɪsəˈleɪniəs/.

! If Sts ask what *QI* stands for, tell them they will find out later in the listening.

b When the time limit is up, put Sts in pairs, **A** and **B**, and tell them to go to **Communication** *QI* **quiz**, **A** on *p.109*, **B** on *p.114*. They will each find detailed answers to half of the questions, which they then tell each other.

Get feedback to find out which pairs answered the most questions correctly, and which answers surprised Sts.

c ◀)) **7.1** Focus on the task. Some Sts may know about *QI*, as the books have been translated into several languages.

Give Sts time to read questions 1–5.

Play the audio once the whole way through for Sts to listen and try to answer the questions.

Get Sts to compare with a partner, and then play the audio again.

Check answers.

EXTRA SUPPORT Read through both scripts and decide if you need to pre-teach any new lexis before Sts listen.

1 Because it stands for *Quite Interesting* and the writers think all the facts are interesting, and it is also *IQ* (= intelligence quotient) backwards.
2 Everything you think you know is probably wrong, and everything is interesting.
3 You are more likely to be killed by an asteroid than by lightning. Julius Caesar was not born by Caesarean section.
4 That human beings, especially children, are naturally curious and want to learn.
5 Schools can make an interesting subject boring by making children memorize facts, and if children are forced to learn something, they will probably be less successful.

◀)) 7.1
(script in Student's Book on *p.136*)
Part 1
When TV producer John Lloyd thought of a formula for a new quiz show, he decided to call it *QI*, which stands for 'Quite Interesting', and which is also *IQ* backwards. It's a comedy quiz where panellists have to answer unusual general knowledge questions, and it is perhaps surprising that it's particularly popular among fifteen to twenty-five-year-olds. Along with co-author John Mitchinson, Lloyd has since written a number of *QI* books, and these have also been incredibly successful. Lloyd's basic principle is very simple: everything you think you know is probably wrong, and everything is interesting. The *QI Book of General Ignorance*, for example, poses two hundred and forty questions, all of which reveal surprising answers. So, we learn, for example, that you are more likely to be killed by an asteroid than by lightning, or that Julius Caesar was not, in fact, born by Caesarian section.
The popularity of these books proves Lloyd's other thesis: that human beings, and children in particular, are naturally curious and have a desire to learn. And this, he believes, has several implications for education. According to Lloyd and Mitchinson, there are two reasons why children, in spite of being curious, tend to do badly at school. Firstly, even the best schools can take a fascinating subject, such as electricity or classical civilization, and make it boring, by turning it into facts which have to be learnt by heart and then regurgitated for exams. Secondly, *QI*'s popularity seems to prove that learning takes place most effectively when it's done voluntarily. The same teenagers who will happily choose to read a *QI* book will often sit at the back of a geography class and go to sleep, or worse still, disrupt the rest of the class.

d 🔊 **7.2** Focus on the task and give Sts time to read the five gapped suggestions.

Play the audio once the whole way through for Sts to listen and complete the gaps.

Get Sts to compare with a partner, and then check answers.

1 play   **2** the children themselves   **3** when and how they learn   **4** theory without practice   **5** stop dead at 17 or 18

🔊 **7.2**
(script in Student's Book on *p.136*)
Part 2
So how could we change our schools so that children would enjoy learning? What would a 'QI school' be like? These are Lloyd and Mitchinson's basic suggestions.
The first principle is that education should be more play than work. The more learning involves things like story-telling and making things, the more interested children will become.
Secondly, they believe that the best people to control what children learn are the children themselves. Children should be encouraged to follow their curiosity. They will end up learning to read, for example, because they want to, in order to read about something they are interested in.
Thirdly, they argue that children should also be in control of when and how they learn. The *QI* school would not be compulsory, so pupils wouldn't have to go if they didn't want to, and there would be no exams. There would only be projects, or goals that children set themselves with the teacher helping them. So, a project could be something like making a film or building a chair.
Fourthly, there should never be theory without practice. You can't learn about vegetables and what kind of plants they are from books and pictures; you need to go and plant them and watch them grow. The fifth and last point Lloyd and Mitchinson make is that there's no reason why school has to stop dead at seventeen or eighteen. The *QI* school would be a place where you would be able to carry on learning all your life, a mini-university where the young and old could continue to find out about all the things they are naturally curious about.

---

e Tell Sts they are going to listen to the audio again and this time, they need to make notes of the reasons for suggestions 1–5 in **d**.

Play the audio again, pausing after each suggestion to give Sts time to write.

Get Sts to compare with a partner, and then check answers.

1 Because learning should never feel like hard work.
2 Because if they follow their curiosity, they will learn things because they are interested in them.
3 Because children shouldn't be made to go to school every day if they don't want to. There shouldn't be any exams, only projects chosen by the children.
4 Because children would learn all theories through practical activities.
5 Because there should be no official school leaving age. Young and old could continue to learn together.

f Get Sts to discuss the suggestions in **d** in small groups. Elicit some opinions.

Finally, ask Sts if they have any other suggestions for improving learning in schools.

2 PRONUNCIATION intonation and linking in exclamations

Pronunciation notes

When we make an exclamation, e.g. using *How* + adjective or *What* + adjective + noun, we usually give the adjective extra emphasis, with a rise-fall intonation. It is important to get the intonation correct because if the adjective is said with a flat or falling tone, it could sound as if you are uninterested or even being sarcastic.

In many of these exclamations, the words are linked together (see **Pronunciation notes** in **5A**). Here Sts also learn that when a word ending in *w*, such as *how*, is followed by a word beginning with a vowel sound, a /w/ sound is inserted between the two words.

a 🔊 **7.3** Focus on the task, making sure Sts know what an *exclamation* is.

Play the audio, pausing for Sts to write down **B**'s exclamations. Play the audio again as necessary.

Check answers and write the exclamations on the board. If Sts want to know, tell them that the other half of the French population spoke a variety of regional languages, like Breton, Basque, Catalan, and Occitan.

1 What a ridiculous idea   **2** How interesting

🔊 **7.3**
1
A Lloyd and Mitchinson think that school shouldn't be compulsory.
B What a ridiculous idea! If it wasn't compulsory, no one would ever go.
2
A Did you know that at the time of the French Revolution, only half the population spoke French?
B How interesting! So what language did the other half speak?

---

b Focus on the task and the questions.

Now play the conversations again for Sts to listen.

Get Sts to discuss what they think, and then check answers.

1 The adjectives (*ridiculous* and *interesting*) have extra stress. The intonation is more exaggerated, with extra stress on the stressed syllable.
2 Because *interesting* begins with a vowel, and when a word ending in *w* is followed by a word beginning in a vowel, the /w/ sound is added.

c Give Sts time to practise saying the exclamations with a partner.

Monitor and encourage them to get the correct intonation.

d Put Sts in pairs, **A** and **B**, preferably face-to-face. Tell them to go to **Communication What a ridiculous idea!**, **A** on *p.111*, **B** on *p.112*.

Go through the instructions. Highlight that Sts can use *How / What* + any adjective or noun phrases they like, e.g. *How awful! What a pity!*, not only the ones they have just practised.

Demonstrate the activity. Invent a piece of news which should elicit one of the exclamations they have just practised. Tell it to them as convincingly as you can (*Did you know that…?*) and elicit an exclamation.

Get Sts to continue in pairs.

Tell Sts to go back to the main lesson **7A**.

3 VOCABULARY word formation: prefixes

a Focus on the task and remind Sts that all *QI* facts are true.

Give them time to read the ten facts.

Put Sts in pairs to discuss what they thought of the facts and to tell each other which they find the most surprising.

Get some feedback.

b Focus on the instructions and give Sts time to look at the highlighted words with a partner.

Check answers.

1 *il, un, in*
2 *anti* = against
   over = too much
   out = more than, better than
   re = again
   mis = wrongly
   sub = under
   micro = very small

Highlight that sometimes there is a hyphen between *anti* and the next word (e.g. *anti-hero, anti-war*), but sometimes not (e.g. *anticlimax*).

c Tell Sts to go to **Vocabulary Bank** Prefixes on *p.169*.

Vocabulary notes

Sts will have come across some common English prefixes before, especially negative prefixes, e.g. *unhappy, impossible*. The aim of this **Vocabulary Bank** is to expand their knowledge of prefixes, and to help them understand what individual prefixes mean, and therefore be able to work out the meanings of other words with these prefixes.

English prefixes can be used before verbs, nouns, adjectives, and adverbs.

There are several common negative prefixes, which are covered in the first part of the **Vocabulary Bank** – which prefix to use is sometimes governed by the spelling of the word, and these patterns are pointed out, so adjectives beginning with *p-* use the prefix *im-*, e.g. *impossible, impure, imperfect*. The second part of the **Vocabulary Bank** deals with prefixes which have specific meanings. Depending on where they are from, Sts may find that many of these have a similar meaning in their L1, although the pronunciation is likely to be different.

Focus on **1 Negative prefixes** and get Sts to do **a** individually or in pairs.

🔊 **7.4** Now focus on **b**. Play the audio for Sts to listen and check.

Check answers, eliciting the meaning of any words your Sts may not be familiar with.

im- + *m* or *p*
il- + *l*
ir- + *r*

🔊 **7.4**
Prefixes
1 Negative prefixes
immobile, immoral, impersonal, impractical
illegitimate, illiterate, illogical
irrational, irregular, irrelevant, irreplaceable
inappropriate, incapable, incoherent, incompetent, inhospitable
unattractive, undo, unhelpful, unofficial
disagree, discontinue, disembark, dishonest

Now either use the audio to drill the pronunciation of the words, or model and drill them yourself. Give further practice of any words your Sts find difficult to pronounce. Point out that these negative prefixes are not stressed, and that the word stress of the original word remains unchanged.

Focus on **2 Prefixes which add other meanings** and get Sts to do **a** individually or in pairs.

🔊 **7.5** Now focus on **b**. Play the first one and pause the audio so that Sts realize they will hear the number and letter, followed by the meaning of the prefix.

Now play the rest of the audio for Sts to listen and check, pausing after each one and checking answers.

🔊 **7.5**
2 Prefixes which add other meanings
1 **D**
  out means 'more than, better than, bigger than, etc.'
2 **I**
  mono means 'one'
3 **U**
  re means 'again'
4 **L**
  out means 'outside, not inside'
5 **Q**
  ill- means 'badly'
6 **C**
  multi means 'more than one, many'
7 **E**
  mis means 'wrongly'
8 **H**
  anti means 'against'

9 O
up means 'higher, towards the top'
10 N
de means 'remove or reduce'
11 K
post means 'after'
12 M
pre means 'before'
13 B
over means 'too much'
14 G
bi means 'two, twice'
15 P
co means 'together'
16 F
sub means 'below'
17 R
inter means 'between'
18 A
under means 'not enough'
19 S
super means 'above average'
20 J
auto means 'by yourself, by itself'
21 T
micro means 'extremely small'

Now focus on the **Prefixes with more than one meaning** box and go through it with the class.

Finally, focus on **Activation** and give Sts time to think of their answers. Highlight that cook and place here are verbs, not nouns.

Put Sts in pairs and get them to compare with their partner.

Check answers, by eliciting the words onto the board and checking their meaning.

-cook: pre, over, under
-lingual: mono, multi, bi
-war: anti, post, pre
-national: multi, inter
-place: re, mis

Tell Sts to go back to the main lesson **7A**.

EXTRA SUPPORT If you think Sts need more practice, you may want to give them the **Vocabulary** photocopiable activity at this point.

d Set the task either for Sts to do individually or in pairs.
If Sts worked individually, get them to compare with a partner.
Check answers.

1 misjudged **2** rewrite **3** illegible **4** inconvenient
5 antisocial **6** ill-equipped **7** uphill **8** undercooked
9 overcharged **10** outdoor

4 READING

a Focus on the task. Highlight that if their partner answers yes to any of the questions, Sts should then ask Did you think you were being treated reasonably?
Put Sts in pairs and get them to answer the questions.
Get some feedback for each question.

b Focus on the task and the questions, and make sure Sts understand them.
Either do this as a whole-class activity, or put Sts in pairs and then get some feedback.

c Focus on the three points and give Sts time to read the three extracts and match each one to one of the points. Tell them not to worry about the gaps.
Check answers.

EXTRA SUPPORT Before Sts read the three extracts the first time, check whether you need to pre-teach any vocabulary.

the rule is based on something which is possible in theory but not in practice   2
no rule actually exists, only advice   3
the rule is based on an outdated rumour   1

d Now tell Sts to read the extracts again and this time complete the gaps with phrases A–J. Remind them that there is one phrase they don't need to use.
Get Sts to compare with a partner, and then check answers.

1 H   **2** A   **3** E   **4** B   **5** I   **6** C   **7** J   **8** D   **9** F

Finally, deal with any other vocabulary problems that arose.

e Do this as a whole-class activity, or put Sts in pairs and then check answers to the first question and elicit opinions to the second.

1 No, it can't.
2 Probably nothing, although some flyers might worry more about security.
3 Not necessarily, as it can be unclear what is actually a rule and what isn't, so people are unsure how to behave.

5 GRAMMAR permission, obligation, and necessity

a Focus on the task and the pairs of sentences.
Give Sts time to discuss each pair with a partner. If necessary, remind them of the meaning of a difference in register, i.e. in the level of formality or informality.
Check answers.

1 Same meaning, but different register. It is not permitted is more formal.
2 Slight difference in meaning: You'd better is stronger than You ought to and implies that something negative may happen if you don't, e.g. They will take your water away.
3 Slight difference in meaning: We aren't supposed to… means it is not allowed, but people sometimes do it.
4 Same meaning and register.
5 Completely different meaning:
We should have left home early = it would have been a good idea, but we didn't do it.
We had to leave home early = it was necessary and we did it.

b Tell Sts to go to **Grammar Bank 7A** on p.154.

Grammar notes

There are many different verbs in English, some of which are modal verbs, used to express permission, obligation, and necessity. The use of the most common ones should be revision for Sts at this level. However, there are areas where there are small differences in meaning and register, e.g. between *have to* and *have got to*, or between *should* and *had better*, *don't need to* and *needn't*, etc., and this is the main focus of this section.

Some Sts may also still make basic errors such as confusing *mustn't* and *don't have to*.

don't need to or needn't?

Highlight that we use *don't need to* (NOT ~~needn't~~) for habitual or general necessity, e.g. *I don't need to wear glasses. My eyesight is still good.* NOT ~~I needn't wear glasses~~.

Focus on the example sentences for **can / could, must, should, ought to, had better** and go through the rules with the class.

Repeat for **mustn't / don't have to**, **need**, and **be able to, be allowed to, be permitted to, be supposed / meant to**.

In the section on **be able to, be allowed to**, etc., you could point out that rule 1 is true particularly when we want to use a form which *can* does not have.

Focus on the exercises and get Sts to do them individually or in pairs. If they do them individually, get them to compare with a partner.

Check answers after each exercise, getting Sts to read the full sentences.

a
1 ✓   2 'd better not   3 shouldn't have   4 not permitted
5 need to   6 ✓   7 didn't need to get   8 ✓
9 don't need to   10 ✓

b
1 You don't **have / need to pay** to go into the art gallery. Entrance is free.
2 Smoking **is not permitted / allowed** anywhere on the aircraft.
3 You'd **better not be** late – you know what Helen is like about punctuality!
4 You **needn't pay me** back until next month.
5 You **shouldn't have said** you didn't like the pasta.
6 It was a difficult journey because we **had to change** trains three times.
7 A lot of people think that governments **ought / need to do** more to protect young people's health.
8 You aren't **allowed / permitted to smoke** e-cigarettes in pubs in the UK.
9 We just looked into each other's eyes – we **didn't need / have to** say anything.
10 Am I **supposed to wear** a suit to the wedding, or is it quite informal?

Tell Sts to go back to the main lesson **7A**.

EXTRA SUPPORT   If you think Sts need more practice, you may want to give them the **Grammar** photocopiable activity at this point.

6 SPEAKING

a Tell Sts they will be talking about rules that they must imagine have been proposed for their country. In the case that such a law or rule actually exists in their country, they should simply discuss whether they agree with it or not.

Now focus on the task and give Sts time to read each rule and decide if they agree with it or not. Depending on the system in the country where you're teaching, you might want to point to the third regulation in the *Public health* section and tell Sts that in the UK and many other countries, healthcare is free and people do not normally need to contribute financially towards their treatment.

EXTRA SUPPORT   Write the following on the board for Sts to refer to:

	PEOPLE SHOULD BE ALLOWED TO…
	WE OUGHT TO BE ENCOURAGED TO…
I THINK	PARENTS SHOULD BE MADE TO…
I DON'T THINK	IT SHOULD BE AGAINST THE LAW TO…
	IT SHOULD BE ILLEGAL TO…
	…OUGHT TO BE BANNED.

Put Sts in small groups of three or four and get them to say what they think of each rule and why. You could remind Sts that they have seen and should try to use expressions for half-agreeing and politely disagreeing (Lesson **1A** on *p.7*).

Monitor and help whilst Sts do the activity.

Get some feedback from various groups. If there's time, you could choose one topic and open it to the class.

EXTRA SUPPORT   You could discuss the first rule in the section *On the road* with the whole class, to get them going.

b Tell Sts to focus on the four categories, and then in their groups, for two categories only, they should think of one new law or regulation they would like to introduce.

c When all the groups are ready, get each group in turn to appoint a spokesperson to present one of their new laws to the class. They need to convince the others to vote for this new law.

With a show of hands, get Sts to vote for the law.

If there's time, when each group has presented one of their laws, get them to present the second law with a different spokesperson.

A masterpiece?

G perception and sensation
V art, colour idioms
P -ure

Lesson plan

In this lesson, the topic is art.

In the first half of the lesson, the focus is on the fourth plinth in Trafalgar Square, London, where different works of public art, mainly sculptures, have been exhibited over the last 20 years. Sts look at three of these, then listen to a documentary about them, and finally give their own opinions. Then in the grammar focus, Sts work on verbs of the senses, *look*, *sound*, *feel*, etc., and the structures which follow them. The pronunciation focus is on the letters *-ure*, which can be pronounced /ə/ or /ʊə/, e.g. *sculpture*, *allure*. The first half ends with Sts learning the words for different kinds of art, discussing public art in their town or city, museums, and art galleries, and images they have in their house or on their computer or phone.

In the second part of the lesson, Sts read an article about a BBC TV programme which tries to prove whether works of art owned by viewers are genuine or fake, and about one work which appeared on the programme. They then listen to a documentary about it, in which the owner of the painting is interviewed about the experience. This leads into a speaking activity about fake items (not just art) and Sts' attitude towards buying something fake. Finally, in Vocabulary, Sts look at some idioms with colours, e.g. *out of the blue*.

More materials
For teachers
Photocopiables
Grammar perception and sensation *p.180*
Communicative Works of art? *p.206* (instructions *p.190*)
For students
Workbook 7B
Online Practice 7B

OPTIONAL LEAD-IN – THE QUOTE

Write the quote at the top of *p.70* on the board (books closed) and the name of the person who said it, or get Sts to open their books and read it.

Point out that Scott Adams is the creator of the *Dilbert* comic strip, and the author of several non-fiction works of satire, commentary, and business.

Get Sts to discuss what they think the quote means and whether they agree with it.

1 LISTENING separating the factual details (names, dates, measurements, etc.) from what the art represents

a Do this as a whole-class activity, or put Sts in pairs and then get some feedback. <u>Don't</u> tell them if they are correct at this stage.

b 🔊 **7.6** Tell Sts when they listen to the first part, they should check their answers to **a** and answer questions 1–4 with a partner. Tell them that the word *plinth* is explained in the documentary. Elicit or model its pronunciation /plɪnθ/.

Play the audio once the whole way through for Sts to check their answers to **a**.

Put Sts in pairs and give them time to answer the four questions. If necessary, play the audio again.

Check answers.

EXTRA SUPPORT Read through the script and decide if you need to pre-teach any new lexis before Sts listen.

a
They have all been shown on the fourth plinth in Trafalgar Square.

b
1 It was originally intended to have a statue of King William IV on a horse.
2 The fourth plinth was empty for over 150 years because people couldn't agree what to put on it.
3 People discussed having permanent statues, e.g. Nelson Mandela or Margaret Thatcher.
4 Some people say this was rejected in order to eventually have a statue of Elizabeth II there.

🔊 **7.6**
(script in Student's Book on *p.136*)
Part 1
Trafalgar Square in London has a plinth, that is, a stone base for a statue, in each of its four corners. On three of them, there are statues of famous historical figures. The fourth plinth was originally intended to hold a statue of King William the Fourth on a horse, but due to insufficient funds, the statue was never built. The use of the fourth plinth was debated for over one hundred and fifty years, and finally, in nineteen ninety-eight, the Royal Society for the encouragement of Arts commissioned three contemporary sculptures to be displayed there temporarily. Shortly afterwards, the authorities decided to seek opinions from public art commissioners, critics, and members of the public as to the future of the plinth. Although various proposals were put forward for permanent statues, such as of Nelson Mandela or Margaret Thatcher, it was finally agreed that, rather than having anything permanent, works of art would be commissioned from leading national and international artists and be displayed there on a temporary basis. In two thousand and five, the first work was unveiled, a sculpture of a pregnant woman by Marc Quinn, and since then, there has been a succession of new works. It is considered the world's most famous public art commission. However, it is thought that the reason for not accepting any permanent statue there may be because the fourth plinth is being reserved for a statue of Queen Elizabeth the Second.

If there's time, you could get Sts to listen again with the script on *p.136*, so they can see exactly what they understood / didn't understand. Translate / Explain any new words or phrases.

c 🔊 **7.7** Focus on the task and go through the **Glossary** with the class.

Give Sts time to read the three information boxes.

Play the audio once the whole way through for Sts to listen, complete the gaps, and match the boxes to the photos in **a**. You could pause the audio after each piece of artwork has been mentioned (see *** in the script).

Get Sts to compare with a partner, and then play the audio again if necessary.

Check answers.

Read through the script and decide if you need to pre-teach any new lexis before Sts listen.

1 B
TITLE *Nelson's **Ship in a Bottle***
BY **British** artist Yinka Shonibare
Displayed from **May 2010** to **January 2012**
2 C
TITLE ***Powerless Sculptures**, Fig. 101*
BY **Scandinavian** artists Michael Elmgreen and Ingar Dragset
Displayed from **February 2012** to **April 2013**
3 A
TITLE *The **invisible enemy** should not exist*
BY **Iraqi-American** artist Michael Rakowitz
Displayed from **March 2018** to **March 2020**

🔊 **7.7**
(script in Student's Book on *pp.136–137*)
Part 2
This sculpture, called *Nelson's Ship in a Bottle*, was unveiled in May twenty ten, and was the first artwork on the fourth plinth to relate directly to Admiral Horatio Nelson, who stands at the top of the column in Trafalgar Square. It was created by the British artist Yinka Shonibare. The ship inside is a model of Nelson's ship HMS *Victory*. The bottle was made out of glass and was constructed by aquarium specialists in Rome, along with the giant cork. Unlike Nelson's ship, however, this ship's sails were made of different African cloths; Shonibare said of his sculpture that it was designed to specifically reflect on the relationship between the birth of the British Empire and Britain's present-day multicultural context. The sculpture, the fourth work of art to be displayed there, was on show until January twenty twelve, and in twenty fifteen it was voted by the public to be the best of all the sculptures that had been displayed up to that point. When the sculpture was removed, money was raised to buy it from the artist, and it was the first of the fourth plinth commissions to be relocated in London. It is now on permanent display in the National Maritime Museum.
***
This statue of a boy on a rocking horse is called *Powerless Sculptures, Figure one oh one*. It was created by two Scandinavian artists, Michael Elmgreen from Denmark and Ingar Dragset from Norway. It was the fifth work to occupy the fourth plinth, and was on display from February twenty twelve to April twenty thirteen. The statue, which is four point one metres high, was made entirely of bronze. The two artists based their concept around the idea of the many memorial statues of men on horseback which celebrate victory in war. This boy on horseback is vulnerable; unlike traditional heroes, he is not competitive or aggressive; rather, he represents the heroism of a child growing up. Talking about their work, the artists said, 'We thought maybe we should celebrate some generations to come and hope that there will be a future where there are not so many war monuments.'
***

Installed in March twenty eighteen, and displayed until March twenty twenty, the ninth work of public art was by Iraqi-American artist Michael Rakowitz. In two thousand and six, Rakowitz started a project to recreate more than seven thousand objects of Iraqi art which had been lost forever, either looted from the Iraq museum in two thousand and three, or destroyed at archaeological sites during the Iraq War. For the fourth plinth commission, Rakowitz created a sculpture that was part of this ongoing project, called *The invisible enemy should not exist*. It was a life-size recreation of the *Lamassu*, the winged god that stood at the entrance to Nergal Gate in Nineveh, in present-day Iraq, from seven hundred BC until it was destroyed in twenty fifteen. This *Lamassu* was made out of ten thousand five hundred empty Iraqi date-syrup cans, which symbolize not only how so much art was destroyed during the war, but also how Iraq's date industry, the country's second-biggest export after oil, was decimated by the destruction of millions of its date palm trees. While his sculpture was on display, Rakowitz also set up a pop-up kiosk across the square, which sold small books of recipes using date syrup, as well as small cakes and biscuits.

d Focus on the task and give Sts time to read the three questions for each work of art.

Play the audio again, pausing after each piece of artwork has been mentioned for Sts to answer the questions.

Get Sts to compare with a partner, and then play the audio again if necessary.

Check answers.

1
a Nelson's ship HMS *Victory*
b The relationship between the birth of the British Empire and today's multicultural Britain
c It was bought from the artist and is on permanent display in the National Maritime Museum.
2
a A rocking horse
b Victory in war
c Future generations, and a time when there are fewer war monuments
3
a To re-create over 7,000 objects of Iraqi art which had been destroyed in the war
b A winged god, which originally stood at the entrance to Nineveh
c Date syrup cans, to symbolize that not only was art destroyed in the war, but also the date industry was decimated.

If there's time, you could get Sts to listen again with the script on *pp.136–137*, so they can see exactly what they understood / didn't understand. Translate / Explain any new words or phrases.

You could elicit / teach Sts more words for materials that sculptures are often made from, e.g. *copper, iron, steel, marble, clay, terracotta*, etc.

Highlight the difference between *made of* and *made out of* when describing an object:

• We use *made of* to talk about the basic material or qualities of something. It has a meaning similar to *composed of*, e.g. *She wore beautiful earrings made of silver*.
• We usually use *made out of* to talk about something that has been changed or transformed from one thing into another, e.g. *My bracelet is made out of rolled magazine pages*.

Elicit or remind Sts that we also use *made from* when we talk about how something is manufactured, e.g. *Plastic is made from oil.*

Finally, you could get Sts to talk about things they own that are made of and made out of the materials.

e Put Sts in pairs and get them to discuss the questions.

Get some feedback from various pairs. For the first question, you could see which is the most popular, with a show of hands for everyone's favourite one. Sts could do the second question in small groups and then present their ideas to the class.

EXTRA IDEA You could also ask Sts *Are there any circumstances in which you think it is acceptable to remove or destroy a statue or monument?* However, this question needs to be managed carefully, as the discussion could veer into sensitive areas.

2 GRAMMAR perception and sensation

a Give Sts time to complete the gaps in 1–4 with the correct form of the verbs in the list.

b ◑ **7.8** Play the audio for Sts to listen and check.

Check answers

> 1 looks like   2 see, look at   3 looks as if   4 seems, looks

---

◑ **7.8**
1 It really looks like the original statue.
2 You can only see what it's made of when you look at it really closely.
3 From a distance, it looks as if it's made of gold and precious metals.
4 The artist seems to be trying not to replicate the lost statue, but to make something which looks similar, but is more connected with modern life.

---

c Give Sts time to answer the two questions in pairs.

Check answers.

EXTRA SUPPORT You could do this as a whole-class activity.

> 1 *look as if* is followed by a clause.
> *looks like* is normally followed by a noun. However, in informal English it can also be followed by a clause (*It looks like it might be a modern cot*).
> **look at** = turn your eyes in a particular direction
> **see** = to become aware of sth using your eyes
> **look** = appear based on what you can see
> **seem** = appear based on any of the senses, e.g. what you hear, taste, etc. or on what you know or think
> 2 hearing, taste, smell, touch

d Tell Sts to go to **Grammar Bank 7B** on *p.155.*

Grammar notes

The basic verbs related to the senses, *see, hear, smell, feel,* and *taste,* do not work in quite the same way in English as in many other languages. They are not usually used in continuous forms, and in order to refer to an action at a particular moment, they are normally preceded by *can* (e.g. *I can smell garlic* NOT ~~I smell garlic~~ or ~~I'm smelling garlic~~). However, there are a few occasions when the present continuous is possible, e.g. *'What are you doing?' 'I'm smelling the milk to see if it's OK.'*

Hear and *see* can also be dynamic verbs and can be used in the continuous form, but with a different meaning. Compare:
I've been hearing good things about you recently. (= been receiving information)
I'm seeing James tonight. (= have arranged to meet him)
The verbs which are used to describe the impression something or someone gives through the senses are the same for smell, taste, and feel (e.g. *It smells awful. They taste nice,* etc.) but for sight we use *look* (*You look exhausted,* etc.) and for hearing we use *sound* (*It sounds like thunder,* etc.).

Focus on the example sentences for **see, hear, smell, feel, taste** and go through the rules with the class.

Repeat for **see / hear / watch / feel + infinitive or gerund, look, feel, smell, sound, taste,** and **seem.**

In the section on **look, feel, smell,** etc. you could point out that we can use *look* in the simple or continuous to talk about temporary appearance, e.g. *You look tired. / You're looking tired.* We can also use *feel* in the simple or continuous to talk about temporary sensation, e.g. *I feel fine / I'm feeling fine.*

Focus on the exercises and get Sts to do them individually or in pairs. If they do them individually, get them to compare with a partner.

Check answers, getting Sts to read the full sentences.

a
1 ✗ he seems very angry
2 ✓
3 ✗ I actually heard the bomb explode.
4 ✗ It sounds like Beethoven's 7th
5 ✓
6 ✗ it feels more like plastic
7 ✓
b
1 ✓   2 looks   3 seem   4 is looking   5 look
c
1 This tastes a bit **like** a soup my grandmother used to make.
2 He **seems / seemed / sounds / sounded** quite nice though.
3 I assume she's gone out because I heard the door **close / shut / slam** about five minutes ago.
4 The engine sounds as **if / though** there's something wrong with it.
5 My favourite perfume is one that smells **of** roses.
6 We saw hundreds of people **taking** selfies instead of enjoying the view.
7 I **can't** hear you very well.

Tell Sts to go back to the main lesson **7B.**

EXTRA SUPPORT If you think Sts need more practice, you may want to give them the **Grammar** photocopiable activity at this point.

e Focus on the questions and give Sts a few minutes to read them and make sure they know all the animals in the last bullet. You could ask Sts to choose one or two of the questions to ask you.

Put Sts in pairs and give them time to answer the questions together. Monitor and correct, especially mistakes with the **bold** verbs of the senses.

Get some feedback.

3 PRONUNCIATION -ure

Pronunciation notes

Sts of many nationalities have problems both with the two different vowel sounds that -ure can produce (/ə/ or /ʊə/) and also with the consonant sounds made by the t as in nature and the s as in pleasure. This exercise gives both the rules and practice of words with this combination of letters.

a Focus on the two sounds and elicit them from the class.

Individually or in pairs, Sts put the words in the correct group.

b 🔊 **7.9** Play the audio for Sts to listen and check.

Check answers and make sure Sts know the meaning of all the words.

🔊 **7.9**

1 computer /ə/

sculpture, picture, architecture, capture, creature, culture, feature, furniture, future, leisure, measure, nature, pleasure, signature, structure, temperature, texture, treasure

2 tourist /ʊə/

allure, endure, immature, impure, obscure, secure, sure

You could play the audio again and get Sts to repeat the words. You may want to point out that when -ure is pronounced /ʊə/, a /j/ sound is usually inserted before it.

c Do this as a whole-class activity.

1 In group 1, the stress is on the first syllable in all the words.
2 The t makes a /tʃ/ sound before -ure and the s makes a /ʒ/ sound.
3 In group 2, the stress is on the last syllable.

d Put Sts in pairs and get them to practise saying the sentences.

EXTRA SUPPORT You could say each sentence first and get Sts to repeat it after you. Then put Sts in pairs to practise saying them.

4 VOCABULARY & SPEAKING art

Vocabulary notes

This vocabulary focus will help Sts to expand the range of language they can use to talk about art. As with the similar 'phones and technology' vocabulary focus on p.60 of the Student's Book, encourage Sts to be as accurate and specific as they can when talking about the differences – this will really stretch their ability to explain themselves in a clear way. (See the answer key in **a** for the kind of language they should be using.)

a Focus on the task and put Sts in pairs to discuss what the difference between the words is.

Check answers. Elicit or model the pronunciation of any tricky words. Sts may have noticed the words portrait and landscape as settings on cameras referring to the shape of the photo. You may also want to point out that the word selfie (= a photo sb takes of him / herself) comes from the word self-portrait.

1 a sculpture = work of art that is a solid figure or object made by carving or shaping wood, stone, clay, metal, etc.
an installation = a piece of modern sculpture that is made using sound, light, etc. as well as objects
2 a statue = a figure of a person or animal in stone, metal, etc.
a monument = a building, column, statue, etc. built to remind people of a famous person or event
3 abstract art = not representing people or things in a realistic way, but expressing the artist's ideas about them
figurative art = showing people, animals, and objects as they really look
4 a landscape = a painting of a view of the countryside
a still life = a painting or drawing of arrangements of objects such as flowers, fruit, etc.
5 a portrait = a picture of a person
a self-portrait = a picture of a person created by the person him or herself
6 a drawing = a picture made using a pencil or pen rather than paint
an illustration = a drawing or picture in a book, magazine, etc., especially one that explains something
7 a poster = a large mass-produced picture printed on paper
a painting = a picture painted by an artist
8 a canvas = the strong cloth artists use to paint on
a frame = a border or structure of metal or wood that holds a picture in position

EXTRA SUPPORT Do this as a whole-class activity.

EXTRA IDEA Other words you might also want to elicit or teach are sketch, oil painting, watercolour, graffiti, palette, print.

b Focus on the task and give Sts time to think of their answers.

Put Sts in small groups to discuss the questions.

Get some feedback from various groups.

EXTRA IDEA If your class are interested in art, you could ask them if there are any works of art or artists that have really made an impression on them. If you have a favourite work of art or a favourite artist, you could tell the class about it / him / her, and if possible, show the class some of the art.

5 READING & LISTENING

a Focus on the task and give Sts time to read the first paragraph.

Elicit the answer.

The programme ends in joy if the masterpiece is genuine and in disappointment if it is a fake.

EXTRA SUPPORT Ask Sts some comprehension questions, e.g. Who is Fiona Bruce? (A TV presenter) Who is Philip Mould? (An art expert) What do Fiona and Philip do in the TV programme? (They try to find out if a piece of art is a genuine or a fake), etc.

EXTRA SUPPORT Before Sts read the article the first time, check whether you need to pre-teach any vocabulary.

b Focus on the task and put Sts in pairs, **A** and **B**.

Give Sts time to read the rest of the article and then, in pairs, to tell each other about Lucian Freud and Jon Turner. You could tell Sts **B** to look at the article and help Sts **A** if they can't remember a fact or date about Lucian Freud, and then they should swap roles for Jon Turner.

Elicit as much information as possible about the two men. It's important that Sts really understand the context of the programme and the people in it in order to then follow the development of the story in the listening sections.

Deal with any vocabulary problems that arose.

c 🔊 **7.10** Focus on the task and go through the **Glossary** of names with the class – these names all come up in the listening.

Now give Sts time to read all the events, making sure they understand all the lexis. Point out that the first one has been done for them.

Play the audio once for Sts to listen and number the events in chronological order.

EXTRA SUPPORT Read through the script and decide if you need to pre-teach any new lexis before Sts listen.

🔊 **7.10**
(script in Student's Book on *p.137*)
P = presenter, I = interviewer, J = Jon Turner
P First of all, the programme needed to know where Jon got the painting from in the first place.
I So Jon, how did you get the painting?
J I was given the painting by Denis Wirth-Miller, who was at the East Anglian School of Painting and Drawing with Lucian Freud, and I was given it when I was staying the weekend at Denis Wirth-Miller's house in Wivenhoe, in Essex.
I So it was a present?
J It was a present. Yep.
P The programme then decided to look into how Denis Wirth-Miller had got hold of the painting, especially since he and Lucian Freud were not friends.
I So Jon, do you think that Freud gave the painting to Denis?
J There was never, there was never a case that Freud had given it to Denis. The case was that Denis had taken it from the barn.
P The story was that during the Second World War, when Denis and Freud were students, it was very difficult to get hold of canvases to paint on, so students often just left their used canvases in a barn at the school, and then the canvases were reused. Denis told Jon that he had just picked up the canvas, Freud's painting, to reuse, but then he didn't; he just kept it.
The next question the programme focused on was who the portrait was of, in case this might give some more clues about the identity of the painter. After some research into the archives, a note in Denis's handwriting was found, which identified the man in the portrait, *The Man in the Black Cravat*, as a certain John Jameson. The programme found letters written by John Jameson which made it clear that he knew Lucian Freud quite well, and had met him on a number of occasions, including at the painting school in nineteen thirty-nine. So, it was perfectly credible that Freud had painted Jameson exactly at the time that Denis had said.
The programme then decided to focus on the canvas itself, and took it to an expert in the scientific analysis of paintings, called Libby Sheldon. Sheldon put the painting under the microscope and made a fascinating discovery. There was a long hair embedded in the picture, which looked like a human hair, and which might give them some DNA evidence. The hair was removed from the picture and taken to be analysed, and at the same time, they were able to get a DNA sample from one of Freud's cousins to compare it with.
I Jon, what did you think when Libby Sheldon found a hair in the painting?
J I was absolutely gobsmacked. I hadn't even thought that there'd be a possibility that anything like that could exist.
I Did you assume it was Freud's hair?
J I didn't. I didn't assume it was Freud's.
I And when the results came back, unfortunately it was not a match. The hair was definitely not Lucian Freud's. How did you feel, Jon, at that moment?

J I was very disappointed when I found that it wasn't a hair from Lucian Freud's head, because I got swept along with adrenalin and excitement that goes with one of these TV shows, because of course you're not only dealing with the presenters, you have the producers and the researchers, and the film crew – we got to know each other so well at this stage – and none of us knew. So, we were all biting our nails at this moment, and as that, when that was delivered, none of us knew the result, and so we'd been sitting in the laboratory for three hours before that was delivered, and I was really biting my fingernails right down.
P The real mystery of course remained – if it really was a Freud painting, why had he denied it? Was it because it was an early work and he was ashamed of it, and didn't want to be associated with it? *Fake or Fortune*'s experts contacted Freud's solicitor, Diana Rawstron, who had known him very well. They had often talked about his paintings, and when she checked back through her records, she found that in two thousand and six they had discussed *The Man in the Black Cravat*, and Freud admitted that in fact he had started the painting – he had painted the body, the shirt, the neck, and part of the face – but that someone else had completed it.
This was very exciting. The programme now had first-hand evidence that the painting was partly by Freud. So, they went back to Libby Sheldon, the expert in the scientific analysis of paintings, and asked her to see whether she thought it was possible that the painting had been made by two different people. After examining all the paint pigments and the brushstrokes, she had no hesitation in saying that she was absolutely certain that the painting was done by a single artist, so she thought that, as Freud admitted to having started it, then he must have finished it, too.
I Jon, what did you think when you heard the news that Freud had admitted to starting the painting?
J I could have fallen over backwards. It was one of those moments when I did the action you're told not to do. I looked off camera straight at the producer, who had been, who had become, actually, a friend and I was very close to at that stage, just looked at her in just utter disbelief that, that this had happened.
P Finally, after collecting together all the evidence they had uncovered, the programme asked three experts on Freud to give their verdict. The letter with their decision was opened live on camera at the end of the programme. And this is what they said…

---

d Get Sts to compare with a partner, and then play the audio again.

Check answers.

EXTRA SUPPORT Read through the script and decide if you need to pre-teach any new lexis before Sts listen.

2 The programme investigated who the subject of the painting was.
3 The programme found letters which confirmed the identity of *The Man in the Black Cravat*.
4 The painting was examined by an expert, who found a long hair embedded in it.
5 DNA analysis proved that the hair did not belong to Lucian Freud.
6 The programme discovered that Freud had admitted to his lawyer that he <u>had</u> started the painting.
7 Scientific analysis proved that the portrait had been painted by only one person.
8 The programme showed the evidence they had uncovered to three Freud experts.

Now ask Sts if they think the experts will say that the painting is genuine.

EXTRA SUPPORT If there's time, you could get Sts to listen again with the script on *p.137*, so they can see exactly what they understood / didn't understand. Translate / Explain any new words or phrases.

e 🔊 **7.11** Give Sts time to read questions 1–5. Make sure they understand *authentication* (= the act of proving that sth is genuine, real, or true).

Play the audio once the whole way through for Sts to listen and answer the questions.

Get Sts to compare with a partner, and then check answers.

EXTRA SUPPORT Read through the script and decide if you need to pre-teach any new lexis before Sts listen, but <u>not</u> the idiomatic expressions in **f**.

1 That the painting was by Lucian Freud
2 Because of his bad relationship with Denis
3 He loves it. It reminds him of Freud's early drawings. He loves the shadows and the exaggerated face.
4 No, he has always loved it, whether it was a fake or not. Because he has been given so many different opinions over the years as to whether it's a fake or not, but has always continued to love it whatever people said about it.
5 He is going to leave it to be sold after he dies and have the money go towards helping young artists.

🔊 **7.11**
(script in Student's Book on *p.137*)
P = presenter, E = expert, I = interviewer, J = Jon Turner
P Finally, after collecting together all the evidence they had uncovered, the programme asked three experts on Freud to give their verdict. The letter with their decision was opened live on camera at the end of the programme. And this is what they said…
E We believe this to be a work that Lucian Freud did at art school, most probably in nineteen thirty-nine.
I Jon, you must have been over the moon! Why do you think Freud denied that he had done the painting?
J I'm absolutely certain that the reason he denied having done the painting to other people was because the war that was going on between him and Denis Wirth-Miller. They fell out when they were aged, when he was seventeen and Miller, Denis Wirth-Miller was twenty-one or so, and there were times when they were together and it was OK. Denis was certainly a very, very difficult character.
I And regardless of the fact that it's by Freud, do you love the painting?
J That's – whether I love the painting or not – is a very interesting question because a lot of people, particularly on social media, when it was seen on the television, were saying, 'But it's hideous; it's absolutely terrible.' I love it. I've always loved it and particularly because it just clicked straight away with me that it was so like Freud's early drawings. I love the shadows; I love the way, the exaggerated face. Everything about it just appeals to me greatly.
I Would your feelings have changed if it had turned out not to be by Freud, or to be a fake?
J My feelings for the painting certainly wouldn't have changed if I'd found it wasn't a Freud, because it mustn't be forgotten that I have been at that stage for many occasions. I've been to meet people, very important people who've told me it is the most wonderful early Freud they've ever seen, and then snapped at me, saying it's a fake, three weeks later, with no explanation as to why we've gone from hot to cold. And, so, my emotions have gone really high, thinking, 'Wow I now know this is a Freud,' to absolutely crashing down to, saying it isn't. And I know from that that my emotion towards the painting has never changed.
I Would you ever sell it?
J What I'd always said that I was going to do with the canvas was put it into my estate and set up a trust to pay for people to go to the Royal College of Art. I was in a situation where there was no money for me to do further education. And I got a bursary, a state bursary, like a scholarship to go to the Royal College of Art, and that saw me through my time there, so it would seem appropriate that it should go towards helping someone who otherwise wouldn't be able to get there to do further education.
I Jon, thank you very much.

f 🔊 **7.12** Focus on the task and then play the audio for Sts to listen and complete the gaps. You could pause the audio after each extract to give Sts time to write.

Now put Sts in pairs and get them to discuss what they think the expressions mean.

Check answers. Remind Sts that *gobsmacked* and *clicked* are informal.

1 gobsmacked (= so surprised that you do not know what to say)
2 swept along (= very interested or involved in sth, especially in a way that makes you forget everything else)
3 biting [our] nails (= very nervous)
4 fallen over backwards (= fainted)
5 clicked (= suddenly became clear)

🔊 **7.12**
1
I Jon, what did you think when Libby Sheldon found a hair in the painting?
J I was absolutely gobsmacked. I hadn't even thought that there'd be a possibility that anything like that could exist.
2
I was very disappointed when I found that it wasn't a hair from Lucian Freud's head because I got swept along with adrenalin and excitement that goes with one of these TV shows.
3
So, we were all biting our nails at this moment, and as that, when that was delivered, none of us knew the result.
4
I Jon, what did you think when you heard the news that Freud had admitted to starting the painting?
J I could have fallen over backwards.
5
I've always loved it, and particularly because it just clicked straight away with me that it was so like Freud's early drawings.

EXTRA SUPPORT Check the answers first. Then put Sts in pairs and get them to discuss the meaning of each expression.

EXTRA SUPPORT If there's time, you could get Sts to listen again with script 7.11 on *p.137*, so they can see exactly what they understood / didn't understand. Translate / Explain any new words or phrases.

g Do this as a whole-class activity, or put Sts in pairs and then get some feedback.

6 SPEAKING

a Put Sts in pairs, **A** and **B**, and tell them to go to **Communication Which is the fake?**, **A** on *p.110*, **B** on *p.115*.

Go through the instructions and make sure Sts understand what they have to do. You could tell Sts before they start that the authentic painting is one of several that the Dutch painter Vincent van Gogh (1853–1890) made in the late 1880s of his bedroom in Arles, in France.

When Sts have finished, elicit the eight differences.

Differences in Sts Bs' painting:
1 A bottle / vase is missing on the small table.
2 The portrait of the blond man is a painting of a boat.
3 There is no door on the right.
4 The small chair by the window is missing.
5 There is an electric socket on the wall by the bed.

6 The red cover / blanket on the bed is blue.
7 One of the prints under the portraits is missing.
8 The middle coat on the rack by the bed is missing.

Finally, get Sts to vote with a show of hands for the painting that they think is the original.

A is the original.

Tell Sts to go back to the main lesson **7B**.

b Focus on the task. You may want to contrast the words *forgery*, *fake*, and *pirate* (*copy* / *version* / *edition*). Fakes and forgeries are similar – they're both made to look as much like the original as possible in order to mislead people. A forgery is usually money, a document, or a work of art, whereas a fake could be almost anything, including watches, handbags, sporting goods, etc. Pirate copies / editions are illegal copies which are sometimes obviously not the original, and are often DVDs, CDs, books, or downloads.

Put Sts in small groups and make it clear that they need to answer questions 1 and 2 for each of the items in the list.

Give Sts time to discuss the four questions. You could do questions 3 and 4 as a whole-class activity.

Monitor and help.

Get some feedback from various groups.

7 VOCABULARY colour idioms

Vocabulary notes
There are a lot of colour idioms in English, but, as with all idioms, it's important to be selective in teaching them. Some idioms can sound rather odd (for example, *I've got the blues* sounds normal in a song, but not in speech) or have a very particular register or meaning (*I was tickled pink* is normally used in a cheerful, humorous way about something small that made you happy, and is quite old-fashioned). Here the focus is on common, 'neutral' colour idioms which Sts will be able to use naturally.

a Focus on the task and remind Sts what an *idiom* is (= a group of words whose meaning is different from the meanings of the individual words).

Give Sts time to complete each idiom with a colour in the list. They could do this individually or in pairs.

Check answers.

1 blue   2 black   3 red   4 white   5 black, white   6 white
7 grey   8 red

b Put Sts in pairs and get them to discuss the meaning of each idiom.

Check answers.

1 **out of the blue** = suddenly, unexpectedly
2 **the black market** = an illegal form of trade in which foreign money, or goods that are difficult to obtain, are bought and sold
3 **red tape** = bureaucracy; official rules that seem more complicated than necessary and prevent things from being done quickly
4 **a white lie** = a harmless or small lie, especially one that you tell to avoid hurting sb

5 (**see everything in**) **black and white** = way that makes people or things seem completely bad or good, or completely right or wrong
6 **a white elephant** = a thing that is useless and no longer needed, although it may have cost a lot of money
7 **a grey area** = an area of a subject or situation that is not clear or does not fit into a particular group and is therefore difficult to define or deal with
8 **a red herring** = an unimportant fact, idea, event, etc. that takes people's attention away from the important ones

EXTRA SUPPORT You could do this as a whole-class activity.

c Focus on the task and give Sts time to choose four colour idioms from **a** and write true sentences about themselves or their country.

Put Sts in pairs and get them to compare their sentences. If Sts come from the same country and the sentences their partner wrote are about their country, they should say whether they agree or not.

Get some Sts to read their sentences to the class.

Lesson plan

In The Interview, the person interviewed is the artist and illustrator Quentin Blake, who is probably the best-known British illustrator of children's books. In this three-part interview, he talks about why he became an illustrator, the relationship between author and illustrator, and in particular his relationship with Roald Dahl, and how he goes about producing his illustrations. This is followed by a language focus on how Quentin Blake uses the verb *get*, which revises and extends what Sts learned in Lesson **3A**.

In The Conversation, Sts watch three people discussing whether the story or the illustrations are more important in an illustrated book. Sts then discuss this question, as well as two other questions related to the topic, focusing on adverbs and adverbial phrases.

More materials
For teachers
Teacher's Resource Centre
Video Colloquial English 6&7
Quick Test 7
File 7 Test
For students
Workbook Colloquial English 6&7
Can you remember? 6&7
Online Practice Colloquial English 6&7
Check your progress

OPTIONAL LEAD-IN (BOOKS CLOSED)

Write the following questions on the board:

DO YOU HAVE A FAVOURITE ILLUSTRATOR / CARTOONIST / CARTOON?

WHAT DO YOU LIKE ABOUT THEM?

Either get Sts to discuss the questions as a class, or put them in pairs and give them a few minutes to discuss the questions, and then get feedback.

Now tell Sts that they are going to watch an interview with a famous illustrator.

If you have internet access in your classroom or Sts have it on their phones, give them a few minutes to google Quentin Blake and find out a bit about him.

1 ▶ THE INTERVIEW Part 1

a Books open. Focus on the photo and the biographical information about Quentin Blake. Give Sts time to read it.

Do the questions as a whole-class activity.

> He has written books and produced art for galleries, museums, and hospitals.

EXTRA IDEA You may want to tell Sts to look at the book covers on *pp.16–17*, both of which are by Quentin Blake.

b Focus on the task and go through the **Glossary** with the class.

Play the video (**Part 1**) once the whole way through for Sts to do the task.

Give Sts time to tell each other what they understood. Check the answer.

EXTRA SUPPORT Before playing the video, go through the listening scripts and decide if you need to pre-teach / check any lexis to help Sts when they watch.

> To learn how to draw and do a lot of drawing

I = interviewer, Q = Quentin Blake
Part 1

I Would you describe yourself as an illustrator or as an artist?

Q I think those are two overlapping categories. I'm, I'm an artist and an illustrator, in the way that one might be an artist and a ceramic artist, or an artist and a sculptor, or something like that, so it's a department of being an artist.

I When did you decide to become an illustrator?

Q I don't think I ever quite decided to become an illustrator. I knew I wanted to draw, and I think I knew I wanted to draw situations. Um, I think it was… First of all, I knew that I could do pictures in magazines, and it was, I suppose, when I was about twenty-something – twenty-three, twenty-four – when I was finding my own way of drawing. I also wanted to get a book to myself, so that I could have the, not only do the drawings, but tell the whole story and design the book that in, in the way that I wanted to.

I And when did you realize that it was going to work out for you as a career?

Q Um, when I was twenty-something, when, no, uh, wait, a bit older than that, when I'd, when I'd left university and art school, I thought – I managed to get a book published in nineteen sixty, and written by John Yeoman, who's a friend, and he didn't know how to write a book and I didn't know how to illustrate it, but we got it published. And I thought, 'Well, I'll, I'll try keep – I'll try and keep on with this until I'm thirty, and if it's not working out, then I'll go back to teaching.' Um, and I got to thirty, but I passed thirty and I didn't notice!

I If a young person who was interested in becoming an illustrator, aged eighteen, say, asked you for any advice you could give them, what would you say?

Q They, they do ask me, actually; it's very, it's very, it's very touching they, they, they still come and say, some of them say, 'I'm doing it because of you,' and but also they, they ask that question. Um, and it's, it's – I mean, I really don't know the answer, but it must be something about drawing and doing a lot of drawing and a lot of different kinds of drawing because then you become completely familiar with the activity, and in a sense, that's the most important thing.

c Focus on the task and give Sts time, in pairs, to see if they can complete any of the sentences.

Play the video again the whole way through.

Get Sts to compare with their partner, and then check answers.

EXTRA SUPPORT You could pause the video after each point has been mentioned and, in pairs, get Sts to compare orally what they have understood.

1 …both an artist and an illustrator.
2 …was finding his own way of drawing and he wanted to illustrate his own book.
3 …had their first book published.
4 …young people ask him for advice.
5 …of him.

If there's time, you could get Sts to watch again with subtitles, so they can see exactly what they understood / didn't understand. Translate / Explain any new words or phrases.

d Do this as a whole-class activity, or put Sts in pairs and then get some feedback.

▶ Part 2

a Focus on the task and the **Glossary**.

Give Sts time to read sentences 1–8. Tell them the first time they watch, they just need to mark each sentence *T* (true) or *F* (False).

Play the video (**Part 2**) once the whole way through for Sts to do the task.

Get Sts to compare with a partner.

You could check answers now, so when Sts are watching again in **b**, they only need to correct the *F* sentences.

Part 2

I How important is the relationship between author and illustrator?

Q Well, in some respects, it has to be terribly important, I think! But it's, it's, um, the thing about it is, is initially, it's, um, collaboration very often isn't what people think it is. Um, you don't spend a lot of time talking much, 'Shall we do this? Shall we do that?' Shall we… ' and I, I never want to do that. Essentially, the collaboration, the relationship, is with the text to begin with, with the book to begin with, and you have to read that first and you have to keep collaborating with – those, those are the messages from the writer, that is the thing that you're dealing with. You may want to talk to the writer as well, but if, if the – if you can establish the, the relationship with, with the words, that's the, the important thing.

I Are there any authors to whom you did talk a lot?

Q With Roald Dahl, I think our view of things, in many respects, is very, very different, and I think we, we did talk a lot and we needed to talk. Um, but it was on the basis of what he'd written, initially, so that I would – the way of going about it, which we established after a while, was that I would draw some pictures of what I thought the characters looked like, and the moments that I thought would be useful to draw and interesting to draw, then I would go and talk to him about it, and he would say, 'Could you do this and could you do this? We need to see more tortoises,' you know, or something like that! But um, er, we talked quite a lot, again, some of it was about the, about the technicalities of the book, getting it to work better, I think. Um, but I think to get, to get into the mood of the book, which is a terribly important thing, it's something you have to do on your own, really, I think. The author can't tell you that.

I I can imagine that an author might ask an illustrator to redraw something. Does it ever work the other way round, that the illustrator asks the author to change things?

Q Er, it can do, yes. Actually, Roald volunteered to alter things; I didn't ask him to. I mean, in the case of *The BFG*, which we spent a long time working on, um, the BFG had a different costume to begin with. Er, he had a long leather apron and long boots, and that sort of thing. Of course, if you say an apron, when the character is introduced you say he was wearing an apron, and you don't talk about it after that probably. But I had to draw it in every wretched drawing – picture, picture that there is in the book! So, he – after a bit he said, 'This apron's getting in the way, isn't it?' because the chap has, you know, the giant has to run and it has to leap in the air, and so on and so on. So, we went back and talked about what he would wear, er, that would keep his character the same, but, um, and, and that – also what came out of that, we couldn't decide what to put on his feet. And I went home, and a day or two later arrived this strange brown paper parcel, which is – was one of Roald's own Norwegian sandals, and of course, that's – it solved the problem as far as what he wears is concerned, but in a funny way it also told you how near he was to his creation.

b Tell Sts that they will watch again and that this time, they need to correct the false sentences.

Play the video again the whole way through.

Get Sts to compare with a partner, and then check answers.

You could pause the video after each point has been mentioned and, in pairs, get Sts to compare orally what they have understood.

1 F (He says that the illustrator may want to talk to the author.)
2 T
3 F (He drew what he thought the characters looked like and then he would talk to Roald Dahl about it.)
4 F (He got into the mood of the books on his own.)
5 T
6 T
7 F (It got in the way / It was problematic.)
8 F (They were based on a pair of Roald Dahl's shoes.)

If there's time, you could get Sts to watch again with subtitles, so they can see exactly what they understood / didn't understand. Translate / Explain any new words or phrases.

c Do this as a whole-class activity, or put Sts in pairs and then get some feedback.

▶ Part 3

a Focus on the task and the **Glossary** and go through it with the class.

Give Sts time to read questions 1–7.

Now play the video (**Part 3**) once the whole way through for Sts to do the task.

Get Sts to discuss the questions and what they understood.

Then play the video again if necessary.

Get Sts to compare with a partner, and then check answers.

1 He has to be able to identify with them.
2 He identifies with them as he is drawing a character.
3 He never draws from life.
4 He drew on a screen in a TV studio about 40 years ago, but he no longer draws digitally.
5 He likes the way they feel on the paper.
6 They influenced him when he started drawing.
7 André François came to the exhibition.

Part 3

I Do you like all the characters you create in an illustration, or are some more interesting to you than others?

Q You have a sympathetic feeling for all of them, I think, but of course some are more interesting than others, I think! Um, that's not a question I've ever thought about, I don't think. Um, yes, I think some are more interesting, but I think the, the, the essence of that question, though I'm not sure I've got this right, is that you have to be able to – whether they're nice or not, or interesting or not – you have to be able to identify with them, um, so that you imagine, in a, some sense, as you're drawing, that you are them, and that's much more important than whether you're interested in them or like them.

I So you're not thinking of the children who are going to be reading the books?

Q What I'm interested in about children is children and about children in books, but I, I'm not illustrating children's books because I love children or because I have children, which I don't, or because, anything of that kind. What you have to do while you're illustrating that book is to identify with them for that moment, in the same way that that's how I know what they're doing, because I just become them for a moment, you know. In the same way that you become the elderly grandparent or you become the dog, or, or whatever the characters are!

I   Do you draw from life?

Q   I never draw from life, no, I make it all up. Um, and, um, I'm, I think I'm fortunate in that respect; I, I can imagine people. I do, I do a rough drawing first to see how, you know, where the gestures are, what the, what the, what the activity is, how the figures relate to each other, what the expressions on their faces are, so I get a rough drawing, and then I, I work from that. But, um, but I, I've mostly just invented.

I   Do you ever draw digitally?

Q   Digitally, curiously enough, I was probably one of the first people who did it, did it, because I did, um, like forty years ago, start – did drawing on a television screen, I mean, in a television studio, so that you could draw on the screen, but I haven't gone on with it. Um, I mean, I wouldn't mind doing it; the disadvantage to it from my point of view is that I like the feeling of the implement on the paper, so that it's, you get with, you know, if you have a quill or a nib or a reed pen, you get a different kind of scratch, but if you're inventing what is happening, the reed pen is actually doing it. It's, it's not copying something, it's actually creating it as you're going along, so that, it's the fact that you can feel it on the paper is enormously helpful.

I   Is there an artist or an illustrator that inspired you?

Q   Er, I mean, I was very influenced by a lot of, of, er, people who were drawing when I started drawing in the fifties, um, I mean, Ronald Searle, for instance, who was, was – who you couldn't avoid being influenced by to a considerable extent – but the person that I think most had an effect on me was a French artist, a contemporary and friend of Searle, André François. When I was a young man, I got his address and went to see him. And, um, then I suppose – but he, he died a few years ago; he was nearly ninety – but, um, just two or three years before that, I had an exhibition in Paris, and it was rather wonderful because he turned up. I mean, I didn't invite him – the gallery owner invited him – um, so it was nice that he hadn't forgotten who I was, exactly.

b   Now tell Sts they will watch again for more details.

Play the video again the whole way through.

Get Sts to compare with a partner, and then check answers.

EXTRA SUPPORT You could pause the video after each point has been mentioned and, in pairs, get Sts to compare orally what they have understood.

1   Some are more interesting than others. He has to imagine that he is them as he draws them.
2   He isn't illustrating children's books because he loves children, and he doesn't have children. He just identifies with them.
3   He invents everything he draws.
4   He wouldn't mind drawing digitally.
5   It helps him to feel the scratch the quills, nibs, and reed pens make.
6   Ronald Searle influenced him a lot in the 50s. André François is probably the artist who had the biggest effect on Quentin Blake. He died a few years ago.
7   The gallery owner invited André François to the exhibition.

EXTRA SUPPORT If there's time, you could get Sts to watch again with subtitles, so they can see exactly what they understood / didn't understand. Translate / Explain any new words or phrases.

c   Do this as a whole-class activity, or put Sts in pairs and then get some feedback.

2 ▶ LOOKING AT LANGUAGE

a   Focus on the **get** box and go through it with the class.

Now focus on the task and give Sts time to read extracts 1–7.

Play the video, pausing after each extract to give Sts time to write.

Get Sts to compare with a partner, and then check answers.

EXTRA CHALLENGE Ask Sts if they can guess any of the missing highlighted words before they listen to the extracts.

1 it published   2 to thirty   3 to work   4 into, mood
5 in, way   6 different kind   7 his address

1   …but we got it published. And I thought, 'Well, I'll, I'll try keep – I'll try and keep on with this until I'm thirty…'
2   Um, and I got to thirty, but I passed thirty and I didn't notice!
3   But, um, er, we talked quite a lot, again, some of it was about the, about the technicalities of the book, getting it to work better…
4   …but I think, to get, to get into the mood of the book, which is a terribly important thing…
5   So he – after a bit he said, 'This apron's getting in the way, isn't it?'
6   …if you have a quill, or a nib, or a reed pen, you get a different kind of scratch…
7   When I was a young man, I got his address and went to see him.

b   Put Sts in pairs and get them to say what each phrase means.

Check answers.

1   Someone published it for us.
2   I reached 30.
3   Making it more successful
4   Feel the atmosphere
5   Preventing sb from doing sth
6   Obtain a different sort of
7   I obtained his address.

3 ▶ THE CONVERSATION

a   Focus on the photo and tell Sts they are going to watch these three people discuss a question. Focus on the task and play the video, pausing after the title screen to give Sts time to read the question.

Then play the video once the whole way through.

Check answers.

EXTRA SUPPORT Before playing the video, go through the listening script and decide if you need to pre-teach / check any lexis to help Sts when they listen.

1 Christian   2 Debbie   3 Lucy

In an illustrated book, for example a comic, graphic novel, or children's book, which do you think is more important, the story or the illustrations?

Lucy   So, I'm a literature student, and I absolutely love books, um, especially classic novels, I absolutely love – and I grew up reading *The Hobbit* over and over again, and *Lord of the Rings*, and dreaming about the fantasy world and imagining what it looked like and I think that was the best part of it, for me, and I remember someone recommended me the graphic novel version of, um, *The Hobbit*, and to see how someone else had depicted it, and what they thought it looked like, almost ruined it for me, and I didn't enjoy it at all, because it takes the magic away of, like, imagination, which I think is really, really important.

But at the same time, I guess, I mean, being a child as well, you do love illustrations.

Christian Yeah, I mean…

Lucy They might be more digestible, so…

Christian I mean, that's the thing, like, if I was – when I was a kid if they had an amazing picture on the front, that's what I'd be like 'Mum, I need to have this book, like, because the picture's so good.' Um, I've, I grew up with dyslexia, so for me, like, reading was always something I struggled with but, um, I'd always have, when I was a kid, my mum would always read me stories, but I'd, um – so, it was always nice to have her reading it with the pictures.

Lucy Yeah.

Christian Um, I would say out of the two, the picture was the thing that I grabbed and be like 'Oh, this is what I want to read, or want to have read to me.' So, yeah.

Debbie I agree with both of you, um, I think it depends on the age of the child it's aimed at.

Christian Yeah.

Debbie If you're looking at pre-school children, I think pictures are vitally important because the story, whoever's reading it is going to bring it to life…

Christian + Lucy Yeah

Debbie …the voices or whatever, 'cause that's what mums do, and grandmas do. I think the picture is something they need to latch on to, like you're saying…

Christian Yeah.

Debbie …because they can't read it for themselves. I think they, they're less important as you get older, and I agree with you, thinking, I mean, I read the Harry Potter books, my boys read them and then I stole the books away from them. And the images that were in my mind when I was reading it were wonderful, and I'm so glad they weren't thrust upon me, …

Lucy Like the films.

Debbie …so much so –

Christian I was gonna say, it's like the films…

Debbie …but when the films came out, that's what was in my head. So, now I think it must have been so well written that everyone sees the same world, and that's quite an exciting thing, I think.

Lucy Yeah.

---

b Focus on the task and give Sts time to read questions 1–3. Play the video again the whole way through, pausing every so often to give Sts time to answer the questions. Play again as necessary.

Check answers.

> 1 She loved reading *The Hobbit* and *Lord of the Rings*. The graphic novel was disappointing because seeing how someone else showed the fantasy world ruined it for her.
>
> 2 He had dyslexia. His mum would read to him and he'd look at the pictures.
>
> 3 Pictures give children something to base things on when they can't read for themselves. The Harry Potter films showed the world just as she'd imagined it when reading the books.

EXTRA SUPPORT If there's time, you could get Sts to watch again with subtitles, so they can see exactly what they understood / didn't understand. Translate / Explain any new words or phrases.

c Do the questions as a whole-class activity, or put Sts in pairs and then get some feedback.

d This exercise focuses on adverbs and adverbial phrases which were used by the speakers. Focus on the extracts and give Sts time to read them.

Play the video, pausing after the first extract and replaying it as necessary. Elicit the missing words. Repeat for the other four extracts.

> 1 absolutely, especially   2 over and over again   3 at all
> 4 really, really   5 vitally

Then do the question as a whole-class activity, or put Sts in pairs and then check the answer.

They are used to add stress and emphasis.

1

Lucy So, I'm a literature student, and I absolutely love books, um, especially classic novels, …

2

Lucy …I absolutely love – and I grew up reading *The Hobbit* over and over again, …

3

Lucy …to see how someone else had depicted it, and what they thought it looked like, almost ruined it for me, and I didn't enjoy it at all, because it takes the magic away…

4

Lucy …it takes the magic away of, like, imagination, which I think is really, really important.

5

Debbie If you're looking at pre-school children, I think pictures are vitally important…

---

e Put Sts in small groups of three if possible. Focus on the questions and then give Sts time to discuss them.

Monitor and help, and encourage them to use the phrases in **d** if they want to add emphasis.

Get feedback from various groups. You could also tell the class what you think.

G advanced gerunds and infinitives
V health and medicine, similes
P /ə/

Lesson plan

In this lesson, the topic is health and medicine.

The first half starts with a quiz on medical vocabulary, which revises vocabulary taught in previous levels of *English File*. Then Sts read an article about treatments or habits that doctors themselves say they would never have or do, and discuss it. This is followed by a listening on five people's experiences of alternative medicine, and Sts then talk about their own experiences and opinions.

The second half of the lesson starts with a grammar focus on gerunds and infinitives, and Sts look at perfect, continuous, and passive gerunds and infinitives, and some new uses. They then listen to a radio interview with a public health scientist about 'social prescribing' – doctors encouraging patients to be more sociable and active instead of prescribing medication. Sts discuss the topic of the interview and whether their government gives advice about how to lead a healthy lifestyle. In Vocabulary, Sts learn some common similes and then end the lesson focusing on the /ə/ sound.

More materials
For teachers
Photocopiables
Grammar advanced gerunds and infinitives *p.181*
Communicative Medical vocabulary definitions game *p.207* (instructions *p.191*)
For students
Workbook 8A
Online Practice 8A

OPTIONAL LEAD-IN – THE QUOTE Write the quote at the top of *p.76* on the board (books closed) and the name of the person who said it, or get Sts to open their books and read it.

Point out that Mark Twain (1835–1910) is best known as the American author of *The Adventures of Tom Sawyer* and *Adventures of Huckleberry Finn*, but in his time was also known as a great humorist and was a popular public figure.

Ask Sts if they agree with the quote.

1 VOCABULARY health and medicine

Vocabulary notes

Sts who have used previous levels of *English File* will have met all the vocabulary in the quiz before. The aim in this section is not only to revise this vocabulary, but also to expand on it by getting Sts to contextualize and explain the lexis. For example, in explaining the symptoms of a cold or the flu, Sts need to know words and phrases like *a sore throat, sneezing, a high temperature / fever, aches and pains*, etc.

This expansion of vocabulary, and the ability to explain it and use it accurately in context, is very valuable at the Advanced level, and you should encourage Sts to ask for and note down any new vocabulary they need to answer the questions.

Give Sts time to read the quiz and make sure they understand all the lexis. Set a time limit (e.g. ten minutes) for Sts to discuss the questions in small groups of three or four.

Check answers, eliciting the meaning of the words and correcting pronunciation where necessary. Find out if any Sts got all the answers correct.

Suggested answers

1 a From a fall, being hit by sb, or knocking against sth, leaving you with a blue, brown, or purple mark
  b As an allergic reaction to sth, or with certain children's illnesses, such as measles. It is an area of red spots on the skin.
  c From walking a long way in uncomfortable shoes, or from wearing shoes that are too tight. It is a swelling on the skin filled with liquid.
  d From a drug that has an unwanted bad effect
2 a A plaster
  b Stitches
  c For a bacterial infection, you might be given antibiotics. For a viral infection (e.g. a cold, flu), there is often no treatment, except for throat sweets and painkillers.
  d An icepack, followed by a tight bandage and putting your foot up
  e Usually an X-ray followed by a plaster cast. If the break is serious, possibly surgery under anaesthetic to insert metal plates or rods.
3 a Sneezing, coughing, a runny nose, a sore throat
  b As for a cold, but also with a temperature / fever, and general aches and pains
  c Vomiting / Being sick, diarrhoea
  d Chest pain, arm pain, fast or irregular heartbeat, sweating, dizziness
  e Speech difficulty, weakness or loss of feeling in one arm, loss of feeling in one side of the face
4 a You might faint.
  b You might have an allergic reaction, get a rash, or your hand might swell up.
  c You might get hypothermia.
5 a For any non-emergency medical problem (*GP* = General Practitioner, i.e. a doctor who deals with general medical problems that don't require a specialist)
  b Because you have a medical problem that requires advice or treatment from a doctor who is an expert in that field.
  c If you need to have an operation. A surgeon is a doctor who performs operations.
  d If you need diagnosis, advice, or treatment for a mental health condition

2 READING identifying reasons and understanding explanations

a Focus on the task and make sure Sts understand all the lexis, e.g. *carb = carbohydrate*.

Put Sts in pairs and give them a few minutes to discuss whether they think doctors would or wouldn't do the things in the list.

Get feedback, asking Sts to give reasons for their opinions.

b Focus on the article and get Sts to read it once and complete headings A–G with a treatment or behaviour from **a**.

Check answers.

EXTRA SUPPORT Before Sts read the article the first time, check whether you need to pre-teach any vocabulary, but not the highlighted phrases.

A have a full health check
B go to the doctor with a long list of symptoms
C sunbathe
D take sleeping tablets
E follow a low-carb diet
F have cosmetic surgery
G see a counsellor

c Focus on 1–7 and tell Sts that these are the reasons given by the doctors. They must read the article again and match reasons 1–7 to paragraphs A–G.

Get Sts to compare with a partner, and then check answers.

1 D **2** B **3** E **4** F **5** A **6** G **7** C

LANGUAGE IN CONTEXT

d Focus on the task and put Sts in pairs to discuss the meaning of the **bold** verbs in the highlighted phrases.

Check answers.

1 **outweigh** /aʊtˈweɪ/ = are greater or more important than sth
2 **sink** /sɪŋk/ = move downwards
3 **underestimate** /ˌʌndərˈestɪmeɪt/ = think that the amount, cost, or size of sth is smaller than it really is
4 **wean themselves off** /wiːn ðəmˈselvz ɒf/ = make themselves gradually stop doing or using sth
5 **stuck to** /stʌk tə/ = continued doing sth despite difficulties
6 **be undertaken** /bi ˌʌndəˈteɪkən/ = be done
7 **varies** /ˈveəriz/ = changes or is different according to the situation

Deal with any other vocabulary problems that arose.

e Finally, focus on the discussion points. With a small class, you may want to do this as a whole-class activity. With larger classes, put Sts in small groups and give them time to discuss the points.

Get feedback from various groups.

3 LISTENING & SPEAKING

a Although Sts may have similar-looking words in their own language, they may find the English words tricky to pronounce. Focus on the words for alternative medicine, and start by eliciting or modelling the pronunciation. Then give Sts, in pairs, a few minutes to say what they think they all are.

EXTRA SUPPORT Do this as a whole-class activity.

Check answers.

acupuncture /ˈækjupʌŋktʃə/ = a Chinese method of treating pain and illness using special thin needles which are pushed into the skin in particular parts of the body
aromatherapy /əˌrəʊməˈθerəpi/ = the use of natural oils that smell sweet for controlling pain or for rubbing into the body during massage
chiropractic /ˌkaɪərəʊˈpræktɪk/ = treating some diseases and physical problems by pressing and moving the bones in a person's spine or joints
herbal medicine /ˈhɜːbl ˈmedsn/ = treating or preventing illness using extracts from plants and herbs
homeopathy /ˌhəʊmiˈɒpəθi/ = treating diseases or conditions using very small amounts of the substance that causes the disease or condition
hypnotherapy /ˌhɪpnəʊˈθerəpi/ = a treatment that uses hypnosis, i.e. putting people into an unconscious state, to help with physical or emotional problems
osteopathy /ˌɒstiˈɒpəθi/ = the treatment of some diseases and physical problems by pressing and moving the bones and muscles

Now ask Sts if they know any other alternative treatments.

b 🔊 **8.1** Focus on the task and the questions. Go through the **Glossary** with the class.

Play the audio once, pausing after each speaker for Sts to answer the questions. You could tell Sts to draw a chart, in order to make it easier for them to complete the task.

Get Sts to compare with a partner, and then play the audio again as necessary.

Check answers.

EXTRA SUPPORT Read through the script and decide if you need to pre-teach any new lexis before Sts listen.

Speaker 1 Yes, acupuncture for back pain. It was successful.
Speaker 2 Yes, herbal medicine for skin problems (tea). It was successful.
Speaker 3 No, she thinks it's a waste of time and doesn't work.
Speaker 4 Yes, hypnotherapy to stop smoking. It wasn't successful.
Speaker 5 Yes, aromatherapy for back and shoulder problems. It was successful.

🔊 **8.1**
(script in Student's Book on *pp.137–138*)
1 Tony
Well, I've had back pain for a while now, and I went to see a chiropractor, who did sort me out partially, but she also does acupuncture, and she said one day would I like to try it, and, well actually, to my surprise it seemed to do some good and for a few days it felt better. Now, I don't know whether it was a real effect or a placebo, but yeah, it did some good. I've had it three times now – I don't know if I'd call it a 'proper' therapy, but yeah, I, I think it worked, and the funny thing is, it's amazing she got me to go back because I have a complete phobia of needles.

2 Katie
So, I went to a Chinese medicine practitioner that I was recommended to me because I had some skin problems, and I went along and it was very nice, sort of a, very calm office – he seemed really professional, anyway. He prescribed me some herbal medicine, it was some tea – a Chinese tea made of bark and leaves and so on – and I had to boil it up three times a day and then drink the liquid, and the liquid just smelled revolting; it was really bad, made the whole house smell and it tasted even worse. It was really expensive as well, the consultations and the dead leaves, but I stuck to it for a few weeks. And I have to say, although I was very sceptical about it, I really do think it made a difference – didn't solve the problem completely, but it did actually improve the quality of my skin. So yeah, maybe I would try it again if I needed to.

3 Jen

I don't use alternative medicine, because I think it's a waste of time and it doesn't work. If alternative medicine worked, it wouldn't be alternative; it would be actual conventional medicine. The reason that it is alternative is because we don't have any solid proof that it works. You only ever hear anecdotal evidence that it's worked for individual people – that's not real evidence, and I would say to anyone who's heard stories like that, look up *the placebo effect*. There's no evidence that alternative medicine works beyond the placebo effect, and so, as far as I'm concerned, it's a waste of time and money, and at its worst, it could even be dangerous or harmful if people are using it in place of real medicine that might cure their very real illness.

4 Chris

My neighbour, who lives in the flat above me, is a homeopathic doctor and also a hypnotherapist, and at one point because I'd been trying to give up smoking for a long time, I decided to try hypnotherapy to see whether it would have any effect. I was pretty sceptical about the whole idea of hypnotherapy, but I very much like and respect my neighbour, so I thought, 'Why not give it a go?' Anyway, I went to her clinic and sat in a chair – there weren't any golden pendulums or anything like that, but she did tell me to close my eyes, and I suppose she asked me several questions or talked to me. But I didn't go into a trance; I was conscious all the time, and the one thing I remember is that she told me to imagine that I was in a forest, walking in a beautiful forest with lots of trees, and green trees, and then to imagine that the forest was slowly dying and that all the trees were dead wood, and that this was the effect that smoking was having on me, and that if I stopped, it would go back into the green beautiful forest that I'd imagined in the first place. Sadly, it had no effect on me whatsoever. Maybe if I'd believed in it – she said that anyway, I wasn't yet ready to stop smoking, so maybe that is the answer, but hopefully one day I will stop smoking.

5 Mary

So, I've used aromatherapy, which I have with a massage whenever I can, because I've got loads of back problems and shoulder problems. Anyway, with an aromatherapy massage, like, they use specific oils from plants which either relax you or they invigorate you, and I always go for the relaxing one because I think that's the whole point of a massage. And so they massage these plant oils and you breathe them in, and then they soak into your skin, and I am pretty sure, I'm, yeah, I'm certain that the oils makes a difference to the effectiveness of this treatment, or you know, it does for me. I don't know if that's a placebo or it's real, but, it's a question worth thinking about. Have I – I don't think anybody really knows; maybe there are some trials. I do know that recently there was a study by some university or, or other on the use of lavender oil for children, and they found that lavender oil really does have a big effect on them, helping them sleep better and on their behaviour – it improves behaviour in over-active children, apparently. So, you know, based on that evidence, I'd, I'd say it's a real therapy; it's just one that doctors don't prescribe, yet – normally, anyway.

c Give Sts time to read the questions.

Play the audio once or twice, pausing after each speaker for Sts to match the speakers and statements.

Check answers.

A Speaker 2 **B** Speaker 4 **C** Speaker 1 **D** Speaker 5
E Speaker 3

d 🔊 **8.2** Focus on the task and give Sts time to read extracts 1–4.

Play the audio, pausing after each extract for Sts to complete the expressions.

Get Sts to compare with a partner, and then check answers. Make sure Sts understand the meaning of the expressions.

1 made a difference **2** anecdotal evidence **3** give it a go
4 had no effect

🔊 **8.2**

1 …although I was very sceptical about it, I really do think it made a difference…

2 You only ever hear anecdotal evidence that it's worked for individual people…

3 …so I thought, 'Why not give it a go?'

4 Sadly, it had no effect on me whatsoever.

EXTRA SUPPORT If there's time, you could get Sts to listen again with script 8.1 on *pp.137–138*, so they can see exactly what they understood / didn't understand. Translate / Explain any new words or phrases.

e You may first like to tell Sts about any experiences you have had with alternative medicine and whether they were successful or not. Then put Sts in small groups to answer the questions.

Get feedback about any good / bad experiences.

4 GRAMMAR advanced gerunds and infinitives

a Do this as a whole-class activity, or put Sts in pairs and then check answers and get feedback.

1 to take **2** going **3** put on

b Focus on the task and give Sts time to write the verbs and verb phrases in the correct column. They could do this individually or with a partner.

EXTRA SUPPORT Tell Sts to do this in their notebooks, so that they end up with a correct list in their Student's Book.

To help Sts, you could tell them how many verbs / verb phrases are in each column: column 1 has eight verbs, column 2 has 13, and column 3 has three.

c 🔊 **8.3** Play the audio for Sts to listen and check. Check answers.

🔊 **8.3**

+ *to* + infinitive
afford, agree, happen, manage, pretend, refuse, tend, threaten
+ gerund
avoid, be worth, can't help, can't stand, deny, imagine, involve, look forward to, miss, practise, regret, risk, suggest
+ infinitive without *to*
had better, needn't, would rather

---

d Tell Sts to go to **Grammar Bank 8A** on *p.156*.

Grammar notes

At this level, Sts should be quite confident about whether they need to use a gerund or infinitive after many common verbs. Here Sts look at some more complex gerund and infinitive constructions (e.g. passive gerunds and perfect infinitives) and also some other uses of gerunds and infinitives not previously covered.

Different forms of gerunds and infinitives

• **Rule 1:**

You may want to remind Sts of the use of *get* instead of *be* in passive constructions, e.g. *I got injured* as an alternative to *I was injured*. See **Grammar Bank 3A**.

• **Rule 3:**

Point out that as well as *I would like to have seen the Eiffel Tower*, you can say *I would have liked to see the Eiffel Tower*.

Focus on the example sentences for **different forms of gerunds and infinitives** and go through the rules with the class.

Repeat for **other uses of gerunds and infinitives**.

Now focus on the **and + verb** box and go through it with the class.

Focus on the exercises and get Sts to do them individually or in pairs. If they do them individually, get them to compare with a partner.

Check answers after each exercise, getting Sts to read the full sentences.

a
1 I was really stupid **to have followed / to follow** my friend's advice.
2 I'd love **to have been** there when you told him you were leaving.
3 If I had a serious illness, I would prefer **to be told** the truth by my doctor.
4 It's no use **running**.
5 I'm not sure who **to ask** for help.
6 By the time I'm 55, I expect **to have saved** enough to be able to just work part-time.
7 The burglar denied **taking / having taken** the jewellery.
8 There will be plenty of time to have something **to eat** at the airport.
9 It's no good **calling** him because he's bound to have switched his phone off.
10 Who was the first woman **to win / to have won** a Nobel Prize?

b
1 We **don't have / haven't got enough time to** do any more shopping.
2 I **hate being woken up** suddenly.
3 **Do you regret not studying / not having studied** harder at school?
4 I love it when people help me in the kitchen **without (even) being asked / having been asked**.
5 I**'d loved to have been able to go to / 'd love to have gone to** your birthday party.
6 **The children seem to be having a good time**, don't you think?
7 My **hope is to have the operation** as soon as possible.

Tell Sts to go back to the main lesson **8A**.

If you think Sts need more practice, you may want to give them the **Grammar** photocopiable activity at this point.

e Put Sts in pairs, **A** and **B**, preferably face-to-face. Tell them to go to **Communication Guess the sentence**, **A** on *p.110*, **B** on *p.115*.

If your Sts are not familiar with this type of activity, you may want to demonstrate it. Write the following sentence on a piece of paper: *I would love to have gone to the concert last night, but I couldn't get a ticket.*

<u>Don't</u> show the sentence to Sts. Then write on the board:

I WOULD LOVE _____ THE CONCERT LAST NIGHT, BUT I COULDN'T GET A TICKET. (+)

Tell Sts that you have this sentence completed on a piece of paper and they have to guess what you wrote. Elicit possible completions with a positive verb. If Sts say something different from what's on your paper, e.g. *to have seen*, say 'Nearly. Try again' or give a clue until someone says the phrase *to have gone to*.

Now go through the instructions. Emphasize that Sts should write their ideas next to the sentence, but not in the gap, and only complete the gap when they have guessed the sentence correctly.

Monitor and help while Sts continue in pairs.

Tell Sts to go back to the main lesson **8A**.

5 LISTENING & SPEAKING understanding the results of research

a Focus on the task and make sure Sts understand what they have to do. You could elicit ideas for the first one by asking the whole class what kind of health benefits dancing might have, e.g. it might improve your fitness, help you to relax, etc.

Then put Sts in pairs and get them to discuss their ideas.

Get some feedback from various pairs.

b Give Sts time to read the extract from the news article and to answer the question.

Check the answer.

Telling people to take up hobbies and other activities rather than taking medicine

❗ Don't ask Sts their opinion on the advice given, as they will be doing this later in the lesson.

c 🔊 **8.4** Focus on the task and the **Glossary**.

Give Sts time to read health benefits A–G.

Play the audio for Sts to listen and match activities 1–7 in **a** to health benefits A–G.

You could pause the audio after each activity has been discussed, to give Sts time to do the matching task.

Check answers.

Read through the script and decide if you need to pre-teach any new lexis before Sts listen, but <u>not</u> the phrases in **e**.

A 2 cycling   **B** 7 knitting   **C** 5 gardening   **D** 3 yoga
E 4 golf   **F** 1 dancing   **G** 6 living with a pet

🔊 **8.4**
(script in Student's Book on *p.138*)
I = interviewer, M = Mark
I So, tell us what you think about it, we'd love to hear from you. Now, you may have heard in the news that the government has been consulting on ways to reduce dependence on prescription drugs, especially those which people take long-term, such as painkillers and antidepressants. Today we have Mark in the studio, and Mark's a research scientist – welcome – and you're going to tell us about something called 'social prescribing'…
M Hi, Liz. Thanks for inviting me on the show. Yes, so my area is public health research, and I've been working with the Department of Health on this issue. Of course, often patients do need to be prescribed drugs, but the concern is that too many people are getting them almost automatically, when in fact there may be other ways to deal with their health problems.
I Right.
M My research has shown that patients who take up social activities or hobbies are far less likely to need some types of prescription medicine, and obviously that's something we want to encourage. So this is what we're calling 'social prescribing', the idea that doctors will suggest to patients that instead of taking medicine, they take up a specific hobby or leisure activity that will improve their particular health issue.
I I see. So, what kind of things are we talking about?
M Well, different hobbies offer different health benefits. Let's take dancing. Dancing of any kind is good for both your fitness and

your mood, but a German study published last year showed that dancing regularly can also slow down brain ageing. In this study, volunteers took part in a dance class once a week for eighteen months. At the end of the eighteen months, the participants showed an increase in the area of the brain that plays an important role in memory and learning.

I Wow.

M So that's clearly something for people to consider as they get older. Another example: cycling. As we get older, the thymus – this is the organ which makes the so-called T-cells that we need to help us resist disease – starts to get smaller, to shrink. But it's now been shown that cycling can actually boost your immune system – recent research has found that the thymus in older cyclists produces as many T-cells as in young people.

I Fascinating. So dancing and cycling are both things that a doctor might consider prescribing for patients to increase their long-term health. Although both of those activities are fairly energetic, and not all patients would be able to do them…?

M Sure. So there's also yoga. It's well known that yoga can improve body flexibility and make you feel calm, but doing yoga regularly can also significantly reduce your blood pressure. It's the stretching and deep breathing that makes a significant difference. Doing yoga for fifteen minutes a day can reduce blood pressure by as much as ten per cent. Then there's golf – already a really popular sport, and there's now evidence that playing golf can actually help to offset the risk of getting diabetes and some types of cancer. In fact, golf can reduce your chances of developing up to forty chronic diseases. Research shows that golfers live longer and feel better than the general population.

I Well, that sounds very positive, but what about people like me who aren't so keen on sporting activities? What could doctors prescribe for them?

M Absolutely. Well, in terms of getting outdoors, how do you feel about gardening?

I Mmm, well, maybe…

M Researchers have repeatedly shown that doing things in the garden will lower levels of stress and anxiety. Looking after your plants for just half an hour a week can almost instantly reduce feelings of tension and fatigue, and make you less likely to suffer from depression. And another really effective thing is owning a pet. You get great exercise from walking a dog, but also, and rather surprisingly, living with a pet really helps reduce the likelihood of allergies. One study showed that stroking a dog for eighteen minutes a day makes a difference to how the body reacts to animals. Children who live with a pet are less prone to developing allergies such as asthma, because they are exposed to fur and animal saliva from a young age.

I And is there anything for the more creative types?

M Yes, one of the most intriguing findings is about knitting, which you might think is a rather old-fashioned hobby, but actually, it's now enjoying a bit of a comeback. A study at Harvard Medical School found that knitting lowers the heart rate by an average of eleven beats a minute, and another trial, involving women with eating disorders who were taught to knit, showed that seventy-four per cent of them said knitting helped them feel better about themselves. And I should just point out that it's not only about being a bit more active – most of the hobbies I've mentioned are things you can do with other people, which in itself has a beneficial effect on your health.

I Well, Mark, I'm totally convinced, so next time I go to the doctor, I'm hoping I'll get a prescription for a course of dance classes and some knitting needles!

M Exactly. Let's hope so…

d Focus on the task and give Sts time to read 1–7.

Play the audio again for Sts to listen and make notes. You could pause the audio after each item has been mentioned to give Sts time to write.

Get Sts to compare with a partner, and then play the audio again if necessary.

Check answers.

1 It causes an increase in the area of the brain that deals with memory and learning.
2 In older people, it produces as many T-cells as in young people.
3 The stretching and deep breathing make a big difference, and 15 minutes of yoga a day can reduce your blood pressure by 10%.
4 It reduces the risk of getting diabetes and some types of cancer; it reduces the chance of developing up to 40 chronic diseases.
5 Half an hour a week reduces tension and fatigue and makes you less likely to get depressed.
6 It makes a difference to how the body reacts to animals.
7 It helped them feel better about themselves.

LANGUAGE IN CONTEXT

e 🔊 8.5 Focus on the task and then play the audio for Sts to listen and complete the gaps in the highlighted phrases.

Put Sts in pairs and get them to discuss what they think each highlighted phrase means.

EXTRA SUPPORT Check the missing words first, and then put Sts in pairs to discuss what the highlighted phrases mean.

Check answers.

1 reduce **dependence on** = make less dependent on
2 **take up** social activities = start doing social activities
3 **plays** an important **role in** = is an important factor in
4 **reduce** blood pressure **by** = make blood pressure go down by
5 offset the **risk of** = do sth to counteract the risk of
6 **suffer from** depression = be ill with depression
7 **prone to** = likely to
8 beneficial **effect on** = a positive effect on

🔊 8.5
1 …the government has been consulting on ways to reduce dependence on prescription drugs…
2 …patients who take up social activities or hobbies are far less likely to need some types of prescription medicine…
3 …the participants showed an increase in the area of the brain that plays an important role in memory and learning.
4 Doing yoga for fifteen minutes a day can reduce blood pressure by as much as ten per cent.
5 …playing golf can actually help to offset the risk of getting diabetes…
6 Looking after your plants for just half an hour a week can almost instantly reduce feelings of tension and fatigue, and make you less likely to suffer from depression.
7 Children who live with a pet are less prone to developing allergies such as asthma…
8 …most of the hobbies I've mentioned are things you can do with other people, which in itself has a beneficial effect on your health.

EXTRA SUPPORT If there's time, you could get Sts to listen again with script 8.4 on p.138, so they can see exactly what they understood / didn't understand. Translate / Explain any new words or phrases.

f Put Sts in pairs to discuss the questions. You could answer some of the questions yourself.

Get some feedback from various pairs. If your Sts come from the same country, you could do the third group of questions as a whole class.

6 VOCABULARY & PRONUNCIATION

similes; /ə/

Vocabulary notes

These similes are all common fixed idiomatic expressions for comparison using either *as…as* or verb + *like*. Sts' languages may have some similar expressions, but the point of comparison may be different – for example, 'deaf as a post' in Spanish is *sordo como una tapia* (= deaf as a wall), 'sleep like a log' in Italian is *dormire come un ghiro* (= sleep like a dormouse), and 'blind as a bat' in Russian is 'blind as a mole'. You could point out that these similes tend to be quite informal, are often intended to be humorous or affectionate, and are best used with or about people you know well. As with all idioms, they shouldn't be overused.

a Put Sts in pairs to tell each other about people they know, giving as much information as possible.

Get some feedback from various pairs.

EXTRA IDEA Get Sts to do **a** and **b** in small groups.

b Focus on the **Similes for comparisons** box and elicit the pronunciation of *simile* /ˈsɪməli/. Go through the box with the class and highlight the meaning of the idioms:

- *as white as a sheet* = extremely pale
- *as quick as a flash* = extremely quickly
- *works like a dream* = works extremely well

You might want to tell Sts that similes are common, but they should take care not to overuse them.

Give Sts time to complete the similes in pairs.

EXTRA CHALLENGE You may want to teach Sts a few more common similes, e.g. *as smooth as silk, as cold as ice, as solid as a rock, as good as gold, fit like a glove, sleep like a baby*, etc.

Check answers, eliciting what each simile means.

1 stubborn (= very stubborn)
2 deaf (= can't hear at all)
3 blind (= can't see at all)
4 fit (= in very good physical condition)
5 thin (= extremely thin)
6 eats (= eats a lot)
7 good (= very well behaved)
8 tough (= very strong and able to deal successfully with difficult conditions or situations)
9 sleeps (= sleeps very well) (You may also want to teach the alternative simile *sleep like a baby*.)
10 drinks (= drinks a lot of alcohol)

EXTRA SUPPORT Go through the words in **bold** first to make sure Sts know what they all mean. A *mule* is an animal which has a horse and a donkey as parents. A *post* is a piece of wood set in the ground vertically, e.g. a lamp post or sth to support a fence. You may want to explain to Sts that in many similes, the **bold** words help with meaning, but occasionally the meaning is less obvious because it refers to an old-fashioned meaning (example: in *fit as a fiddle, fit* meant 'fit for purpose / suitable' and a *fiddle* (violin) is specially designed to make the sound).

c In their pairs, Sts now do **a** again, but this time using similes, as in the example.

Get some feedback from various pairs.

Pronunciation notes

As Sts should know at this level, /ə/ is the most common sound in English. /ə/ can be spelled by any vowel. It always occurs in unstressed syllables in multi-syllable words, e.g. <u>surgeon</u>, or it is the vowel sound in many unstressed words, such as articles, prepositions, *was / were, than*, etc.

Encouraging advanced Sts to make the /ə/ sound correctly is one way of instantly improving their sentence rhythm and general pronunciation, and making their speech sound more natural.

d Focus on the task and tell Sts they might find it easier if they say the sentence out loud to themselves.

e 🔊 **8.6** Play the audio for Sts to listen and check.

Get Sts to compare with a partner, and then check answers.

1 to, to, the, about, as, as, a
2 doctor, stubborn – the /ə/ sound is on the unstressed syllable.

🔊 **8.6**
See sentence in **d** in Student's Book on *p.79*

Get Sts to practise saying the sentence.

EXTRA IDEA Put Sts in pairs and get them to practise sentences 2–10 in **b**, focusing on the /ə/ sound.

f 🔊 **8.7** Focus on the task and play the audio, pausing after each sentence to give Sts time to write.

Get Sts to compare with a partner, and then play again if necessary.

Elicit the sentences onto the board.

🔊 **8.7**
a He's lost a lot of weight since September.
b It's about time he saw an optician.
c She never complains about taking her medicine.
d He's never had a problem with insomnia.
e My grandmother's ninety-four and never catches a cold.

Now get Sts to match each sentence to a simile in **b**. They could work individually or in pairs.

Check answers.

a He's lost a lot of weight since September. = 5 He's as thin as a rake.
b It's about time he saw an optician. = 3 He's as blind as a bat.
c She never complains about taking her medicine. = 7 She's as good as gold.
d He's never had a problem with insomnia. = 9 He sleeps like a log.
e My grandmother's 94 and never catches a cold. = 8 She's as tough as old boots.

Give Sts time to practise saying both the sentence and the simile. They could work individually or in pairs.

EXTRA IDEA Sts could write sentences for the other five sentences not covered on the audio, i.e. 1, 2, 4, 6, and 10.

G expressing future plans and arrangements
V travel and tourism
P homophones

Lesson plan

The topic of this lesson is travel and tourism.

In the first half, Sts begin by looking at photos and descriptions of six famous tourist attractions. Then they read an article about how underwhelmed some people were when they visited these places. This leads to vocabulary, where Sts learn new travel-related words and phrases. They then discuss places they have been to that have been a disappointment and also ones that were better than expected, as well as places they want to visit, and sights in their own area.

In the second half of the lesson, Sts listen to a story about a disastrous flight. Then they move on to the grammar, language for expressing future plans and arrangements, which is presented through extracts from the listening. The pronunciation focus is on homophones (words pronounced the same but spelt differently, e.g. *site* and *sight*). In the Video Listening, Sts watch a documentary about Cornwall and Belfast, two places that have to deal with the positive and negative effects of tourism. The lesson ends with a writing focus on a discursive essay, in which the writer argues in favour of or against a statement – in this case, the topic is tourism.

More materials
For teachers
Photocopiables
Grammar expressing future plans and arrangements *p.182*
Communicative Travel role-plays *p.208* (instructions *p.191*)
Vocabulary Travel and tourism *p.226* (instructions *p.215*)
For students
Workbook 8A
Online Practice 8A

OPTIONAL LEAD-IN – THE QUOTE

Write the quote at the top of *p.80* on the board (books closed), or get Sts to open their books and read it.

Ask Sts whether they agree with the proverb.

1 READING identifying negative reactions

a Do this as a whole-class activity, or put Sts in pairs and then check answers and find out what else Sts know about the places.

! Don't ask Sts if they have been to any of the places, as they will be doing this later in the lesson.

1 New York, USA **2** Copenhagen, Denmark **3** Peru
4 Hawaii, USA **5** South Dakota, USA **6** Bolivia

b Focus on the title of the article, and ask Sts *If someone asked that question about a famous monument, what would it imply that they felt about it?* (That they were unimpressed.) Then give Sts time to quickly read the article and match each comment to a photo in **a**.
Check answers.

EXTRA SUPPORT Before Sts read the article the first time, check whether you need to pre-teach any vocabulary, but not the highlighted expressions or the words focused on in **2a** or **b**.

A 3 **B** 4 **C** 1 **D** 6 **E** 2 **F** 5

c Focus on the task and give Sts time to read the article again and answer the questions. Tell them to use their own words when answering the questions, and not just lift chunks of text.

Get Sts to compare with a partner, and then check answers.

A It was just big stones.
B It was empty and soulless; there was no white sand, but had tacky hotels.
C There were long queues to get in and go up. You can't see the iconic building because you're on it.
D It was not remote, but near the shore, run-down, and local people don't want tourists there.
E It is a long way from the city centre, surrounded by tourists, small, and unimpressive.
F It is very boring – just flat, with trees on the top of the mountain.
The only positive comment is about Machu Picchu: breathtaking location, beautiful hill behind.

LANGUAGE IN CONTEXT

d Focus on the task and tell Sts to try to work out the meaning from the context before matching the highlighted expressions to meanings A–F.

Get Sts to compare with a partner, and then check answers.

A 4 **B** 5 **C** 6 **D** 1 **E** 3 **F** 2

EXTRA SUPPORT Get Sts to work in pairs.

Deal with any vocabulary problems that arose.

e Focus on the task and give Sts time to complete the comments with the places or things in the photos.

Get Sts to compare with a partner, and then check answers. You might want to point out that *bathroom* in 5 means *toilet* and is commonly used in American English.

1 the Sphinx **2** The *Mona Lisa* **3** Stonehenge
4 the Australian Outback **5** Times Square on New Year's Eve

Deal with any vocabulary problems that arose.

f Do this as a whole-class activity, or put Sts in pairs or small groups and then get some feedback. If you have been to any of the places mentioned, you could tell the class what you thought.

2 VOCABULARY travel and tourism

a Do this as a whole-class activity.

imposing = impressive to look at

b Do this as a whole-class activity, or put Sts in pairs and then check answers. Elicit or model their pronunciation. Point out that *tacky* is informal.

breathtaking: positive – very impressive or exciting; to describe, e.g. a view, an experience
iconic: positive – acting as a classic symbol of sth; to describe, e.g. a building, a painting
run-down: negative – in very bad condition; to describe, e.g. a building, an area in a city
soulless: negative – depressing; to describe, e.g. a city, a building, a monument
tacky: negative – cheap and lacking in taste; to describe, e.g. souvenirs, a hotel or restaurant

Get various pairs to give examples of a place or thing for each adjective.

c Tell Sts to go to **Vocabulary Bank Travel and tourism** on *p.170*.

Vocabulary notes
Describing places
Highlight that *off the beaten track* comes from the idea that the *beaten* (i.e. flattened by thousands of footsteps) *track* is the road where many people walk. A place which is *off the beaten track* is away from where most people go and is therefore more remote, unspoilt, etc.

With the negative adjectives, remind Sts of the meaning of the prefix *over* (= too much) in *overcrowded* and *overrated*.

Verb phrases
Make sure to also highlight the synonyms in 1, 5, 7, and 8, e.g. *set out*, etc.

Focus on **1 Describing places** and get Sts to do **a** individually or in pairs.

🔊 **8.8** Now focus on **b**. Play the audio for Sts to listen and check.

Check answers.

🔊 **8.8**
Travel and tourism
1 Describing places
1 The view is absolutely breathtaking.
2 It's a really **lively** area at night.
3 We found a tiny café in the back streets of Venice, right **off the beaten track**.
4 We went to a very **picturesque** little fishing village yesterday.

5 It's a lovely city, almost completely **unspoilt** by tourism.
6 The site of the temple is extremely **remote** – you can only get there on foot and it takes four hours.
7 The enormous statue at the entrance to the palace is very **imposing**.
8 The Leaning Tower of Pisa is one of Italy's most **iconic** sights.
9 I think that restaurant's **overrated**.
10 The museum's pretty **dull**, but the café's good.
11 The shops are quite **touristy**, but we bought some nice things.
12 The seafront has been **spoilt** by all the new hotels.
13 The hotel pool is always **overcrowded**.
14 The souvenirs were all plastic Eiffel Towers and key rings, really **tacky** stuff.
15 The main square is quite smart. But the buildings behind are very **run-down**.
16 The old town has a lot of character, but the modern part of the city is mainly **soulless** office blocks.
17 The hotel breakfast was a bit **pricey**, but it was worth it.
18 The hotel entrance is **unimposing**, but the lobby inside is spectacular.

Highlight any words your Sts may have problems pronouncing correctly, e.g. *picturesque* /ˌpɪktʃəˈresk/.

Focus on **2 Verb phrases** and get Sts to do **a** individually or in pairs. You might want to remind Sts that *SYN* stands for *synonym* and *IDM* stands for *idiom*.

🔊 **8.9** Now focus on **b**. Play the audio for Sts to listen and check.

Check answers.

The three idioms mean:
hit the shops = go shopping as a fun / leisure activity
get away from it all = to have a holiday in a place where you can really relax
recharge your batteries = to get back your strength and energy by having a holiday

🔊 **8.9**
2 Verb phrases
1 set off on a journey
2 **extend** a trip
3 **go** camping
4 **go on** holiday
5 **postpone** a trip
6 **wander round** the old town
7 **chill out** after a tiring day
8 **soak up** the atmosphere
9 **sample** the local cuisine
10 **hit** the shops
11 **get away** from it all
12 **recharge** your batteries

Now either use the audio to drill the pronunciation of the verb phrases, or model and drill them yourself. Give further practice of any words your Sts find difficult to pronounce. You might want to highlight that the *t* in *postpone* /pəˈspəʊn/ is silent.

Focus on **Activation** and give Sts time to think about places in their country that could be described using the adjectives in **1**, and verb phrases in **2** that could be used to describe their last holiday. As there are 18 adjectives in **1**, you might want to suggest that Sts choose ten only.

Put Sts in pairs and get them to tell each other about the places they thought of and their last holiday.

Get some feedback.

Tell Sts to go back to the main lesson **8B**.

3 SPEAKING

Give Sts time to look at the questions and think of their answers. Make it clear that in the first section, the five questions with bullet points (*Where was it?*, etc.) should be answered for both of the options above (a disappointing place and a wonderful place).

Put Sts in pairs and get them to talk to their partner.

Get some feedback from various pairs. If your Sts come from the same area, you could do the last two groups of questions as a class. You could also ask Sts if concerns about the environmental impact of flying have changed their attitudes to travel or long-distance tourism, either in general or for themselves personally.

4 LISTENING & SPEAKING understanding an anecdote

a Focus on the task and the words. Elicit / Explain that Gatwick Airport is a major international airport near London. You may want to tell Sts that Clive is one of the co-authors of *English File*, and this is a true story.

Elicit some ideas about where Clive was travelling to, why, and the kind of problems he might have had.

b ◉ **8.10** Focus on the task and on the **Glossary**.

Tell Sts that they are going to hear the story in four parts, and after each part they will answer questions and predict what happens next. Play **Part 1** of the audio once the whole way through.

Get Sts to retell the story so far, using the words in **a**.

Elicit what Sts think is going to happen next.

◉ **8.10**

(script in Student's Book on *p.138*)

CN = Clive narrating, C = Clive, K = kids, MA = Maria Angeles, A = announcer

CN *So I was living in Spain at the time, and I was travelling back from Spain to the UK with my wife and two young children. It was two days before Christmas, and we were travelling back to London to visit my family there, it was an evening flight, from Valencia to London Gatwick.*

C Come on, kids, are you nearly ready? We're leaving for the airport in fifteen minutes.

K Coming, Daddy!

MA What time do we need to check in?

C Well, the flight leaves at ten fifteen. Don't worry, we've got plenty of time.'

A Departure for flight Iberia 6845 - please passengers proceed to gate number A6.

CN *The weather in Spain was really good, but just before we were going to take off, I was just reading my messages at the last minute, and I saw there was a message from my brother, Russ.*

C Oh look, there's a message from Russ – oh, he's asking whether the flight's been cancelled – apparently, there's a really bad storm in London, with gale-force winds.

MA Oh, really? That doesn't sound good.

C I know. Anyway, we're about to take off. I'll let him know we're already on the plane.

CN *So we took off, but obviously, we were a bit worried about what the weather was going to be like when we got there. It was a two-hour flight, and everything was fine until we were approaching Gatwick, when the pilot made an announcement.*

---

c ◉ **8.11** to ◉ **8.13** Give Sts time to read questions 1–6, making sure they understand all the lexis, e.g. *started circling*.

◉ **8.11** Play **Part 2** of the audio once the whole way through for Sts to listen and answer the questions.

Get Sts to compare with a partner.

Check answers 1–6 and elicit their ideas in response to the question in **bold**.

1 He warned them about the windy weather at Gatwick Airport, and the fact that it might be quite bumpy.
2 There was terrible turbulence, and the plane was dropping down and rising again.
3 They could see that the wind was very strong, and the wings were moving up and down.
4 They all thought they were going to crash.
5 The plane suddenly went up again.
6 That the wind made it too dangerous to land, and that all the airports in the UK were now closed.

◉ **8.11**

(script in Student's Book on *pp.138–139*)

P = pilot, CN = Clive narrating, Pa = passenger

P Ladies and gentlemen, this is your pilot speaking. We're about twenty minutes from Gatwick, but unfortunately, we can't land yet because we've been told that there's really windy weather there, so we're going to circle for a while and assess the situation. Please make sure that your seatbelts are fastened, as it may be a bit bumpy.

CN *So the plane started circling, and then we started getting the worst turbulence I've ever, ever experienced. The plane just seemed to be going up in the air, then dropping down, then rising up again, then dropping.*

P Ladies and gentlemen, thank you for your patience. We're going to attempt a landing now.

CN *We could see now that the wind was incredibly strong – we could see the wings of the plane moving up and down out of the window. I'm sure everyone on the plane was thinking the same thing: 'He's never going to be able to land the plane. We're going to crash.'*

Pa We're going to crash!

CN *Then just at the very last moment, the pilot obviously realized that it was impossible to land, and he changed his mind and the plane suddenly rose back up into the air.*
It was an absolutely terrifying moment. The plane just kept climbing and climbing, going further and further away from the airport. Then the pilot made another announcement.

P Ladies and gentlemen, well, I'm very sorry, but it was too dangerous to land; it was too windy, and I'm afraid we can't land at Gatwick now because the airport's been closed. In fact, I have to tell you that we can't land anywhere in the UK because all the airports are closed.

◉ **8.12** Repeat the same process for **Part 3**.

7 In Paris
8 Amsterdam, Schiphol Airport
9 Because it was less windy than at Gatwick
10 They stood up and started to get their things from the overhead lockers.
11 That the flight was going to refuel and then go back to Gatwick
12 To stay on the plane or to get off

◉ **8.12**

(script in Student's Book on *p.139*)

MA = Maria Angeles, C = Clive, CN = Clive narrating, P = pilot,
Pa = passengers, CC = cabin crew

MA So, where are we going to land if the airports are closed?

C I've no idea – maybe Paris?

MA Paris?! What if we don't have enough fuel to get there?

CN *Then the pilot made another announcement.*

P Ladies and gentlemen, we're going to try to land at Amsterdam because the weather conditions there are a little better, so we're heading towards the Netherlands now. We're due to land at Schiphol in approximately one hour.

CN *After that, we had about an hour's journey to Holland. That was OK – fairly normal – and then as we got closer to Amsterdam, the pilot came back on again.*

P Good evening, everyone. We'll be landing shortly at Schiphol Airport. It's going to be a bit windy here, too, but not as bad as at Gatwick, you'll be happy to hear.

Pa Thank goodness!

CN *And it was quite a good landing – a little bit bumpy – but everyone was very, very relieved to get down on the ground. And we all started getting up – to be honest, we couldn't wait to get off, to get our feet back on firm ground again – and we got up and we started to get all our things from the overhead locker. But then there was another announcement…*

CC Your attention, everyone. We aren't going to disembark here in Amsterdam. We're going to refuel, and then we'll be flying back to the UK, because we've been told that in a couple of hours, the weather may be a bit better at Gatwick.
…However, ladies and gentlemen, if you want to get off, you can get off, but unfortunately, there won't be a hotel for you to stay at tonight, because this plane's travelling back to Gatwick.

🔊 **8.13** Repeat the same process for **Part 4**.

13 Because they didn't want to be stuck in Amsterdam over Christmas.
14 They got off the plane.
15 They spent the night at the airport, then got a train to Belgium, and took the Eurostar from Brussels to London.
16 At 7.00 p.m. on Christmas Eve

🔊 **8.13**
(script in Student's Book on *p.139*)

CN *So basically, then everyone had a dilemma – to stay on the plane or to get off and spend the rest of the night in Amsterdam.*

C What do you want to do? Get off here? Or try getting back to London tonight? To be honest, I think we should get off.

MA Yes, absolutely, let's get off now – I don't want to be on this plane a minute longer. Come on, kids, get your things.

CN *More or less everyone with children got off the plane, but a lot of the passengers stayed on board. I suppose for some people, the idea of being stuck in Amsterdam on Christmas Eve was even worse than flying back to Gatwick and trying to land again. But personally, we were really happy to get off that plane, and we spent the night in Amsterdam airport, then in the morning we got a train from Amsterdam to Belgium. In Brussels, we picked up the Eurostar, and that took us through France, under the Channel, and safely back to London. So, after travelling all day, we finally got to my parents' house at around seven o'clock in the evening on Christmas Eve, just in time for the children to hang up their stockings. That flight was definitely the most frightening experience I've ever had.*

EXTRA SUPPORT If there's time, you could get Sts to listen again with the scripts on *pp.138–139*, so they can see exactly what they understood / didn't understand. Translate / Explain any new words or phrases.

d Do this as a whole-class activity, and tell Sts what you think you would have done.

e Focus on the task and the plan for telling the story.

Give Sts time to try to think of a journey and make a few notes. Stress that it doesn't need to be a flight or long journey – it could just be a short journey to work or school, or to visit friends or family, as long as something bad happened.

If you have a good story, tell Sts. Then put them in small groups and get them to tell each other their stories.

Encourage Sts to listen 'actively' and interact with the person telling the story with exclamations and further questions.

Get some feedback from various groups.

5 GRAMMAR expressing future plans and arrangements

a 🔊 **8.14** Focus on the task and then play the audio, pausing after each extract to give Sts time to write. Check answers.

1 're leaving **2** leaves **3** to take off **4** 're going to try
5 to land **6** 'll be landing

🔊 **8.14**
1 …are you nearly ready? We're leaving for the airport in fifteen minutes.
2 …the flight leaves at ten fifteen. Don't worry, we've got plenty of time.
3 Anyway, we're about to take off.
4 …we're going to try to land at Amsterdam.
5 We're due to land at Schiphol in approximately one hour.
6 Good evening, everyone. We'll be landing shortly at Schiphol Airport.

b Put Sts in pairs to discuss whether any other forms could be used in the sentences in **a**.
Check answers.

1 're going to leave, 'll be leaving **4** 're trying
6 're going to land

EXTRA SUPPORT Do this as a whole-class activity.

c Tell Sts to go to **Grammar Bank 8B** on *p.157*.

Grammar notes

Sts should be very familiar with the different verb forms used to express future plans and arrangements. Here they are pulled together and contrasted. Other ways of expressing this aspect of the future, such as *be due to* and *be about to*, may be new for Sts.

Advanced Sts should now realize that in any given situation, there are often several different ways of expressing a future plan or arrangement. The form we use depends on many factors, including how we view the future event, how we feel about it, and how fixed or definite it is. For example, in the section of the **Grammar Bank** about 'other ways of expressing future arrangements', sentence 1 (*My sister is due to arrive*) could also be *My sister arrives / is arriving / is going to arrive / will be arriving*, depending on our personal 'view' of the event. At this level, Sts should be becoming more comfortable with these options, and the idea that there isn't only one 'answer'.

Focus on the example sentences for **present and future forms** and go through the rules with the class.

Now focus on the ***be going to* or the present continuous?** box and go through it with the class.

Repeat for **other ways of expressing future arrangements**.

Focus on the exercises and get Sts to do them individually or in pairs. If they do them individually, get them to compare with a partner.

Check answers after each exercise, getting Sts to read the full sentences.

> **a**
> 1 be having   2 going to watch   3 going to ask   4 ✓
> 5 ✓   6 I'll be wearing   7 ✓   8 ✓   9 ✓   10 closes
> **b**
> 4 no difference
> 5 *is due to arrive* is more formal
> 7 *is to open* is more formal
> 8 *I'll be writing up* implies it's sth you know will happen, but that you've probably not planned yourself. *I'm going to write up* implies you've planned it.
> 9 no difference
> **c**
> 1 **We're about to leave**.
> 2 **Her new album is due to be released** next month.
> 3 **Will you be going to the canteen at lunchtime**?
> 4 **The ministers are on the point of signing** a new agreement.
> 5 **The manager will be responding to your complaint** in the near future.
> 6 **Are you going to meet us** at the hotel?

Tell Sts to go back to the main lesson **8B**.

EXTRA SUPPORT If you think Sts need more practice, you may want to give them the **Grammar** photocopiable activity at this point.

6 PRONUNCIATION homophones

Pronunciation notes
Homophones are words with different meanings and spellings, but the same pronunciation (e.g. *wait* and *weight*). Even at this level, Sts often doubt whether two words are pronounced exactly the same when their spelling is different. Homophones may also occasionally cause confusion for Sts when they hear one word but imagine that they have heard the other.

a 🔊 **8.15** Focus on the **Homophones** box and go through it with the class, stressing that the pronunciation of the words is <u>identical</u>.

Focus on the task and make sure Sts understand what they have to do.

Put Sts in pairs, give them time to look at the phonetics in 1, then play the audio, pausing after each pair of sentences to give Sts time to write.

Repeat the process for 2–10.

Check answers, getting Sts to spell the words.

1	**a** wait	**b** weight
2	**a** board	**b** bored
3	**a** piece	**b** peace
4	**a** caught	**b** court
5	**a** brake	**b** break
6	**a** fair	**b** fare
7	**a** plane	**b** plain
8	**a** through	**b** threw
9	**a** site	**b** sight
10	**a** suite	**b** sweet

🔊 **8.15**
1 **a** We've got a three-hour wait before the flight leaves.
  b What's the maximum weight for hand luggage on this flight?
2 **a** Flight EZ four seven two is now ready to board. Will passengers please proceed to Gate ten.
  b We're bored! We don't want to visit any more museums!
3 **a** Where's the piece of paper with the address of the hotel?
  b We're going off the beaten track for a bit of peace and quiet.
4 **a** There was terrible traffic on the way to the airport and we only just caught the flight.
  b It's a four-star hotel and it's even got a tennis court.
5 **a** The airport bus had to brake suddenly when a lorry pulled out.
  b We're going to break the journey in Milan.
6 **a** My ticket cost twice as much as yours. It's not fair!
  b How much is the airfare to Peru?
7 **a** The pilot landed the plane very smoothly, and everyone clapped.
  b The cabin crew uniform is a dark blue suit with a plain white shirt.
8 **a** When we arrived in the States, it took us ages to get through Immigration.
  b They threw away my perfume at security because it was two hundred mill.
9 **a** We visited an archaeological site on the banks of the Nile.
  b My first sight of the Pyramids completely took my breath away.
10 **a** The hotel gave us the honeymoon suite – it was the only room available!
  b I don't like the local white wine. It's too sweet for me.

EXTRA CHALLENGE Elicit other meanings for the following words:

board:
as a noun = in a classroom, a whiteboard or blackboard; a large piece of strong, hard material, especially wood, used, for example, for making floors or building walls and roofs; a group of people who have power to make decisions and control a company or other organization

as a verb = to live and take meals in sb's home, in return for payment; to live at a school during the school year

fair:
as a noun = an entertainment or event where people can go on rides and play games

as an adjective = pale in colour for hair or skin; bright and not raining for weather

as an adjective or adverb = according to the rules; in a way that is considered to be acceptable and appropriate, e.g. *The punishment was fair*.

court:
as a noun = the place where legal trials take place and where crimes, etc., are judged; a large open section of a building, often with a glass roof, e.g. *a food court*

b Put Sts in pairs, **A** and **B**. Sts **B** (books closed) listen to Sts **A**, who say homophones 1–5, and Sts **B** must give both spellings and meanings. Then Sts swap roles and Sts **B** say 6–10.

c 🔊 **8.16** Focus on the task and explain to Sts that the sentences include the homophones in **a** in the same order.

Play the audio, pausing after each sentence to elicit whether Sts heard word **a** or **b** from the sentences in **a**.

> 1 a 2 b 3 b 4 a 5 b 6 a 7 b 8 a 9 b 10 b

◀)) 8.16

1 We had to queue for ages to get in, but it was worth the wait.
2 Don't forget to take your iPad, or you'll be bored on the journey.
3 We couldn't get any peace on the flight because we were sitting next to a crying baby.
4 I caught a terrible stomach bug while I was on holiday in India.
5 We're going on a city break to Prague in April.
6 I think it would be fair if we split the cost.
7 The hotel food was rather plain, but delicious nevertheless.
8 Please could you come through here, Sir, and open your suitcase?
9 I've never been to Paris, so I'm looking forward to seeing the sights.
10 It was a wonderful trip – short but sweet.

EXTRA CHALLENGE You could ask Sts if they know any more homophones, e.g. *sent / cent / scent*; *flower / flour*; *waste / waist*; *new / knew*; *aloud / allowed*, etc.

7 ▶ VIDEO LISTENING

a Focus on the task and do the questions as a whole-class activity, or put Sts in pairs and then get some feedback. You could also answer the questions yourself.

b Tell Sts they are going to watch a documentary about screen tourism. You could tell them that Cornwall is a county in the far south-west of England. Then give Sts time to read items 1–10, making sure they understand all the lexis, e.g. *infrastructure*.

Play the video once the whole way through for Sts to watch and answer the questions.

Get Sts to compare with a partner, and then play again if necessary.

Check answers.

EXTRA SUPPORT Read through the script and decide if you need to pre-teach any new lexis before Sts watch the video.

1 Porthcurno Beach is a *Poldark* location, and lots of people visit the beach because they've seen the TV series.
2 The '*Poldark* Effect' has greatly increased tourist numbers in Cornwall.
3 The National Trust owns Porthcurno Beach.
4 The Cornish economy depends very heavily on the tourism industry, which brings in £2 billion a year.
5 500,000 people visit Charlestown every year.
6 High visitor numbers put pressure on the local infrastructure, especially roads and beaches.
7 Northern Ireland is one of the principal locations for *Game of Thrones*.
8 Political violence in the past meant that Northern Ireland wasn't a tourist destination.
9 The Northern Irish Government contributed £9 million to the building of Titanic Studios, and *Game of Thrones* has since brought £65 million into Northern Ireland.
10 *Outlander* and *Downton Abbey* are other TV programmes which have had a similar effect to *Poldark* and *Game of Thrones* (in Scotland and at Highclere Castle).

Following in their footsteps: the pros and cons of screen tourism

N = narrator, S = Simon Hocking, I = Ian Lay, T = Tania Plowright,
H = Huey Park, J = Jessica Lawrence, B = Bridgeen Barbour

N *This is Porthcurno Beach in Cornwall. On this breathtaking beach, we are almost at the south-western tip of England. It may not look like it today, but this beach has always been popular with visitors, and tourist numbers have increased over the past few years because it is one of the many locations used in the hugely successful British TV series,* Poldark. Poldark *is a period drama, set in the late eighteenth and early nineteenth centuries. It follows the fortunes*

of the determined Cornish landowner, tin miner, and farmer, Ross Poldark, and his charming and courageous wife, Demelza. The series was watched by as many as five million people in the UK and many millions more around the world, and the 'Poldark Effect' has had a striking impact on tourism numbers in Cornwall. But for Porthcurno Beach, and indeed for other Poldark *locations, there are both pros and cons. Whilst visitors may rave about the beach on social media, there are some local people who are less keen on the sudden influx of tourists. Porthcurno Beach is owned and managed by the National Trust, an independent charity which preserves beautiful houses, coastlines, and other areas of outstanding natural beauty.*

S I think Porthcurno and the rest of Cornwall really was the star of *Poldark*. People got a chance to see Cornwall's enchanting landscapes on screen and were really captured by it and wanted to see it for themselves. Obviously, Cornwall as a whole is really dependent on tourism, with approximately two billion pounds coming into the Cornish economy from tourism directly and much more indirectly.

N *This money brings in much needed revenue for an area like Cornwall, where older, local industries like mining, farming, and fishing can no longer provide enough employment.*
Other locations in the county were also central to the Poldark *series and are very popular with visitors in the summer, like these former tin mines on the coast at Botallack and, further east, the wild and windswept Bodmin Moor.*
But the most filmed location in Cornwall is the picturesque coastal town of Charlestown, a principal location for the Poldark *story. Charlestown has a population of only five hundred people, but each year half a million people visit the town. So, can this huge visitor influx be put down to the 'Poldark Effect'?*

I I think it's the harbour itself – the beauty of it, the way it's been preserved over its two hundred years of operation. That's what attracts people here. I think there are people that do come down and realize this is where *Poldark* was filmed or this is where one of their favourite celebrities has been filmed before. As an area and as Cornwall as a whole as a filming location, it's positive. It does bring people down here, whether it's into the museum or not. It does bring people to Cornwall. It encourages the tourism trade. In Charlestown, the eateries – the restaurants – I think they are probably benefitting the most out of the footfall.

N *Around four point five million people visit Cornwall each year. When the weather is good, this figure rises by twenty per cent. And this can mean huge numbers of people on the roads, putting the local infrastructure under pressure, not to mention the overcrowded beaches. While those in the tourist industry see only positives in the summer boom in visitor numbers, some local residents take a slightly different view.*

T I wouldn't choose to live anywhere else. On a beautiful day, standing on a clifftop, overlooking a white sand beach, with the waves crashing down below, there is no greater place. But, like anything, you choose to live somewhere beautiful, you've got to put up with the downfalls to that and, in Cornwall's case, that means the swell in population and the associated pressures of that. Cornwall is a very rural county and its roads are very, very narrow; it's a – it is a – it can be very, very difficult to get around, even in wintertime, and of course tourists come with caravans, big camper vans, big cars and aren't used to the narrow roads. So, for the local people, if I wanted to go to the beach for the morning, in the summertime, I'd have to think very seriously whether I can actually be bothered because it will take me double the amount of time.

N *But Cornwall isn't the only place in the UK to be affected by an increased number of visitors as a result of a film or and television series, a phenomenon known as 'screen tourism'. Nowhere is this phenomenon more pronounced than in Northern Ireland. For nearly ten years, the province has been the base, and one of the principal locations, for the blockbuster US TV series,* Game of Thrones.
The main studios are here in the Titanic Quarter in Belfast and there are numerous other locations elsewhere in the province, including Winterfell, which is Castle Ward in County Down, and this, perhaps the most famous of them all, the location for the Dark Hedges in Armoy, County Antrim.
Due to political troubles and violence in the past, Northern Ireland wasn't a traditional tourist destination like Cornwall. But since the

Troubles ended, tourism has increased, and peace has allowed for more inward investment, like the building of TV studios. Since the series began, the Northern Irish Government estimates that Game of Thrones *has brought in sixty-five million pounds from visitors to the province, useful money, especially as the same government contributed nine million pounds to the building of the studios. The local tourist board estimates that three hundred and fifty thousand visitors come to Northern Ireland every year solely as a result of the TV series, and a brief survey of visitors seems to confirm the* Game of Thrones *Effect.*

H We are *Game of Thrones* fans!

J Yes!

H We've seen some of the some of the *Game of Thrones* art in the city, around the city.

J We saw the studios.

H That was very cool. We saw Titanic Studios where it was produced, that was, we thought that was very cool. And we've looked into doing one of the *Game of Thrones* tours that goes, that goes around to see Winterfell and, and some of the other places that we would, you know, where our favourite characters are from.

N *The increase in tourism has been good for local businesses, too. Established Coffee started in twenty thirteen and its owner, Bridgeen Barbour, is grateful for the* Game of Thrones *Effect, which brought the cast of the series into her café.*

B Oh, I, I think it's been great for the city, for the country. It's – sometimes it's hard to believe how big it's actually been and I think it's incredible. We've just come out of a conflict after a long time and to have, to see our city thrive the way it is now and seeing the opportunities, I think, from lots of different areas, I think, has just been incredible. How could you not win with something like this coming to such a small place?

N *Screen tourism is felt all over the UK. The TV series,* Outlander, *has had a similar effect to* Game of Thrones *in parts of Scotland. Downton Abbey – a TV series and a film – has made the actual house, Highclere Castle in Hampshire, a magnet for visitors. In Cornwall, it is slightly different. The county was always a popular place for visitors and the 'Poldark Effect' has only increased the numbers. But of course, the upside of living in a place that attracts so many visitors is that you're living all year round in a fabulously beautiful place. Here at Porthcurno and at other stunning beaches around the county – you can see why visitors can't stay away.*

c Focus on the task and give Sts time to read the questions. Play the video again, pausing if necessary to give Sts time to write.

Check answers to question 1 and elicit opinions for 2.

1

Simon Hocking is in favour of screen tourism because it brings a lot of money into the local economy.

Ian Lay is positive about it because it brings people to Cornwall and is very good for the local restaurants.

Tania Plowright thinks it can cause problems, especially with increased traffic.

Bridgeen Barbour thinks it's been great for Belfast and has created lots of opportunities.

2 Generally good:

Cornwall: screen tourism has been generally good, bringing in lots of visitors and money and boosting the local economy, though with some downsides like heavy traffic and crowded beaches.

Northern Ireland: screen tourism has been very beneficial, bringing in lots of visitors and investment, and helping Northern Ireland to recover from a troubled political past, with no obvious downsides.

EXTRA SUPPORT You could get Sts to watch again with subtitles, so they can see exactly what they understood / didn't understand. Translate / Explain any new words or phrases.

d Do this as a whole-class activity, or put Sts in pairs and then get some feedback.

8 WRITING a discursive essay (2): taking sides

In this lesson, the focus is on the second type of discursive essay, where Sts decide to argue either in favour or against a statement (the balanced approach was covered in **6B**). The writing skills focus is on topic sentences and using synonyms, and the **Useful Language** section covers common expressions for giving personal opinions, and for expressing opposite arguments and refuting them.

Tell Sts to go to **Writing** A discursive essay (2): Taking sides on *p.126.*

ANALYSING A MODEL TEXT

a Focus on the text type (*a discursive essay where you take one side*). Remind Sts of the balanced approach, which they covered in Lesson **6B**. Point out that sometimes an essay title simply asks them if they agree with a statement or not. As an alternative to the balanced approach, they can argue in favour of or against the statement, rather than giving both sides of the argument. They can also include a typical counterargument which they then refute (prove that it is wrong), although this may not always be necessary or appropriate.

Focus on the **Key success factors** and go through them with the class. Then focus on the task, and give Sts time, in pairs, to discuss the essay title and decide whether, generally speaking, they agree or disagree with it.

Get feedback to find out what the majority of the class thinks.

b Focus on the **Topic sentences** box and go through it with the class.

Now focus on the task and give Sts time to read A–E and, in pairs, discuss how the paragraphs are likely to continue.

Check answers.

A We expect the rest of the paragraph to give examples of this, e.g. better public transport, better water systems, etc.

B We expect the paragraph to develop this argument and give more examples, e.g. overcrowding, excess traffic, etc.

C We expect some information about tourism in general.

D We expect specific examples of what governments are doing and the results of this, e.g. creating conservation areas.

E We expect the paragraph to elaborate further, e.g. jobs are created in hotels and restaurants.

Elicit whether the essay will be for or against tourism.

It will be for tourism – topic sentences A, D, and E introduce paragraphs in favour of tourism; only B introduces an argument against.

c Now focus on the model essay. Tell Sts to read it once and then read it again, completing each paragraph (1–5) with the appropriate topic sentence (A–E).

Get Sts to compare with a partner, and then check answers.

1 C 2 E 3 A 4 D 5 B

d Focus on the task and give Sts time to discuss the questions in pairs.

Check answers.

1 In paragraphs 1 and 6 (the introduction and the conclusion)
2 Three – jobs and the economy, better infrastructure, better conservation
3 To give an opposing opinion, and then refute it

USEFUL LANGUAGE

e Focus on the **Using synonyms and richer vocabulary** box (this was also focused on in Lesson **2A**) and go through it with the class.

Now focus on the task and tell Sts to look for the synonyms in the topic sentences as well as the paragraphs.

Check answers.

1 holidaymakers, visitors 2 influences 3 for instance
4 generally, on the whole

f Finally, focus on the expressions and get Sts to complete them.

Get Sts to compare with a partner, and then check answers.

1 believe 2 feel 3 view 4 opinion 5 Personally
6 argue 7 claimed 8 those 9 may have, nowadays
10 flaws 11 case

PLANNING WHAT TO WRITE

a Focus on the task. Tell Sts to read the two essay titles and decide which side of the arguments they take and why, and make notes of three or four reasons for each.

b Now put Sts in pairs and get them to share their ideas, but point out that they don't have to agree. They should also think of typical opposing arguments.

Get feedback from individual Sts, finding out if they agree or disagree, what their reasons are, and if they can refute a typical opposing argument.

c Now get Sts to decide which essay they are going to write and to write topic sentences for the introduction and the main paragraphs.

Then get them to compare with a partner and comment on, and improve where possible, each other's sentences.

EXTRA SUPPORT If a pair has chosen the same essay title and agreed with each other when they discussed it, they could write the topic sentences together.

Finally, go through the **Tips** with the class.

WRITING

Go through the instructions, and set the writing for homework.

For instructions on how to use these pages, see *p.43*.

More materials
For teachers
Teacher's Resource Centre
Video Can you understand these people? 7&8
Quick Test 8
File 8 Test
For students
Online Practice Check your progress

GRAMMAR

a
1 Do you think I ought **to have apologized** to Mario yesterday?
2 You'd better **go** to the doctor about that cough.
3 You're not supposed **to use** your phone at work, but everyone does.
4 Alex seems **to be going out** a lot at the moment.
5 Isn't there anywhere **to sit down** here?
6 Rick hates **being criticized** by his boss.
7 I would love **to have seen** the installation, but it finished the day before we arrived.
8 There's no point **calling** him.
9 It's important for celebrities **to be seen** at all the right parties.
10 The meeting isn't due **to start** until 10.30.

b
1 not permitted 2 You should have listened 3 didn't need to get up 4 ✓ 5 ✓ 6 I can hear 7 tastes like 8 ✓
9 about to 10 ✓

VOCABULARY

a
1 misspelled / misspelt 2 demotivated 3 outnumbered
4 overrated 5 undercharged 6 discontinued
7 rescheduled 8 illogical
b
1 still 2 portrait 3 herring 4 elephant 5 market
6 tape
c
1 blister 2 stroke 3 surgeon 4 rash 5 mule 6 post
7 log 8 dream
d
1 beaten 2 set 3 hit 4 touristy 5 postpone
6 recharge 7 breathtaking 8 sample

CAN YOU understand this text?

a Eat probiotics; wash your hands, take multivitamins and Omega-3; sit in the right place, close your eyes or look at the horizon, distract yourself; use insect repellent, wear suitable clothing
b
1 c 2 b 3 a 4 a 5 b 6 a 7 b 8 c

▶ CAN YOU understand these people?

1 b 2 b 3 a 4 c

🔊 8.17
1
I = interviewer, S = Sean
I Are there any rules or restrictions in your daily life that you find really annoying?
S I find restrictions on creating passwords really frustrating and really annoying. Um, everything about one upper case and one lower case character and a number and, um, you can't use anything that you've used for the last six months, I think. So, it means that I always end up creating a, a password that I have no chance of remembering next time I need it.
2
I = interviewer, C = Claire
I Do you ever go to museums or art galleries in your home town or when you are on holiday?
C I do. I like both at home and when abroad. We've just been to the Tate Gallery and when at home, I would visit our local galleries also.
I Do you have a favourite?
C I like the National Gallery of Ireland and the Natural History Museum. They're both together, side by side, on the same street. And I suppose the reason why I like them, they bring back a lot of happy memories, when our children were small, they used to love going to those two galleries.
3
I = interviewer, H = Helen, S = Simon
I Do you believe in alternative medicine?
H No. Er, because if it wasn't, if it worked, it would just be medicine rather than alternative, and no, I don't. No.
S I have more of an, of an open mind because I think, er, if someone believes in it, then their, their brain will help them get better anyway so it has a role, but perhaps it isn't the medical bit itself that's working.
I What alternative medicine have you tried?
S Um, you've done acupuncture.
H Um, I, I tried acupuncture, but no, it had no effect, so…
S I haven't, no.
4
I = interviewer, R = Rob
I Have you ever visited a famous tourist site and been really disappointed by it?
R Um, the Pyramids is both one of the most awe-inspiring places I've ever been, yet the most disappointing places I've ever been, the amount of rubbish there is horrendous. Er, that's quite saddening.

Pet hates

G ellipsis
V animal matters
P auxiliary verbs and *to*

Lesson plan

The topic of this lesson is animals. In the first part, the focus is on pets, and in the second on veganism and various controversial issues relating to animals.

In the first half of the lesson, Sts read a newspaper article about a journalist's attitude to pets. Sts then expand their knowledge of vocabulary related to animals and the natural world, which they put into practice in a speaking activity, followed by a focus on idioms and sayings with animals.

The second half of the lesson begins with a grammar focus on ellipsis, followed by the pronunciation of weak and strong forms of auxiliary verbs and *to*. Sts then listen to a radio programme where two people debate the pros and cons of being vegan. A second visit to the Vocabulary Bank, looking at animal issues, sets up the discussions in Speaking, where Sts debate various animal issues, such as pet ownership and hunting.

More materials
For teachers
Photocopiables
Grammar ellipsis *p.183*
Communicative Animal quiz *p.209* (instructions *p.191*)
Vocabulary Animal matters *p.227* (instructions *p.216*)
For students
Workbook 9A
Online Practice 9A

OPTIONAL LEAD-IN – THE QUOTE

Write the quote at the top of *p.86* on the board (books closed) and the name of the person who said it, or get Sts to open their books and read it. Elicit / Explain what a *rattlesnake* is (= a poisonous American snake that makes a noise like a rattle with its tail when it is angry or afraid).

Point out that Lance Morrow is an American writer. He writes mainly for *Time* magazine.

Ask Sts what they think Morrow meant by the quote and whether they agree.

1 READING understanding complex language

EXTRA IDEA Before beginning **a**, you may want to focus on the lesson title and ask Sts what they think *pet hates* means (= things that you particularly dislike).

a Focus on the questions and put Sts in pairs. Elicit / Explain the meaning of *to be attached to something*.

Give Sts a few minutes to answer the questions.

Get some feedback from various pairs.

b Do this as a whole-class activity. Then ask Sts if they think this is typical or unusual of British people (*Unusual, as they have the reputation of being animal lovers*).

It implies that the writer dislikes animals.

c Focus on the **Glossary** and go through it with the class.

Now focus on the task and set a time limit for Sts to read the article and match each paragraph to its topic.

Get Sts to compare with a partner, and then check answers.

EXTRA SUPPORT Before Sts read the article the first time, check whether you need to pre-teach any vocabulary.

1 his current feelings about kittens
2 his general attitude to cats
3 his attitude to dogs
4 his childhood experience of pets
5 people's preference for animals over children
6 his children's attitude to animals
7 future plans about pets in his household

d Explain to Sts that the writer of this article uses complex sentence structures and vocabulary to express his ideas in a memorable and entertaining way. This approach is common in articles where the writer is expressing an opinion. Focus on extracts 1–7 and explain that these are a summary of the main idea of their respective paragraphs.

Now give Sts time to read the article again and circle the **bold** phrase which explains what each extract means.

Check answers.

1 good reasons   2 more annoying than loveable   3 dogs even more than cats   4 I'm not used to   5 completely normal   6 inconsistent   7 prepared to tolerate having

EXTRA SUPPORT Get Sts to work in pairs.

Finally, deal with any other vocabulary problems that arose.

e This exercise focuses on the advanced skill of understanding the tone of the article, not just the information in it. Put Sts in pairs and get them to discuss the three questions. Make sure they understand the three options in 2.

Check the answer to the first question and get some feedback for the other two. You could give your opinion, too.

1 a

2 VOCABULARY & SPEAKING animal matters

a Focus on the task and tell Sts to write down the three animals that first come to mind.

Put them in pairs and get them to compare their lists.

Now tell them to go to **Communication Three animals** on *p.108*.

Give Sts time to read the information and then tell their partner whether they agree with the results.

Get some feedback from various pairs.

Tell Sts to go back to the main lesson **9A**.

b Tell Sts to go to **Vocabulary Bank Animal matters** on *p.171*.

Vocabulary notes

Sts should know the names for most common animals. Here in the first section of the **Vocabulary Bank**, they learn the words for animal young, where they live, the noises they make, and animal parts. The second section, which covers animal issues, is done later in the lesson.

When they return to the main lesson after **Part 1**, they focus on some animal idioms. As with the colour idioms in Lesson **7B**, there are a lot of animal idioms in English. We've avoided animal idioms that are less used, or that have a slightly comic or informal register, like *the cat's whiskers* or *the bee's knees*, and have focused on idioms which can be used in a variety of contexts without sounding unnatural or too informal.

Focus on **1 Animals, birds, and insects**, **Young ones** and get Sts to do **a** individually or in pairs.

🔊 **9.1** Now focus on **b**. Play the audio for Sts to listen and check.

Check answers. You may want to point out that when we talk about baby animals in the plural, we often simply use the adjective *young* and talk about their young. Point out also that *chick* is used for the young of most wild birds, and that *cub* is used for the young of all felines, e.g. tigers, leopards, etc.

A b**aby bear or a fox is called a** *cub*, a **young whale or elephant is a** *calf*, **and a young donkey is a** *foal*.

🔊 9.1
Animal matters
1 Animals, birds, and insects
Young ones
1 dog, puppy
2 goat, **kid**
3 horse, **foal**
4 cow, **calf**
5 hen, **chick**
6 lion, **cub**

Now either use the audio to drill the pronunciation of the words, or model and drill them yourself. Give further practice of any words your Sts find difficult to pronounce. Highlight the silent *l* in *calf*.

EXTRA CHALLENGE You could elicit / teach expressions for groups of animals, e.g. *a swarm of bees, a herd of cows / elephants, a flock of sheep / goats / birds*, etc.

Focus on **Where they live** and get Sts to do **c** individually or in pairs.

🔊 **9.2** Now focus on **d**. Play the audio for Sts to listen and check.

Check answers, and for each one, elicit other animals that might live in the same place (not all of them have more than one answer).

3 canary (also many animals kept in captivity, and pets like guinea pigs, hamsters, other birds, etc.)
5 goldfish (also all other fish, turtles, etc.)
6 blackbird (also other birds, and some insects, e.g. wasps, and small mammals, e.g. mice)

🔊 9.2
Where they live
1 a hive, bee
2 a stable, **horse**
3 a cage, **canary**
4 a kennel, **dog**
5 a tank, **goldfish**
6 a nest, **blackbird**

Now either use the audio to drill the pronunciation of the words, or model and drill them yourself. Give further practice of any words your Sts find difficult to pronounce.

Focus on **The noises they make** and get Sts to do **e** individually or in pairs.

🔊 **9.3** Now focus on **f**. Play the audio for Sts to listen and check.

Check answers.

🔊 9.3
The noises they make
1 squeak, mouse
2 bark, **dog**
3 neigh, **horse**
4 meow, **cat**
5 roar, **lion**
6 grunt, **pig**
7 twitter, **bird**

Now either use the audio to drill the pronunciation of the words, or model and drill them yourself. Give further practice of any words your Sts find difficult to pronounce.

Focus on **Animal parts** and get Sts to do **g** individually or in pairs.

🔊 **9.4** Now focus on **h**. Play the audio for Sts to listen and check.

Check answers.

🔊 9.4
Animal parts
5 a beak
1 claws
2 a fin
7 fur
8 hooves
6 horns
10 paws
9 a shell
4 a tail
3 wings

Now either use the audio to drill the pronunciation of the words, or model and drill them yourself. Give further practice of any words your Sts find difficult to pronounce.

Finally, focus on **Activation** and make sure Sts know what a mind map is. Demonstrate first on the board with 'dog'. Write the word in a circle and elicit the following words onto lines coming off the circle: *tail / claws / paws / fur*, etc.

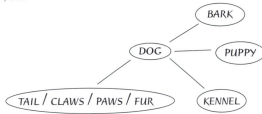

Then give them time to make mind maps for the other three animals. They could do this in pairs or individually.

If Sts worked individually, get them to compare their mind maps.

Elicit each mind map onto the board.

Tell Sts to go back to the main lesson **9A**.

▪ Don't do the **Vocabulary** photocopiable now, as Sts do **Part 2** of the **Vocabulary Bank** later in the lesson.

c Focus on the task and the topics. Give Sts time to read them. Demonstrate the activity by telling the class about people you know.

Put Sts in pairs to do the activity.

Get some feedback from the class by saying, e.g. *Who knows somebody who prefers animals to people? Who are they?*, etc.

d Focus on the ten idioms, highlighting that there are many English idioms which involve animals. You could remind Sts that they looked at colour idioms in Lesson **7B**, and that two of the colour idioms also involved animals – *a white elephant* and *a red herring*. Ask Sts if they can remember what they mean.

Individually or in pairs, Sts choose the correct word from the list to complete the idioms.

Check answers.

1 donkey **2** duck **3** fish **4** chickens **5** horse **6** lion
7 rat **8** birds **9** bark **10** tail

You may want to point out that:

- the origin of the idiom *water off a duck's back* is because water runs off a duck's back without affecting or bothering it, in the same way that criticism does not affect or worry certain people.
- although the full expression is *Don't count your chickens before they hatch*, we usually just say the first part, *Don't count your chickens*.

e Do this as a whole-class activity.

3 GRAMMAR ellipsis

a 🔊 **9.5** Focus on the task and get Sts to complete each gap with one word. Point out that the first one (*to*) has been done for them.

Get Sts to compare with a partner.

Then play the audio for Sts to listen and check.

Check answers, and then ask Sts what the function of these words is.

2 to **3** is **4** does **5** should **6** have **7** so **8** are
The function of these words is to avoid repetition.

 9.5
W Have you ever had a pet?
M Sadly not. I've always wanted to, but I've never been able to because I'm allergic to cats and dogs.
W Are you? I'm not, but my sister is, which is why we never had them either. But my kids really want a puppy, and so does my husband.
M I think you probably should, then. What's stopping you? You ought to go to a rescue centre for abandoned dogs.
W I already have.
M So, you really are going to get one, then?
W I suppose so. I'm not a hundred per cent convinced, but the children are.

b Tell Sts to go to **Grammar Bank 9A** on *p.158*.

Grammar notes

Sts at Advanced level will already have an instinctive feel for the aspects of ellipsis covered here, but they probably will not have totally assimilated them into their own English. The emphasis in this lesson is to look overtly at the theory, thus making Sts feel more confident when they speak.

Ellipsis with *so* and *not*

- **Rule 1:**
  There are occasions when you can also use *I don't suppose so*, e.g.

A *You won't be around tomorrow, then?*

B *I don't suppose so.*

Focus on the example sentences for **ellipsis after linkers** and go through the rules with the class.

Repeat for **ellipsis after auxiliaries or with infinitives** and **ellipsis with *so* and *not***.

Focus on the exercises and get Sts to do them individually or in pairs. If they do them individually, get them to compare with a partner.

Check answers after each exercise, getting Sts to read the full sentences.

a
1 Everyone else liked the hotel, but I didn't ~~like it~~.
2 Nobody expects us to win, but we might ~~win~~.
3 I didn't take the job in the end, but now I think I should have ~~taken it~~.
4 I went to the gym every week and ~~I~~ played basketball when I was living in the USA.
5 **A** Would you like to come for dinner tomorrow?
  B I'd love to ~~come to dinner~~, but I'm afraid I can't ~~come~~.
6 We don't go to the theatre very often, but we used to ~~go~~ before we had children.
7 I won't be able to go to the concert, but my wife will ~~be able to go~~.
8 We didn't enjoy the film because we arrived late and ~~we~~ missed the beginning.

b
1 I'm not vegetarian, but my wife **is**.
2 I would love to fly a plane, but I know that I never **will**.
3 Nobody believes me when I say that I'm going to resign, but I **am / will**.
4 We thought that Karen would get the job, but she **didn't**.
5 In the end they didn't come, even though they had promised that they **would**.

6 If you haven't seen the film yet, you **must / should / ought to**.
7 If I could help you I would, but I'm afraid I **can't**.
8 I don't speak French, but my friend **does**.

c
1 I **hope not**. I want to do some gardening.
2 I **used to**, but I stopped going last month.
3 I **suppose not**. She might give it to the other children.
4 No, but I'**ll try to** after the meeting.
5 I **guess so**, though I'm really enjoying myself.
6 I don't know. I'**ve always wanted to**.
7 Yes he has, even though I **asked him not to**.
8 Yes, I **imagine so**.

Tell Sts to go back to the main lesson **9A**.

EXTRA SUPPORT If you think Sts need more practice, you may want to give them the **Grammar** photocopiable activity at this point.

4 PRONUNCIATION auxiliary verbs and *to*

Pronunciation notes

Encouraging Sts to distinguish between strong and weak forms of the auxiliary and *to* in the infinitive form is a clear and motivating way of improving their pronunciation at this level.

You could point out the following:
- auxiliary verbs are stressed in question tags, short answers, negative sentences, when they are used for emphasis, and when they come as the last word in a sentence.
- auxiliary verbs are unstressed in *wh-* questions and with *so* and *neither*.
- the auxiliary verb in *yes / no* questions, e.g. *Do you like dogs? Did you go on safari?* is usually unstressed.
- unstressed auxiliaries usually have the /ə/ vowel sound. The exceptions are *did*, which is pronounced /dɪd/ even when it's unstressed, and *do* in the phrases *So do I* and *Neither do I*, where it is pronounced /duː/.
- *to* is pronounced /tə/ when it is unstressed and /tuː/ when it is stressed.
- *to* is stressed when it is used in ellipsis (e.g. *I wanted to, but it was a business trip*).

a ◑ 9.6 Focus on the instructions and the three conversations. Give Sts time to do the task in pairs. Encourage them to read the conversations out loud to decide when the auxiliary verbs or *to* are stressed.

Play the audio once the whole way through for Sts just to listen.

Then play it again, pausing after each conversation for Sts to listen and check.

Check answers.

◑ 9.6
1 A Do you like dogs?
  B No, I <u>don't</u>, but my husband <u>does</u>.
  A So does mine. We have three Alsatians.
2 A I went to Kenya last summer.
  B Lucky you. I'd love to go there. Did you go on safari?
  A No. I wanted <u>to</u>, but it was a business trip and I <u>didn't</u> have time.
3 A Allie <u>doesn't</u> eat meat or fish, <u>does</u> she?
  B She <u>does</u> eat fish sometimes. She loves shellfish.
  A Ugh. I <u>don't</u> like shellfish.
  B Neither do I. It's so difficult to eat.

Then get Sts to practise saying the conversations, stressing the correct words.

EXTRA SUPPORT You could play the audio line by line and get the class to copy the stress and sentence rhythm.

b Put Sts in pairs, **A** and **B**, preferably face-to-face. Tell them to go to **Communication** **Match the sentences**, **A** on *p.111*, **B** on *p.113*.

Go through the instructions. You could get a strong pair to demonstrate the activity. Get **A** to say his / her first sentence, *Have you seen the latest James Bond film?*, for **B** to find the correct response, *No, but I'd love to*. Correct **B**'s pronunciation if necessary.

Get Sts to continue in pairs. Monitor and correct any pronunciation errors.

2 A I absolutely hate getting up early.
  B So do I. Luckily, I don't often have to.
3 A Is Lina coming swimming this afternoon?
  B She isn't, but her children are. She didn't want to.
4 A Your brother lives in Liverpool, doesn't he?
  B Yes, and so does my sister.
5 A Your aunt doesn't eat much, does she?
  B No, she doesn't, but she drinks like a fish.
6 A You do like cabbage, don't you?
  B I love it. It's cauliflower I can't stand.
7 B Are you going to go skiing at Christmas?
  A We'd like to, but we aren't sure if we can afford to.
8 B Katie doesn't look like her parents, does she?
  A No, and neither does her brother. Maybe they were adopted.
9 B Were there many people waiting at the doctor's?
  A No, there weren't. I was the only one.
10 B Do you do a lot of gardening?
  A I don't, but my partner does. I'm too lazy!
11 B Erica did say she was coming, didn't she?
  A She said she wanted to, but she wasn't sure if she'd be able to.
12 B Adam isn't particularly good at tennis, is he?
  A He is! He won the under-18 cup this year.

When they have finished, Sts can repeat the exercise, concentrating on correct pronunciation of auxiliaries and *to*.

Tell Sts to go back to the main lesson **9A**.

EXTRA SUPPORT You could elicit the matched pairs of sentences before getting Sts to practise the mini-conversations a final time.

5 LISTENING understanding contrasting points of view, agreement / disagreement / partial agreement

a Focus on the task and put Sts in pairs to discuss what the people in the list eat and don't eat.

Check answers. You could tell Sts that being vegan has implications beyond just the food you eat, as some vegans do not use animal products such as silk or leather, or ride animals.

an omnivore = sb who eats anything
a flexitarian = sb who has a mainly vegetarian diet, but occasionally eats meat or fish
a pescatarian = sb who doesn't eat meat, but does eat fish
a vegetarian = sb who doesn't eat meat or fish
a vegan = sb who doesn't eat or use any animal products

With a show of hands, you could find out how many Sts there are in the class for each category.

b Focus on the task and give Sts time, in pairs, to do the task.

c 🔊 **9.7** Play the audio for Sts to listen and check.
Check answers.

1 500,000 **2** 500% **3** 20%

🔊 **9.7**
P = presenter
P   Good afternoon, and welcome to *A Question of Food*, where each week we look at a different aspect of food and the food industry. This week we're talking about veganism. Well over half a million people in the UK now describe themselves as vegan, an increase of over five hundred per cent in ten years, and twenty per cent of people under the age of thirty-five have tried a vegan diet.

Now ask Sts if they think the statistics would be similar in their country.

Finally, ask them how easy it would be for a vegetarian or a vegan to eat in restaurants where Sts live.

d 🔊 **9.8** Focus on the task and 1–6 in the chart, making sure Sts understand all the lexis, e.g. *immoral*, *diet* (here = the food that you eat and drink regularly), etc. Go through the **Glossary** with the class.

Play the audio once the whole way for Sts to listen and complete the chart.

Get Sts to compare with a partner, and then check answers.

EXTRA SUPPORT Read through the script and decide if you need to pre-teach any new lexis before Sts listen, but <u>not</u> the collocations in **f**.

	agrees	partly agrees	disagrees
1 Eating meat is immoral.	J		S
2 Veganism is good for the environment.	J	S	
3 Vegans have to be careful with their diet.	S	J	
4 Being vegan is a healthy choice.	J	S	
5 Vegans have problems eating out.	S		J
6 Vegans make difficult dinner guests.	S		J

🔊 **9.8**
(script in Student's Book on *p.139*)
P = presenter, J = Jimmy, S = Simone
P   Good afternoon and welcome to *A Question of Food*, where each week we look at a different aspect of food and the food industry. This week we're talking about veganism. Well over half a million people in the UK now describe themselves as vegan, an increase of over five hundred per cent in ten years, and twenty per cent of people under the age of thirty-five have tried a vegan diet. So, what are the arguments for and against veganism, and is it here to stay? We have two experts here to explore the arguments: Jimmy, a vegan activist who also runs a vegan restaurant in East London – hello, Jimmy–
J   Hello.
P   – and Simone, a dietician and omnivore.
S   Hello.

P   Jimmy, let me start with you. What, in your view, are the main reasons for the explosion of interest in veganism?
J   For me, there are two main reasons. The most obvious reason for veganism is to do with animal rights, and this argument has been around for a long time. In fact, writer Leo Tolstoy had this to say in eighteen eighty-six, and it sums up my feelings very well: 'A man can live and be healthy without killing animals for food; therefore, if he eats meat, he participates in taking animal life merely for the sake of his appetite. And to act so is immoral.' I think this is at the heart of why so many people are now becoming vegans, the idea that killing and eating animals, and modern farming practices, are simply immoral. And the second big reason is that being a vegan helps the environment: it reduces your carbon footprint. There was a recent study at Oxford University which concluded that adopting a vegan diet can reduce your carbon footprint by seventy-three per cent, which is far more significant than cutting down on flights or buying an electric car.
P   Simone, can I bring you in here? These both seem pretty strong arguments; what do you think of those two points?
S   Well, the first point, the point about your moral position, I do think that's a very personal decision, whether to eat meat or not, and I personally, I don't think it's immoral. But I think everybody needs to decide for themselves. An unfortunate aspect of veganism is that it's easy for vegans to believe that their position is morally superior, and so they make meat-eaters feel morally inferior, which of course meat-eaters resent, so immediately you have this conflict, which I really think is unfortunate.
P   Jimmy, can I ask you, do you feel morally superior to Simone?
J   Yes, yes, I do feel superior. I do think that veganism is a morally strong position, but it's not about being better than other people, it's just about doing what's right.
P   And Simone, what about Jimmy's second point, about the environment?
S   Well, broadly speaking, Jimmy is right: being a vegan can reduce your carbon footprint. But it isn't quite as simple as that. Some foods that are a real favourite with vegans, like avocados and quinoa and soybeans, are grown a long way from the UK. I mean, the biggest producers of quinoa are Peru and Bolivia, and avocados come to the UK from Mexico, the Caribbean, Africa, and soybeans from Brazil. And there's a significant environmental impact associated with bringing those foods to Britain, and they are often not grown in a sustainable way – growing food crops can be just as damaging to the environment as farming animals. And there's also the problem that demand for those foods is now so high in, for example, Britain and the States, that there isn't enough left for the country that actually grows the food – so, for example, Kenya has recently banned the export of avocados because they were all going abroad, with none left for the Kenyans.
P   OK, Simone, that's a valid point. As a dietician, what do you think are the health implications of being vegan? We hear a lot about vitamin deficiency and so on, is that something we should be concerned about?
S   Yes, it is true that it's harder to maintain a balanced diet if you're vegan, and that may present a serious health risk, especially for children and teenagers, who I absolutely believe should not be vegan. Humans are designed to be omnivores, so obviously if you eat a bit of everything, like me, then you get plenty of vitamins and minerals and so on, but vegans have to really make sure that they get enough of these things. The classic example is vitamin B twelve. If you're vegan, you need to take B twelve supplements, or eat food fortified with B twelve. If you don't, you can become quite ill quite quickly.
J   Of course you do need to take a bit of care, but that goes without saying. There's nothing wrong with taking vitamin supplements, and lots of people who aren't vegans do the same thing. But I think you're missing the important point, which is that overall, being vegan is hugely positive for your health. Less risk of heart disease, less risk of diabetes, and how many vegans do you know who are overweight?
S   That may be true to some extent, but fundamentally, I still don't see why anyone would choose to eat a diet that doesn't deliver the right nutritional balance for the human body.
P   One thing I want to ask you both about is what you could call the social side of being vegan. I mean eating out – that can be very difficult.

J Well, actually, I think that problem has disappeared now. Being vegan is becoming more and more mainstream, and most restaurants offer vegetarian and vegan options.

P Well, one if you're lucky!

S Yes, and that's only true in big cities and in certain countries. I mean, there are some countries where avoiding all animal-based food is more or less impossible.

P And Jimmy, what about when you go round to somebody's house for dinner? Does that create problems?

J Not at all. Most of my friends are vegan anyway, and all my other friends are really getting into trying vegan recipes.

S I'm afraid you'd have a problem if you came to my house – I think it's really inconsiderate to expect the host to cook something specially for you, or for everybody to have to eat the food that only you actually want. You'd expect me to cook something special for you, but would you be prepared to cook a steak for me?

J I'm sorry, but I wouldn't.

P So can I ask you both, just to round off, is veganism the future?

J Absolutely it is.

S I think it'll always be an option, but it'll never be for everyone.

e Now tell Sts they are going to listen again, and this time, they need to note the reasons Jimmy and Simone give for their beliefs.

Play the audio again, pausing after each argument has been made to give Sts time to write.

Get Sts to compare with a partner, and then play the audio again if necessary.

Check answers.

1 Jimmy says it's immoral to kill animals and eat them.
Simone says it isn't immoral; it's a personal decision.

2 Jimmy says it reduces your carbon footprint much more than flying less or getting an electric car.
Simone says it can reduce your carbon footprint, but many vegan-friendly foods, e.g. quinoa and avocados, come from very far away; also, growing food crops can be as damaging to the environment as farming animals.

3 Jimmy says you need to take a bit of care, but there's nothing wrong with taking vitamin supplements, and many non-vegans do it.
Simone says it's harder to maintain a balanced diet if you're vegan, especially with vitamin B12.

4 Jimmy says overall, being vegan is hugely positive for your health: less risk of diseases, and vegans are not overweight.
Simone says it may be partially true, but basically, a vegan diet doesn't give your body what it needs to be healthy.

5 Jimmy says most restaurants now offer vegetarian and vegan food.
Simone says this is only true in big cities and in some countries.

6 Jimmy says most of his friends are vegan and all his friends enjoy cooking vegan food.
Simone says it's inconsiderate to expect people to cook vegan food just for you.

Finally, with a show of hands, find out whose side Sts are on – Jimmy's or Simone's. Ask Sts if they have any reasons other than the ones mentioned on the audio.

LANGUAGE IN CONTEXT

f ◗ **9.9** Focus on the task and give Sts time to complete the collocations with the words in the list. They could do this individually or in pairs.

Play the audio for Sts to listen and check.

Check answers, making sure Sts understand all the collocations.

1 rights 2 footprint 3 position 4 impact 5 deficiency
6 diet 7 risk

◗ **9.9**
1 The most obvious reason for veganism is to do with animal rights…
2 And the second big reason is that it reduces your carbon footprint.
3 …the point about your moral position, I do think that's a very personal decision…
4 And there's a significant environmental impact associated with bringing those foods to Britain…
5 We hear a lot about vitamin deficiency and so on…
6 …it's harder to maintain a balanced diet if you're vegan…
7 …and that may present a serious health risk, especially for children and teenagers…

EXTRA SUPPORT If there's time, you could get Sts to listen to the discussion again with script 9.8 on *p.139*, so they can see exactly what they understood / didn't understand. Translate / Explain any new words or phrases.

g Do this as a whole-class activity, or put Sts in pairs and then get some feedback.

6 VOCABULARY & SPEAKING

a Tell Sts to go to **Vocabulary Bank** **Animal matters** on *p.171*.

Vocabulary notes
Animal issues
The lexical set here focuses on expressions used when discussing topical issues related to animals and the environment.

You may want to point out:

• that the infinitive of *bred* is *breed*.

• the difference between *inhuman* (= lacking the qualities of kindness and pity, very cruel) and *inhumane* (= not caring about the suffering of people or animals).

◗ **9.10** Now focus on **2 Animal issues**. First, play the audio for Sts to listen and read at the same time.

◗ **9.10**
See questions in Student's Book on *p.171*

Now put Sts in pairs and get them to tell each other what the **bold** words and phrases mean.

Check answers. Highlight any words your Sts may have problems pronouncing correctly, e.g. *species* /ˈspiːʃiːz/.

1 **protect** = to make sure that sb or sth is not harmed or injured
environment = the natural world in which people, animals, and plants live
animal charities = organizations which collect money to help animals, e.g. the World Wildlife Fund

2 **animal rights activists** = people who demonstrate for the rights of animals to be treated well, e.g. by not being hunted or used for medical research

3 **treated cruelly** = handled in a cruel or violent way

4 **live in the wild** = live in their natural environment – not in zoos, etc.

5 **endangered species** = kinds of animals that may soon no longer exist, e.g. the tiger, the polar bear, etc.

6 **hunted for sport** = killed for enjoyment rather than for food
7 **bred in captivity** = kept in order to reproduce
8 **inhumane conditions** = very cruel conditions

Focus on **Activation** and give Sts time to answer the questions in pairs or small groups.

Get some feedback.

EXTRA SUPPORT Ask the questions to the whole class and elicit examples.

Tell Sts to go back to the main lesson **9A**.

EXTRA SUPPORT If you think Sts need more practice, you may want to give them the **Vocabulary** photocopiable activity at this point. This covers the vocabulary in both parts of the **Vocabulary Bank**.

b ◑ **9.11** This exercise focuses on how we frequently collocate certain adverbs with other words when we give our opinion, e.g. *I feel very **strongly** about this* or *I'm **totally** / **completely** against hunting. I'm **quite** sure that…*, etc.

Focus on the task and on the **Common adverb collocations** box and give Sts time to read the phrases.

Play the audio for Sts to listen and complete the gaps.

Get Sts to compare with a partner, and then play the audio again as necessary.

Check answers. Remind Sts that *I don't entirely agree* is used when you half-agree. Highlight that *quite* in the phrase *I'm quite sure = completely*, and is another very common collocation. You might also want to highlight the use of *Well…* used here by two of the speakers to give themselves time to think.

1 very strongly   2 particularly strongly   3 completely
4 entirely   5 absolutely   6 quite

◑ **9.11**
Common adverb collocations
1 It's something I feel very strongly about.
2 Well, I don't feel particularly strongly about it either way.
3 I have to say, I am completely against zoos nowadays.
4 I don't entirely agree with you.
5 Well, I'm absolutely convinced that the animal does not want to be there.
6 I'm quite sure that kids could get the same amount of pleasure from seeing animals in the wild.

Play the audio again for Sts to focus on the rhythm and intonation of the phrases. Elicit / Point out that the adverbs are stressed more strongly. You could get Sts to practise saying the phrases.

EXTRA SUPPORT Play the audio again for Sts to listen and copy the rhythm and intonation.

c Focus on the instructions and the tweets. Make sure all the lexis is clear, e.g. *exploit, to object to sth*, etc.

Put Sts in small groups of three or four. Tell them to choose one issue each to talk about, and then to agree with the other members of their group so that each student opens the discussion on a different issue.

Give Sts time to make notes, helping with vocabulary where necessary.

d Set a time limit for each discussion. Then tell one student from each group to start.

Monitor and make a note of any mistakes you think would be useful to deal with when they have finished the discussions.

e Get feedback to find out which issues everybody generally agreed about in each group, and which ones created the most controversy.

EXTRA IDEA You could make these discussions into more formal debates, where one person or pair proposes and one opposes the issues.

G nouns: compound and possessive forms
V preparing food
P words with silent syllables

Lesson plan

The topic of this lesson is food and eating out.

In the first half of the lesson, the focus is on cooking. Sts begin by expanding their lexis related to ways of preparing food, which will also help them to understand menus in English. This is followed by Pronunciation, where they focus on words with silent syllables, e.g. *vegetables*, *chocolate*. Sts then read an extract about making boiled eggs from *The Food Lab: Better Home Cooking Through Science*, a best-selling cookery book. This is followed by two more extracts about how to make perfect fried eggs and scrambled eggs. The first half of the lesson ends with a vocabulary section on food adjectives ending in -y, e.g. *salty*, *creamy*, etc.

In the second half of the lesson, the focus shifts to eating out. Sts first study the grammar of compound and possessive forms, e.g. *a recipe book, a chef's hat*. They then listen to some tips about eating out from a book written by a well-known British food critic, discuss them, and talk about their own experiences of eating out. The lesson ends with Sts writing a formal email of complaint.

More materials
For teachers
Photocopiables
Grammar nouns: compound and possessive forms *p.184*
Communicative Talk for one minute *p.211* (instructions *p.191*)
Vocabulary Preparing food *p.228* (instructions *p.216*)
For students
Workbook 9B
Online Practice 9B

OPTIONAL LEAD-IN – THE QUOTE

Write the quote at the top of *p.90* on the board (books closed) and the name of the person who said it, or get Sts to open their books and read it.

Point out that Abraham Maslow (1908–1970) was an American psychologist, best known for his work on what people need to realize their full potential.

Ask Sts what they think he means by the quote and whether they agree.

1 VOCABULARY preparing food

a Focus on the instructions and give Sts two minutes, in pairs, to think of as many ways as possible to cook the five items.

b Elicit the different cooking methods Sts thought of, and then find out which pair got the most.

The following are common ways of cooking these foods, but there are lots of other acceptable answers:
fried / roast / grilled chicken
boiled / fried eggs
baked / boiled / fried / roast potatoes
baked / fried / grilled / steamed fish
boiled / fried / steamed rice

You could have a class vote for the favourite way of preparing the food items.

c Tell Sts to go to **Vocabulary Bank Preparing food** on *p.172*.

Vocabulary notes
How food is prepared

You may want to highlight some of the following information:

- common herbs include parsley, rosemary, thyme, basil
- *chop* and *slice* both mean *cut*, but *chop* means to cut into (very) small pieces, e.g. *to chop herbs*, and *slice* means to cut into thin, flat pieces, e.g. *to slice bread*. You could contrast *chop an onion* and *slice an onion*.
- *baked* and *roast* are similar (both mean cooked in the oven), but *roast* = with fat, e.g. oil or butter. *Roast potatoes* are potatoes which are peeled and then cooked in the oven with oil. *Baked potatoes* are cooked in their skins in the oven, without fat.

If your Sts don't cook themselves, point out that this vocabulary is also very helpful for understanding restaurant menus.

Utensils

You could tell Sts that the phrase *pots and pans* is often used to refer to a mixture of cooking utensils. A *pot* is any kind of deep round container used for cooking.

You could point out that *sieve* and *whisk* can also be verbs.

Focus on **1 How food is prepared** and get Sts to do **a** individually or in pairs.

🔊 **9.12** Now focus on **b**. Play the audio for Sts to listen and check.

Check answers.

🔊 **9.12**
Preparing food
1 How food is prepared
18 baked figs
7 barbecued pork ribs
11 boiled rice
1 chopped parsley
2 deep-fried onion rings
10 grated cheese
9 grilled fillet of fish

17 mashed potatoes
8 melted chocolate
4 minced beef
16 peeled prawns
3 poached egg
6 roast lamb
20 scrambled eggs
5 sliced bread
12 steamed mussels
15 stewed plums
19 stuffed chicken breast
13 a toasted sandwich
14 whipped cream

Now either use the audio to drill the pronunciation of the words, or model and drill them yourself. Give further practice of any words your Sts find difficult to pronounce.

Focus on **2 Utensils** and get Sts to do **a** individually or in pairs.

🔊 **9.13** Now focus on **b**. Play the audio for Sts to listen and check.

Check answers.

🔊 **9.13**
2 Utensils
5 a baking tray
10 a chopping board
1 a colander
3 a food processor
2 a frying pan
11 a bowl
6 a saucepan
7 scales
8 a sieve
4 a spatula
9 a whisk

Now either use the audio to drill the pronunciation of the words, or model and drill them yourself. Give further practice of any words your Sts find difficult to pronounce.

Finally, focus on **Activation** and give Sts time to think of their answers.

Put Sts in pairs and get them to compare with their partner.

Elicit answers to both questions.

Utensils needed for…
an omelette: a bowl, a whisk, a spatula, a frying pan
spaghetti: a saucepan, a colander
biscuits: a baking tray, a bowl, a sieve, scales, a spatula

Tell Sts to go back to the main lesson **9B**.

EXTRA SUPPORT If you think Sts need more practice, you may want to give them the **Vocabulary** photocopiable activity at this point.

d Focus on the task and give Sts time to think of a popular regional or national dish.

Monitor and help.

Put Sts in pairs and get them to tell each other the ingredients needed and how to prepare the dish. You could also get Sts to say which utensils are needed.

Get some feedback from various pairs.

EXTRA SUPPORT If your Sts come from the same region or country, you could do this as a whole-class activity.

2 PRONUNCIATION words with silent syllables

Pronunciation notes

As well as words having silent consonants, there are also words in English which have silent vowels, which result in the words having a silent syllable such as those in *literature* /ˈlɪtrətʃə/, *interesting* /ˈɪntrəstɪŋ/, and *comfortable* /ˈkʌmftəbl/. Sts will sound more natural if they don't pronounce these silent syllables, and should be advised to cross them out when they're recording new vocabulary. Sts should be encouraged to fine-tune their pronunciation of common words with silent syllables (like the ones in the exercise), which some Sts may have been mispronouncing for years. This can be hard for them, especially if they have a similar word in their language where the silent syllable in English is stressed in their language, e.g. *historia* in Spanish

a Give Sts time to read the two sentences out loud and count the syllables. They could do this individually or in pairs.

Check answers.

Sentence 1 has more syllables, with 11 syllables whereas sentence 2 has 9 syllables.

EXTRA SUPPORT Read the two sentences out loud for Sts to hear them first.

b 🔊 **9.14** Focus on the task and emphasize that Sts don't have to write the whole sentence, just the last word.

Play the audio for Sts to listen and write the last words. Play the audio again as necessary.

Check answers, eliciting the spelling of the words onto the board. Don't worry about pronunciation at this stage.

1 restaurant **2** comfortable **3** medicine **4** different
5 temperature **6** dictionary **7** miserable **8** separate
9 family **10** ordinary

🔊 **9.14**
1 Do you remember the name of that new Mexican restaurant?
2 The table over there in the corner might be a bit more comfortable.
3 I can't drink any alcohol because I've just taken some anti-allergy medicine.
4 Are you going to have the steak again, or do you want to try something different?
5 When you're baking a cake, it's really important to preheat the oven to the right temperature.
6 If you don't know what *courgette* means, look it up in the dictionary.
7 I always want to eat something sweet when I'm feeling miserable.
8 If you have cooked and raw meat in your fridge, it's important to keep them separate.
9 I love having Sunday lunch with all the family.
10 It was a really expensive restaurant, but I thought the food was pretty ordinary.

c Focus on the **Fine-tuning your pronunciation: silent syllables** box and go through it with the class.

Give Sts time to cross out the vowels which they think are not pronounced in the words they wrote in **b**.

Get them to compare with a partner.

d Play the audio again for Sts to listen and check.

Check answers and cross out the vowels that are not pronounced in the words on the board (they are marked in colour in the key).

1 rest**au**rant   2 comf**or**table   3 med**i**cine   4 diff**e**rent
5 temp**e**rature   6 diction**a**ry   7 mis**e**rable   8 sep**a**rate
9 fam**i**ly   10 ordin**a**ry

Get Sts to practise saying the words to themselves quietly. Finally, elicit them from individual Sts.

3 READING & SPEAKING following instructions / a recipe, reading and explaining, rebuilding instructions from notes

a Put Sts in small groups of three or four and get them to discuss the questions.

Get some feedback from various groups. Check Sts know the meaning of *yolk*, *white*, and *shell*. You could also tell the class how you cook boiled eggs.

b Focus on the task and do the question as a whole class.

The author uses scientific methods to work out how to cook things better.

c Focus on the task and the verbs in the list.

Get Sts to read the extract and complete the gaps. Point out that the first one (*lower*) has been done for them.

Check answers.

EXTRA SUPPORT Before Sts read the extract the first time, check whether you need to pre-teach any vocabulary, but not the highlighted adjectives in **g**.

2 add   3 drop   4 heat   5 bring   6 stick   7 remove
8 peel

Then elicit the answer to the question *What makes hard-boiled eggs difficult to cook well?*

Suggested answer
Hard-boiled eggs are difficult to cook well because if you put the eggs into boiling water, the white cooks much faster than the yolk, and if you start them in cold water, the shell sticks to the egg.

You could also ask Sts if they noticed a deliberately misspelt word in the extract, and why it's misspelt (the author spells *exact* as *eggsact* as a joke).

d Before getting Sts to read the recipe, you might want to check they understand the meaning of *foolproof* (= very well designed and easy to use, so that it cannot fail), and some cooking verbs, e.g. *pour*, *simmer*, etc.

Give Sts time to read the recipe and then do the questions as a whole-class activity. Make sure Sts understand *give it a go* (= try it).

e Focus on the task and give Sts time to read both extracts.

Get Sts to compare with a partner, and then check answers, eliciting how Sts guessed.

EXTRA SUPPORT Before Sts read the extracts the first time, check whether you need to pre-teach any vocabulary, but not the highlighted adjectives in **g**.

1 fried eggs: He mentions heating oil in a pan and spooning it over the eggs.
2 scrambled eggs: He uses the words *dense / creamy* and *light / fluffy*.

f Put Sts in pairs, **A** and **B**, and tell them to go to **Communication** Cooking eggs, **A** on *p.107*, **B** on *p.111*.
Sts **A** read the recipe for scrambled eggs and Sts **B** read the recipe for fried eggs. They then tell each other the recipes and make notes, so that they can check they understood the recipes correctly.

Finally, Sts discuss how they make scrambled and fried eggs (if they ever do).

Get feedback as to what Sts thought of the recipes and encourage them to try them out!

Tell Sts to go back to the main lesson **9B**.

LANGUAGE IN CONTEXT

g Put Sts in pairs to discuss the meaning of the four highlighted adjectives, and to decide which three are positive and which one is negative.

Check answers.

rubbery = feeling like rubber – negative
creamy = thick and smooth, like cream – positive
fluffy = soft and light, containing air – positive
crispy = pleasantly hard and dry – positive

Deal with any other new vocabulary. Elicit or model the pronunciation of any tricky words.

h Focus on the **Describing texture** box and go through it with the class. Elicit the meanings of the adjectives in the list. Point out to Sts that the adjectives in **g** and the information box mostly describe texture, but also that lots of food words + *-y* can be adjectives to describe taste. Common examples include *buttery*, *cheesy*, *chocolatey*, *fishy*, *fruity*, *herby*, *lemony*, *meaty*, *peppery*, *salty*, *spicy*, and *sugary*. You may want to point out that we can also use *crisp* as an adjective without the *-y*.

Tell Sts to use the adjectives in **g** as well as the ones in the **Describing texture** box to describe the food items in the list.

Put Sts in pairs to complete the task.

Get some feedback from various pairs.

an apple – crunchy, juicy
chips – greasy, crispy
honey – sticky
an omelette – fluffy, greasy
an oyster – slimy
a sauce – creamy, lumpy, watery
squid – rubbery

4 GRAMMAR nouns: compound and possessive forms

a Focus on the task and give Sts time to go through the phrases with a partner.

Check answers.

1 a recipe book
2 a tuna salad
3 children's portions
4 Both are possible, but with a different meaning: *a coffee cup* = a cup used for coffee; *a cup of coffee* = a cup with coffee in it
5 a chef's hat
6 a tin opener
7 Both are possible and mean the same.
8 a friend of John's

b Tell Sts to go to **Grammar Bank 9B** on *p.159*.

Grammar notes

This is a complicated area of grammar where Sts will still have doubts as to when they should use a compound noun, a possessive *'s* or an *of*-structure (*the car door*, *the car's door*, or *the door of the car*) and when they are all possible.

Your Sts' own language might use an *of*- or *for*-structure where English uses a compound noun, e.g. *a recipe book*, or a possessive noun like *children's portions*.

Compound nouns

*   **Rule 2:**
    Explain that in rule 2, we say *story book* because this is an example of a common type of book; in contrast, we say, e.g. *a book about insects* NOT ~~an insect book~~, because this is a less common / more specific type of book.

Focus on the example sentences for **apostrophe s** and go through the rules with the class.

Repeat for **using *of* (instead of apostrophe s)** and **compound nouns**.

Go through the **One word, two words, or hyphenated?** box with the class.

Focus on the exercises and get Sts to do them individually or in pairs. If Sts do them individually, get them to compare with a partner.

Check answers, getting Sts to read the full sentences.

a
1 ✓ **2** ✓ **3** the end of the story **4** the wife of my friend who lives in Australia **5** hers **6** a bottle of milk
7 photo of the house **8** story book **9** a box of old photographs **10** ✓ **11** ✓
b
In 1, *my friend's* = one friend; *my friends'* = more than one friend
In 2 and 10, there is no difference in meaning.
In 11, *a wine glass* = a glass for wine; *a glass of wine* = a glass with wine in it
c
1 I can't find the **bottle opener**.
2 It's **Alice and James' wedding / Alice and James's wedding** next weekend and I don't have anything to wear yet.
3 There's shepherd's pie on **today's menu**.
4 Can I introduce you to Jess White, our **marketing manager**?
5 Don't forget to lock the **garage door** when you take the car out.
6 We would like a room with a **sea view** if that's possible.
7 The **government's proposal** to freeze MPs' salaries has been met with criticism.
8 Make sure you fill the **cats' bowls** with water every day…

Tell Sts to go back to the main lesson **9B**.

5 LISTENING extracting and understanding the main points of an argument

a Do this as a whole-class activity, or put Sts in pairs and then get some feedback. Encourage Sts to try to use compound nouns, e.g. *chocolate and almond tart* not *a tart of chocolate and almonds*, *herb butter* not *butter with herbs*.

A avocado, tomato, and onion salad
B grilled lamb chops
C chocolate and almond tart
D herb butter
E onion rings
F orange and strawberry sorbet

b Focus on the instructions and elicit / explain any vocabulary Sts ask about, or get them to look the words up in their dictionaries.
You may want to explain that:
*   *tofu* is a soft white substance that is made from soya and used in cooking, often instead of meat.
*   *a kebab* is small pieces of meat and / or vegetables cooked on a wooden or metal stick.
*   *hollandaise sauce* is a French sauce made with butter, egg yolks, and lemon juice or vinegar.
*   *New York strip steak* is considered among the higher-end cuts of beef.
*   *jasmine rice* is a long-grain rice with a nutty flavour, used in Thai cooking.
*   *lentils* are a small green, orange, or brown seed that is usually dried and used in cooking, for example in soup or stew.
*   *custard* is a sweet yellow sauce made from milk, sugar, eggs, and flour.
*   *crème brûlée* is a cold dessert made from cream, with burnt sugar on top.
*   *sorbet* is a sweet frozen dessert made from sugar, water, and fruit juice.

Give Sts time to read the menu and make their choices.

c Get Sts to compare their choices with a partner and discuss the questions.
Get feedback from various pairs. You could tell the class your answers to the questions.

d Focus on the task and make sure the subject of the book is clear to Sts. You might want to tell Sts that Giles Coren, apart from being *The Times* newspaper's restaurant critic, has also made several TV shows related to food and cooking. Sts might remember Giles Coren's article about the Hater app from Lesson **3A**.

Put Sts in pairs to decide what the missing words in the seven tips might be. Tell them <u>not</u> to write in the gaps.

e 🔊 **9.15** Play the audio once the whole way through for Sts to listen and complete the gaps.
Check answers. Find out how many Sts had guessed some correctly.

1 fish **2** bread **3** vegetarian **4** outside **5** tap
6 complain **7** staff

Now elicit which two items Giles would never order on the *Henry's* menu.

Giles would never order the New York strip steak or the sourdough bread.

9.15
(script in Student's Book on *pp.139–140*)
How to Eat Out

Tip one Always order the fish.
Really good fresh fish is very hard to find, very hard to store and keep fresh – you've got to really cook it as soon as you buy it or there's no point. It's often fiddly to prepare and very smelly to cook. It's what restaurants are FOR! It just amazes me that people will go into a restaurant and order the steak. A thing you can buy almost anywhere, keep for weeks, and cook however you like without doing anything to it and it'll always basically be OK.

Tip two Never eat the bread.
An ex-girlfriend of mine eats nothing all day. She claims she doesn't get hungry. So, whenever we meet for dinner, she is utterly starving and gobbles up the entire bread basket and three pats of butter without pausing for breath. Then halfway through her main course she starts poking about and saying, 'I don't know why they give you such large portions. I'll never eat all this!' I just don't know why people eat the bread. You shouldn't be that hungry. Ever. Bread is not a first course. It's a breakfast food, an accompaniment to certain terrines. But in an expensive place with a TV chef and a whole range of exciting things to chew on for the next couple of hours, why would anyone want to fill up with bread? I always tell them, as soon as I arrive, to bring no bread. But sometimes they do, and you must tell them to take it away.

Tip three Have the vegetarian option – but not in a vegetarian restaurant.
As a rule, the best vegetarian food is cooked by meat-eating chefs who know how to cook, rather than by bearded hippies. For this reason, if you want good vegetarian food, go to a normal, that is, omnivorous, restaurant. There may not be much choice, but personally, I would much rather restaurants focused on doing one or two things brilliantly than offered a whole load of stuff that was just about OK.

Tip four Never sit at a table outside.
Why on earth would you want to eat outside? I suppose in a hot country where there's no air conditioning, it might be nice to sit outside in the shade overlooking the sea. But on a busy London street? Crazy. Go indoors. Also, in most restaurants the outside tables are ruined by smokers. If you want to eat outside in London, take sandwiches and eat them in one of the wonderful parks.

Tip five Insist on tap water.
We have invested years and years and vast amounts of money into an ingenious system which cleans water and delivers it very cheaply to our homes and workplaces through a tap. And yet last year, we bought three billion litres of bottled water. That's just free money for the restaurant, so don't order mineral water! Ask for a jug of tap.

Tip six How to complain – and get a result.
Complain nicely, politely, apologetically. But firmly, and at the very moment of disappointment. 'I'm awfully sorry to make a fuss,' you might say, 'but this fish really isn't as fresh as I'd hoped. I really can't eat this. What else might I have as a replacement that can come quickly?'
There's simply no way you can lose with that. The end result is likely to be free main courses, a jolly time, and an amicable departure.

Tip seven Be nice to the staff.
Just be nice to them, that's all. You should always be nice to everybody, obviously, but if you're not, make being nice to staff in restaurants your only exception. Don't flirt with them, and don't ask foreign staff where they're from. Just smile, and say please and thank you, and look at them when you're ordering. And then shut up and eat.

f Play the audio again, pausing after each tip has been mentioned to give Sts time to write Giles's reasons.
Get Sts to compare with a partner, and then play again if necessary.
Check answers.

1 Fresh fish is much harder to buy and cook well yourself than steak.
2 Bread fills you up and then you don't want all the much more exciting food on offer.
3 The best vegetarian food is cooked by good chefs who are not necessarily vegetarian.
4 Sitting outside in London is noisy and that's where the smokers sit.
5 Tap water is fine and it's free.
6 If you're polite but firm, you'll probably get the replacement food free and everyone will feel relaxed, rather than angry or upset.
7 It's just important to be polite.

LANGUAGE IN CONTEXT

g   **9.16** Focus on the task and give Sts time to read the seven extracts.

Play the audio once the whole way through for Sts to listen and complete the gaps.

Get Sts to compare with a partner, and then play again as necessary.

Check answers, eliciting the words onto the board.

1 fiddly to prepare   2 utterly starving, gobbles up
3 such large portions   4 chew on   5 whole load of stuff
6 jug of tap   7 make a fuss

 9.16
1 It's often fiddly to prepare and very smelly to cook.
2 So, whenever we meet for dinner, she is utterly starving and gobbles up the entire bread basket and three pats of butter without pausing for breath.
3 I don't know why they give you such large portions.
4 But in an expensive place with a TV chef and a whole range of exciting things to chew on for the next couple of hours…
5 …personally, I would much rather restaurants focused on doing one or two things brilliantly than offered a whole load of stuff that was just about OK.
6 …so don't order mineral water! Ask for a jug of tap.
7 'I'm awfully sorry to make a fuss,' you might say, 'but this fish really isn't as fresh as I'd hoped.'

Now either put Sts in pairs and get them to discuss what they think the words mean, or do it as a whole class.
Check answers.

1 **fiddly** (adj) **to prepare** = difficult to do (here because of the bones, etc.)
2 **utterly starving** = very hungry
    gobble up = to eat sth very fast, in a way that people consider rude or greedy
3 **large portions** = big amounts of food
4 **chew on** = to bite food into small pieces in your mouth with your teeth to make it easier to swallow
5 **whole load of stuff** = used to refer to a substance or things when you don't know the name, the name is not important, or when it's obvious what you are talking about (here it refers to food)
6 **jug of tap** (water) = a container with a handle and a lip, for holding and pouring liquids
7 **make a fuss** = make unnecessary excitement, worry, or activity

EXTRA SUPPORT If there's time, you could get Sts to listen again with script 9.15 on *pp.139–140*, so they can see exactly what they understood / didn't understand. Translate / Explain any new words or phrases.

Point out that Giles Coren's tone is deliberately exaggerated in order to be funny. You could ask Sts to find examples of this from the script (e.g. *whenever we meet for dinner, she is utterly starving and gobbles up the entire bread basket and three pats of butter without pausing for breath*; *You shouldn't be that hungry. Ever*; *As a rule, the best vegetarian food is cooked by meat-eating chefs who know how to cook, rather than by bearded hippies*).

6 SPEAKING

Focus on the questions and give Sts time to read them and think of their answers. For question 4, encourage them to talk about specific restaurants, cafés, etc. that they know and would recommend.

Get Sts to discuss the questions in small groups.

Get some feedback from various groups. If your Sts come from the same country, you could discuss questions 1, 2, and 3 as a class.

7 WRITING a formal email

In this section, Sts write an email complaining about a bad experience at a hotel. Sts have already written a formal email of application in **File 1**, so here the focus is on the specific language relating to a complaint. Although this is something Sts may have looked at in previous years, this text type often comes up in advanced exams, and the language Sts would be expected to use is more sophisticated. The writing skills focus is on getting the correct style and register, and the writing task involves expressing information in a more formal way.

Tell Sts to go to **Writing A formal email** on *p.128*.

ANALYSING A MODEL TEXT

a Focus on the text type (*a formal email*). Remind Sts of the importance of being able to write a formal letter or email in English, and point out to them that one context in which they may need to write one in English is if they have had a problem, e.g. with an airline or a hotel, while travelling. A letter of complaint is also a common exam question.

Go through the **Key success factors** with the class.

Focus on the questions, and do them as a whole-class activity, or put Sts in pairs and then get some feedback.

b Now focus on the email, and set a time limit for Sts to read it. Tell them not to worry about the gaps.

Check the answer.

The service was very slow, but they were still asked to leave the table by 9.00, when they hadn't really finished their meal. The waiter's recommended dishes were more expensive than the ones on the menu, but the waiter didn't point this out when they ordered.

c Set a time limit for Sts, in pairs, to read the email again and choose the best phrase for each gap.

Check answers, eliciting why one phrase is better than the other.

1 b (more formal and avoid using contractions)
2 a (avoid emotional language)
3 a (more formal verb)
4 b (formal fixed phrase)
5 b (more formal adjective, more precise, less vague)
6 a (formal phrase)

7 a (use of passive is less confrontational)
8 b (passive is less personal and confrontational)
9 a (more formal verb)
10 a (less aggressive and demanding)

Highlight the use of the passive rather than the active in 3, 7, 8, and 9. The passive is often used in an email / letter of complaint, as it is less accusatory and distances the complaint from any individual.

Test Sts on the phrases by saying the informal phrase and getting them to say the more formal one.

USEFUL LANGUAGE

d Focus on the task. Get Sts to read the email again, and with a partner, try to remember the six phrases that were used.

Check answers.

1 I am writing to complain…
2 …according to our online reservation…
3 …the waiter not only brought us the bill, but also asked us to hurry…
4 I feel strongly that if customers are given a table…
5 Under the circumstances…
6 I look forward to hearing your views on this matter.

PLANNING WHAT TO WRITE

a Focus on the message Hannah wrote. Tell Sts to read it carefully and then to discuss the question with a partner. Check the answer.

The hotel was turning into a B&B, so there were noisy builders, a cold breakfast as the kitchen wasn't open, no room service or evening meal, and the manager wasn't available.

b Focus on the task and give Sts time to discuss it with a partner.

Get feedback. Accept all reasonable suggestions for compensation, e.g. free night at the new B&B or a refund of the amount it cost. As regards the threat to put the experience on Twitter, in real life many people would threaten to write a bad review online, e.g. on a travel website like Tripadvisor, or to tweet about it, as it is often the only way to elicit a response. Tell Sts that if they do decide to include it, it should not be expressed in an aggressive way, but simply in a firm, matter-of-fact way, e.g. *If I do not hear from you in the very near future, I will write about my experience on Twitter.*

Details that Sts should include in their email would be:

• the date of their stay
• the information on the website at the time of booking
• the number of people travelling together, and the children's ages
• the time at which the builders started
• the lack of a cooked breakfast
• the unavailability of evening snacks
• the unavailability of the manager

Finally, go through the **Tips** with the class.

WRITING

Go through the instructions and set the writing for homework.

Lesson plan

In The Interview, the person interviewed is George McGavin, a well-known entomologist. In this three-part interview, he talks about why he became interested in arthropods (insects, spiders, and crustacea), why he thinks people have phobias of insects, and how he feels about killing and eating insects. This is followed by a language focus on the informal and vague language which he uses.

In The Conversation, Sts watch three people discussing if they ever watch wildlife programmes on TV and why they think this kind of programme is so popular. Sts then discuss these questions as well as two other questions related to the topic, focusing on words and phrases to check whether the other speakers agree.

More materials
For teachers
Teacher's Resource Centre
Video Colloquial English 8&9
Quick Test 9
File 9 Test
For students
Workbook Colloquial English 8&9
Can you remember? 8&9
Online Practice Colloquial English 8&9
Check your progress

OPTIONAL LEAD-IN (BOOKS CLOSED)

Put Sts in pairs and set a time limit for them to write as many names of insects as they can come up with.

When the time is up, elicit the names and write them on the board (if someone suggests *spider*, write it up, but elicit that it isn't an insect as it has eight legs).

Then tell Sts they are going to watch an interview with a well-known naturalist whose particular area of interest is insects and arthropods (including spiders).

If you have internet access in your classroom or Sts have it on their phones, give them a few minutes to google George McGavin and find out a bit about him.

1 ▶ THE INTERVIEW Part 1

a Books open. Focus on the biographical information about George McGavin. Give Sts time to read it.

  Now focus on the photos. Drill the pronunciation of the insects where necessary, and then do the question as a whole-class activity.

b Focus on the task and go through the **Glossary** with the class.

  Play the video (**Part 1**) once the whole way through for Sts to watch and answer the question.

  Get Sts to compare with a partner, and then check answers.

EXTRA SUPPORT Before playing the video, go through the listening scripts and decide if you need to pre-teach / check any lexis to help Sts when they watch.

Arthropods are animals with lots of hinged legs (legs with joints in them) and hard outsides, e.g. crustacea, spiders, and insects. They are important because they make up three quarters of all animals in the world. / They are the biggest animal group in the world.

I = interviewer, G = George McGavin
Part 1

I Professor McGavin, you're an expert in arthropods. Could you start by telling us what arthropods are?

G Well, arthropods are, are this really enormous group of animals; I mean, they're, they're much bigger than any other animal group on Earth. They comprise about, you know, three quarters of, of all animals and they're the, they're the animals that have lots of hinged legs: so, crustacea, spiders, insects – that sort of thing. Hard outsides, lots of hinged legs.

I And what is it about them that interests you?

G Arthropods have got to interest everybody because they are, to all intents and purposes, the, the major animal group on Earth. So, if you call yourself a zoologist and you don't know anything about arthropods, you really don't know anything about anything because they are the majority! Everybody gets very excited about, er, backboned animals, things with a spine: er, bats, cats, rats, mammals, amphibians, fish, birds. They only comprise two point nine per cent of all species, whereas arthropods comprise about sixty-six per cent of all species. So, you know, uh, in terms of, of, of species, they are immensely important. In terms of what they do, they are immensely important.

I Were you interested in them right from the start, from when you were a child?

G When I was very young, I, I knew that the natural world was the most interesting thing around. So I wanted to be outside, and you don't have to be outside very long before you find, you know, insects and spiders and things, you know, doing interesting things. But I was interested more generally as a kid, and it was only when I got to Edinburgh for my first degree that I realized that actually, insects were the major player in any habitat. And we were on a field trip to the west coast of Scotland, when all my classmates were looking for badgers and owls and eagles, and failing to find them, but at our feet were hundreds of thousands of ants doing very interesting things, and I thought, 'Well, the, the – surely this is easier to work on?'

I I understand that there are several species that are named after you. Could you tell us a bit about them?

G One of the great things about being in a field for long enough is that people will eventually describe a new species and think, 'Oh, what on earth am I going to call this?', you know, and normally they're, they're named after the country, or how they look, or something like that. But five people around the world have named, er, an insect in my honour, and a spider, I think, so I have a, a plant hopper in Africa, I've got a shield bug from Borneo, er, I think an ant from Africa as well, a cockroach from south-east Asia, which is, is great, and they have my name, er, attached to them! What's making me slightly depressed is the fact that, er, these things may not survive. Er, even though they've been named in my, my honour, we're losing species at a quite alarming rate now, be, because of habitat loss. And the sad truth is that although we are pretty sure there are eight million species of arthropods out there unknown, our chances of ever finding them and naming them are probably pretty slim because they will come and they will go without us ever knowing they were there.

c Focus on the task and give Sts time, in pairs, to see if they can answer any of the questions.

  Play the video again the whole way through.

  Get Sts to compare with their partner, and then check answers.

You could pause the video after each point has been mentioned and, in pairs, get Sts to compare orally what they have understood.

1 Examples of animals with a spine: bats, cats, rats, mammals, amphibians, fish, birds
   He thinks they are less important because they make up only 2.9% of all species.
2 When he was on a field trip at university (for his first degree). Ants caught his attention.
3 Normally, new species are named after the country they are found in or how they look.
   He has five named after him.
4 Their habitat is being destroyed and they are disappearing very quickly, and we may never even discover some of them.

If there's time, you could get Sts to watch again with subtitles, so they can see exactly what they understood / didn't understand. Translate / Explain any new words or phrases.

d Do this as a whole-class activity, or put Sts in pairs and then get some feedback.

▶ Part 2

a Focus on the task and the **Glossary** and go through it with the class.

   Play the video (**Part 2**) once the whole way through for Sts to do the task.

   Give Sts time to tell each other what they understood.

   Check answers.

He isn't particularly sympathetic.
Yes, once. He was afraid of a fer-de-lance snake in the Amazon.

Part 2
I Quite a lot of people have phobias of insects and spiders. Why do you think that is?
G I sometimes wonder why people have a phobia. I mean, they, they say it's because they're unpredictable, they, they move in a strange way, they've got lots of legs – well, you know, I, I don't know. It's, it's, it – I think it's passed on. I think if you're a kid growing up, you have a fascination with, with the thing arou– all the animals around you, and I think adults sometimes pass their fears on by, by going, 'Oh, what's that?', you know, 'Oh, it's a spider', you know. In some parts of the world it, it's perfectly justifiable to, to have a fear of spiders, because there are many places in the world where, you know, spiders can injure you severely, you know. In the UK, however, there are no spiders which can injure you at all. You might get a slight irritation or, you know, a swelling, but, but still there are something like seven million people in the United Kingdom who are terrified of spiders, and, and moths.
I Do you think it's possible for them to be cured of their phobia?
G It is possible to, to train people out of fears, er, by, by simply exposing them to something, you know, on, on a regular basis, and perhaps if they have a spider phobia, you start with a very small spider and you say, well, 'Have it on your hand, look at it, examine it, you know, it's fine.' And I've, I've actually cured a girl who had a spider phobia in a, in a day, and by the end of the day, she was able to hold a tarantula. Um, and I, I think it's – you know, I think if people look at the natural world, if they look at insects or spiders, and they understand them, then you begin to, to really enjoy them. And it, but, but if you just cut yourself off, which is what most people do, they say, you know, 'I'm going to have an insect-free zone around me', it, it's not possible.
I I'm assuming you're not afraid of any insects or spiders, but have you ever been in a situation where you were genuinely frightened of an animal?

G We were filming in the Amazon after dark because it was a programme about animals after dark, and I saw a, a head of a snake poking out from under a leaf, and of course I thought, well, 'This is great, you know. Quick, the camera! Come on, let's get down and have a look at this thing.' You know, I'm not stupid, so I, I got a stick and I, I lifted this leaf up gingerly, and of course it was a fer-de-lance, which is, uh, one of the most dangerous snakes in the whole of South America, responsible for more human deaths than probably any other snake. And as I lifted it up, it sort of looked at me, you know, and they don't like head torches, so I'm wearing a head torch shining right in its face! It does this, you know! And then I realize that it's four feet long; it's twice as long as my stick, which means that it could get me very easily indeed. So I, I, I just sort of froze; I could feel my heart pounding, and I just gent– gingerly put the leaf down and said, 'We'll just leave this one I think!' That could have been very nasty.

b Focus on the task and give Sts time to read sentences 1–8. Remind them to correct the ones that are false.

   Play the video again the whole way through.

   Get Sts to compare with a partner, and then check answers.

You could tell Sts that the first time they watch, they just need to write *T* or *F*. Check answers, then play the video again and get Sts to correct the *F* sentences.

1 T
2 T
3 F (He thinks it is justifiable for people who live in countries with dangerous spiders.)
4 F ('In the UK, however, there are no spiders which can injure you at all.')
5 F (He cured one girl of her phobia in a day.)
6 T
7 F (The snake didn't like the head torch.)
8 F (He froze and then put the leaf back on the snake.)

If there's time, you could get Sts to watch again with subtitles, so they can see exactly what they understood / didn't understand. Translate / Explain any new words or phrases.

c Do this as a whole-class activity, or put Sts in pairs and then get some feedback.

▶ Part 3

a Focus on the task and the **Glossary** on *p.95* and go through it with the class.

   Give Sts time to read questions 1–7.

   Now play the video (**Part 3**) once the whole way through for Sts to do the task.

Part 3
I Would you ever just kill an insect that was in your house?
G Well, in my career I have killed millions of insects. As part of my work is, you have to collect them, er, because you can't name them, or describe them, or work on them unless you kill them. In my home, uh, that's a different thing. If it's a, if it's a bee that has come in by accident, or a wasp or something like that, I will catch it and outside it goes. Fleas, however – if you have a cat and you don't control the fleas – are a bit of a pest, and I will definitely get rid of the fleas.
I Eating insects has recently become quite fashionable. Is it a realistic solution to the problem of world nutrition, or is it just a flash in the pan, for want of a better phrase?
G I don't think it's a flash in the pan because you can farm them in, in, in a very easy way. And as long as you can make the food available in a palatable form, er, I mean, I've, I've eaten insects for, for years and years, fry them up and grind them into flour and

make, you know, bread out of it. No, it, it isn't a flash in the pan; um, we will have to, to address this quite seriously in the next, you know, hundred or so years.

I   Why do we not eat insects in Europe?

G In the West we, we tend to not eat insects and, and lots of people say it's because insects are dirty, or they look funny, or whatever. It's actually not anything to do with those things: it's, it's about, uh, ecology – it's about a thing called 'optimal foraging theory', which simply says if you use up more energy collecting food to feed yourself and your family than you get back from eating it, it won't happen; it's, it's not a thing that will, will occur in that area of the world. So, in the West, where it's cold and insects are relatively small, it's, it's not a very sensible idea. However, in hot countries where insects are larger and swarm and can be collected very, very easily – and that's anywhere from Mexico, Japan, South America, you know, any of these, uh, countries – it makes sense. It's very easy to harvest enough food, er, in a relatively short time – half an hour, an hour – which will provide a, a sizeable meal. And it's, it's a thing that, that we've been doing as a species for a million years.

I   If you were trying to convert someone to insect-eating, what would be the first thing you would cook them?

G Well, you, you would have to make the food appealing and interesting and, er, you know, attractive, so I would start with a, with a mealworm, er, in a snack! Roasted mealworms are awfully good!

I   How often do you cook insects?

G As often as I can! I cook, I cook insects as often as I can! I like to open audiences' eyes to the possibility of eating insects. We eat prawns; we eat lots of things – you know, snails – but I mean, insects are essentially flying prawns. OK, they, they tend to be smaller. But I, I had an audience once in, in Oxford of two hundred eight-, eight- to twelve-year-olds, and at, at the end of my lecture, I cooked up a big wok of, of, of crickets – fried them up with some garlic and a bit of salt and pepper, handed them round, and the kids went wild! They, they ate the whole lot. From the back of the audience came a mum with a face like thunder, she came down to the front of the, of the auditorium and said, 'My son's just eaten six crickets!' I went, 'Yeah, and your point is?' She was like, 'At home he doesn't even eat broccoli.' And I just went, I said, 'Well, clearly it's the way you cook your broccoli.'

b Get Sts to discuss the questions and what they understood.

EXTRA SUPPORT You could elicit answers now before playing the video again for more details.

1 He has killed millions.
2 He doesn't do it unless they are fleas.
3 It is an ecological theory.
4 We don't do it in cold countries. In hot countries it makes sense.
5 He says it's delicious.
6 He did it at the end of a lecture.
7 One boy's mother came to talk to him after her child had eaten crickets.

Now tell Sts they will watch again for more details.

Play the video again the whole way through.

Get Sts to compare with their partner, and then check answers.

EXTRA SUPPORT You could pause the video after each point has been mentioned and, in pairs, get Sts to compare orally what they have understood.

1 He has killed millions because he has to, so that he can work on them and describe them.
2 He will catch the insect and let it go outside the house. He kills fleas as they are a pest.

3 It is an ecological theory meaning if you use more energy collecting food to feed yourself and your family than you get back from eating it, it isn't worth it.
4 People don't eat insects in cold countries because they say they are dirty and look strange. Also, insects in the West are small, so they aren't worth eating. Insects in hot countries are large and swarm, so can be collected very easily. People have been doing this for millions of years.
5 He thinks a mealworm in a snack is a good way to start eating insects.
6 He cooked the crickets with some garlic, salt, and pepper. He then gave them to the children, who ate all of them.
7 The mother couldn't believe her son had eaten crickets as he refuses to eat broccoli at home.

EXTRA SUPPORT If there's time, you could get Sts to watch again with subtitles, so they can see exactly what they understood / didn't understand. Translate / Explain any new words or phrases.

c Do this as a whole-class activity, or put Sts in pairs and then get some feedback.

2 ▶ LOOKING AT LANGUAGE

a Focus on the **Informal and vague language** box and go through it with the class.

Now focus on the task and give Sts time to read extracts 1–8.

Play the video, pausing after each extract to give Sts time to write.

Get Sts to compare with a partner, and then check answers.

EXTRA CHALLENGE Ask Sts if they can guess any of the missing highlighted words before they watch.

1 pretty, out 2 going 3 something 4 bit 5 so
6 whatever 7 whole 8 went, like

1 And the sad truth is that although we are pretty sure there are eight million species of arthropods out there unknown…
2 …and I think adults sometimes pass their fears on by, by going, 'Oh, what's that?', you know, 'Oh, it's a spider…''
3 …but, but still there are something like seven million people in the United Kingdom who are terrified of spiders, and, and moths.
4 …however, if you have a cat and you don't control the fleas, are a bit of a pest…
5 No, it, it isn't a flash in the pan; um, we will have to, to address this quite seriously in the next, you know, hundred or so years.
6 …lots of people say it's because insects are dirty, or they look funny, or whatever.
7 …and the kids went wild! They, they ate the whole lot.
8 I went, 'Yeah, and your point is?' She was like, 'At home he doesn't even eat broccoli.'

b Put Sts in pairs and get them to say how each highlighted phrase could be said using more formal or neutral lexis.

Check answers.

1 pretty sure = quite sure / certain
    out there = in the natural world
2 by going = by saying
3 something like = approximately / about
4 bit of a pest = rather
5 hundred or so = approximately / about

6 or whatever = something like that
7 the whole lot = all of it / everything
8 I went = I said
  She was like = She replied

EXTRA IDEA You may want to point out that the past of *to be + like* is often used by native speakers to report speech, especially when telling a story, but that it is very informal, for example:

She was like, 'I never want to see you again!' (= She said that she never wanted to see me again.)

We were like, 'Where's your car?' (= We asked (them) where their car was.)

3 ▶ THE CONVERSATION

a Focus on the photo and tell Sts they are going to watch these three people discuss two questions. Focus on the task and play the video, pausing after the title screen to give Sts time to read the questions.

Then play the video once the whole way through.

Check the answer.

EXTRA SUPPORT Before playing the video, go through the listening script and decide if you need to pre-teach / check any lexis to help Sts when they listen.

The programmes are of such a high quality now.

Do you ever watch wildlife programmes on TV? Why do you think they are so popular?

Sean I love wildlife programmes, um, and when, when I see there's a new one coming on I get really excited about where we might be going. It's almost like going on safari, or going on a, on a diving holiday, or something like that, I think, they're just so immersive, I guess, that…

Joanne Yes.

Sean …you feel that, you know, you do feel that you're there, somehow.

Joanne No, I think that's true. Um, for me, I love that sort of, technical bit. You know, I love finding out the bit at the end, how they actually filmed it, and, um, and appreciating quite how difficult that it would have been…

Emma Takes ages, doesn't it?

Joanne Absolutely, to put something like that together, and the fact that it really is…

Sean Yeah.

Joanne …a serious expedition for many of these things. And so I think it, they kind of appeal to people on, of different ages…

Emma Mmm.

Joanne …and across a spectrum. You know, my eight-year-old will want to watch it because he's fascinated by animals generally and wildlife, my eleven-year-old because he, too, loves that behind the cameras idea. Um, and also, sometimes there's a bit of a, there's about learning something and reconnecting us with nature, maybe?

Emma Yeah.

Sean I think that's true, yeah.

Emma I know why they're popular, I just, I don't tend to watch them…

Joanne Right.

Emma …that religiously, I suppose. Um, if they're on, I'll put them on in the background and, like David Attenborough's voice is really relaxing, I think.

Joanne Maybe that's one of the reasons they're so popular, David Attenborough's voice is amazing, and he has this great way of just putting things across to us, doesn't he, in a way that we can all relate to, maybe?

Emma Yeah.

Sean I think so, I think they just keep getting better and better, that's the thing, really.

Joanne Yes.

Sean You see – you can watch something on a subject that you've seen before, and the next time they go there the cameras are better…

Joanne Yes.

Sean …the techniques are better, and it's a whole, whole new experience.

Joanne Absolutely.

Emma And they're almost becoming more extreme, as well, aren't they, with all the kind of different areas, like the, under the sea, and then the jungle ones that you've mentioned, it's just so – there's so much variety, isn't there?

Joanne It's an adventure every time.

---

b Focus on the task and give Sts time to read sentence stems 1–5.

Play the video once the whole way through, pausing after each speaker to give Sts time to do the task. Play again as necessary.

Check answers.

1 going on a safari or a diving holiday.
2 how they filmed the programmes.
3 he's fascinated by animals and wildlife.
4 doesn't watch them regularly.
5 wildlife programmes becoming more extreme.

EXTRA SUPPORT If there's time, you could get Sts to watch again with subtitles, so they can see exactly what they understood / didn't understand. Translate / Explain any new words or phrases.

c Do the questions as a whole-class activity, or put Sts in pairs and then get some feedback. You could also tell the class if you watch wildlife programmes.

d This exercise focuses on words and phrases used by the speakers to check whether the other speakers agree. Focus on the extracts and give Sts time to read them.

Play the video, pausing after the first extract and elicit the missing words. Repeat for the other four extracts.

1 doesn't it   2 maybe   3 doesn't he, maybe   4 aren't they
5 isn't there

Now do the question as a whole-class activity, or put Sts in pairs and then check the answer.

The speakers use question tags to check others agree with their points / to invite agreement, and *maybe* to add a tentative point of their own.

1
Joanne You know, I love finding out the bit at the end, how they actually filmed it, and, um, and appreciating quite how difficult that it would have been…

Emma Takes ages, doesn't it?

2
Joanne …Um, and also, sometimes there's a bit of a, there's about learning something and reconnecting us with nature, maybe?

3
Joanne Maybe that's one of the reasons they're so popular, David Attenborough's voice is amazing, and he has this great way of just putting things across to us, doesn't he, in a way that we can all relate to, maybe?

4
Emma And they're almost becoming more extreme, as well, aren't they, with all the kind of different areas,…

5

Emma   …like the, under the sea, and then the jungle ones that you've mentioned, it's just so – there's so much variety, isn't there?

---

e Put Sts in small groups of three if possible. Focus on the questions and make sure they understand them. Then give Sts time to discuss them.

Monitor and help, and encourage them to use words and phrases to confirm or check information where appropriate.

Get feedback from various groups. You could also tell the class what you think.

10A On your marks, set, go!

G relative clauses
V word building: adjectives, nouns, and verbs
P homographs

Lesson plan

This lesson focuses on two different angles on sport.

In the first half of the lesson, Sts discuss various sport-related choices. They then read an article, *Battle of the workouts*, which compares similar activities (weights and circuits, yoga and Pilates, etc.) that people might decide to take up if they want to get fit, and looks at the pros and cons of each. Then there is a focus on word building, forming nouns and verbs from common adjectives, e.g. *strong / strength / strengthen*, etc.

In the second half of the lesson, Sts start by listening to some sports commentaries and identifying the sport. They then listen to an interview with a professional sports commentator, Olly Hogben, in which he talks about why he became a commentator, what the job involves, and a memorable moment in his career. This leads to Sts talking about sports commentators and some sports issues raised in the interview. Sts then work on relative clauses, both defining and non-defining. Finally, there is a pronunciation focus on homographs, words which are spelt the same but pronounced differently according to the meaning, e.g. *row*.

More materials

For teachers

Photocopiables
Grammar relative clauses *p.185*
Communicative What's wrong with sport? *p.212*
(instructions *p.192*)

For students
Workbook 10A
Online Practice 10A

OPTIONAL LEAD-IN – THE QUOTE
Write the quote at the top of *p.96* on the board (books closed) and the name of the person who said it, or get Sts to open their books and read it.

Point out that Kapil Dev is a former Indian cricket player and is regarded as one of the greatest captains India ever had.

Ask Sts if they agree with the quote.

1 SPEAKING

EXTRA IDEA Before beginning **a**, you may want to focus on the lesson title and ask Sts what they think the phrase means and when it is used (*to tell runners in a race to get ready and then to start*).

a Focus on the task and make sure Sts understand all the lexis, e.g. *a (yoga) retreat, ballroom dancing*, etc.

Give Sts time to choose the option they'd rather do in each question. Stress that even if they hate sport and don't like either option, they have to choose one.

b Put Sts in small groups and focus on the two examples.

Now get them to explain their choices to each other. Encourage them to give as much information as they can.

Get some feedback from various groups, and find out what Sts disagreed about. You could also tell the class your own choices.

2 READING scanning for specific information

a Focus on the task and do this as a whole-class activity, or put Sts in pairs. Highlight the pronunciation of *circuits* /ˈsɜːkɪts/, *Pilates* /pɪˈlɑːtiːz/, and *spinning* /ˈspɪnɪŋ/. Some Sts may not be familiar with all the activities. You could elicit / explain the following:

- *circuits* (or *circuit training*) is a type of gym training in which different exercises are each done for a short time.
- *Pilates* is a physical fitness system (developed by Joseph Pilates in the early 20th century) which focuses on the core postural muscles that help keep the body balanced and that are essential to providing support for the spine. Point out that it always has a capital *P* as it is named after someone.
- *spinning* is a type of indoor exercise performed in a class on a stationary bicycle, usually with music.

If Sts worked in pairs, elicit some feedback. If Sts do or have done any of the activities, ask if they enjoyed them and why (not). You could tell the class about your own experiences.

b Now focus on the title of the article and elicit / explain what a *workout* is (= a period of physical exercise that you do to keep fit). Tell Sts to look through the article quickly to find the answers to the six questions (you could set a time limit). If they can't find the answer to one of the questions, tell them to go on to the next one, and return to the one they couldn't answer at the end.

Get Sts to compare with a partner, and then check answers.

EXTRA SUPPORT Before Sts read the article the first time, check whether you need to pre-teach any vocabulary, but <u>not</u> the nouns in **d**.

1 Pilates **2** step **3** yoga **4** circuits **5** weights
6 spinning

c Focus on the task. Explain that in the original article, for each pair of activities, one was declared the winner by a sports expert.

Get Sts to read each pair of activities carefully and guess which was judged the winner.

Get them to compare with a partner.

Elicit opinions before giving the answer.

The winners were circuits (burns more calories, interesting and varied, has a wider range of benefits), Pilates (burns slightly more calories, is addictive, improves strength as well as posture), and spinning (less boring, very good for your heart and lungs).

LANGUAGE IN CONTEXT

d Focus on the definitions and tell Sts, in pairs, to see if they can remember any of the nouns.

Set a time limit for them to find the nouns in the article. Tell Sts that they are in the order that they appear in the article.

Check answers.

> **1** training **2** flexibility **3** skipping rope **4** stretching
> **5** press-ups **6** sit-ups **7** trunk **8** spine

Deal with any other vocabulary problems that arose.

e Focus on the task and give Sts time to prepare their answers.

Put Sts in small groups to describe their chosen activity.

Get feedback by asking some groups to talk about their chosen sports.

3 VOCABULARY word building: adjectives, nouns, and verbs

Vocabulary notes

The adjectives in this section are very straightforward, but at this level, Sts should be expanding their knowledge to include related nouns and verbs. A common suffix for nouns formed from adjectives is *-ness*, but several nouns end in *-th*. Most of these are connected with dimensions, e.g. *width*, *depth*, and may involve a spelling change, e.g. *long* → *length*. All the verbs here end in the suffix *-en*, but some are formed from the adjective (e.g. *weak* → *weaken*) and some from the noun (e.g. *strength* → *strengthen*). *Height* is an exception here, both in the form of the noun and because the verb has a different, though related, meaning.

You could point out that all the verbs in this section could be replaced by *make* + comparative adjective, e.g. *Pilates can strengthen your back / make your back stronger*.

a Focus on the task. You could elicit that in the first sentence a noun is needed, and in the second a verb.

Get Sts to complete the sentences.

Check answers.

> **1** strength **2** strengthening

b Focus on the task. Elicit / Explain that with *strong*, the verb is formed by adding *-en* to the noun. Point out that with the other words in the chart, sometimes the verb is formed from the adjective + *-en*, and sometimes from the noun, and Sts should try out both ways to see which sounds correct.

Put Sts in pairs and give them time to complete the chart.

Check answers. You could tell Sts that *thicken* is often used in cookery, e.g. with soups and sauces. Elicit or model the pronunciation of any tricky words.

adjective	noun	verb
strong	strength	strengthen
long	length	lengthen
deep	depth	deepen
wide	width	widen
high	height	heighten
weak	weakness	weaken
short	shortness	shorten
thick	thickness	thicken
flat	flatness	flatten

c Focus on the sentences and get Sts to complete them with words from the chart in **b**. They can do this in pairs or individually and then compare answers with a partner.

Check answers, eliciting pronunciation. You might want to tell Sts that some of the words cannot only be used in a physical sense, but they also have non-literal / metaphorical uses, e.g. *to strengthen understanding, the depths of despair, a weakness for chocolate, the height of her powers*, etc.

> **1** shorten **2** length, width **3** height **4** weaken **5** depth
> **6** thicken **7** flattened **8** weaknesses **9** widened
> **10** strengthened **11** lengthened **12** strength

4 LISTENING & SPEAKING

a 🔊 10.1 Focus on the task. You might want to tell Sts that the vocabulary in the audio is very specialized, so the aim here is to focus on getting the gist of the commentaries.

Play the audio once the whole way through for Sts to listen and match each commentary to a photo.

Check answers.

EXTRA SUPPORT Before playing the audio, elicit what the sports in the photos are and write them on the board.

> **1** 100 metres (the only possibility for 10.72 seconds)
> **2** golf **3** (road) cycling **4** judo **5** basketball **6** ice-skating

---

🔊 10.1
(script in Student's Book on *p.140*)
1
Off and running! Brilliant start from Lorraine Stewart – she's flying out. Browning's getting into her stride; she's trying to chase her down. Now Harris is coming up in lane six; she's coming up on Stewart; she's coming hard, but Stewart is going to get there – she dips for the line. Ten point seven-two! Stewart takes the gold in a new championship record.
2
Brian Marks to putt now, and he, he's had a tough time in this competition: nothing has gone right for him. And we haven't seen him make a long putt in a while. He would love this to go in for a birdie and try to get his round back on track. It must be thirty, thirty-two feet, with a slight break to the left, and he needs enough speed on it. He's hit it well; it's looking good – come on, come on – and he makes it! That was beautiful!
3
Surely the attack is going to come soon: Fernández can't afford to wait any longer. She doesn't have a sprint finish; she needs to go now. Coming to the foot of the final climb of the day, eight kilometres at an average gradient of twelve per cent, this could be very interesting. And she's gone! Fernández has gone! Brankart is trying to follow, but the gap is opening! And Fernández has twenty

metres, thirty metres, and she looks round once, and she knows this is her chance.

4

The Cuban has got the arm lock, Asaka desperately trying to keep his elbow turned. That was a moment of real danger; he needs to settle himself here. He might have hurt his arm. Thirty seconds to go now. This is fraught with danger: every time you take a step towards your opponent, you put yourself in danger, but you've got to take that step to win the gold.

5

What has happened to Australia? They cannot contain Brazil; they're trying to come back at them, but Australia have lost their rhythm. Very consistent throwing from Brazil – there's another three-pointer; that's a nice move; they're running away with this now. Only a few seconds left – and that's it, it's two more points to Brazil and it's all over. Brazil are safely through to the semi-final, seventy-one to forty.

6

Fantastic start from Ivanova – triple Salchow, triple toe, great elevation on both jumps. And again, amazing elevation – that was a flip. She looks so relaxed; she's completely in control here. Triple flip, double toe, ooh, a little bit of a stumble, but she comes out of it well. Last jump coming up now; it's a double Axel, and oh no! She's down on the ice, and she's back up, but that's going to be the end of her hopes for a medal. That is a disaster for Ivanova.

b Focus on the task and give Sts time to match two phrases to each sport they made a note of in **a**. Sts can do this individually or in pairs.

Play the audio again for Sts to listen and check.

Get Sts to compare with a partner, and then check answers. Make sure Sts understand all the lexis.

A 3   B 6   C 5   D 6   E 2   F 4   G 1   H 5   I 2   J 4
K 1   L 3

EXTRA SUPPORT If there's time, you could get Sts to listen again with the script on *p.140*, so they can see exactly what they understood / didn't understand.

c ◀)) **10.2** Focus on the photo of Olly Hogben and the task. Give Sts time to read all the topics.

Play the audio once the whole way through for Sts to listen and tick the topics Olly mentions.

Get Sts to compare with a partner, and then check answers.

EXTRA SUPPORT Read through the script and decide if you need to pre-teach any new lexis before Sts listen.

He talks about:
his family background
why he became a sports commentator
how commentary should interact with pictures
a sport that he's an expert in
cheating in football
the value of good commentary
his most memorable sporting occasion

◀)) **10.2**
(script in Student's Book on *pp.140–141*)
I = interviewer, O = Olly Hogben
I   So, Olly, have you always been interested in sport?
O   Yes, I have. I was always a huge sports fan as a child, particularly tennis and football. They were the ones that I played. My mother was a tennis player; my dad was a footballer. So they, those were the sports that I got into. But I always loved watching most sports. My grandfather – both of my grandfathers – were huge fans of sport. So watched a lot and, and then just became very curious about the language of television, sometimes even more than the action of the sport.

I   Do you do a lot of sport or exercise yourself?
O   I could tell you yes, but that would be a lie. Especially about the exercise bit. I do probably not enough exercise. I play football, I play tennis a little bit, but that's about it. And I would never – because I'm a sports commentator – I would never call myself an athlete because I know what an athlete really is, and it isn't me.
I   What made you want to be a commentator?
O   When I was a child, I commentated on everything that was happening. That, that's the thing that unites all sports commentators. When you go back to their childhood, they're the ones that commentated when people were playing football in the playground. I, when I was playing sport in the back garden, I would add in a running commentary to it. I made cassette tapes that I've still got, when I was eleven years old, of radio broadcasts of pretend football matches. So, I always had this love of language. My grandfather was somebody who absolutely loved words, and I think in my family we grew up with a passion, a curiosity, for language, so that was always there. And then when my love of sport developed, I think the two married together very nicely.
I   What's your favourite sport to commentate on?
O   My number one is definitely gymnastics, which I love because of the variety: there's just so many different forms of gymnastics. It could be trampolining or aerobics, or rhythmic gymnastics – that's beautiful and exciting to do so many different things.
I   Do you have to be an expert in all the sports you commentate on?
O   There are some sports that you have to have extremely strong knowledge of. Gymnastics is full of technical moves, complex rules, complex scoring; you have to know the vocabulary, you have to understand it.
I   I'm sure.
O   There are other sports that are definitely something you can commentate without being an expert. For example, a race. Now if you're doing a race – in swimming, in horseracing, in athletics – it's still just a race. The most important thing is: tell the story of the race.
I   What would you say is the most difficult thing about commentating?
O   Shutting up is definitely the hardest thing about commentating, because pictures are beautiful. Sound is beautiful. The sound of a crowd is a beautiful thing; the sound of a player screaming with excitement when they hit the winning point is wonderful. It's very easy as a commentator to forget that there are pictures, and we use a phrase in the broadcasting world – we say, 'Let the picture breathe,' and I think that's really important to do.
I   That's so interesting. Do you ever disagree with the referee or the judges when you're commentating?
O   Absolutely, but the important thing is: do not destroy them. As a broadcaster, do not attack referees or judges. They are human beings; they are doing a job. They get it right sometimes; they get it wrong sometimes. Unless a referee is obviously cheating, which is very, very, very unusual, then you have to be understanding and kind, because athletes make mistakes, referees make mistakes, commentators make mistakes.
I   So, have you ever seen anyone, a player or an athlete, cheating during an event?
O   Very occasionally. I would say that most athletes actually have great integrity. They are very honest people. It's rare that it happens. When it does happen, it can be quite difficult, actually. You have to choose your words very carefully because to, maybe to me or to you, it's very obviously cheating, but it's not to them. Sometimes a footballer dives. But did they dive or did they fall? And actually, I – it's not my job to try to inhabit the mind of the athlete and tell you what they were thinking at the time. Where it is also difficult is maybe if an athlete has returned after a ban because they had taken drugs or they had cheated, then you have to refer to that ban, but it's important not to be stuck in the past too much.
I   What do you think commentary adds to the experience of a television viewer?
O   Commentary should be furniture, not wallpaper; I think that's a term that we use quite often in broadcasting. It should make it easier for the viewer to place themselves in the action. It shouldn't just be decoration; it shouldn't be something that distracts you from the really important things. If you use too

many words, if you start to tell meaningless stories, then the viewer will switch off from the things that you're saying. I think the point of commentary is to provide drama, it is to help explain why things have happened, and it's also to introduce new viewers to a sport.

I   I see. What are the most memorable moments of your career so far?

O   You never forget your first Olympic Games. The feeling of arriving at the stadium, staring up at the Olympic rings, probably the most famous logo in all of sport; you look at it and you realize this is what you are doing. You are part of the Olympic movement, and that's incredible. And the Olympic Park is full of energy; the atmosphere is unbelievable there. And you get to broadcast the greatest moments of people's careers at the Olympic Games, which is an incredible feeling.

d Focus on the task and give Sts time to read sentences 1–10. Remind Sts to correct the false statements.

Play the audio again, pausing after Olly Hogben answers each question to give Sts time to complete the task.

Get Sts to compare with a partner, and then check answers.

EXTRA SUPPORT You could tell Sts that the first time they listen, they just need to mark each statement *T* (true) or *F* (false). The second time, they will need to correct the false ones. You could also check answers between listenings.

1   F (He played tennis and football, but loved watching all sports.)
2   F (He plays a bit of football and tennis, but he doesn't do enough exercise and he's no athlete.)
3   T
4   T
5   F (You need specialist knowledge for some sports, but not all. For example, a race is a race, whether it's swimming, running, or horse racing, and you tell the story.)
6   F (He thinks you need to give some space to the pictures and sounds of what's happening, rather than talk over everything.)
7   F (He disagrees with them, but he doesn't attack them for it.)
8   T
9   T
10 F (The feeling that you're part of it is incredible, and the Olympic park is full of energy.)

EXTRA SUPPORT If there's time, you could get Sts to listen again with the script on *pp.140–141*, so they can see exactly what they understood / didn't understand. Translate / Explain any new words or phrases.

e 🔊 **10.3** Focus on the task and photo of Stig-André Berge and make sure Sts know what a *wrestler* is. Elicit or model its pronunciation /ˈreslə/.

Give Sts time to read the events they need to number in the correct order, and point out that the first one has been done for them.

Play the audio once the whole way through for Sts to listen and number the events.

Get Sts to compare with a partner, and then play the audio again if necessary.

Check answers.

EXTRA SUPPORT Read through the script and decide if you need to pre-teach any new lexis before Sts listen.

2   He found out that his mother was seriously ill.
3   He saw his mother for the last time.
4   He went to the Rio Olympics.
5   He won the bronze medal.

🔊 **10.3**
(script in Student's Book on *p.141*)
I   Can you tell us about one really special moment that you remember?
O   There was one very special moment for me that happened in the Rio twenty-sixteen Olympics. Sometimes it's not the biggest moments – they're not always the most memorable. Sometimes it's small things that have a particular story. And there was a Norwegian wrestler, a gentleman called Stig-André Berge. He was thirty-three, it was his third Olympic Games, and he had never even come close to winning a medal in his previous attempts. He was a very good wrestler, but he had never come close. Just before the Olympic Games, he discovered that his mother had terminal cancer, and he made it home from the qualification tournament for the Olympic Games in time to see her for the last time.
I   Wow.
O   And he promised her in that last meeting that he would win her an Olympic medal. And we got to the Olympic Games in Rio a few months later, and every match he won by the most narrow of margins; it was so tight and so close. And then he won the crucial match that gave him a chance to go for the bronze medal. And when he won that match, he looked up into the sky and he just pointed upwards. And I realized that this was now the time to start telling that story. Because I didn't want to start telling it too early or make it too sentimental, so I mentioned the story about his mother. And then he won the bronze medal. And it was so close. And at the end, his coaches ran– he burst into tears, his coaches ran on, they were three of them lying on the ground, holding each other, crying. And I was able to put into words that story of the promise he'd made to his mother. I felt very honoured to be the person trusted to tell his story.
I   Wow, what a moment that must have been. Thank you so much, Olly, and thank you for sharing that story with us.

EXTRA SUPPORT If there's time, you could get Sts to listen again with the script on *p.141*, so they can see exactly what they understood / didn't understand. Translate / Explain any new words or phrases.

f Put Sts in small groups and give them time to discuss the questions.

Get some feedback from various groups. You could do some of the questions as a whole-class discussion.

5 GRAMMAR relative clauses

a Focus on sentences 1–7 and get Sts to cross out the relative clauses that are not possible.

Get them to compare with a partner, and then check answers.

1   ~~that~~ / who / ~~whom~~   2   ~~that~~ / ~~what~~ / which
3   that / who / ~~(–)~~   4   ~~that~~ / ~~who~~ / whose   5   that / who / (–)
6   ~~that~~ / what / ~~which~~   7   that / which / (–)

b Tell Sts to go to **Grammar Bank 10A** on *p.160*.

Grammar notes
Defining relative clauses
Sts at this level should be confident with basic defining relative clauses, i.e. with *who / which / that* (**rule 1**). They have also been introduced to the use of *whose*, and relative clauses where the relative pronoun is left out (**rules 3** and **4**), but will still need practice of these kinds of sentences.

- **Rule 4:**

  Here Sts learn two ways to say the same thing. Preposition + *whom* is rather more formal than using *who / which* and a verb + preposition. *Whom* is still sometimes used when the person it refers to is the object of the relative clause, e.g. *The person whom I saw yesterday*, but this is very formal and normally we would either use *who / that* or leave the relative pronoun out altogether.

- **Rule 5:**

  Sts may still confuse *what* (= the thing / things that) and *that* as relative pronouns, often because of L1 interference.

Non-defining relative clauses

  Sts have already been introduced to non-defining relative clauses, but will probably need reminding of what they are and how to use them (**rule 1**).

- **Rule 2:**

  This use of *which* is probably new for Sts, who may try to use *what* in these kinds of sentences.

- **Rule 3:**

  This use of *of which / of whom / of whose* may be new for Sts. The structure is easy to understand.

Focus on the example sentences for **defining relative clauses** and go through the rules with the class.

Repeat for **non-defining relative clauses**.

Focus on the exercises and get Sts to do them individually or in pairs. If Sts do them individually, get them to compare with a partner.

Check answers, getting Sts to read the full sentences.

a
1 ✓
2 ✗ that goes to Birmingham
3 ✗ which was absolutely true
4 ✗ who is very bright
5 ✗ The employee to whom I spoke / (who / that) I spoke to
6 ✓
7 ✓
8 ✗ eats what I cook
9 ✓
10 ✗ whose fans sing the best
11 ✗ What we love about living in Paris
12 ✗ none of which I enjoy

b
1 They gave us a present, which was a complete surprise.
2 My girlfriend, who is an architect, is very intelligent. / My girlfriend, who is very intelligent, is an architect.
3 It's too hot in my flat, which makes it impossible to sleep.
4 The car which / that crashed into mine was a Mini.
5 The police officer (who / that) I spoke to was working on the reception desk. / The police officer to whom I spoke was working on the reception desk.
6 Our computer, which we only bought two months ago, keeps on crashing.
7 The things (which / that) I left on the table aren't there any more.
8 That's the electrician who / that did some work for my mother.
9 I've got two brothers, neither of whom can swim.
10 The houses, many of which were built in 1870, are still in very good condition. / Many of the houses, which are still in very good condition, were built in 1870.

Tell Sts to go back to the main lesson **10A**.

EXTRA SUPPORT If you think Sts need more practice, you may want to give them the **Grammar** photocopiable activity at this point.

c Focus on the **Defining relative clauses in spoken English** box and go through it with the class.

  Now focus on the task and make sure Sts understand what they have to do.

  Give Sts time to write their five definitions. Make sure they don't write the word.

  Put Sts in pairs and get them to swap definitions and guess the words.

  Get some Sts to read their definitions for the class to guess.

EXTRA SUPPORT Sts can choose the five words and write the definitions in pairs. Then put two pairs together and get them to swap pieces of paper.

6 PRONUNCIATION homographs

Pronunciation notes

Homographs (words with different meanings which have the same spelling but different pronunciation) cause problems, as in many cases, Sts are not aware that a word like *row* has more than one possible pronunciation.

This exercise focuses on some common homographs, and you should encourage Sts to note any others they come across.

❗ Sts should already be aware of one kind of homograph, i.e. two-syllable words which can be verbs or nouns, and where the stress shifts, e.g. *contract* (verb) and *contract* (noun).

a Focus on the **Homographs** box and go through it with the class.

  Focus on the task and get Sts, in pairs, to try saying the two pronunciations first, using the phonetics, and then match them to the correct sentence.

b 🔊 **10.4** Play the audio for Sts to listen and check.

  Pause after each group of sentences and elicit the answer. Then move on to the next group.

1 b **2** a **3** a **4** b **5** a **6** b **7** a **8** a **9** b **10** b
11 a **12** b **13** a **14** a **15** b

🔊 **10.4**
See sentences in Student's Book on *p.99*

Finally, get Sts in pairs to practise saying the sentences.

EXTRA SUPPORT If your Sts seem to have particular problems with some of the pairs of words, you could use the audio to model and drill the different pronunciations and get them to say the sentences.

EXTRA CHALLENGE Sts could choose some homographs and make their own sentences for their partner to guess.

G adding emphasis (2): cleft sentences
V words that are often confused
P intonation in cleft sentences

Lesson plan

The topic of this lesson is living in another country, emigration, and identity.

The lesson begins with listening and speaking, where Sts hear a British couple who emigrated to Spain in 1997 talking about their experiences. Sts then talk about people they know who have gone to live in another country, and the pros and cons. This is followed by the grammar section, where Sts work on adding emphasis by using clauses or phrases which emphasize one part of a sentence, sometimes called *cleft sentences*. In Pronunciation, they work on the intonation patterns in this kind of sentence. The first half ends with a speaking activity in which Sts complete some cleft sentence stems with their own ideas and then compare them with a partner.

In the second half of the lesson, Sts read and discuss an article by Michal Iwanowski, a photographer who was born in Poland, lives in Wales, and recently walked from Cardiff to his hometown. This leads to a discussion about Michal's conclusions about where home is, and about what people are like. The vocabulary focus is on words which are often confused, e.g. *foreigner*, *stranger*, and *outsider*. The lesson ends with a documentary on Ellis Island.

Immigration is very much part of the modern world, but it can be a sensitive topic. Although the lesson does not ask Sts to talk about immigration in their country directly, you may need to be alert to the background of Sts in your class, and to be aware that discussions may go in unpredictable directions.

More materials
For teachers
Photocopiables
Grammar adding emphasis (2): cleft sentences *p.186*
Communicative About the UK quiz *p.213*
(instructions *p.192*)
For students
Workbook 10B
Online Practice 10B

OPTIONAL LEAD-IN – THE QUOTE

Write the quote at the top of *p.100* on the board (books closed) and the name of the person who said it, or get Sts to open their books and read it.

Point out that Malala Yousafzai is a Pakistani activist for female education and the youngest Nobel Prize laureate – she won the Nobel Peace Prize at 17.

Get Sts, in pairs, to say whether they agree with the quote.

1 LISTENING & SPEAKING

a Do this as a whole-class activity and elicit reasons.

b Focus on the task and then give Sts time to read the extract and complete the gaps with the adjectives from the list. Point out that the first one (*dramatic*) has been done for them.
Check answers.

2 lovely   3 far   4 seasonal   5 intimate   6 warm
7 winning

Elicit the meaning of *nooks and crannies* (= small, quiet places or corners that are sheltered or hidden from other people) in the first paragraph.

Now get Sts to quickly read the extract again and decide what would attract them there and what they might do once there.

Get Sts to tell a partner.

Elicit ideas.

c 🔊 10.5 Focus on the task and tell Sts that David and Emma are both British.

Give Sts time to read 1–8, making sure they understand all the lexis, e.g. *integrate*.

Play the audio for Sts to listen and answer the questions.

Get Sts to compare with a partner, and then check answers.

EXTRA SUPPORT When playing audio 🔊 10.5 and 🔊 10.6, pause after each question has been answered to give Sts time to write.

EXTRA SUPPORT Read through the scripts and decide if you need to pre-teach any new lexis before Sts listen, but *not* the idioms and phrasal verbs in **f**.

1 D   2 E   3 B   4 B   5 D   6 D   7 E   8 B

🔊 10.5
(script in Student's Book on *p.141*)
I = interviewer, E = Emma, D = David
Part 1
I   Why did you decide to leave the UK and live abroad?
E   Well, actually, it was David who convinced me it was a good idea. A long time ago, going back, I was studying at the, my final year at University of Warwick, and David was working at that time in Majorca. And we met in England and then he returned to work in Majorca. And then it was, it was very, we kept in touch by letters and it was very easy to be seduced by the, the lifestyle he had there: the lovely swimming, the barbecues in the mountains, the, the fishing for octopus. So I was sitting finishing my le– my essays in the, the library, windows covered with rain and, yes, so when I graduated I, I went very happily out to, to Spain to be with him. And we both got jobs in Vigo in, in Spain, working as language teachers in a private school, and we had a lovely time. We just, we worked, and when we weren't working, we spent the time discovering the area, going out on our bikes, and learnt to windsurf. Yes, that was a great year.
I   So a very happy introduction to Spain for you. And, and how did you both end up in Mairena?
D   Well, it was by chance, really. We'd, we'd been working as English teachers for, for several years – ten years perhaps in my case – and we realized that we had the opportunity to, to take a year off, a

sabbatical year as it were, with a view to then going back to, to teaching again. And we had a friend who had a, a small house in the, in, in a village in the mountains south of Granada, and he'd agreed to, to let us rent his house for, for next to nothing for a year. So that's what we did, but whilst we were there, we wandered around and cycled around and finally stumbled on this little village of Mairena, where we live now, and fell in love with the village, fell in love with the house that we, we lived in for a while at first, and realized at the end of the year that we were, we were having a ball and enjoying it too much, really, to, to want to go back. So at that point, we realized that we had to, to find a way of earning a living because we didn't have any money, and so we, I, I got a job in Granada, in fact, just teaching for a year or so, and then we opened what's now Las Chimeneas, our little hotel and restaurant.

I   How integrated do you feel in the local community?
D   Well, one of the things that made me feel very integrated and indeed very, very proud in fact was, was being invited to, to join the local council. And I worked for six years as the, the Deputy Mayor, and not necessarily a very good Deputy Mayor, but I kind of enjoyed it, and it was, you know, I consider it as an honour to be, to be involved and asked to get involved in, in local politics. And it's, it's a useful thing as well, rather than just being on the outside protesting at decisions taken after the event, it's quite useful to be part of the decision-making process as well. And…
E   I think for me the, the thing that really made a difference was when we had children, because especially as being, being, you know, a mother in the village, it meant that you met other mothers and people felt it was a reason to talk. And our children are friends with the other kids; they come round to play now – so yeah, that was a big difference for me.
D   And having a business as well because we, you know, people can see that we're, we're actually working, and we're working alongside our neighbours, because, you know, we're lucky, we're, enough to be in a position where we've been able to employ quite a lot of the local villagers as, you know, as cooks, and chefs, and taxi drivers, and so on.

---

d   Focus on the task and tell Sts they are going to listen to **Part 1** of the interview again. Give them time to read questions 1–4.

Play the audio again.

Get Sts to compare with a partner, and then play again as necessary.

Check answers.

1   The swimming, barbecues in the mountains, fishing for octopus
2   They rented a cheap house in the mountains, and did lots of walking and cycling.
3   He considered it an honour to be involved in local politics and be part of the decision-making process.
4   People can see they're working, and they employ local people.

e   🔊 **10.6** Focus on the task and tell Sts they are now going to listen to the rest of the interview. Give them time to read the questions and their options.

Play the audio for Sts to listen and complete the task.

Get Sts to compare with a partner, and then play again if necessary.

Check answers.

1 b   2 c   3 a   4 c   5 b

🔊 **10.6**
(script in Student's Book on *p.141*)
Part 2
I   What do you like most about living in Mairena?
E   The obvious thing, and almost a cliché, is the weather – you can't underestimate that; I mean, the weather does affect your

everyday life – and also simple things like the incredible clear skies and the light. But I think it's something more than that. As long as I can remember, I always had a hankering, I really wanted to live in a very small community. I remember even as a child it was something that I always had an ambition to do. And I think something about living in a very small village – everything seems very kind of human, very manageable: you, you know everybody, you literally know everybody in the village. And what's also been great the last few years is that we bought some land which is filled with almonds and olive and fruit trees, so we spend a lot of tr– time down there, and learning how to farm like the locals do, because they have very complicated watering techniques, so we've had to speak to locals and learn how to farm the land.
I   Are there any downsides to living there?
E   It's the travelling, isn't it? We have to spend probably more time than we would like in a car to, to buy something simple. On, on the one hand, it's great being away from shops – it's like a kind of a, real kind of consumer detox – but on the other hand, when you actually have to buy something, it means you have a long journey, which I could do without.
D   And there's lots of paperwork as well: Spain is a very heavily bureaucratic country as well, and so there is lots of certification and permits and so on that we've got to, we've got to get together, and that always means a drive of a couple of hours to, to get to, to Granada, the local centre, to, to get paperwork sorted out.
I   Is there anything you miss about the UK?
D   Well, obviously, we miss friends and family – I mean, that's the, the big thing – but we're lucky we live in a nice part of the world, and so we, we get lots of visitors who come out and, and stay with us, which is nice. And then, you know, often it's very trite, silly little things that you miss – I mean, I miss pubs with carpets and soft lighting and, you know, polite dog walkers – that kind of thing.
E   The fact that, actually, when we come back, we often come back to London, so, what I really like about the UK is, is that sense of cultural diversity. Just travelling on public transport in London, you're very aware of the, the, the very wide range of people living here, which obviously you wouldn't get in a, a small rural community. And, of course, the, the great thing about that is being in London is, yeah, you can choose the, the, you know, rest– any kind of restaurant. That's a big treat to come back and be able to choose what kind of food you want to eat.
I   Do you think you'll come back to the UK one day?
D   Well, you never know. I mean, we, we, we never took a, a decision that we would stay in Spain forever, so it was kind of by chance – by accident – that we've been in Spain so long, so we, we've never really ruled it out. It would be tricky, I think, to come back, largely for economic or financial reasons. Britain is a very expensive place to buy a house at the moment, and then of course there's the boys – the boys, our two sons, are now aged seven and thirteen, so they were born and brought up in Spain. So it would be, they would be really uprooted for them to take them back to the UK, I think, now – that would be perhaps a, a bigger hurdle.
E   Yeah, for sure, that's the main reason why, why I can't see us going back is definitely Dan and Tom, but of course, I think once you've spent fifteen years building up a business, then also that's something you don't want to, to easily turn your back on. Of course the other thing we need to think about is the impact of Brexit. It might be that we end up applying for Spanish nationality. I think for now we're just going to see how things go.

LANGUAGE IN CONTEXT

f   🔊 **10.7** Focus on the task and give Sts time to read the extracts.

Play the audio once the whole way through for Sts to listen and complete the gaps.

Get Sts to compare with a partner, and say what they think the idioms and phrasal verbs mean.

Check answers.

EXTRA SUPPORT   Check the missing words first, then put Sts in pairs to say what they think the idioms and phrasal verbs mean.

1 next, nothing (*next to nothing* = almost nothing)
2 stumbled on (= to discover sth unexpectedly)
3 having, ball (*have a ball* = enjoy yourself a lot)
4 had, hankering (*have a hankering* = have a strong desire)
5 consumer detox (= a removal of the desire to buy things)
6 ruled, out (*rule sth out* = to decide that sth is not possible)
7 bigger hurdle (= a bigger problem that must be solved or dealt with before you can achieve sth)
8 turn, back (*turn your back on sth* = to reject sth that you have previously been connected with)

🔊 10.7

1 …he'd agreed to, to let us rent this house for, for next to nothing…
2 …we wandered around and cycled around and finally stumbled on this little village of Mairena, where we live now…
3 …we were having a ball and enjoying it too much, really, to, to want to go back…
4 As long as I can remember, I always had a hankering – I really wanted to live in a very small community…
5 …on the one hand, it's great being away from shops – it's like a kind of a, real kind of consumer detox…
6 …so we, we've never really ruled it out. It would be tricky, I think, to come back, largely for economic or financial reasons.
7 …to take them back to the UK, I think, now, that would be perhaps a, a bigger hurdle.
8 …I think once you've spent fifteen years building up a business, then also that's something you don't want to, to easily turn your back on.

EXTRA SUPPORT If there's time, you could get Sts to listen to the interview again with scripts 10.5 and 10.6 on *p.141*, so they can see exactly what they understood / didn't understand. Translate / Explain any new words or phrases.

g Focus on the task and point out the *Yes* and *No* sections under the question.

Put Sts in pairs and get them to tell their partner their answers.

Get some feedback from each section if possible.

2 GRAMMAR adding emphasis (2): cleft sentences

a Focus on sentences 1–4 and give Sts time to try to complete them with a partner, preferably in pencil or on a piece of paper.

b 🔊 10.8 Play the audio for Sts to listen and check, pausing and playing again as necessary.

Get Sts to compare with their partner, and then check answers.

See script 10.8

Elicit that the second versions give more emphasis to a particular part of the sentence, e.g. in the first sentence, *It was David who convinced me…* gives more emphasis to her husband than *David convinced me…* In the second sentence, putting *The thing that…* at the beginning gives more emphasis to this.

🔊 10.8

1 It was David who convinced me it was a good idea.
2 The thing that really made a difference was when we had children.
3 What I really like about the UK is, is that sense of cultural diversity.
4 The main reason why, why I can't see us going back is definitely Dan and Tom.

c Tell Sts to go to **Grammar Bank 10B** on *p.161*.

Grammar notes

When we want to focus attention on or emphasize one part of a sentence, we can do this by adding certain words or phrases to the beginning of the sentence, as a kind of introduction or build-up. For example, *What I enjoyed most about the film was*… or *The reason I was late was*… These kinds of sentences are often referred to in grammar books as *cleft sentences* (from the old-fashioned verb *to cleave* = to cut) because the sentence is divided into two parts. Cleft sentences are useful in writing because we can't use intonation to add emphasis.

Focus on the example sentences for **adding emphasis (2): cleft sentences** and go through the rules with the class.

Go through the **It was me who… or It was I who…?** box with the class.

Focus on the exercises and get Sts to do them individually or in pairs. If they do them individually, get them to compare with a partner.

Check answers after each exercise, getting Sts to read the full sentences.

a
1 It 2 What 3 reason 4 happens 5 All 6 place
7 What 8 me
b
1 The reason (why) she left her husband was…
2 The place (where) we stopped for lunch was…
3 What happened was that…
4 What really annoyed me was that…
5 It was your brother who…
6 All I said was…
7 The person (who / that) I like best of all my relatives is…
8 What happens is…
9 What you need to do right now is…
10 The first time I met Serena was…

Tell Sts to go back to the main lesson **10B**.

EXTRA SUPPORT If you think Sts need more practice, you may want to give them the **Grammar** photocopiable activity at this point.

3 PRONUNCIATION & SPEAKING intonation in cleft sentences

Pronunciation notes

Cleft sentences have a specific intonation pattern, which Sts should be made aware of. Encourage them to imitate it, as this will make their English sound more natural. If they find the technical expressions (fall-rise-fall tone, etc.) difficult to understand, tell them not to worry and to simply try to copy the intonation on the audio.

a 🔊 10.9 Focus on the **Fine-tuning your pronunciation: intonation in cleft sentences** box and go through it with the class.

Play the audio for Sts to listen to the example sentences in the box and try to grasp the two different intonation patterns.

🔊 10.9

See sentences in Student's Book on *p.101*

b ⏺ **10.10** Focus on sentences 1–6.

Play the audio, pausing after each sentence for Sts to listen and repeat. You could point out that the parts of the sentences that Sts should focus on are highlighted. Play the audio again as necessary.

⏺ **10.10**
See sentences in Student's Book on *p.101*

---

c Focus on the task and give Sts time to complete the sentences.

Monitor and help.

Put Sts in pairs and get them to take turns to read their sentences to each other and explain why or give more details. Monitor and check their intonation, correcting it where necessary.

Get some Sts to read their sentences and explain them to the class. You could find out if any pairs wrote similar endings to some of the sentences.

4 READING & SPEAKING

a Focus on the task, the photos, and the first two paragraphs of the article. Give Sts time to read and answer the questions.

Get Sts to compare with a partner, and then check the answer to the first question.

He saw some graffiti which made him question where his home was.

Now ask Sts what they think Michal might have learned from his walk to Poland.

Finally, elicit why they think he is holding a bird's nest in one of the photos.

The nest probably represents the concept of 'home'.

You may want to explain that *the Brexit referendum* refers to the vote held in the UK in June 2016 in which 52% of voters decided that the UK should leave the European Union.

b Focus on the task and the **Glossary**.

Give Sts time to read the article and put the paragraphs in the correct order.

Get Sts to compare with a partner, and then check answers.

EXTRA SUPPORT Before Sts read the article the first time, check whether you need to pre-teach any vocabulary.

1 E 2 A 3 G 4 B 5 C 6 F 7 D

c Focus on the seven situations and make sure Sts understand all the lexis.

Get Sts to read the article again and then, in pairs, to describe in their own words how Michal felt.

Check answers.

Suggested answers
1 Surprised, upset
2 Pleased, relieved when he got a positive reaction; upset when a man shouted at him
3 Hot, exhausted, depressed
4 Depressed
5 Relieved, a bit strange
6 Pleased with himself / satisfied
7 Angry

Deal with any other new vocabulary. Elicit or model the pronunciation of any tricky words.

d Do this as a whole-class activity, or put Sts in pairs and then get some feedback.

5 VOCABULARY words that are often confused

Vocabulary notes
All languages have words which learners may find confusing, and English is no exception. Sometimes this is because two words look similar, even though the meaning is completely different – some Elementary Sts mix up *kitchen* and *chicken*. At higher levels, this may still be true (e.g. the homophones *principal / principle* or *stationary / stationery*), and is sometimes caused by L1 interference (*extranjero* in Spanish looks more like *stranger*, but means *foreigner*). Confusion also arises because words have similar meanings, and this is the focus in this Vocabulary section. It's important for Advanced Sts both to understand nuances of meaning, and to be able to use the exact words required by the context, in order to express themselves accurately and effectively.

a Focus on the task and give Sts time, in pairs, to discuss the difference between the three words in 1–8.

Check answers, eliciting the exact meaning of each word. When looking at number 2, you could also elicit the difference between *emigration* (= the act of leaving your own country to go and live permanently in another country) and *immigration* (= the act of coming to live permanently in a country that is not your own).

1 **foreigner** = a person who comes from a different country; **stranger** = a person that you don't know; **outsider** = a person who is not accepted as a member of society, group, etc.
2 **emigrant** = a person who leaves their own country to go and live permanently in another country; **immigrant** = a person who has come to live permanently in a country that is not their own; **migrant** = a person who moves from one country or region to another, especially in order to find work
3 **journey** = act of travelling from one place to another; **trip** = a journey to a place and coming back again, especially a short one for pleasure or a particular purpose; **voyage** = a long journey, especially by sea or in space
4 **walk** = move or go somewhere by putting one foot in front of the other; **stroll** = walk somewhere in a slow, relaxed way; **wander** = walk slowly around or to a place, often without any purpose or direction
5 **reclusive** = living alone and avoiding other people; **reserved** = slow or unwilling to show feelings or express opinions; **shy** = nervous or embarrassed about meeting or speaking to other people
6 **achieve** = attain a particular goal, status, or standard, especially by making an effort for a long time; **succeed** = have the result that was intended, achieve sth that you've been trying to do or get; **reach** = arrive at the place you have been travelling to, achieve a particular aim
7 **ground** = the solid surface of the Earth; **floor** = the surface of a room that you walk on; **soil** = the top layer of earth in which plants, trees, etc. grow
8 **deplore** = strongly disapprove of sth and criticize, especially in public; **deny** = say that sth is not true; **decline** = refuse politely to accept or do sth (also = become smaller / fewer / weaker)

EXTRA SUPPORT Do the first one as a whole-class activity.

b Focus on the task and give Sts time to complete the sentences with the words from **a**. Remind them to put the word in the correct form.

Check answers.

1 stranger 2 migrant 3 voyage 4 walked 5 reserved
6 reached 7 soil 8 deplore

6 ▶ VIDEO LISTENING

a Focus on the task and tell Sts they are going to watch a documentary about Ellis Island. Find out what they already know.

Play the video once the whole way through for Sts to watch and find out why all the names are mentioned.

Get Sts to compare with a partner, and then check answers.

EXTRA SUPPORT Read through the script and decide if you need to pre-teach any new lexis before Sts watch the video.

Bursorsky   It was the presenter's original surname.
Annie Moore   She was the first immigrant to be processed at Ellis Island.
Isaac Asimov, **Max Factor**, and **Elia Kazan**   They are famous people who came through the immigration centre at Ellis Island.

Ellis Island

Hi, I'm Amy Burser. Like most Americans, my family background is quite diverse. My surname was originally Bursorsky, which is Russian, but my ancestors came here from all over the world, including Austria and Puerto Rico. And many of them came through the immigration station here at Ellis Island.

The island's first immigration point opened on New Year's Day eighteen ninety-two, when a young Irish woman called Annie Moore became the first immigrant to be processed here.

From eighteen ninety-two to nineteen fifty-four, twelve million people passed through here, and today an estimated forty per cent of America's population can trace their ancestry to this tiny island in New York harbour.

Nineteen oh seven was the busiest year with over one million immigrants processed here. The largest number came from Italy, but there were many from Poland, Germany, Hungary, and Scandinavia, too. As they sailed past the Statue of Liberty, many of them must have been filled with hope and joy. After all, they had just spent weeks – if not months – in cramped conditions aboard overcrowded ships. Finally, they had arrived. But for most of them, their ordeal wasn't quite over. The ships moored in Manhattan. The first- and second-class passengers could disembark here, along with any American citizens. But passengers in steerage – the poorest on the ship, all of whom were immigrants – were ferried over to this building for further inspection. The building – built in nineteen hundred, after the first station burned down in eighteen ninety-seven – was very impressive. It had a large dining hall and kitchen, dormitories with six hundred beds, a hospital, and a roof garden with a play area for children.

But the jewel in the crown was this – the Great Hall. With its sixty-foot vaulted ceiling, it resembles an old-fashioned ballroom, but from nineteen hundred to nineteen twenty-four, this was the Registry Room. Each day it was filled with new arrivals. On some days, five thousand people waited here. The noise was deafening and the atmosphere chaotic. Dozens of languages filled the air as each person fearfully awaited a series of citizenship tests. In fact, each person had undergone a 'six-second medical exam' before they had even entered the hall. Here, doctors checked for signs of physical weaknesses or illnesses, especially tuberculosis or trachoma, an infectious disease of the eye. If they failed, they were marked with a chalk letter and were sent to the hospital for a full examination. If they passed, they shuffled into the Great Hall and

waited on benches like these. On average, this wait lasted three and four hours, but could take much longer. Those still here in the evening had to sleep in the dormitory and start the process again the next morning. Eventually they were called by the clerks, who stood at desks like these, with a full list of each ship's passengers. They found each person's name and then asked twenty-eight further questions. It was their job to find out if the person could work and had money to support themselves. They also had to weed out any 'undesirables', including criminals and political radicals.

If someone failed these tests, they were sent back home. This only happened to around two per cent of the passengers, but for the unlucky ones and their families, it was a traumatic experience – a dispiriting end to a long and arduous journey.

But those that were approved could walk through the doors, out into their new lives. Some were met by relatives here at the 'kissing post'; others emerged alone into a completely new world. Around a third stayed in the New York area, while the rest scattered across the country.

The Immigration Act of nineteen twenty-four effectively ended the era of mass-immigration. But for just over three decades, Ellis Island was America's gateway for millions of people. Some became authors, like science fiction writer Isaac Asimov, who came here from Russia. Others became successful businessmen, like the cosmetics giant Max Factor, whose real name was Maksymilian Faktorowicz and who moved to America in nineteen oh four. And some worked in film, like Elia Kazan, a Greek-American who directed classic films such as *On the Waterfront* and *A Streetcar Named Desire*. Others became doctors, shopkeepers, and builders. They all settled down and started families. And they all created the country we know today.

b Give Sts time to read sentences 1–10, making sure they understand all the lexis. Tell them that the answers are all types of numbers, e.g. standard numbers, but also dates, ordinals, etc.

Play the video again, pausing if necessary, for Sts to complete the gaps.

Get Sts to compare with a partner, and then check answers.

1 1892   2 12 million   3 40   4 first; second   5 1924; 5,000
6 six   7 three; four   8 28   9 2; third   10 1924

EXTRA SUPPORT You could get Sts to watch again with subtitles, so they can see exactly what they understood / didn't understand. Translate / Explain any new words or phrases.

c Do this as a whole-class activity, or put Sts in pairs and then get some feedback.

❗ Please note that this could be a sensitive topic of discussion.

EXTRA IDEA After doing the **Revise and Check** lesson, you could give Sts one or all of the three **Vocabulary** Revision photocopiable activities (Revision 1: Describing game, Revision 2: Phrasal verbs, Revision 3: Idioms), which include questions to revise all the vocabulary lexis they studied in this level.

For instructions on how to use these pages, see *p.43*.

More materials
For teachers
Teacher's Resource Centre
Video Can you understand these people? 9&10
Quick Test 10
File 10 Test
Progress Test Files 6–10
End-of-course test
For students
Online Practice Check your progress

GRAMMAR

a
1 ✓ 2 because she had never expected 3 I hope not
4 a tin opener 5 a glass of wine 6 which is a bit strange
7 ✓

b
1 so 2 have 3 ✓ 4 ✓ 5 car key 6 ✓ 7 what 8 who

c
1 The **reason (why) I didn't bring sunscreen was** / **is** because the weather forecast said rain.
2 The **person I spoke to was** the head of Customer Services.
3 **What I don't like about him is** the way he blames other people for his mistakes.
4 **All I said was (that)** I thought that she was making a big mistake marrying him.
5 **It was a girl from my school who** / **that** was chosen to carry the Olympic torch.

VOCABULARY

a
1 calf 2 kennel 3 neigh 4 claws 5 species 6 hunt
7 beak 8 chopping board 9 simmer 10 grate 11 stuff
12 melt 13 whip 14 mince

b
1 strength 2 shorten 3 height 4 thicken 5 depth
6 weakened 7 width 8 lengthen

c
1 trip 2 an outsider 3 wandering 4 declined
5 immigrants 6 achieved 7 ground 8 reclusive

CAN YOU understand this text?

b
1 c 2 b 3 b 4 c 5 a

▶ CAN YOU understand these people?

1 c 2 b 3 a 4 c

🔊 **10.11**

1
I = interviewer, A = Alicia
I Do you have any friends who are vegan?
A Yes.
I Does it cause any problems?
A It does because I always forget that cheese is not allowed in the vegan diet. So just trying to find things that are filling to cook for someone that doesn't have any animal products, yeah, is difficult.
I Have you found any good recipes?
A I've found a way to make cheese out of soy, so it's not cheese in my book, but it's definitely edible for a vegan, yeah.

2
I = interviewer, V = Vicky
I Do you enjoy cooking?
V I love cooking. Yeah, yeah.
I Do you have a speciality?
V Um, I, I tend to just throw things together. I'm not a very scientific cook. I never follow a recipe. It's a kind of open the fridge, see what's in there, and see what I can make happen.

3
I = interviewer, H = Hywel
I Do you watch much sport on TV?
H I wouldn't say I'm religious in my sport watching, but I like a range of things, like the Tour de France, or international football, athletics. So, I like a wide range of things. Um, but I don't watch every day or every week.
I Do you find that commentators help you to enjoy it or do they annoy you?
H Generally speaking, I like what commentators have to say, especially if they give background about the, um, about the sportsman or the sportswoman. Um, I find it a little bit annoying if they repeat what everybody's just seen. Um, but usually they, they talk around it, and they find ways of asking good questions.

4
I = interviewer, C = Claire
I Would you ever consider going to live permanently in another country?
C That's a really interesting question. In fact, it's something we've talked about quite recently, and yes I would seriously consider moving to another country.
I Why?
C The country in particular, I might as well say, is Germany and I like the way the people are, um, they are very positive in the manner in which they deal with things. Their public service is very efficient, um, they seem to do things right. They never throw litter on the ground, now maybe I have a, a warped view of it. I've only been there on holidays, but they're the little things that I like. And the fact that you have beautiful summers, nice winters. You can ski, you can sun, and it's, it just covers a lot of, ticks a lot of boxes for me, yeah.

Photocopiable activities

Overview

- There is a **Grammar activity** for each main (A and B) lesson of the Student's Book.
- There is a **Communicative activity** for each main (A and B) lesson of the Student's Book.
- There is a **Vocabulary activity** for each Vocabulary Bank in the Student's Book. There are also some revision activities for **Vocabulary**.

The photocopiable material is also available on the **Teacher's Resource Centre** (TRC) and the **Classroom Presentation Tool** (CPT), allowing you to display the worksheets on an interactive whiteboard or projector. This will make it easier to set up and demonstrate the activities, and show answers.

Using extra activities in mixed ability classes

Some teachers have classes with a very wide range of levels, and where some Sts finish Student's Book activities much more quickly than others. You could give these fast finishers a photocopiable activity (Grammar, Vocabulary, or Communicative) while you help the slower Sts. Alternatively, some teachers might want to give faster Sts extra oral practice with a communicative activity while slower Sts consolidate their knowledge with an extra grammar activity.

Tips for using Grammar activities

- The grammar activities are designed to give Sts extra practice in the main grammar points from each lesson. How you use these activities depends on the needs of your Sts and the time available. They can be used in the lesson if you think all of your class would benefit from the extra practice or you could set them as homework for some or all of your Sts.
- Before using the worksheets in class, check for any vocabulary that may be either new or difficult for your Sts.
- All of the activities start with a writing stage. If you use the activities in class, get Sts to work individually or in pairs. Allow Sts to compare before checking answers.
- If Sts are having trouble with any of the activities, make sure they refer to the relevant Grammar Bank in the Student's Book.
- All of the activities have an **Activation** section. Some of them have a task that gets Sts to cover the sentences and test their memory. If you are using the activities in class, Sts can work in pairs and test their partner. If you set them for homework, encourage Sts to use this stage to test themselves. Alternatively, you could set the main activity

for homework and then get Sts to do the **Activation** at the start of the next class.
- Make sure that Sts keep their worksheets and that they review any difficult areas regularly. Encourage them to go back to activities and cover and test themselves.

Tips for using Communicative activities

- Before using the worksheets in class, check for any vocabulary that may be either new or difficult for your Sts.
- We have suggested the ideal number of copies for each activity. However, you can often manage with fewer, e.g. one worksheet per pair instead of one per student.
- When Sts are working in pairs, if possible get them to sit face to face. This will encourage them to really talk to each other and also means they can't see each other's worksheet.
- If your class doesn't divide into pairs or groups, take part yourself, get two Sts to share one role, or get one student to monitor, help, and correct.
- If some Sts finish early, they can swap roles and do the activity again, or you could get them to write some of the sentences from the activity.

Tips for using Vocabulary activities

- These worksheets are intended to recycle and consolidate Sts' understanding of the vocabulary in the Student's Book Vocabulary Banks. As such, we suggest not using them directly after doing these exercises. Instead, get Sts to do them in a subsequent lesson.
- If Sts are having trouble with any of the activities, make sure they refer to the relevant Vocabulary Bank page.
- You could ask Sts to check their answers by referring to the relevant Student's Book Vocabulary Bank.
- All the activities are suitable for use in class. However, you may wish to set some of the tasks for homework.
- Most of the Vocabulary worksheets have an **Activation** task and this can be treated in a similar way to the Grammar ones.
- Make sure that Sts keep their worksheets and that they review any difficult areas regularly. Encourage them to go back to activities and cover and test themselves.

Customisable worksheets

There are customisable versions of some of the Grammar, Communicative, and Vocabulary activities on the **Teacher's Resource Centre**. These allow you to adapt the material to make it more applicable and/or relevant to your Sts. For instance, you could:

- change some of the names to the names of Sts in your class.
- change place names to ones that are more relevant and/or familiar to your Sts.
- change items of grammar or vocabulary to focus on the needs and interests of your Sts and/or adapt the level of challenge.
- reduce the number of items if you are short of time.

Grammar activity answers

1A *have*: lexical and grammatical uses
a 2 a   3 a   4 b   5 c   6 b   7 c   8 a
b 2 haven't   3 got / had   4 've   5 been   6 taking   7 hasn't
  8 haven't   9 've   10 got
c 2 always **have** such a laugh   3 have it **out** with them
  4 willing to have **a** go   5 really had **it** with them
  6 teacher has really **got** it in for him   7 was he having us **on**

1B discourse markers (1): linkers
a 2 consequently   3 so as not to   4 in case   5 though
b 2 but   3 As a result   4 so that   5 However
c 2 As / Since / Because   3 to / so as to / in order to
  4 so / so that   5 but   6 because of / due to

2A the past: habitual events and specific incidents
2 didn't have   3 was playing   4 interrupted
5 'd, wanted   6 had, been allowed
7 got / would get / used to get
8 fed / used to feed / would feed   9 didn't want
10 used to be / was   11 was taking   12 bit   13 dropped
14 wasn't / didn't use to be   15 used to cry / cried
16 had gone   17 was explaining   18 had happened
19 spoke   20 'd ever experienced / 'd experienced

2B pronouns
a 2 one another   3 They   4 it's   5 you   6 It's   7 you
  8 There's   9 their   10 there's   11 them   12 yourself
b 2 one   3 it   4 There   5 they   6 yourself   7 themselves
  8 it   9 you   10 It   11 there   12 you

3A *get*
a 2 broken   3 to tidy   4 used   5 paid   6 to check
  7 redesigned   8 to call   9 to agree   10 made
b 2 Some business owners have got rich at the expense of their
    workforce.
  3 You need to get your eyes tested.
  4 He got ten years in prison for fraud.
  5 Getting food from farmers' markets is eco-friendly, but much
    more expensive.
  6 He's getting used to the weather here. / He's getting more
    accustomed to the weather here.
  7 My bike got stolen last night.
  8 You'll never get him to understand.

3B discourse markers (2): adverbs and adverbial expressions
2 Obviously   3 that is to say   4 in fact   5 By the way
6 Anyway   7 Basically   8 As far as   9 at least   10 All in all

4A adding emphasis (1): inversion
a 2 when   3 Rarely   4 again   5 Never   6 Only   7 but
  8 until
b 2 have I had the opportunity to eat
  3 does the novel have an implausible storyline, but the
    characters are also
  4 will I read another book
  5 had the film started when I was
  6 you've watched the film two or three times can you fully
    understand
  7 did my head hit the pillow than I
  8 were we given

4B speculation and deduction
a 2 might / may / could have left   3 can't be
  4 might / may / could have taken
  5 might / may / could be trying   6 shouldn't be
  7 must have fallen   8 must have (done)
b 2 the disease **is** likely to   3 you probably **won't** be able
  4 is unlikely **to** be   5 we **'re / are** bound to
  6 it's very **unlikely** that   7 she's bound **to** be
  8 she**'ll / will** definitely

5A distancing
a 2 It seems that men are more at risk from this disease than
    women.
  3 It appears that she has changed her mind since I last spoke to
    her.
  4 It seems that you are unable to deal with this problem
    effectively.
  5 It seems that the weather is about to improve.
  6 It appears that the robbers were wearing face masks.
    would seem / appear is also possible where the context is more
    formal.
b 2 A spokesperson is expected to make an announcement later
    today.
  3 More than half of the population is believed to suffer from
    headaches.
  4 St Petersburg is said to be one of the most majestic cities in
    the world.
  5 At least 70 people are understood to have been injured as a
    result of the explosion.
  6 There are reported to be around 250 fake universities in the UK.

5B unreal uses of past tenses
2 c   3 b   4 c   5 a   6 c   7 a   8 b   9 b   10 c   11 a
12 b   13 b   14 c   15 a   16 b

6A verb + object + infinitive or gerund
a 2 us to take   3 you to be offended   4 ✓
  5 my grandmother teaching me   6 you to feel
  7 ✓   8 for our children to go   9 ✓
b 2 to retake   3 to get   4 to attend   5 stopping   6 do
  7 using   8 to leave   9 not to arrive   10 taking

6B conditional sentences
a 2 would / could go down   3 'd / had suggested
  4 would have laughed   5 would have been
  6 wasn't   7 'd / had known   8 would have brought
  9 'll / will lend   10 want   11 don't make
  12 will probably change
b 2 My dad says that I can borrow the car on condition (that) I
    promise to drive carefully.
  3 I'm going to go to the party whether I'm invited or not.
  4 The exam will be fine providing (that) you do enough revision.
  5 Supposing you hadn't found your passport, what would you
    have done?
  6 I'm in favour of contact sports as / so long as nobody gets
    seriously injured.
  7 I would never wear fur, even if it was very cold.
  8 You can go out tonight provided (that) you're back by
    midnight.

7A permission, obligation, and necessity

a 2 ✗ had better not ask her 3 ✓ 4 ✗ mustn't download
5 ✓ 6 ✗ ought to study more 7 ✗ 'd / had better watch out
8 ✓ 9 ✗ ought to have thought 10 ✓

b 2 shouldn't 3 ✓ 4 mustn't 5 don't need to 6 ✓
7 could 8 ✓ 9 should

7B perception and sensation

2 smells like garlic
3 as if she had
4 been hearing good things about you
5 ice cream really tastes of
6 see anyone leave / leaving the house
7 sounds like a violin
8 to have changed much
9 heard the alarm go off
10 looks as if / as though / like he didn't sleep very well / hasn't slept very well
11 as though she was / were delighted
12 heard the couple arguing

8A advanced gerunds and infinitives

a 2 ✓ 3 ✗ being spoken to 4 ✗ to have been able to
5 ✗ to understand 6 ✓ 7 ✗ inviting 8 ✓
9 ✗ to be trying 10 ✓

b 2 feeling 3 being told 4 have been informed 5 to do
6 to be searching 7 to be / to have been
8 not having been contacted

c 1 d 2 e 3 a 4 c 5 f 6 g 7 h 8 b

8B expressing future plans and arrangements

a 2 to 3 be 4 on 5 going 6 begins / starts

b 2 2 ✓ 3 ✗ we're going / we're going to go
4 ✗ Wendy's due to go 5 ✓ 6 ✓
7 ✗ are you and Jennifer doing / going to do 8 ✓ 9 ✓
10 ✗ they're going to lose / they'll lose 11 ✓
12 ✗ I'm going to paint

9A ellipsis

a The second paragraph has no ellipsis.

b Nicky's father gave her his phone number and ~~he~~ said she could contact him whenever she wanted to ~~contact him~~. Nicky said goodbye and then ~~she~~ hung up. At first, she was angry that he had got in touch and ~~she~~ wished that he hadn't ~~got in touch~~. But a few weeks later, she called him and ~~she~~ arranged to see him because she felt they needed to talk. She got on well with him, although she hadn't expected to ~~get on well with him~~. Nicky decided that she wanted them to meet regularly, and her father promised that they would ~~meet regularly~~. Five years later, when Nicky got married, no one imagined that her father would be walking her up the aisle, but he was ~~walking her up the aisle~~.

c 2 I'm afraid **not**.
3 I guess **so**, …
4 I suspect **not**.
5 I don't imagine **so**. / I imagine **not**.
6 I suppose **not**. / I don't suppose **so**.

9B nouns: compound and possessive forms

2 ✗ other people's business 3 ✓ 4 ✗ tin opener
5 ✗ an hour's walk 6 ✓ 7 ✓
8 ✗ the high point of her career 9 ✓ 10 ✗ kitchen cupboard
11 ✗ champagne glasses 12 ✓ 13 ✗ the middle of the room
14 ✓

activation
Possible answers:
chocolate cake, birthday cake, lemon cake, etc.
coffee cup, tea cup, egg cup, etc.
bread knife, steak knife, fish knife, etc.
CD player, DVD player, football player, etc.
coffee machine, running machine, fruit machine, etc.
city centre, health centre, sports centre, etc.
surf board, chopping board, message board, etc.
story book, address book, physics book, etc.
car key, house key, back door key, etc.
mineral water, sea water, tap water, etc.
credit card, birthday card, identity card, etc.
picture frame, photo frame, window frame, etc.

10A relative clauses

a 2 whose 3 who 4 which 5 where 6 which 7 What
8 who / that 9 which 10 what 11 who / that / whom
12 whose 13 who 14 What 15 whom 16 which
17 whose 18 which

10B adding emphasis (2): cleft sentences

a 2 The reason (why) he married her was for her money.
3 The person (who / that) she loves more than anyone else in the world is her niece.
4 The last time (that) I saw her was in October.
5 The person who / that really understands how I feel is my sister.
6 The reason (why) we retired early was in order to have time to enjoy life.
7 The place (where) I relax most is (in) the garden.
8 The first time (that) I met David was just after I graduated.

b 2 What my son is crazy about is skateboarding.
3 All they want (to do) is to lie on a beach and relax.
4 What I'm desperate for is a nice cup of tea.
5 It was the atmosphere that / which made the restaurant special rather than the food. / It was the atmosphere rather than the food that / which made the restaurant special.
6 What I don't want is to be late for work tomorrow.
7 All she asked for was a glass of water.
8 It was Alec who was a professional footballer when he was young, not Darren.
9 What happened was (that) I asked her a question, but she refused to answer it.

1A GRAMMAR *have*: lexical and grammatical uses

a (Circle) the correct answer.

1 Would it be OK if I left work a bit early this afternoon? I _____ go to the dentist's.
   a got to   **(b)** have to   **c** 'm having to

2 _____ an umbrella? I can lend you one, if you like.
   a Don't you have   **b** Haven't you   **c** Hadn't you

3 I wouldn't get them a toaster as a present because they _____ one.
   a already have   **b** have already had   **c** are already having

4 If you want to get rid of those stains, I reckon you'll need to _____ professionally.
   a clean the carpet   **b** have the carpet cleaned   **c** have cleaned the carpet

5 Would you mind not calling me between seven and eight, because I _____ dinner?
   a 'll have   **b** 'll have had   **c** 'll be having

6 Once the kids were older, we _____ give them a lift to school every day.
   a hadn't got to   **b** didn't have to   **c** hadn't to

7 I _____ loads of friends when I was at school, but I've lost touch with most of them now.
   a had got   **b** was having   **c** used to have

8 Did you hear about Sally? She _____ last night.
   a had her car broken into   **b** broke into her car   **c** had broken into her car

b Read the conversation below. Complete each gap with one word (contractions count as one word).

Doctor Good morning. So, why ¹*have* you come to see me today

Patient Well, I ² _____ been feeling very well recently.

Doctor What symptoms have you ³ _____ ?

Patient I ⁴ _____ had a terrible headache for the last few days and my eyes hurt a lot. It's worse when I read or watch TV.

Doctor Have you ⁵ _____ taking anything for the headache?

Patient I've been ⁶ _____ paracetamol every four hours, but it ⁷ _____ made any difference yet.

Doctor OK. Can you look at the eye chart and read this line for me?

Patient Oh, I ⁸ _____ a clue what those letters are! They're all blurred!

Doctor I think I ⁹ _____ found the problem! The first thing you've ¹⁰ _____ to do is go to the optician's for an eye test. I think you need glasses!

c Add one word to the idioms to make the sentences correct.

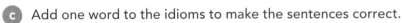

1 To be honest, I'm not sure Sarah has got it in/to go travelling alone.   *her*

2 I love spending time with my old school friends. We always such a laugh together.

3 If you think your colleagues are treating you unfairly, you should have it with them.

4 I've never ridden a horse before, but I'm willing to have go.

5 I can't believe the neighbours are having another party! I've really had with them.

6 My brother's teacher has really it in for him because he's failed his exams again.

7 Is Tom really taking dancing lessons or was he having us?

ACTIVATION

Work in pairs. Tell your partner about the following:

someone you have a close relationship with

something you've had done recently

a time you had it out with a friend

something you've got to do after class today

something you've wanted to do for ages

an activity you'd like to have a go at

1B GRAMMAR discourse markers (1): linkers

a (Circle) the correct linker.

I would say that the most challenging period in my career so far was my first junior management position in the company where I still work today. I had always wanted to be an accounts manager, ¹(so)/ although / despite I was thrilled when I got the job, but little did I know what was waiting for me on my first day. The office environment was rather disorganized, and to make matters worse, my boss was completely unsupportive of me. For some reason, he just refused to take any responsibility for dealing with the clients, and ² consequently / so as to / although, I was forced to deal with all the problems by myself. I used to stay late at the office almost every night ³ because of / so that / so as not to miss any of the clients' deadlines. It seems ridiculous now, but I was so stressed that I used to check my emails every five minutes, even at weekends, ⁴ so that / in case / as a result there was an urgent message asking me to sort something out. It was worth it in the end, ⁵ though / but / as, because eventually my boss was fired and I got promoted in his place!

b Complete the text with a linker from the list. There are two you don't need to use.

~~although~~   as   as a result   but   despite   however   so that

The toughest time I've ever had was definitely my first term here at university. ¹ _Although_ I really love student life now, it wasn't so easy in the beginning. My bad luck started on the very first day. My parents had just dropped me off with all my stuff when some of the guys whose rooms were on the same corridor as mine suggested going to play basketball in the park nearby. I don't know exactly how it happened, ² _____ somehow, during the game, I tripped and fell really hard on my right arm and broke it. Apart from not being able to play any sports for weeks, it was especially annoying because my injury meant I wasn't able to write properly. ³ _____, I got really behind with my essays and I had to take an extra class later in the year ⁴ _____ I could catch up. On top of that, it wasn't as easy as I had expected to find friends, and I was pretty homesick for a while. ⁵ _____, things got better eventually. Once my arm was better, I managed to get into the university basketball team and made loads of new friends.

c Complete the text with a suitable linker. Sometimes more than one answer is possible.

Most people can't wait until the day they retire, but I can tell you it's not as simple as you might think. ¹ _Despite_ all the free time, retirement isn't just a question of enjoying yourself and feeling happy that you never have to work again. When my husband Frank retired after 40 rewarding years as a lawyer, he had terrible trouble adjusting to his new lifestyle. ² _____ he had always been committed to his career, it wasn't easy just to give it up overnight. We decided to move to the countryside ³ _____ be nearer to our daughter and her family, but when we arrived, we found that they were all so busy with their own lives that they didn't have much time for us. Of course, we did babysit for our daughter sometimes ⁴ _____ she could go out in the evenings, but somehow it wasn't the life we had imagined. Just when we were feeling really down, a friend of ours invited us along to a ballroom dancing class in the village. Frank wasn't keen at first, ⁵ _____ once we got there, we had a wonderful time. Now we go three times a week and it's changed our lives. We keep fit and we've met so many fantastic people. And it's all ⁶ _____ the dance class. I don't know what we would have done without it!

ACTIVATION

Write a paragraph about a challenging experience you have faced. You could write about your work, studies, or family. Explain what the challenge was and how you overcame it. If you can't think of anything from your life, write about a friend or relative.

In your paragraph, make sure you use at least five linkers.

2A GRAMMAR the past: habitual events and specific incidents

● Read the story and put the verb in brackets in the most appropriate form. Sometimes more than one answer is possible.

I started school at the age of four at my local primary. I ¹ *'d been looking forward* (look forward) to starting school for some time because I ² _____ (not have) any siblings, so I thought it was going to be the perfect opportunity to make new friends and have fun. On the first day, I ³ _____ (play) with my new classmates when the teacher ⁴ _____ (interrupt) us and asked us to pay attention. We all stopped what we had been doing and she introduced us to the class pet – Hammy the Hamster. He was the pet I ⁵ _____ always _____ (want), but ⁶ _____ never _____ (allow) to have.

The teacher told us that each child – in strict alphabetical order – could take Hammy home with them for one weekend and then bring him back the following Monday. I could hardly wait for it to be my weekend. I ⁷ _____ (get) to school very early every day and I ⁸ _____ (feed) and play with him. I ⁹ _____ (not want) to let the other children near him because I wanted Hammy to be my new best friend!

After three weeks, my weekend finally arrived. My mum hadn't been too keen on having a hamster in the house, but I'd been very persuasive – I ¹⁰ _____ (be) very resourceful as a child – and finally she agreed. I was so happy.

Saturday was a beautiful, sunny day, so I thought Hammy would appreciate a morning walk in the garden. However, as I ¹¹ _____ (take) him out of his cage, he ¹² _____ (bite) me, I ¹³ _____ (drop) him, and Hammy ran away!

I ¹⁴ _____ (not be) a child who ¹⁵ _____ (cry) very often, but on that occasion I spent all weekend crying and looking for Hammy. Sadly, though, Hammy ¹⁶ _____ (go) forever and I never saw him again.

The worst was yet to come, however. On Monday, I had to go back to school with an empty cage. As I ¹⁷ _____ (explain) to the teacher what ¹⁸ _____ (happen), I realized that the rest of the class were looking at me with hatred in their eyes; after all, I had lost the adored class pet! Nobody ¹⁹ _____ (speak) to me for at least a week and I remember it being the worst feeling I ²⁰ _____ (experience) in the four short years of my life.

> **ACTIVATION**

Think of a time in your childhood when you did something wrong.
Write a paragraph describing the incident.

2B GRAMMAR pronouns

a Read the travel guide and (circle) the correct pronoun.

Why visit

[1] **There's** / **It's** often referred to as the world's 'coolest little capital' and for good reason. Despite its compact size, Wellington offers tourists a vibrant arts scene, world-class dining options, and excellent outdoor activities. It's also a safe city with a great atmosphere; a place where locals are always ready to help [2] **one another** / **themselves** and visitors.

When to visit

[3] **They** / **You** say that you can't beat Wellington on a good day. However, [4] **it's** / **there's** hard to say when that day might be. The city is renowned for its wild, windy weather, which [5] **they** / **you** can be subjected to in any season. Generally speaking, though, late January and February provide the sunniest, calmest days.

Getting around

One of the best ways to explore Wellington is on foot. [6] **There's** / **It's** only two kilometres from one side of the city centre to the other, meaning [7] **you** / **they** can walk across it in under half an hour. [8] **It's** / **There's** also an excellent, well-used public transport system.

What to see and do

Naturally, everyone has [9] **his** / **their** own idea about what constitutes a great day out, but you'll find that [10] **there's** / **it's** plenty to do in Wellington, whatever your interests. If history is your thing, a trip to *Te Papa* Museum is a must. Active travellers may like to climb to the top of Mount Victoria and appreciate the 360-degree views around [11] **them** / **themselves**. If you're into good food, you should make your way to Cuba Street to try out some of the city's best restaurants and cafés. However you decide to spend your time in Wellington, you can't fail to enjoy [12] **you** / **yourself**.

b Complete the travel guide with a suitable pronoun.

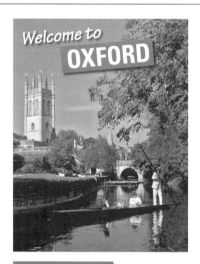

Why visit

[1] *They* say that one always learns something when [2] _____ visits Oxford. With its world-famous university and numerous other institutes of learning, [3] _____ can't be denied that the 'city of dreaming spires' is significant not only academically, but also historically and culturally.

When to visit

[4] _____ really isn't a bad time of year to visit the city, since the weather is rarely extreme. As with much of the UK, however, it can be unpredictable, so anyone planning a trip ought to check the forecast before [5] _____ arrive.

Getting around

Due to its modest size, the simplest ways to get around the city's streets are walking or cycling. And while in Oxford, you must of course have a go at punting (boating) on the River Thames. You can either hire a punt with a chauffeur or, if you're more adventurous, you can do the punting [6] _____ .

What to see and do

Oxford is home to one of Europe's oldest libraries – the fascinating Bodleian Library. Unfortunately, visitors cannot look around the library by [7] _____; [8] _____'s necessary to join a guided tour. However, these are reasonably priced and very informative. If [9] _____ enjoy being outdoors, head to Christ Church Meadow. [10] _____'s a popular spot for tourists, students, and locals, with riverside walking trails and stunning views back to the city. If you fancy a drink, [11] _____'s a fabulous, traditional British pub – *The Eagle and Child* – that's well worth a visit. The pub has been a favourite with famous writers, such as J.R.R. Tolkien and C.S. Lewis, since the seventeenth century, so you never know who might end up sitting next to [12] _____!

ACTIVATION

Write your own travel guide about a city you know well. Use the same headings as above. Try to include at least six of the pronouns from **a** and **b**.

3A GRAMMAR *get*

a Complete the sentences with the correct form of a word from the list.

| agree break call check ~~do~~ make pay redesign tidy use |

1 She was in the middle of getting her hair *done*, so I said I'd call her back.
2 Quite a few of our things got _____ when we were moving into our new house.
3 I got the children _____ their rooms whilst I put away the shopping.
4 It took my brother a long time to get _____ to living in a different country.
5 Top bosses often get _____ substantial bonuses at the end of the year.
6 I was wondering if you could get Elena _____ the figures for me.
7 We got the kitchen _____ by a professional.
8 Do you think you could get Paul _____ me later?
9 The meeting wasn't great; we couldn't get the managers _____ to our plans.
10 Unfortunately, Martin got _____ redundant when the factory closed.

b Rewrite the sentences using a form of *get*.

1 Women should always receive the same pay as men.
  Women should always get paid the same as men.
2 Some business owners have enriched themselves at the expense of their workforce.
  _____
3 You need to go for an eye test.
  _____
4 He received ten years in prison for fraud.
  _____
5 Buying food from farmers' markets is eco-friendly, but much more expensive.
  _____
6 He's becoming more accustomed to the weather here.
  _____
7 Someone stole my bike last night.
  _____
8 You'll never make him understand.
  _____

ACTIVATION

Write six sentences using *get* where the meaning is different in each one.

3B GRAMMAR discourse markers (2): adverbs and adverbial expressions

Complete the extracts from the presentation with a discourse marker from the list.

~~after all~~   all in all   anyway   as far as   at least   basically   by the way   in fact   obviously   that is to say

A

Hi, everyone. The historical figure I've chosen for my mini-presentation today is Guy Fawkes. I'm pretty sure the name will be familiar to you. [1] *After all*, we do have a well-known celebration named after him. I expect, however, that you might not know much about his story. [2]_____, I don't have time to tell you everything about him in just five minutes, but let's start with some information about his early life…

B

…Despite his parents being members of the Church of England, [3]_____ Protestants, Fawkes's mother remarried a Catholic after his father's death. Several years later, Fawkes became influenced by his stepfather's religious practices, and those of his school friends, and converted to Catholicism, even though it was [4]_____ a crime to be a Catholic at that time in England…

C

…While fighting for the Spanish in 1604, Fawkes met Thomas Wintour, who encouraged him to join a group of conspirators in a plot to assassinate the new Protestant king of England. [5]_____, interestingly, the king was both James VI and I. He was King of Scotland as James VI and then later King of England as James I. [6]_____, back to what I was saying about Guy Fawkes…

D

…So, over the next 18 months, Fawkes and 12 others worked out a careful plan. [7]_____, they plotted to blow up the Houses of Parliament, kill the King, and replace him with a Catholic monarch. [8]_____ the method was concerned, they decided to use gunpowder. Thirty-six barrels of it, to be precise. They placed these in the cellar and planned to set them alight when the King opened parliament on 5 November. The plan was bound to succeed, or [9]_____ that's what the conspirators thought!

E

…Fawkes was sentenced to death and executed. Now, every year on 5 November, people mark the anniversary of the failure of the Gunpowder Plot by setting off fireworks and building large bonfires. And that brings me to the end of my presentation. [10]_____, I think it's fair to say that Guy Fawkes led a very eventful life, driven by his cause. If you have any questions, I'll do my best to answer them.

ACTIVATION

Prepare a five-minute mini-presentation about a famous historical figure who interests you. If you need to find information, try searching on the internet in English. Use discourse markers in your mini-presentation.

4A GRAMMAR adding emphasis (1): inversion

a Read the online reviews. Complete them with a word from the list. There are four words you don't need to use.

again but hardly never no not only rarely ~~sooner~~ than until when

Restaurant reviews

Fantastic service! No ¹*sooner* had we sat down at our table than we were offered a drink. ★★★★

Hardly had we finished our starters ²_____ the waiter brought us our main courses. It was almost as if they wanted to get rid of us! ★★

Film reviews

³_____ have I seen such a moving film. There are only a few that can compare. ★★★★★

Never ⁴_____ will I watch a war film on a laptop. I think it's essential to see them at the cinema to appreciate the special effects. ★

Book reviews

⁵_____ have I read such a gripping book. I just couldn't put it down! ★★★★★

⁶_____ when I compared the original to the translated version did I see just how bad the translation really was. ★

Hotel reviews

Not only were our rooms not available when we arrived, ⁷_____ there was also nowhere to leave our luggage. ★★★

Not ⁸_____ you stay at this hotel do you really understand the meaning of the word 'luxury'. 10/10. ★★★★★

b Rewrite the sentences to make them more emphatic.

1 We only received our drinks when we reminded the waiter for the third time.
Only when *we reminded the waiter for the third time did we receive* our drinks.

2 I've rarely had the opportunity to eat at such a high-class restaurant.
Rarely _____ at such a high-class restaurant.

3 The novel has an implausible storyline and the characters are really dull as well.
Not only _____ really dull.

4 I'll never read another book by that author again.
Never again _____ by that author.

5 The film had scarcely started when I was moved to tears.
Scarcely _____ moved to tears.

6 Until you've watched the film two or three times, you can't fully understand the plot.
Not until _____ the plot.

7 The bed was so comfortable! I fell asleep as soon as my head hit the pillow.
The bed was so comfortable! No sooner _____ fell asleep.

8 We were only given a different room after we asked to speak to the manager.
We asked to speak to the manager. Only then _____ a different room.

ACTIVATION

Write a short online review about a restaurant / film / book / hotel experience you have had. In your review, use one or two negative adverbial expressions followed by inversion to emphasize your point.

4B GRAMMAR speculation and deduction

a Complete the conversation. Rewrite the phrases in brackets using *must*, *may*, *might*, *can't*, *could*, or *should*, and a verb.

Paul   What's wrong, Helena? You look a bit worried.

Helena   I think I [1] *must have lost* (am almost sure I lost) my phone. I can't find it anywhere.

Paul   Isn't it in your bag?

Helena   No, I don't think so. I've double-checked.

Paul   You [2]_____ (perhaps left) it at work.

Helena   No, it [3]_____ (almost certainly isn't) there because I remember having it when I was shopping after work today.

Paul   Somebody [4]_____ (perhaps took) it from your bag in the supermarket.

Helena   Oh no! I hope it's not a hacker who [5]_____ (is perhaps trying) to steal my identity.

Paul   You'd better contact the bank and cancel all your credit cards just in case. It [6]_____ (probably won't be) a problem if you tell them what's happened – they can just block your account.

Helena   Good idea. Can I use your phone?

Paul   Here you are. Hey! Isn't that your ringtone? It's coming from the sofa.

Helena   Ah, thank goodness! Here it is. It [7]_____ (almost definitely fell) out of my pocket when I sat down after I came home from work.

Paul   Yes, it [8]_____ (almost certainly did). Lucky you didn't ring the bank!

b Add one word in the right place to make the sentences correct.

1 The traffic is heavy today, so they're sure ~~be~~ *to* be late for the meeting.

2 Medical experts say that the disease likely to spread all over the world.

3 Without an experienced guide, you probably be able to get to the top of the mountain.

4 The company is unlikely be in a position to make a profit this year.

5 If we play as badly as we did last week, we bound to lose in the semi-final.

6 It's very that you'll win anything. I'd say there's only a two per cent chance.

7 With her presentation skills, she's bound be able to convince the company to choose her proposal.

8 If Sophie doesn't get to the gate in the next ten minutes, she definitely miss the flight.

ACTIVATION

Prepare a short presentation about what you think life might be like in 20 years' time. Try to use the grammar from **a** and **b** above. Include two or three of these topics:

Entertainment   Family and friends   Shopping   The economy   The environment   Technology   Transport   Work

---

'First of all, I think **it's very likely** that 20 years from now I'll still have a small group of very close friends, although if I'm married, **I might not** see them as often as I do now. People will **definitely** still want to meet each other face to face, and I don't believe that email or chatting online will ever replace that. Families are **bound to** become smaller in the future as nowadays people are having fewer children and I think that the tradition of a large extended family **is likely** to disappear. Moving on to work, I think…'

5A GRAMMAR distancing

a Rewrite the sentences with *It* + clause.

1 The government appears to be planning to raise taxes.
It appears that the government is planning to raise taxes.

2 Men seem to be more at risk from this disease than women.

_____

3 She appears to have changed her mind since I last spoke to her.

_____

4 You seem to be unable to deal with this problem effectively.

_____

5 The weather seems to be about to improve.

_____

6 The robbers appear to have been wearing face masks.

_____

b Rewrite the sentences beginning with the **bold** phrases.

1 It is thought that **the finance minister** is about to resign from his post.
The finance minister is thought to be about to resign from his post.

2 It is expected that **a spokesperson** will make an announcement later today.

_____

3 It is believed that **more than half of the population** suffers from headaches.

_____

4 It is said that **St Petersburg** is one of the most majestic cities in the world.

_____

5 It is understood that **at least 70 people** have been injured as a result of the explosion.

_____

6 It is reported that **there are** around 250 fake universities in the UK.

_____

ACTIVATION

You are a TV newsreader. Use the following pieces of gossip to prepare an official news report about a famous actress, Blanche Devoy. Be careful to distance yourself from the people's claims using a range of structures from **a** and **b** above.

Actress Blanche Devoy was said to be close to a nervous breakdown last night. It has been suggested that…

> She's close to a nervous breakdown because the paparazzi follow her everywhere.

> Her husband Jeff left her last week, and she was seen at a party last night with another man.

> Jeff's going to file for divorce and Blanche won't have anything left after she's paid the lawyers.

> Blanche doesn't have any real friends, only people who want to be famous like her.

> The box office earnings from her new film were very low and her career is in ruins.

> There are rumours that a former personal assistant is taking her to court.

5B GRAMMAR unreal uses of past tenses

● Circle the correct answer.

1 That job of yours is so dead-end. Isn't it time _____ a new one?
　a you found
　b you find
　c you had found

2 If only our neighbours _____ a dog, life would be much more peaceful.
　a wouldn't have
　b don't have
　c didn't have

3 What a lovely view! I wish _____ my camera.
　a I brought
　b I'd brought
　c I've brought

4 I'm too tired to go out tonight. I'd rather _____ at home.
　a we would stay
　b we'd stayed
　c we stayed

5 If only _____ Mike the car, we'd be able to drive there.
　a you hadn't lent
　b you lent
　c you didn't lend

6 Come on, kids! It's time _____ for school.
　a you leave
　b you had left
　c you left

7 I'd rather _____ your shoes off at the door, if you don't mind.
　a you took
　b you take
　c you had taken

8 I'd love to be able to sing in a choir. If only _____ a better voice!
　a I'd have
　b I had
　c I have

9 As soon as I said it, I wished _____ .
　a I wouldn't
　b I hadn't
　c I didn't

10 Diane thinks it's high time her daughter _____ out.
　a had moved
　b moves
　c moved

11 Those children look freezing. I bet they wish _____ indoors.
　a they were
　b they had been
　c they would be

12 As you're busy, _____ we postponed the meeting?
　a had you rather
　b would you rather
　c do you rather

13 I'd wear these jeans more often if only _____ so tight.
　a they were
　b they weren't
　c they wouldn't be

14 I've just had a text from Anna. She'd rather _____ at 6.30, as she's running late.
　a we had met
　b we were meeting
　c we met

15 I wish those people in the front row _____ talking. I can't hear the film!
　a would stop
　b stopped
　c will stop

16 I'd rather _____ anything to him – he's such a gossip!
　a you not to say
　b you didn't say
　c you wouldn't say

ACTIVATION

Look at the context in brackets and complete the sentences in a logical way.

1 It's high time _____. (parent to teenager)

2 I wish you _____. (wife to husband)

3 I'd rather you _____. (boss to employee)

4 If only our teacher _____. (student to student)

5 If you hadn't _____. (doctor to patient)

6A GRAMMAR verb + object + infinitive or gerund

a (Circle) the correct form. Tick (✓) if both are possible.

1 Our teacher taught **us that we should check / us to check** new words in a dictionary. ✓

2 Mark begged **us that we took / us to take** him to the nearest village.

3 I didn't mean **you be offended / you to be offended**. I'm very sorry.

4 Luckily the doctor didn't advise **me to change / me that I should change** my lifestyle.

5 I vividly remember **my grandmother to teach / my grandmother teaching** me how to cook.

6 I would hate **you to feel / that you feel** uncomfortable about the proposed changes.

7 Having an extra team member helped **us complete / us to complete** the project ahead of schedule.

8 We'd always planned **our children to go / for our children to go** to university.

9 Phil persuaded **me that I should give up / me to give up** riding my motorbike.

b Complete the sentences with the verb in brackets in the infinitive (with or without *to*) or the gerund.

1 I'm afraid I can't let you _check_ (check) in until I see proof of your identity.

2 Any student who fails will be made _____ (retake) the test.

3 It shouldn't take you more than five minutes _____ (get) here. We're just round the corner.

4 We have arranged for Jack _____ (attend) the meeting.

5 I really dislike people _____ (stop) me in the street to ask for money.

6 My dad would always make us _____ (do) our homework before watching TV.

7 Any task that involves my mother _____ (use) a computer makes her panic.

8 We strongly advise guests _____ (leave) their valuables in the hotel safe.

9 Henry reminded everyone _____ (not arrive) late for the welcome tour.

10 Fortunately, her injury won't prevent her from _____ (take) part in the competition.

ACTIVATION

Choose one of the questions and write a paragraph giving your opinion.

- Do you mind buskers playing music on the street?
- Should we really expect students to be responsible for their own learning?
- Should local governments force people to use public transport in cities where there is a traffic problem?
- How can governments encourage people to respect the environment?
- Can you imagine yourself living in another country for the rest of your life?

6B GRAMMAR conditional sentences

a Complete the conversation with the correct form of the verb in brackets.

Sara What are you up to, Rosie?

Rosie I'm just having a look at some vegetarian recipes. I was reading somewhere recently that if everyone [1] _gave up_ (give up) eating meat, the world's carbon emissions [2]_____ (go down) by about 60%.

Sara Wow! So does that mean you and Ben are becoming vegetarians?

Rosie No, but we're going to have a go at not eating meat on Mondays. Today's the first day!

Sara Oh, good on you! If I [3]_____ (suggest) the same thing to Robert, he [4]_____ (laugh) in my face. Was it difficult to persuade Ben?

Rosie It was pretty tough. It [5]_____ (be) far easier to convince him if he [6]_____ (be) such a big meat lover, of course!

Sara Definitely! Anyway, I've got a fantastic veggie cookbook at home. If I [7]_____ (know) about this sooner, I [8]_____ (bring) it in for you. I [9]_____ (lend) it to you tomorrow though if you [10]_____ (want).

Rosie That would be great, thanks. In the meantime, I'd better get on with finding a dish to cook tonight. If I [11]_____ (not make) something really tasty, Ben [12]_____ (probably / change) his mind about the whole idea!

b Rewrite the sentences using the word in **bold**.

1 Had we been aware of the situation, we would have changed our plans. **if**
   If we had been aware of the situation, we would have changed our plans.

2 My dad says that I can borrow the car provided that I promise to drive carefully. **condition**
   _____

3 I'm going to go to the party – it doesn't matter if I'm invited or not. **whether**
   _____

4 The exam will be fine as long as you do enough revision. **providing**
   _____

5 If you hadn't found your passport, what would you have done? **supposing**
   _____

6 I'm in favour of contact sports providing nobody gets seriously injured. **long**
   _____

7 I would never wear fur, however cold it was. **even**
   _____

8 You can go out tonight as long as you're back by midnight. **provided**
   _____

ACTIVATION

Write a paragraph on one of the following topics. Give clear examples to support your ideas.

- If everyone were forced to give up eating meat one day a week, what impact would this have?
- Do you agree that if people in the past had been more careful with our planet's resources, the environment would be in a better state today?
- Supposing everybody earned the same amount of money, do you think the world would be a happier place today?

7A GRAMMAR permission, obligation, and necessity

a Right (✓) or wrong (✗)? Correct the mistakes in the **bold** phrases.

1 These shoes are too tight. I **should have tried** them on before buying them. ✓
2 Emma's still very upset about the argument, so you **hadn't better ask her** about it.
3 The invitation said we **didn't need to wear** formal clothes, so we wore jeans.
4 Employees **don't have to download** any software as it's against company rules.
5 We**'re supposed to finish** early on Fridays, but we always end up staying late.
6 If you want to be sure of passing your exam, you really **ought study more**.
7 The boss is in a bad mood today, so you **better watch out**.
8 You **don't need to show** your passport for domestic travel within the UK.
9 We **ought to think** of that solution earlier. It's too late now.
10 You **needn't have washed up**, but thank you anyway.

b ⬭Circle the correct alternative in each pair. Tick (✓) if both are possible.

Customer Hi, my laptop hasn't been working properly for a few days now. Could you help?

Technician Yes, of course. First of all, I'd ¹**need to** / **need** look at it. Have you brought it with you?

Customer Yes, here it is. It's been really slow since I opened up an email attachment. I know I ²**mustn't** / **shouldn't** have done that, but I did and now I feel really stupid – I just wasn't thinking.

Technician Mmm, we always tell people that you're ³**not supposed to** / **not meant to** open up attachments unless you know who the sender is, but people do. The other thing we always tell customers is that they ⁴**mustn't** / **don't have to** forget to back up their files before they bring a laptop in, just in case we have to reinstall programs. You have backed yours up, haven't you?

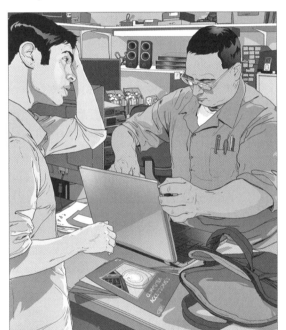

Customer Oh yes, I've done that. But what do you think the problem is?

Technician I'm just having a look now, but you ⁵**needn't to** / **don't need to** worry…Right, got it. The memory on the laptop is full and that's why it's been working so slowly. Try restarting it first. That will clear the memory and reset the programs. Also, you ⁶**should** / **ought to** delete any apps that you don't need. That will free up some memory.

Customer Is there anything else that I ⁷**could** / **may** do?

Technician It's probably worth scanning for viruses.

Customer Can you recommend some software for that?

Technician Well, I'm not really ⁸**permitted to** / **allowed to** recommend one brand over another, but perhaps do an internet search to see which providers are trustworthy. That ⁹**should** / **must** help you decide which one to use.

Customer That's great, thanks.

 ACTIVATION

Write five rules that you think would make your English class (even) better! Use the grammar from **b** above.

I think it would be really good if we were allowed to use our phones more in class.

7B GRAMMAR perception and sensation

● Complete the sentences using the word in **bold**.

1 The situation sounds worse than we'd expected. **though**

It sounds *as though the situation is worse* than we'd expected.

2 This herb has a similar smell to garlic, but it isn't garlic. **like**

This herb _____ , but it isn't garlic.

3 I could see that she had probably been crying. **if**

She looked _____ been crying.

4 Your manager has been telling me good things about you. **hearing**

I've _____ from your manager.

5 You can really taste the almonds in this ice cream. **tastes**

This _____ almonds.

6 The neighbour says that no one left the house after 9.00 p.m. that night. **see**

The neighbour says she didn't _____ after 9.00 p.m.

7 A viola makes a noise similar to a violin, but its range is lower. **sounds**

A viola _____ , but its range is lower.

8 It seems as though the city hasn't changed much since I left. **have**

The city doesn't seem _____ since I left.

9 The alarm went off at exactly eight o'clock. **heard**

I _____ at exactly eight o'clock.

10 Adam seems not to have slept very well judging by the amount he's yawning. **looks**

Adam _____ judging by the amount he's yawning.

11 She seemed to be delighted with the outcome of the meeting. **though**

It seemed _____ with the outcome of the meeting.

12 According to neighbours, the couple were arguing for more than an hour. **heard**

Neighbours _____ for more than an hour.

ACTIVATION

Read the following poem.

Sitting in my kitchen

I can	**see**	sunbeams dancing on the curtains.
The birds outside	**sound**	as if they're having a serious conference today.
The air	**smells**	of the coffee I've just made.
The cup	**feels**	warm in my hand,
And the coffee	**tastes**	deliciously sweet.

Now write your own poem about any place you like or dislike. Write a title and five lines, one for each of the senses, paying particular attention to the grammar in the exercise above. Use this table to help you:

(your title)		
I can	see	
	sound(s)	
	smell(s)	
	feel(s)	
	taste(s)	

8A GRAMMAR advanced gerunds and infinitives

a Right (✓) or wrong (✗)? Correct the mistakes in the **bold** phrases.

1 I expect **to have finished** the report by Friday afternoon. ✓
2 It's no use **sitting** around talking about it. We need actions, not words.
3 Your remarks really offended me. I will not put up with **speaking to** like that.
4 We would love **to be able to** stay longer in Bangkok, but it just wasn't possible.
5 Julia doesn't have much experience, so it's difficult for her **understanding** your point of view.
6 I wasn't aware of **having been introduced** to her before.
7 There's no point **to invite** George because he never goes to parties.
8 **Having studied abroad** will certainly be an advantage when you come to apply for a job.
9 What's that noise? Someone seems **to try** to open the door.
10 We quite enjoyed the holiday, but to be honest, we would rather **have stayed** at home.

b Complete the second sentence with a gerund or infinitive so that it means the same as the first.

1 We can't get a taxi because we don't have enough cash.
We don't have enough cash _to get_ a taxi.
2 It won't do you any good to feel guilty about what happened.
It's no good _____ guilty about what happened.
3 He was fed up with his mum telling him what to wear.
He was fed up with _____ what to wear by his mum.
4 It would have been better if the director had informed me personally.
I would rather _____ by the director in person.
5 He's unsure about what he should do after he graduates.
He's unsure about what _____ after he graduates.
6 It is thought that the police are searching the whole area.
The police are thought _____ the whole area.
7 She was the first female prime minister.
She was the first woman _____ elected prime minister.
8 I'm concerned that I haven't been contacted about an interview yet.
I'm concerned about _____ about an interview yet.

c Match 1–8 to a–h to make questions.

1 | d | How easy is it for you   a to have achieved by the time you're 50?
2 | | Do you think there is any point in   b have gone to a different university?
3 | | What do you hope   c telling a white lie is ever justifiable?
4 | | Do you think   d to tell people how you really feel?
5 | | What would it have been like   e regretting something after you've done it?
6 | | Do you mind   f to have lived 100 years ago?
7 | | Would you admire someone for   g being asked about your age?
8 | | Would you rather   h dedicating their whole life to their career, but neglecting their family?

ACTIVATION

Choose a question from **c** and write a paragraph answering it.

8B GRAMMAR expressing future plans and arrangements

a Complete the news report with one word in each gap.

One of the most talked-about matches in the history of tennis ¹ *is* due to take place this afternoon in New York. Current world number one Arturo Villa is ² _____ face his long-term rival Bill Everard in what is going to ³ _____ a long and tough struggle for the top spot, according to commentators. Their last match was a narrow defeat for Everard. 'I have worked so hard to get this far, and I'm ⁴ _____ the point of becoming the most highly-ranked player in the world,' he commented in a pre-match press conference. When asked about his predictions for the match, Villa replied: 'I've never been in better shape and I'm ⁵ _____ to show him who's boss, just like last time.' The match ⁶ _____ at 5.00 p.m. local time.

b Right (✓) or wrong (✗)? Correct the mistakes in the **bold** phrases.

Keith So, what ¹**are you and Wendy doing** this weekend? ✓

Tom Well, ²**the school holidays start** on Friday and ³**we will go** to the seaside with the kids. We can't stay away for long, though. ⁴**Wendy's due go** into hospital on Monday.

Keith Really? ⁵**Is she having** an operation?

Tom Yes, but it's nothing serious. It's just a minor operation on her wrist. ⁶**She'll be home** again in the evening. What ⁷**do you and Jennifer do** this weekend?

Keith Unfortunately, ⁸**Jennifer is working** all weekend. ⁹**Her company is about to be** taken over by a big multinational, so everyone is worried ¹⁰**they're losing** their jobs. So it looks like ¹¹**I'll be spending** the weekend on my own. I've decided that ¹²**I'm painting** the outside of the house if the weather stays nice.

Tom That doesn't sound like much fun!

ACTIVATION

Use the information below to write a one-paragraph local news report about a planned museum opening. Use some of the structures from **a** and **b**.

11.30 a.m.	Arrival of mayor and husband at museum, greeted by director
12.00 p.m.	Tour of museum for mayor and husband
1.30 p.m.	Formal lunch with staff and volunteers
3.00 p.m.	Official opening ceremony by mayor
3.30 p.m.	Drinks reception with members of the public
5.00 p.m.	End of visit; departure of mayor and husband

*The mayor and her husband **are due to** arrive at the museum at 11.30 a.m. and **are to be** greeted by the director. At 12.00 p.m., they **will be having** a tour of the museum, and then…*

9A GRAMMAR ellipsis

a Read the story. What difference do you notice between the two paragraphs?

A happy ending

Ever since she had been a small girl, Nicky had wanted to get to know her father, but she had never been able to. Whenever Nicky used to ask about him, her mother would shake her head and look angry. Every year on her birthday, Nicky used to hope that he would come to visit, but he never did. Nicky's mother told her he was always busy working abroad, but Nicky didn't believe he was. She was constantly talking about him, even though her mother begged her not to. Although Nicky had never met her father, she always felt that one day she would. Sometimes she used to close her eyes and wish that he would contact her. But when he finally phoned on her 21st birthday and asked her if she wanted to see him, Nicky wasn't sure if she did.

Nicky's father gave her his phone number and he said she could contact him whenever she wanted to contact him. Nicky said goodbye and then she hung up. At first, she was angry that he had got in touch and she wished that he hadn't got in touch. But a few weeks later, she called him and she arranged to see him because she felt they needed to talk. She got on well with him, although she hadn't expected to get on well with him. Nicky decided that she wanted them to meet regularly, and her father promised that they would meet regularly. Five years later, when Nicky got married, no one imagined that her father would be walking her up the aisle, but he was walking her up the aisle.

b Read the second paragraph again and ~~cross out~~ any words that can be left out.

c Rewrite the **bold** sentences using *so* or *not*.

1 **A** Do classes start at the usual time next week?
   B I presume ~~they do start at the usual time.~~ Otherwise the director would have mentioned it. *(so)*

2 **A** Do you have any batteries?
   B I'm afraid we haven't got any batteries. We sold the last pack yesterday.

3 **A** Are you going to go skiing next week?
   B I guess I'll go skiing, though I'm not very excited about it.

4 **A** Do you think they'll accept the contract as it is?
   B I suspect they won't accept it. They'll ask us to change some sections.

5 **A** Do you think Chris and Angie will come tomorrow?
   B I don't imagine they will come. They're very busy right now.

6 **A** John won't be interested in coming along, will he?
   B I suppose that he won't be interested in coming along. He has other plans for the summer.

ACTIVATION

Complete the sentences about yourself.

- _____ , but I've always wanted to.
- _____ , but my parents didn't.
- _____ , but I'm not.
- _____ , but I used to.
- _____ , even though I should have.
- _____ , but my friend can.

9B GRAMMAR nouns: compound and possessive forms

● Right (✓) or wrong (✗)? Correct the mistakes in the **bold** phrases.

1 There's a small garden at **the back of the house**. ✓

2 She's always sticking her nose into **other peoples' business**.

3 We're going to be at **Paula and James's house** for dinner tonight.

4 Does anyone have a **tins opener**? I want to open this soup.

5 I'd say it's at least **an hours walk** to the city centre from here.

6 Mrs Ramirez has always been **a very dear friend of my aunt's**.

7 Have you got a **coat hanger**? This jacket creases easily.

8 This painting is regarded as **her career's high point**.

9 Opticians usually sell accessories like **glasses cases** and cleaning products.

10 Please put the sugar back in the **kitchen's cupboard** when you've finished with it.

11 Be careful when you wash the **glasses of champagne** as they're very fragile.

12 I'm just going to **the doctor's**. I'll be back in an hour.

13 To play this game, we need to form a circle in **the room's middle**.

14 His partner is a **physics teacher** at one of the local high schools.

ACTIVATION

Try to think of at least two nouns that collocate with the **bold** words to make compound nouns.

	_____	**knife**	_____	**book**
	_____	**player**	_____	**key**
traffic *street*	**lights**	_____ _____ **machine**	_____ _____ **water**	
	_____ _____ **cake**	_____ _____ **centre**	_____ _____ **card**	
	_____ _____ **cup**	_____ _____ **board**	_____ _____ **frame**	

● Complete the article with relative pronouns.

The story behind the photo

This photo, [1] *which* shows a destitute woman with her children, was taken in 1936 by the photographer Dorothea Lange. Only three of the woman's seven children, [2]_____ ages ranged from a few months to ten years, can be seen in the photo. The woman, [3]_____ was 32 years old at the time, and her children became the subjects of the photo, [4]_____ later came to be known as 'Migrant Mother'. The camp [5]_____ they were staying was located in California, and after the publication of this photo in the newspapers, the US government was prompted to deliver food aid to the camp, in [6]_____ several thousand hungry people were living in squalid conditions. [7]_____ was ironic was the fact that the woman and her family [8]_____ had caused the government to react were no longer at the camp. They had moved on.

Lange's photo, [9]_____ became a defining image of the Great Depression in the US, was, in a sense, a mystery. For decades, no one knew [10]_____ had become of this woman and her family. Why? Well, because the woman [11]_____ Lange had talked to and photographed had never told Lange her name. Lange had never asked her for it, either.

In the late 70s, a reporter tracked down the 'mystery' woman, [12]_____ last name was then Thompson, at her California home. Thompson was critical of Lange, [13]_____ had died in 1965, saying she had felt exploited and wished the photo had never been taken. [14]_____ she and her children, some of [15]_____ were still alive, also regretted was that none of them had made any money from the image. It seems unfair that 'Migrant Mother', [16]_____ is one of the most iconic photos in American history, was able to help so many people, yet did nothing for the woman [17]_____ face was able to express so much.

In 1998, 15 years after Thompson died at the age of 80, a print of the image, [18]_____ had been signed by Lange, sold for $244,500 at auction.

ACTIVATION

Write a short description of a photo or painting that you like based on the article above. Try to use a variety of relative pronouns.

10B GRAMMAR adding emphasis (2): cleft sentences

a Rewrite the sentences starting with *The person*, *The place*, *The first / last time*, or *The reason*. Keep the emphasis on the **bold** word or phrase.

1 I've always wanted to visit **Istanbul** more than anywhere else.

The place I've always wanted to visit more than anywhere else is Istanbul.

2 He married her **for her money**.

_____

3 She loves **her niece** more than anyone else in the world.

_____
_____

4 I saw her for the last time in **October**.

_____

5 It's **my sister** who really understands how I feel.

_____
_____

6 We retired early **in order to have time to enjoy life**.

_____
_____

7 I relax most in **the garden**.

_____

8 I met David for the first time **just after I graduated**.

_____
_____

b Complete the second sentence so that it emphasizes the **bold** phrase.

1 **His unhealthy diet** really worries me.

What *really worries me is his unhealthy diet.*

2 My son is crazy about **skateboarding**.

What _____.

3 They just want to **lie on a beach and relax**.

All _____.

4 I'm desperate for a **nice cup of tea**.

What _____.

5 The restaurant was made special by **the atmosphere** rather than the food.

It _____
_____.

6 I don't want to **be late for work tomorrow**.

What _____.

7 She only asked for **a glass of water**.

All _____.

8 **Alec** was a professional footballer when he was young, not Darren.

It _____
_____.

9 I asked her a question, but **she refused to answer it**.

What happened _____
_____.

ACTIVATION

Complete the sentences about yourself.

- The reason I'm learning English is _____.
- What I most like about my English class is _____.
- The thing that bothers me most in the cinema, theatre, or at a concert is _____.
- The person I spend the most time with is _____.
- What really annoys me on trains, planes, or buses is when people _____.
- When I'm on holiday, all I want to do is _____.

Communicative activity instructions

1A Families

A pairwork discussion activity

Sts describe and compare photos, and then discuss family-related issues. Copy one worksheet per pair and cut into **A** and **B**.

LANGUAGE

agreeing, half-agreeing, and politely disagreeing
I see what you mean, but… etc.

- Put Sts in pairs, **A** and **B**, ideally face to face, and give out the worksheets. Tell them not to look at their partner's photo.
- Focus on **a**. Tell Sts that when they describe their photo they should not just comment on what they can see, but also say what they think of the photo, and what the image communicates.
- Set a time limit (e.g. two minutes) for Sts **A** to describe their photo. Sts then swap roles. When they have finished, tell them to discuss how the photos illustrate ways in which family life has changed over the past 60 years. When Sts have done this, they can show each other their photo.
- Now focus on **b**. Give Sts five minutes to read their statements, choose the three they would like to talk about, and to think of some ideas. They can take notes if they wish. Help with any vocabulary as necessary.
- Finally, focus on **c**, and set a time limit for Sts to discuss their statements. When the time is up, get feedback from various pairs to find out which statements they both agreed with and why.

EXTRA SUPPORT Get Sts to look at the phrases for half-agreeing and politely disagreeing on p.7 in the Student's Book and encourage them to use these phrases.

1B Have I got the job?

A job interview role-play

Sts take the roles of interviewers or candidates in a series of quick job interviews. Copy one worksheet per 12 Sts. Cut off the candidate's role card and make five more copies of this. Then cut up all the cards.

LANGUAGE

question formation, work vocabulary

- Divide the class in half. One group will be interviewers and the other candidates. If you have an uneven number, double up on one of the interviewers. With a very large class, you may want to have interviewers work in pairs, interviewing individual candidates together.
- Give each interviewer (or pair of interviewers) and each candidate a role card. Give them five minutes to prepare their questions and answers. Interviewers should think of questions to elicit whether candidates fit the profile of the ideal candidate.

- Arrange the class so that the interviewers for the different jobs aren't sitting too close together. They should have an empty chair across from or next to them for the candidates.
- Send one candidate to each interviewer (or pair of interviewers), and tell them to start. Remind interviewers to take notes to help them to remember the strengths / weaknesses of each candidate. After exactly three minutes, stop the interviews and get the candidates to move on to the next interviewer. Continue until each candidate has been interviewed for all the jobs, or until you run out of time.
- Give the interviewers time to decide who they thought was the best candidate, and get the candidates to discuss which job they think they would prefer.
- Finally, get the interviewers to say who they would like to offer the job to and why. The chosen candidate must say if he / she will accept the job or not. If a candidate is offered more than one job, he / she must choose between them, and the interviewer should select another candidate for the job, giving reasons for his / her choice.

2A Childhood questionnaire

A pairwork questionnaire

Sts choose six questions to ask each other from a questionnaire about childhood. Copy one worksheet per student.

LANGUAGE

narrative tenses, *used to / would* + infinitive

- Put Sts in pairs and give out the questionnaires. Focus on **a**, and give Sts time to read the questions and choose six to ask their partner. Elicit the meaning of *look up to* in 6 (= admire or respect sb) and *chores* in 8 (= small jobs in the house, e.g. doing the washing-up).
- Then get Sts to ask and answer their questions alternately. Sts **B** should turn their worksheet face down when Sts **A** ask the first question. Highlight that most of the questions have one or two follow-up questions, and Sts should ask the first one, wait for their partner to answer it, and then ask the follow-up questions. Sts then swap roles.
- Monitor and correct any mistakes in the use of tenses, and help with vocabulary.
- When Sts have finished, get some feedback on the most interesting answers.

2B All about English

A reading and discussion activity

Sts read and discuss issues related to learning and using English. Copy one worksheet per student.

> **LANGUAGE**
>
> expressions related to language learning, giving opinions

- Give out the worksheets. Focus on **a** and tell Sts to read all the comments.
- Put Sts in pairs and focus on **b**. Encourage them to give reasons for their answers and to tell each other how they feel about it.
- When Sts have discussed all eight comments, get feedback on each comment from the whole class.

EXTRA IDEA You could get Sts to discuss a comment in pairs for a set time (e.g. three minutes), then get feedback before getting Sts to discuss the next comment.

3A Reconciliation?

A role-play activity

A free-speaking activity to promote fluency in which Sts role-play a conversation between a couple who have split up, but are considering getting back together again. Copy one worksheet per pair and cut into **A** and **B**.

> **LANGUAGE**
>
> arguing, persuading, making suggestions, and reaching an agreement

- Put Sts in pairs, **A** and **B**, and give out the worksheets. Make sure Sts can't see each other's worksheets. If you have odd numbers, take part in the role-play yourself, or ask the extra student to act as 'counsellor' for one pair, to mediate and advise after they have discussed each point.
- Give Sts time to read their worksheets. Encourage them to underline the most important information. Tell them to think about their role and what they are going to say. They should decide on their priorities, and if there is anything they are not prepared to give up.
- When Sts are ready, get them to sit face to face with their partner, and tell them to imagine that they have just arrived at a café. They must discuss the four areas on the worksheet. You may want to remind them of the difference between *discuss* and *argue*. Emphasize that Sts should go through the areas one by one, first giving their own points of view, and then listening to their partner and trying to reach agreement. Highlight …*try to keep calm and don't lose your temper* at the end of their worksheets.
- Set a time limit, but be flexible depending how the conversations are going.
- Finally, get feedback from various pairs and ask if they reached any kind of agreement or reconciliation. You could find out how many 'couples' have decided to reconcile.

EXTRA IDEA If you feel your Sts would be uncomfortable performing the role-play, they could instead work in pairs to write the conversation dialogue rather than role-playing it.

3B Classic historical films

A group quiz

Sts work in groups to complete a quiz about historical films. Copy one worksheet for each group of three or four Sts.

> **LANGUAGE**
>
> expressions related to historical films, speculating and guessing

- Put Sts in groups of three or four, and give each group a worksheet face down. Set a time limit (e.g. ten minutes) and tell Sts to answer as many questions as possible in the given time. Stress that if they don't know the answers, they should speculate and make guesses.
- Tell Sts to turn over the worksheet and start. When the time is up, say *Stop* and check answers. The group with the most correct answers is the winner.

1 **a** Ancient Greece **b** World War II **c** Ancient Rome **d** World War I **e** the 1970s (during the last part of the Vietnam War)
2 **a** 2 **b** 5 **c** 3 **d** 1 **e** 4
3 **a** Vincent van Gogh **b** Che Guevara **c** Nelson Mandela **d** Jackie Kennedy **e** Neil Armstrong
4 **a** 3 **b** 1 **c** 2 **d** 5 **e** 4
5 **a** **Seven** Samurai **b** **Mary** Queen of Scots **c** The Theory of **Everything** **d** The **Iron** Lady **e** The **King's** Speech

EXTRA IDEA You could give Sts two points for a correct answer and one point for an intelligent guess.

4A First or last?

A reading and discussion activity

Sts read lines from famous novels and decide if they are the first or the last ones in the book. Copy one worksheet per student.

> **LANGUAGE**
>
> describing books and films, speculating

- Give out the worksheets and focus on **a**. Tell Sts to write *F* (first line) or *L* (last line) for 1–10. Tell them to think of reasons for their choices.
- Put Sts in pairs and focus on **b**. Give them time to compare answers, then ask them to match the lines to novels a–j.
- Check answers. For each line, first find out what most Sts think and why, and then tell them whether it was the first or last line. Then check if they got the novel correct.

1 L, h   2 L, i   3 F, d   4 F, c   5 F, j   6 L, g   7 L, b   8 F, a   9 F, e   10 L, f

- Finally, focus on **c**, and set a time limit (e.g. five minutes) for Sts to discuss the questions in their pairs. Encourage them to use adjectives for describing books and films from p.37 of the Student's Book.
- Get some feedback from various pairs.

EXTRA SUPPORT You may want to revise some expressions for speculating.

4B Sound or noise?

A pairwork activity

Sts choose sounds / noises they like and don't like, and explain why to a partner. Copy one worksheet per student.

LANGUAGE

sounds and the human voice vocabulary

- Give out the worksheets. Focus on **a**, and give Sts time to choose the sounds they like and don't like. Help with any vocabulary as necessary.
- Put Sts in pairs, and set a time limit (e.g. ten minutes) for them to compare and explain their choices.
- Get feedback on which sounds most Sts like / don't like.

5A Managing time

A pairwork questionnaire

Sts fill in a questionnaire about time management and discuss their results. Copy one worksheet per student.

LANGUAGE

expressing frequency, expressions with *time*

- Tell Sts that they are going to do a questionnaire to find out how good they are at time management.
- Put Sts in pairs and give out the worksheets. Tell them to fold their worksheet along the line where it says **FOLD** and not to look at the score descriptions yet.
- Focus on **a** and give Sts time to tick the appropriate box for each statement.
- When Sts have finished, focus on **b** and get Sts to compare their answers with their partner. They should read out the statement incorporating the adverb of frequency they have ticked, e.g. *'I never make a list…'*, and then give reasons or examples.
- When Sts have finished, focus on **c** and tell them to look at the folded part of the worksheet to work out their scores and read the results. Get them to tell their partner their score, and whether they agreed with the description or not.
- Get some quick feedback to find out who's the best / worst at time management.

5B Money

A pairwork activity

Sts interview each other to find out about their attitude towards money. Copy one worksheet per student.

LANGUAGE

money vocabulary

- Put Sts in pairs, **A** and **B**, and give out the worksheets.
- Give Sts time to read the questions and choose two from each section to ask their partner.
- Tell Sts **B** to put their questionnaire face down. Sts **A** start by interviewing Sts **B**, and then they swap roles.
- Get feedback to find out which questions they found most interesting.

EXTRA IDEA   When they have finished, ask Sts to write their own set of money questions to ask their partner.

6A Ask me a question

A group card game

Sts ask and answer questions using verb + object + infinitive or gerund. Copy and cut up one worksheet per group.

LANGUAGE

verb + object + infinitive or gerund
let sb do sth, imagine yourself doing, etc.

- Put Sts into groups of three or four and give out a set of cards to each group, face down in a pile.
- Tell Sts to take turns to pick up a card and ask the question to one person in the group.
- Remind Sts to ask each other for more information and encourage them to ask *How about you?* to other members of the group as a way of extending communication. Monitor and correct any grammar mistakes.
- Finally, get feedback from various groups on some of the most interesting answers.

NON-CUT ALTERNATIVE   Put Sts in pairs. Copy one worksheet per student and fold it down the middle. Sts take turns to ask their partner a question from their list.

6B Case studies
A reading and discussion activity

Sts read and discuss some case studies about people with obsessions. Copy one worksheet per student.

> **LANGUAGE**
>
> language related to obsession

- Give out the worksheets and focus on **a**. Tell Sts that all the case studies are based on real people, although the names have been changed. Set a time limit (e.g. five minutes) for Sts to read each case study and think of answers to the questions.
- When the time is up, put Sts in pairs and focus on **b**. Get them to share their ideas.
- Get feedback by finding out which obsessions Sts think are the most common. Then find out if any Sts know anyone with a similar obsession.

7A Let's change the rules
A reading and discussion activity

Sts read and discuss some proposals and suggestions related to education. Copy one worksheet per student.

> **LANGUAGE**
>
> verbs to express permission, obligation, and necessity; education

- Give out the worksheets. Focus on **a** and give Sts some time to read the proposals and suggestions (e.g. five minutes). Tell them to decide how they feel about each one and remind them that they should support their opinion with reasons.
- Put Sts in pairs and focus on **b**. Tell them to discuss each proposal or suggestion with their partner, giving reasons for their opinions. Monitor and correct any mistakes with verbs of permission, obligation, and necessity.
- When Sts have finished, get some feedback from various pairs to find out which of the proposals or suggestions Sts feel most strongly about.

EXTRA IDEA Get the class to vote on which two of the proposals they would most like to see implemented in their country.

7B Works of art?
A pairwork activity

Sts look at photos and decide whether they think each is a famous work of art or an ordinary object. They then exchange information about the real works of art. Copy one worksheet per pair and cut the texts into **A** and **B**.

> **LANGUAGE**
>
> art vocabulary

- Put Sts in pairs, **A** and **B**, ideally face to face, and give out the top half of the worksheet.
- Explain that Sts have the same photos, and that two are famous works of art and four are not. Together they should look at each photo and decide which two they think are the real works of art. Encourage them to give reasons for their choices.
- Now hand out the texts and give Sts time to read the information. Sts **A** then tell Sts **B** in their own words about their work of art.
- Sts then swap roles.
- Get feedback to find out who guessed the real works of art correctly and what information they found most interesting.

EXTRA IDEA Get pairs to tell each other which of the real works of art they like the best and the reason for their choice.

8A Medical vocabulary definitions game

A pairwork activity

Sts extend their knowledge of medical vocabulary by describing medical-related words to each other and teaching each other new words. Copy one worksheet per pair and cut into **A** and **B**.

> ### LANGUAGE
> health and medicine vocabulary

- Put Sts in pairs, **A** and **B**, ideally face to face, and give out the worksheets. Make sure they can't see each other's worksheets.
- Give Sts time to look at their pictures and words. Explain that half the pictures are labelled, and the other half are not (their partner will have these labelled). Tell them to make sure they can pronounce all their labelled words.
- Sts **B** start by asking Sts **A**, e.g. *What do you call the woman who helps deliver a baby?* Sts **A** should identify the picture that their partner is describing and then tell him / her what the word is, giving both the spelling and pronunciation. Sts **B** then write the word down. They then swap roles.
- When Sts have labelled all their pictures, they should compare their worksheets to make sure they have spelled the words correctly. Check answers.

8B Travel role-plays

A role-play activity

Sts role-play being a dissatisfied tourist with some complaints, and a travel agency representative responding to their client's complaints. Copy one worksheet per pair and cut into **A** and **B**.

> ### LANGUAGE
> making complaints, travel and tourism vocabulary

- Put Sts in pairs and give out the worksheets. Focus on **Role-play 1** and give Sts time to read their role card and make some notes about what they are going to say.
- Set a time limit for Sts to do the first role-play (e.g. five minutes). Monitor and make a note of any problems to deal with later.
- When the time is up, stop the role-play and find out what agreement, if any, was reached.
- Now repeat the process for **Role-play 2**.

EXTRA SUPPORT Before Sts begin, you could write the following phrases on the board to help Sts.
Making complaints: I'M VERY UNHAPPY ABOUT / DISSATISFIED WITH…; I THINK THIS IS UNACCEPTABLE / OUTRAGEOUS…
Responding to complaints: I SEE WHAT YOU MEAN / I UNDERSTAND WHAT YOU'RE SAYING / I CAN SEE WHY YOU FEEL LIKE THIS, BUT…; I'LL DO MY BEST TO…

9A Animal quiz

A pairwork quiz activity

Sts ask and answer questions about unusual animal facts. Copy one worksheet per student (there are separate **A** and **B** worksheets).

> ### LANGUAGE
> animal vocabulary

- Put Sts in pairs, **A** and **B**, ideally face to face, and give out the worksheets. Make sure Sts can't see each other's worksheets as their questions are different. Set a time limit (e.g. five minutes) for Sts to read through their questions. Help with any vocabulary problems as necessary.
- Focus on **a** and tell Sts that the objective is to see who knows more about animals. Sts **A** ask Sts **B** their questions first and Sts **B** answer. If the answer is correct, Sts **B** get one point. If the answer is wrong, Sts **A** must give the correct answer. Remind Sts to explain the correct answer with the additional information underneath each question. Encourage them to use their own words rather than simply reading out the information. When Sts **A** have finished asking their questions, Sts swap roles.
- When both Sts have finished asking their questions, get feedback to see who got more correct answers in each pair. Find out if anyone got all answers correct.

9B Talk for one minute

A group board game

Sts move around the board and talk about a topic for one minute. Copy one worksheet per group of three or four Sts. You also need one dice or coin per group and one counter per student.

> ### LANGUAGE
> food vocabulary

- Put Sts in groups of three or four. Give each group the worksheet, a dice, and enough counters. If you don't have a dice, give each group a coin. Sts toss the coin for their go and move 1 for heads and 2 for tails.
- Each student puts their counter on **START**.
- Explain the rules of the game. Sts take turns to throw the dice and move their counter. When they land on a circle, they must talk for one minute about the topic.
- If a student is unable to talk for one minute, he / she moves back a circle. If a student is able to talk for one minute, they stay on the circle.
- Monitor and help if necessary. The first student to reach **FINISH** wins. If a group finishes very quickly, tell them to go around the board again.
- Get feedback on some of the more interesting answers.

10A What's wrong with sport?

A groupwork discussion activity

Sts read statements about the negative influences of sport and then discuss to what extent they agree or disagree with each one. Copy one worksheet per student.

> **LANGUAGE**
>
> agreeing, half-agreeing, and politely disagreeing; sports vocabulary

- Give out the worksheets. Focus on **a** and give Sts time to read the statements and write the number which best indicates to what extent they agree or disagree with each according to the scale at the top of the worksheet. Remind them that they should think of reasons to support their opinions.
- Put Sts in groups of three or four. Focus on **b** and give Sts time to discuss each statement and decide how far, as a group, they agree or disagree with each one. You could tell them that they don't have to agree with each other.
- When Sts have finished, get some feedback from various groups to find out which of the statements Sts agreed or disagreed with most strongly.

EXTRA SUPPORT   Remind Sts that when sharing opinions, it's important to remain polite. Refer Sts back to the phrases for half-agreeing and politely disagreeing on p.7 in the Student's Book and encourage them to use these phrases.

10B About the UK quiz

A quiz activity

Sts complete a quiz about life in the UK. Copy one worksheet per student.

> **LANGUAGE**
>
> general revision

- Give out the worksheets. Focus on **a** and explain that these questions are typical of the ones that are asked in the 'Life in the UK' test – a test which people over 18 and under 65 have to do if they want to become a British citizen.
- Set a time limit (e.g. ten minutes) for Sts to complete the quiz individually. Monitor and help with any vocabulary as necessary.
- When Sts have finished, put them in pairs. Focus on **b** and get Sts to compare their answers with their partner. Encourage them to give reasons for choosing their answers.
- When Sts have finished comparing and discussing their answers, check answers and ask Sts to score their tests, with one point for each correct answer. Then find out if anyone got all the answers correct.

Politics	**1** c (elections can be called earlier under special circumstances) **2** c **3** b **4** c **5** a
History	**1** b **2** b **3** c **4** c **5** a
The arts	**1** a **2** b **3** a **4** b **5** b
Geography	**1** b **2** c **3** b **4** a **5** a
Sport	**1** a **2** c **3** c **4** b **5** a

EXTRA IDEA   When they have finished, ask Sts what questions about their country they would ask people who wanted to come and live there.

1A COMMUNICATIVE Families

Student A

a Describe your photo to **B** in detail. Then listen to **B** describe his / her photo. Discuss in what ways the photos show how family life has changed over the past 60 years.

b Read the five statements and choose three you would like to talk about. Decide if you agree, disagree, or half-agree and think of reasons.

1 There should be at least one hour every evening when all members of the family turn off their electronic devices and talk to each other.
2 Ideally, new parents should be over 20 and under 40.
3 How to be a parent and bring up children should be part of the school curriculum.
4 An only child is a lonely child.
5 There is a lot of truth in the saying 'Blood is thicker than water'.

c Read your chosen statements to **B** one by one. Say what you think and ask if they agree with you.

- -

Student B

a Listen to **A** describe his / her photo. Then describe your photo to **A** in detail. Discuss in what ways the photos show how family life has changed over the past 60 years.

b Read the five statements and choose three you would like to talk about. Decide if you agree, disagree, or half-agree and think of reasons.

1 One of the parents of children under five should not go out to work.
2 Even if parents are unhappy, they should stay together because of their children.
3 Marriage should be a five-year renewable contract.
4 People who decide not to have children should pay less tax than people who have them.
5 The position of a child in a family (e.g. first born, middle child, etc.) definitely has an influence on their personality.

c Read your chosen statements to **A** one by one. Say what you think and ask if they agree with you.

● Role cards for interviewers

 1 You are interviewing for a part-time **assistant librarian** position. It will be a short-term contract to cover maternity leave.

Profile of the ideal candidate:
- book lover
- prepared to work flexible hours
- previous experience not essential, but desirable
- able to work well alone
- organized

You have three minutes to speak to each interviewee. You have to decide who you would like to employ. At the end of the interviews, you will be asked to explain who you chose and why. Before you begin, think about and write down the questions you are going to ask.

 2 You are interviewing for a **telemarketing position** for a well-known mobile phone company. It is a three-month, non-renewable contract. There will be a basic salary with additional commission.

Profile of the ideal candidate:
- good interpersonal skills and telephone manner
- no experience necessary, but experience in sales or marketing a bonus
- determination and drive essential
- able to work well under pressure

You have three minutes to speak to each interviewee. You have to decide who you would like to employ. At the end of the interviews, you will be asked to explain who you chose and why. Before you begin, think about and write down the questions you are going to ask.

3 You are interviewing for a **toy shop supervisor** position. It is a three-month trial period leading to a permanent, full-time contract. A job share would be possible.

Profile of the ideal candidate:
- proven team leader
- excellent organizational skills
- basic accounting knowledge
- some knowledge of what toys are popular at the moment is desirable

You have three minutes to speak to each interviewee. You have to decide who you would like to employ. At the end of the interviews, you will be asked to explain who you chose and why. Before you begin, think about and write down the questions you are going to ask.

 4 You are interviewing for a **car park attendant** position. It is a full-time job that involves 12-hour shifts, both day and night. A permanent contract will be offered.

Profile of the ideal candidate:
- would suit a solitary person who isn't easily bored
- numerate
- able to make on-the-spot decisions
- able to deal with difficult or aggressive customers
- physically fit

You have three minutes to speak to each interviewee. You have to decide who you would like to employ. At the end of the interviews, you will be asked to explain who you chose and why. Before you begin, think about and write down the questions you are going to ask.

 5 You are interviewing for a **bike messenger** for a company that uses bicycles and motorcycles to deliver letters and packages. It is a six-month contract with possibility of extension, and involves some Saturdays.

Profile of the ideal candidate:
- able to ride motorcycle (licence required) or bicycle in city centre
- reliable and trustworthy with confidential documents
- organized and punctual
- good knowledge of the city

You have three minutes to speak to each interviewee. You have to decide who you would like to employ. At the end of the interviews, you will be asked to explain who you chose and why. Before you begin, think about and write down the questions you are going to ask.

 6 You are interviewing for the position of a **care assistant at a retirement home**. It involves alternate morning / evening shifts one weekend a month.

Profile of the ideal candidate:
- caring personality, with experience of working with older people
- first aid knowledge an advantage
- able to make decisions on own
- must be a team player
- available to work overtime

You have three minutes to speak to each interviewee. You have to decide who you would like to employ. At the end of the interviews, you will be asked to explain who you chose and why. Before you begin, think about and write down the questions you are going to ask.

● Role card for candidates

You are out of work and desperate for any job (you really need the money). You are going to be interviewed for some of the following jobs:
- assistant librarian
- bike messenger
- car park attendant
- care assistant at a retirement home
- telemarketing position
- toy shop supervisor

The interviews will last three minutes each. You really want to sell yourself well at the interview! Think about the following questions you might be asked and make some notes. You can use real information about yourself, or invent some. Once you have decided on your answers, you can't change them.

- What do you consider to be your main skills?
- What previous work experience do you have?
- How physically fit are you?
- What kind of work situation would you prefer (part-time / full-time / temporary / permanent)?
- Are you prepared to work overtime and at weekends?

2A COMMUNICATIVE Childhood questionnaire

a Read the questionnaire and choose six questions to ask a partner.

b Ask the questions and answer the ones your partner asks you.

1 Are there any clothes you had as a child that you particularly loved or hated? Did you use to have to wear clothes that belonged to your older brothers or sisters?

2 Did you have any favourite places where you used to like going to play? Did you go alone or with your friends? What did you do there?

3 What was your favourite sweet or chocolate bar? Can you describe it? Why did you like it so much?

4 Who were the people you felt closest to as a child? What do you remember about them?

5 Did you get pocket money? How much? Did you use to spend it immediately or did you sometimes save it? What for?

6 When you were growing up, was there anybody you really looked up to or wanted to be like?

7 Did your parents use to read you a story before you went to sleep or did you read stories yourself? What was your favourite story?

8 Did you have to do any chores while you were growing up? What were they? How did you feel about having to do them?

9 Who was the oldest member of your immediate or extended family when you were a child? What do you remember about him / her?

10 As a child, what did you want to be when you grew up? Do you still have the same ambition or did you change your mind? Why?

11 What were your typical family meals like? Did you use to all eat together? Where? Who used to cook?

12 As a child, what was your favourite special occasion, e.g. birthday, holiday? How did you use to celebrate it?

13 If you did something naughty, how did your parents punish you? Can you remember which type of punishment was the most effective?

14 Were you ever a member of a youth club or organization, e.g. the Scouts? How long did you belong to it for? Did you enjoy it?

2B COMMUNICATIVE All about English

a Read the comments from around the world about learning or using English. Is the situation the same or different in your country? How do you feel about it?

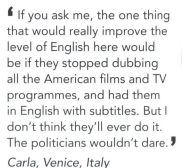

' If you ask me, the one thing that would really improve the level of English here would be if they stopped dubbing all the American films and TV programmes, and had them in English with subtitles. But I don't think they'll ever do it. The politicians wouldn't dare. '

Carla, Venice, Italy

' At a lot of secondary schools in my country, the main aim is to get the children to pass written exams in English – spoken English isn't given enough importance. I feel that's a mistake because later on in life it's more important to speak the language rather than write it. '

Raquel, Seville, Spain

' Some of my friends have studied English abroad in the summer holidays. The ones who did courses in the UK when they were younger are the ones whose level of English is really good. Personally, I feel that if you haven't studied English in an English-speaking country, you're at a bit of a disadvantage. '

Ahmad, Istanbul, Turkey

' Some people don't have the time or money to go to a language school to study English – I'm one of those. Luckily, there are so many great language learning apps and tutorials to watch online. I think you can learn English without going to classes. However, you need to have quite a lot of motivation to do this. '

Alejandro, Puebla, Mexico

' In my opinion, nowadays, people in public life really ought to be able to speak good English. I feel really embarrassed when I hear how some of our politicians or public figures speak. '

Akiko, Osaka, Japan

' Personally, I think that pop groups in my country shouldn't sing in English. I mean it's more universal, but they aren't English, and not everybody in Hungary understands English. I think they should sing in Hungarian. '

András, Debrecen, Hungary

' In some secondary schools in my country, they are now teaching other subjects like maths and science in English, as well as the normal English language classes. In general, I think it's a really good idea – as long as the teachers' English is good enough, of course. '

Karolina, Brno, Czech Republic

' In French, we use a lot of English words like *weekend*, *news*, *leader*, *cool*, *OK* – words like that. I personally hate it. I think we ought to use our own words for these things, not just borrow from English. '

Marc, Grenoble, France

b Talk to a partner and compare your ideas.

3A COMMUNICATIVE Reconciliation?

Student A

You're Nicole and you went out with Steve for two years. About six months ago you mutually agreed to split up, but you have kept in touch. Recently, you've discussed the possibility of getting back together again. You've agreed to meet to talk through the reasons why you split up, and to see whether solutions can be found to make a reconciliation possible.

1 Attitude to appearance
When you first started going out, Steve loved going to the gym and shopping for clothes. Over the two years you were together, you felt he'd started to let himself go, e.g. he stopped going to the gym with you, and started to wear any old thing!

2 Helping in the house
You know that your way of doing things is the best way. It used to drive you mad when Steve did things his way (the wrong way), e.g. when he was preparing a meal or doing the washing-up. So, when you saw him doing things incorrectly, you'd try and put him right. Steve used to get very annoyed by this, but you can't see why.

3 Your friend Max
One of the main reasons why you split up was because Steve was jealous of your friendship with Max – your ex-partner. Although you get on really well with Max and he's one of your closest friends, you certainly don't have any romantic feelings for him anymore. You meet Max about once a month for a drink, or to go to the cinema (you and Max have the same taste in films, unlike you and Steve).

4 The spoilt child
Steve has a nine-year-old daughter (Nina) from his previous marriage. He has Nina for a weekend once a fortnight. You think she is immensely spoilt, manipulative, and badly behaved. Initially, you spent time as a threesome, but you felt this wasn't working, so you used to go away with friends for the weekends when Steve had Nina.

Talk to Steve about these problems and try to find a way forward. Remember you want to get back together with him, so try to keep calm and don't lose your temper!

Student B

You're Steve and you went out with Nicole for two years. About six months ago you mutually agreed to split up, but you have kept in touch. Recently, you've discussed the possibility of getting back together again. You've agreed to meet to talk through the reasons why you split up, and to see whether solutions can be found to make a reconciliation possible.

1 Attitude to appearance
You think that when you're in a relationship, you need to be able to be yourself, and that includes your appearance, but Nicole was always going on about the clothes you wore and the fact that you weren't as fit as you used to be. You think Nicole is rather obsessed with the gym, and she spends a fortune on clothes.

2 Unwanted advice
You've managed to survive perfectly well all these years cooking and cleaning in your own way. One of the reasons you broke up with Nicole was because she was always telling you a 'better' way of doing things (in other words, her way) when you hadn't asked her for advice, and it used to really get on your nerves.

3 Her ex
Nicole's ex-partner is called Max. They often go out to the cinema, talk on the phone, and have a drink together. You don't understand why she still needs him in her life. You're not jealous of Max, it's just that you don't like him and you really don't think it's healthy for Nicole to stay in touch with him.

4 Your daughter
You have a nine-year-old daughter (Nina) from your previous marriage who you have every other weekend. Nina can be a bit difficult at times, and you know that you do tend to spoil her and need to be stricter – but that's only because you see her so little. You're aware that Nicole doesn't get on with Nina, but you think that she didn't really give Nina a chance. She just started going away with friends when Nina was around. It is really important for you that Nina and Nicole get on well.

Talk to Nicole about these problems and try to find a way forward. Remember you want to get back together with her, so try to keep calm and don't lose your temper!

3B COMMUNICATIVE Classic historical films

1 In which historical period are the following films set?
a *Clash of the Titans* _____
b *Dunkirk* _____
c *Pompeii* _____
d *War Horse* _____
e *Apocalypse Now* _____ ___/5

2 Match quotes a–e to films 1–5.

a ☐ 'They may take our lives, but they'll never take our freedom.'

b ☐ 'I'm the king of the world.'

c ☐ 'I don't want to survive. I want to live.'

d ☐ 'Sometimes it's the very people who no one imagines anything of who do the things no one can imagine.'

e ☐ 'An eye for an eye only ends up making the whole world blind.' ___/5

1 *The Imitation Game*
2 *Braveheart*
3 *12 Years a Slave*
4 *Gandhi*
5 *Titanic*

3 Which important figures do you associate with these films?
a *Loving Vincent* _____
b *The Motorcycle Diaries* _____
c *Invictus* _____
d *Jackie* _____
e *First Man* _____ ___/5

4 Who played the US presidents below? Match photos a–e to actors 1–5.

☐ Dwight D. Eisenhower in *The Butler* (2013)

☐ George W. Bush in *Vice* (2018)

☐ Abraham Lincoln in *Lincoln* (2012)

☐ Franklin D. Roosevelt in *Hyde Park on Hudson* (2012)

☐ Lyndon B. Johnson in *LBJ* (2016)

1 Sam Rockwell   2 Daniel Day-Lewis   3 Robin Williams   4 Woody Harrelson   5 Bill Murray
___/5

5 Correct the film titles by changing one word.
a *Three Samurai* _____
b *Margaret Queen of Scots* _____
c *The Theory of Something* _____
d *The Tin Lady* _____
e *The Queen's Speech* _____ ___/5

Total score ___/25

4A COMMUNICATIVE First or last?

a Look at some famous first and last lines from novels. Try to decide which are first lines and which are last lines. Write **F** (first) or **L** (last).

1 ☐ 'He was soon borne away by the waves and lost in darkness and distance.'

2 ☐ 'I'm so glad to be at home again.'

3 ☐ 'It's a funny thing about mothers and fathers. Even when their own child is the most disgusting little blister you could ever imagine, they still think that he or she is wonderful.'

4 ☐ 'James Bond, with two double bourbons inside him, sat in the final departure lounge of Miami airport and thought about life and death.'

5 ☐ 'Somewhere in La Mancha, in a place whose name I do not care to remember, a gentleman lived not long ago, one of those who has a lance and ancient shield on a shelf and keeps a skinny nag and a greyhound for racing.'

6 ☐ 'Then with a profound and deeply willed desire to believe, to be heard, as she had done every day since the murder of Carlo Rizzi, she said the necessary prayers for the soul of Michael Corleone.'

7 ☐ 'Tomorrow, I'll think of some way to get him back. After all, tomorrow is another day.'

8 ☐ 'Many years later, as he faced the firing squad, Colonel Aureliano Buendía was to remember that distant afternoon when his father took him to discover ice.'

9 ☐ 'Mr Phileas Fogg lived, in 1872, at No.7, Saville Row, Burlington Gardens, the house in which Sheridan died in 1814.'

10 ☐ 'The creatures outside looked from pig to man, and from man to pig, and from pig to man again; but already it was impossible to say which was which.'

a ☐ *One Hundred Years of Solitude*
Gabriel García Márquez

b ☐ *Gone With The Wind*
Margaret Mitchell

c ☐ *Goldfinger*   Ian Fleming

d ☐ *Matilda*   Roald Dahl

e ☐ *Around the World in Eighty Days*
Jules Verne

f ☐ *Animal Farm*   George Orwell

g ☐ *The Godfather*   Mario Puzo

h ☐ *Frankenstein*   Mary Shelley

i ☐ *The Wonderful Wizard of Oz*
L. Frank Baum

j ☐ *Don Quixote*   Miguel de Cervantes

b Compare your answers with a partner. Then match lines 1–10 to novels a–j.

c Talk to a partner.

1 Which do you think is the best first line? Does it make you want to read the book? What do you think the book will be like?

2 Have any of the last lines spoilt the book for you?

3 Have you seen the film of any of these books?

4 Which (if any) of these books have you read? What did you think of it / them?

a Look at the list of sounds. Tick (✓) the five you like most and cross (✗) the five that most annoy you.

b Compare your list with a partner and explain your choices. How do these sounds make you feel?

church bells ringing

children splashing in a swimming pool

the wind whistling at night

the pop of a champagne cork

fireworks going off

someone crunching crisps

a fly or a bee buzzing

someone clicking their fingers

the crash of thunder

a dog barking

people whispering in the cinema

someone near you snoring

the hum of air conditioning

an owl hooting

someone chewing gum and blowing bubbles

other people's strange ringtones

audience applause or laughter during a TV show

someone tapping their fingers on the table

the rattle of plates and cutlery being piled up when someone is washing up

the sound of your phone alarm

the roar of an underground train approaching

5A COMMUNICATIVE Managing time

a Read the questionnaire and put a tick (✓) in one of the boxes for each statement.

	always	sometimes	never
1 I make a list of things I have to do each week.	☐	☐	☐
2 I leave things to the last minute.	☐	☐	☐
3 I turn off my electronic devices (e.g. phone) when I'm working on something important.	☐	☐	☐
4 I arrive late for meetings or classes.	☐	☐	☐
5 I make time to be with my friends and family.	☐	☐	☐
6 I do two or three things at the same time.	☐	☐	☐
7 I deal with difficult or unpleasant tasks straight away.	☐	☐	☐
8 I have trouble saying 'no'.	☐	☐	☐
9 I control my phone, it doesn't control me.	☐	☐	☐
10 I skip meals or exercise so that I can work or study.	☐	☐	☐
11 When I have a lot to do, I prioritize tasks.	☐	☐	☐
12 I work or study on my days off.	☐	☐	☐
13 When I'm travelling or waiting, e.g. for an appointment, I use the time to work or study.	☐	☐	☐
14 I'm stressed about the deadlines I have to meet.	☐	☐	☐
15 My desk is tidy.	☐	☐	☐
16 I ask for extensions to deadlines.	☐	☐	☐
17 I open any emails / messages as soon as they arrive.	☐	☐	☐
18 Thinking about the things I have to do worries me.	☐	☐	☐
19 I know the time of day I'm most productive.	☐	☐	☐
20 I have problems finding time to relax.	☐	☐	☐

b Compare with a partner. Give examples to explain your answers.

c Work out your score and read your description. Do you agree?

- FOLD -

Scoring system

odd numbers *always* = 2 points   **even numbers** *always* = 0 points
sometimes = 1 point   *sometimes* = 1 point
never = 0 points   *never* = 2 points

0–17 You really need to organize your time more effectively. How about setting yourself some goals and planning what to do each week? If you do this, you'll be able to see what you're doing with your time and you'll know exactly what needs to be done. You'll make more efficient use of your time. Honestly!

18–30 You sometimes have trouble finding time to relax and switch off from the stress of everyday life. How about developing some new strategies to help you with this? You could start by planning times during the day which are dedicated to checking / answering emails and messages (stick to those times!), or take up yoga or meditation. You'll soon notice the difference and find that you're more relaxed and making more efficient use of your time.

31–40 Congratulations! You're an excellent time manager and you really know how to organize yourself and your time effectively. You know exactly where you're going and what needs to be done on a daily, weekly, and yearly basis. Keep on doing what you're doing!

5B COMMUNICATIVE Money

● Choose two questions from each section to ask a partner.

Saving money

1 Would you say you are good at saving money? Why (not)?
2 Do you have any strategies for saving money, e.g. when you are shopping?
3 Are you saving for anything at the moment? What for?
4 What factors might influence your decision to keep your money in a specific bank?

Losing and winning money

Do you know anyone who…?
1 has been a victim of credit card fraud
2 found that money had been mistakenly paid into their bank account
3 lost or made a large amount of money on the stock market
4 won a substantial amount of money in the lottery

Earning money

1 Did you have a Saturday job or a summer job when you were younger? What kind of work did you have to do?
2 Do you have any skills that could bring in extra income if you needed it?
3 How would you feel about earning a lot less than your partner?
4 In what jobs do you think people can justify earning huge salaries?

Spending money

1 When you go shopping, do you prefer paying with cash or by card?
2 Do you prefer spending money on things (e.g. clothes, gadgets, etc.) or experiences (e.g. holidays, concerts, etc.)?
3 Is there anything you feel guilty about spending money on? Why?
4 Have you ever bought something that you now think was a complete waste of money?

Giving money

1 Do you donate to any charities? Which ones? Why did you choose them?
2 Where and when do you tend to give tips? What factors influence your decision to give a tip or not?
3 Do you ever give money to people begging on the street?
4 Do you often give money as a present, e.g. for a birthday or wedding present? Do you prefer being given money yourself, or would you rather have an actual present?

Borrowing or lending money

1 Do you think it's better to borrow money from friends or family?
2 Have you ever lent someone some money and never been paid back?
3 Do you currently have a bank loan or a mortgage? What for?
4 Do you think the government should give young people loans for higher education or grants which they don't have to pay back?

6A COMMUNICATIVE   Ask me a question

When you have a technical problem, e.g. with a phone or tablet, do you ask someone to help you or do you try to sort it out yourself?	Which aspects of your daily life involve you speaking English?
Do you prefer shop assistants to help you choose new clothes or leave you alone to choose yourself?	What kinds of excuses do you give when someone invites you to do something or go somewhere and you don't really feel like it?
Which three places would you recommend visiting if someone was in your town for 24 hours?	If a friend wanted to make a good impression at an interview, what would you advise them to do or not to do?
What kinds of situations cause you to feel stressed? What are the best ways to cope with stress?	Is there anything that sometimes prevents you from sleeping at night? What do you do when you can't sleep?
How would you try to persuade someone to do you a really big favour?	If you have to do something you don't really want to, like homework or housework, what 'distractions' do you find to stop yourself from having to do it?
What sorts of things do you dislike your neighbours doing? How can we build good relationships with neighbours?	How could governments encourage citizens to use public transport rather than cars?
If a friend wanted to contact you, would you prefer them to call you or message you? Why?	Who taught you to swim? How quickly did you learn?
Do you mind people asking you your age? What other questions is it sometimes inappropriate to ask someone?	Do you think playing too many computer and video games might make young people behave violently?
What things did your parents let you do as a child that parents probably wouldn't allow their children to do nowadays?	What apps or websites do you use which help you improve your English outside the classroom?
How do you think local councils could encourage people to recycle more?	What gadgets or techniques do you use to help you remember important dates like birthdays?

6B COMMUNICATIVE Case studies

a Read the case studies. How do you think each obsession may affect the person's daily life? Which of the obsessions do you think are the most common? Do you know anyone with a similar obsession?

b Talk to a partner and compare your ideas.

Case study 1
Mark, 21, has an obsession with double-checking. Before leaving his flat each morning, he goes around twice, sometimes three times, to make sure that all the appliances are turned off and unplugged. It's not uncommon for him to have to turn back after leaving home to check one more time. Sometimes, he even gets on the bus to work and then has a doubt – 'Did I leave the iPad charging?' or 'I don't think I turned the iron off'. On those occasions, he gets off the bus and goes back home to check.

Case study 2
Maggie, 23, is obsessed with the singer Taylor Swift. Swift has been her favourite performer ever since she saw her in London seven years ago. Since then she's been to see her more than 40 times, including a two-week holiday to the States where she went to nine concerts in different cities. She spends all her money on Swift merchandise and music, and says she 'just couldn't live without her – she knows how I feel about everything'.

Case study 3
Phil, 25, has an 'order' obsession. He puts all the books on his bookshelves in strict order according to their publication date. Similarly, all the magazines in the rack at his home have to be chronologically ordered. He admits to feeling 'seriously stressed' if someone takes out a book or magazine and then puts it back in the wrong place.

Case study 4
Karen, 19, has been obsessed with 'single food eating' for the last three years. Basically, this means she can only eat one certain food type at a time – that's to say she can't mix textures or flavours, and she has to brush her teeth after each different food she eats. So, for example, if she has chicken, potatoes, and peas, she will eat all the peas first, then all the potatoes, and finally the chicken.

Case study 5
Amanda, 29, has an obsession with germs. She is unable to shake hands with anyone because she knows that is how germs are transmitted from person to person. She can't even cope with holding her child's hand, or her partner's. She cleans the bathroom and kitchen twice a day from top to bottom, and won't have carpets or rugs in her house because she believes that this is where germs breed. She also disinfects all her daughter's toys every evening to prevent her catching anything.

Case study 6
Simon, 36, is obsessed with Arsenal, the football team he supports. He goes to all their home games and travels all over the country to see them when they play away. All the rooms in his house are painted in red or white, the Arsenal colours, and there are pictures of the players, past and present, on all the walls. His two young boys are named after famous Arsenal players. His wife likes football and is an Arsenal fan, but only goes to some of their home games. 'Arsenal are my life,' says Simon.

Case study 7
Sean, 18, has had an obsession with car number plates since he was five or six years old. Whenever he sees a car, he automatically looks at the number plate, and starts adding up the digits. 'I find it impossible to watch a car go by without trying to see the number plate and adding up the numbers,' he says.

Case study 8
Maria, 28, is obsessed with going to the gym and healthy eating. She works night shifts at a call centre. She sleeps during the morning and then spends every afternoon at the gym, six days a week. She works out in the weight room and also does aerobics or spinning. She follows a strict vegetarian diet and carefully monitors her daily intakes of sugar, fat, and salt.

7A COMMUNICATIVE Let's change the rules

a Read the following proposals and suggestions related to education. For each one, decide whether you agree, disagree, or half-agree and why.

1 Schoolchildren ought not to be given grades on tests, only general comments, so that they can't compare themselves with other children.

2 Teachers should not be allowed to use red pens to correct exercises as this is psychologically harmful to students.

3 Secondary school teachers should never be made to teach more than four hours a day, so that they have enough time to prepare classes and correct homework.

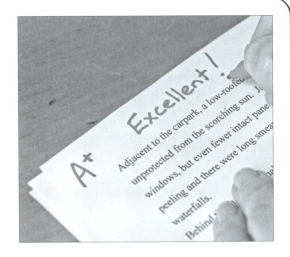

4 Children don't need to be 'streamed' at school. Stronger pupils can learn as much in a class with weaker pupils as they would with those of their own level.

5 The fact that everyone uses keyboards to write means that it's no longer important to teach handwriting.

6 Competitive sport should be banned in schools, so that children's self-esteem is not affected by losing.

7 Science teachers should be paid more than arts teachers as it is much harder to recruit them.

8 Online learning and coursework can never totally replace traditional learning methods.

9 The people who decide on new education laws should be teachers, not politicians.

10 The best way to motivate children to pass exams is to give them money as a reward.

11 Continuous assessment and project work is fairer than traditional written exams.

12 With so much information available on their phones and computers, children don't need to memorize facts like multiplication tables and important historical dates.

b Compare your answers with your partner. Discuss the pros and cons of each proposal or suggestion.

7B COMMUNICATIVE Works of art?

a Look at the photos with a partner. Together, decide which two are famous works of art and which four are ordinary objects. Explain your choices.

b Now read your text about one of the real works of art and tell your partner about it. Did you guess correctly?

A

B

C

D

E

F

- -

Student A

Artwork B

Kobe Frog was created by Dutch artist Florentjin Hofman. It is an inflatable, ten-metre high sculpture and is displayed on the roof of the Museum of Art in Kobe, Japan. Kobe was the site of a very severe earthquake in 1995. The frog wears a party hat and sits very close to the edge of the roof. The artist says that the work is about enjoying life and having a flexible attitude in times of disaster.

- -

Student B

Artwork D

Incommunicado is a sculpture by British Palestinian artist Mona Hatoum. Born in Beirut, Hatoum was left stranded in London whilst on a short visit, due to the outbreak of the Lebanese Civil War in 1975. The piece consists of an altered infant's cot. The bare metal bars resemble those of a prison cell and, where mattress springs would usually be, there are very sharp wires. A cot is normally thought of as a protective, safe place. However, this one symbolizes danger and discomfort. It provides a metaphor for the suffering of political prisoners who are imprisoned and tortured. The relationship of 'parent' (state) to 'child' (citizen) is presented as cruel and abusive, rather than warm and loving.

Student A

crutches /ˈkrʌtʃɪz/ _____

a stretcher /ˈstretʃə/ _____

a first-aid kit /fɜːst ˈeɪd kɪt/ _____

an operating theatre /ˈɒpəreɪtɪŋ θɪətə/ _____

a fracture /ˈfræktʃə/ _____

a midwife /ˈmɪdwaɪf/ _____

take somebody's pulse /teɪk ˈsʌmbədis pʌls/ _____

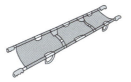

a hospital ward /ˈhɒspɪtl wɔːd/ _____

Student B

a plaster /ˈplɑːstə/ _____

a wheelchair /ˈwiːltʃeə/ _____

a dressing /ˈdresɪŋ/ _____

a drip /drɪp/ _____

a sling /slɪŋ/ _____

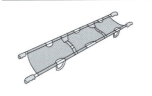

a syringe /sɪˈrɪndʒ/ _____

a plaster cast /ˈplɑːstə kɑːst/ _____

a scar /skɑː/ _____

8B COMMUNICATIVE Travel role-plays

Role-play 1

You're a travel agency representative at a popular tourist resort on the coast. The resort has several hotels, all of which are full because it's peak season. All hotels have swimming pools and cater for families. It's your first week in this job. You want to make sure you don't get anything wrong, and that you are very clear about any problems clients may have, so that there aren't any misunderstandings later on. You've been trained to use the customer's first name wherever possible in a conversation to personalize things more. You don't have much authority as yet – especially not when it comes to promising refunds.

B is a client who arrived at one of the resort's hotels last night and has asked to speak to you.

- You begin. Introduce yourself by your first name and ask what **B**'s first name is.
- Remember to use it throughout the conversation! Ask how you can help **B**.
- Listen to **B**'s complaints and ask for more specific details. Then rephrase and repeat the information back to **B** to show you fully understand.
- Try to think of solutions, but under no circumstances promise any kind of discount or refund.

Role-play 2

You're a tourist on a one-week city break. Your trip was expensive and included transport, a four-star hotel, and various excursions.

You were not satisfied with the hotel and asked to be moved on the first day, which eventually you were. However, you are still unsatisfied for the following reasons:

- The restaurant at the new hotel is not very good (why?).
- There is no wi-fi in your room, only in the lobby.
- The excursion to the museum was very unsatisfactory (why?).

B is the local travel agency representative.

You don't feel that he / she was particularly sympathetic with your original problem at the first hotel, and today you're determined to make him / her take you seriously. You're not going to be satisfied with vague promises. You arranged to meet him / her and you want to have a long conversation.

- You begin. Inform **B** of your three new complaints, giving as many details as possible.
- Insist on **B** providing concrete solutions.
- Try to prolong the conversation as much as possible, and only accept the solutions you think are convincing.

Role-play 1

You're a tourist. You arrived last night with your family at a popular tourist resort.

There are already three complaints you need to make, so you have arranged to speak to your representative:

- Your room is unsatisfactory (why?).
- The swimming pool is much smaller than the brochure showed, and is always crowded.
- Your children aren't happy with the Kids Club (why?).

A is the travel agency representative at the resort.

He / She looks very young and inexperienced, so you're sure you're going to have the upper hand. You just hope he / she's not one of those over-friendly people who use your first name all the time (you hate that), and pretend they're listening to your complaints and then do absolutely nothing!

- **A** will start.
- Explain your three complaints. Be more specific when asked.
- Be firm, but without losing your temper. Demand some kind of financial compensation.
- Be prepared to accept other solutions, but only if you absolutely have to.

Role-play 2

You're a travel agency representative in a popular tourist city.

You've just had the worst day of your life at work and you're about to finish an 18-hour shift. You're used to dealing with complaints, and know that the best way is to use a lot of vague expressions like 'I'll get back to you on that one' or 'I'll see what I can do'.

A is a client of the travel agency and is in the city.

He / She is a difficult client and complained on the first day about the hotel. You managed, with great difficulty, to get him / her moved to another hotel. A few minutes ago, **A** called you and said he / she needed to talk to you. Your heart sinks because you really want to go home, but you go and meet him / her.

- **A** will start.
- Listen to **A**, but keep looking at your watch, and try to cut short long and involved explanations.
- Make vague promises and try to get rid of him / her as quickly as possible.

9A COMMUNICATIVE Animal quiz

a Ask **B** the questions. Then confirm if he / she chose the correct answer and explain the answers to them.

1 Which of the following encourages cows to produce more milk?
 a listening to classical music
 b listening to people talking
 c listening to pop music

 answer: a Research has shown that classical music reduces a cow's stress levels in the same way as it does in humans. Favourites are Beethoven's *Pastoral Symphony* and Haydn's *Symphony no.7.*

2 How many hearts does an octopus have?
 a 1
 b 2
 c 3

 answer: c They need three hearts to pump blood to their eight limbs.

3 Which of these animals cannot jump?
 a an elephant
 b a goat
 c a hamster

 answer: a Although elephants have the same number of bones in their feet as other mammals, those bones are very close together. This means that they don't have the flexibility to enable them to jump.

4 Which creature did the Americans try to train to drop bombs in the Second World War?
 a eagles
 b pigeons
 c bats

 answer: c The plan was to release 'bat bombs' over major Japanese cities. Bats were an ideal choice to carry the 28-gram incendiary bombs because they can carry more than their own weight in flight.

5 In which direction can a pig not look?
 a to the left
 b to the right
 c upwards

 answer: c A pig's spine limits its movement and doesn't let it look up to the sky. In spite of this, pigs have a very good sense of direction!

6 Which of these animals kills the most people in Africa per year?
 a tigers
 b hippos
 c lions

 answer: b Although you might think hippos are docile, watch out! They are considered the most dangerous animal in Africa. An average of 3,000 people are killed by them each year compared to 70 by lions. There are no tigers in Africa.

7 How long can most sharks live without eating?
 a up to six weeks
 b up to one week
 c up to 72 hours

 answer: a They can survive on the oil that's stored in their livers for six weeks. When the oil gets low, they have the instinct to hunt again.

8 How many eyes does a dolphin close when it sleeps?
 a neither of them
 b one of them
 c both of them

 answer: b Its left eye closes when the right part of its brain sleeps and vice versa. During this time, the other half of the brain monitors what's going on in the environment and controls breathing functions.

9 What do butterflies taste with?
 a their feet
 b their wings
 c their antennae

 answer: a They have tiny, hair-like sensors on their feet. By standing on a leaf, a female can 'taste' and see if it's good to lay eggs on.

10 Which European city is said to have more dogs than children?
 a Stockholm
 b London
 c Paris

 answer: c France has one of the highest people / dog ratios in the world with 17 dogs to every 100 people. The country has an unofficial dog population of 10 million with over 500,000 dogs living in Paris.

b Now answer **B**'s questions. Who knows more about animals?

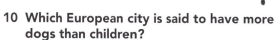

Student B

a Answer **A**'s questions.

b Now ask **A** the questions. Then confirm if he / she chose the correct answer and explain the answers to them. Who knows more about animals?

---

1 How intelligent are dogs?
a as intelligent as a 2–3-year-old child
b as intelligent as a 4–5-year-old child
c as intelligent as a 6–7-year-old child

answer: a Research has shown that dogs can understand about 165–200 words, signs, or signals – about the same as a 2.5-year-old child.

2 Which animal produces mohair?
a a rabbit
b a goat
c a sheep

answer: b Mohair is made from the hair of the Angora goat, which is farmed mainly in South Africa, the USA, and Turkey.

3 In ancient Rome, which animal was a symbol of liberty?
a the cat
b the wolf
c the eagle

answer: a In ancient Rome, cats were a symbol of liberty. In ancient Egypt, they were sacred animals, and anyone who killed a cat (even accidentally) was executed.

4 Which animal can't taste sweet things?
a a dog
b a bear
c a cat

answer: c A human has 9,000 taste buds whereas a cat only has 470, and their sweet buds are not very reactive, so, unlike humans, they will not be tempted by chocolate or cake!

5 What do male (but not female) elephants do at the age of 13?
a go back to the place where they were born
b leave their herd forever to live alone
c become the leader of the herd

answer: b Although female elephants spend all their lives living with their herd, once a male reaches about the age of 13, he will leave the rest of the herd, and will live a solitary life from then on.

6 Which of these animals have 'friends'?
a bears
b chickens
c cows

answer: c Cows are incredibly sociable animals. Research shows that their stress levels go down when they are put with a 'friend' in comparison to when they are alone or paired with a random cow.

7 On average, how long does a housefly live for?
a 15 minutes
b 15 hours
c 15 days

answer: c Houseflies live for 15 days, and are only active during the daytime. They are capable of carrying over 100 diseases such as cholera and TB.

8 What colour of clothing will make a mosquito more likely to bite you?
a pale yellow
b dark blue
c red

answer: b You're twice as likely to be bitten if you're wearing dark blue because dark colours trap carbon dioxide, which is what attracts a mosquito to you in the first place. Yellow is the best colour to wear as it's a colour they can hardly see and they get confused by it.

9 Which creature would survive the shortest time if it were sent into space?
a a bird
b a tortoise
c a rabbit

answer: a A bird would soon die because it needs gravity in order to be able to swallow.

10 Which of these creatures doesn't sleep?
a ants
b crabs
c bees

answer: b Crabs 'relax' as opposed to sleep. However, if they detect light or movement, they get active again very quickly.

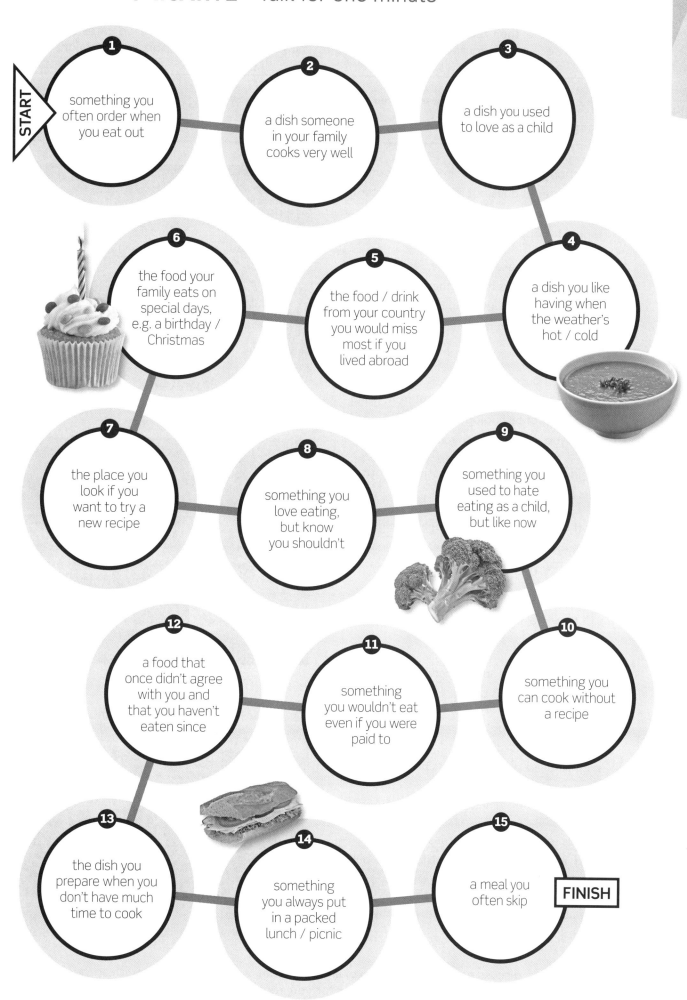

START

1. something you often order when you eat out

2. a dish someone in your family cooks very well

3. a dish you used to love as a child

4. a dish you like having when the weather's hot / cold

5. the food / drink from your country you would miss most if you lived abroad

6. the food your family eats on special days, e.g. a birthday / Christmas

7. the place you look if you want to try a new recipe

8. something you love eating, but know you shouldn't

9. something you used to hate eating as a child, but like now

10. something you can cook without a recipe

11. something you wouldn't eat even if you were paid to

12. a food that once didn't agree with you and that you haven't eaten since

13. the dish you prepare when you don't have much time to cook

14. something you always put in a packed lunch / picnic

15. a meal you often skip

FINISH

10A COMMUNICATIVE What's wrong with sport?

a Look at the scale, then read the statements. Write the number (1–5) which best indicates to what extent you agree or disagree with each statement. Think of reasons to support your opinion.

1 ◄————— 2 ————— 3 ————— 4 ————— 5 ►

Strongly disagree **Strongly agree**

1 Sport brings out the worst in people, both fans and athletes. It does not improve character or help to develop virtues such as fair play and respect for opponents. ☐

2 Sport doesn't make you happy. Spectators as well as participants have higher than average levels of stress, anxiety, and hopelessness because of their engagement with professional sport. ☐

3 Doping is no worse than any other kind of cheating and is really no different from using other kinds of technology to gain an advantage, e.g. high-tech running shoes. ☐

4 It's ridiculous to expect professional sports stars to be role models. ☐

5 Sport occupies a disproportionately high place in the media, often making headlines in papers and on TV. ☐

6 Large-scale sports tournaments have a detrimental impact on a host city's economy. ☐

7 The massive pay disparity between female and male competitors is unjust. ☐

8 Team sports diminish personal responsibility and lead to 'pack behaviour', where no single individual feels responsible for his / her actions. ☐

9 Sponsorship of sports clubs and events by brands representing industries such as fast food, alcohol, or gambling misleads the public about making healthy lifestyle choices. ☐

10 The use of animals in sport is exploitative and cruel. ☐

b In small groups, discuss each statement, explaining to what extent you agree or disagree and giving examples. Try to decide as a group how far you agree or disagree with each one.

10B COMMUNICATIVE About the UK quiz

a How much do you know about the UK? Read the questions and choose the correct answer.

POLITICS

1 How often must general elections be held in Britain?
   a every three years
   b every four years
   c every five years

2 What is the Shadow Cabinet?
   a It's the name of the office where the public has to wait before entering the Houses of Parliament.
   b It's a cupboard in the Prime Minister's office which holds important documents and is unlit.
   c It's the name for the senior members of the main opposition party.

3 When were women first allowed to vote in parliamentary elections in the UK?
   a 1882
   b 1918
   c 1948

4 Stormont is the name of the parliament buildings in
   _____.
   a Scotland
   b Wales
   c Northern Ireland

5 The House of Lords is
   _____.
   a independent from, and checks the work of, the government
   b made up of members elected by the government
   c made up of members elected by the public

HISTORY

1 For how many years did the Romans remain in Britain?
   a 200 years
   b 400 years
   c 600 years

2 Queen Elizabeth I was the younger daughter of
   _____.
   a Edward VI
   b Henry VIII
   c Richard III

3 Which of the following was a British invention?
   a the mobile phone
   b the diesel engine
   c the World Wide Web

4 The 'suffragettes' were women who campaigned for the right to _____.
   a work outside the home
   b get divorced
   c vote

5 Big Ben is the name of the famous _____ next to the Houses of Parliament.
   a bell
   b bridge
   c tower

THE ARTS

1 Who designed St Paul's Cathedral?
   a Sir Christopher Wren
   b Sir Norman Foster
   c Sir Walter Raleigh

2 Which of the following is a British fashion designer?
   a Ralph Lauren
   b Stella McCartney
   c Donna Karan

3 The Proms are a series of _____ which take place in the Royal Albert Hall during the summer.
   a classical music concerts
   b pop music concerts
   c sporting events

4 Which of the following novels was written by Charles Dickens?
   a *Dracula*
   b *Oliver Twist*
   c *Pride and Prejudice*

5 What was the artist William Turner famous for painting?
   a portraits
   b landscapes
   c seascapes

GEOGRAPHY

1 What is the capital city of Scotland?
   a Aberdeen
   b Edinburgh
   c Glasgow

2 Which of the following is not part of the United Kingdom?
   a Wales
   b Scotland
   c The Republic of Ireland

3 Devon and Cornwall are in the _____ of England.
   a south-east
   b south-west
   c north-west

4 What is the second-biggest city in England?
   a Birmingham
   b Manchester
   c Brighton

5 The highest mountain in the UK, Ben Nevis, is _____ high.
   a 1,345 metres
   b 2,345 metres
   c 3,345 metres

SPORT

1 The sport of rugby is named after _____.
   a the school where it was invented
   b the town where it was first played
   c the person who invented it

2 How long can a cricket test match last?
   a up to six hours
   b up to two days
   c up to five days

3 What sport is played at Wimbledon?
   a basketball
   b golf
   c tennis

4 What are the Derby and the Grand National?
   a athletics events
   b horse races
   c football tournaments

5 What football team plays at Stamford Bridge?
   a Chelsea
   b Manchester City
   c Arsenal

b Compare your answers with a partner. Who knows the most about the UK?

Vocabulary activity instructions

1A Personality

A crossword

Sts read the definitions and write the answers into the crossword. Copy one worksheet per student.

LANGUAGE
personality adjectives, phrases, and idioms

- Give out the worksheets to individual Sts or to pairs. Focus on the instructions and set a time limit (e.g. five minutes) for Sts to fill in the words.
- If Sts worked individually, they can compare with a partner when they've finished.
- Check answers. Elicit or model the pronunciation of the words and phrases.

ACROSS
5 down to earth **7** resourceful **8** gentle **10** sympathetic
12 bright **13** spontaneous **14** self-sufficient

DOWN
1 deep down **2** soft touch **3** thorough **4** conscientious
6 steady **9** sarcastic **11** determined

- Now focus on **Activation** and put Sts in pairs, **A** and **B**. Sts **A** read a clue from the worksheet, replacing the gaps with a 'beep'. Sts **B** (not looking at the worksheet) guess the word(s). They can look at the **Vocabulary Bank** on p.162 if they need to. Make sure they swap roles.

1B Work

A paraphrasing activity

Sts rewrite sentences to practise expressing work-related concepts in different ways. Copy one worksheet per student.

LANGUAGE
adjectives describing a job, collocations, words and phrases that are often confused

- Give out the worksheets and focus on the instructions. Elicit the answer to **1** (maternity leave). Then set a time limit for Sts to complete the sentences.
- Get Sts to compare with a partner, and then check answers.

2 work experience **3** off work **4** fixed-term
5 career ladder **6** freelance **7** colleagues / co-workers
8 academic qualifications **9** made redundant / laid off
10 staff **11** perks / benefits **12** resign **13** out of work
14 civil servant **15** dead-end **16** repetitive

- Now focus on **Activation**. Give an example of a sentence using one of the gapped words (*My sister has very good academic qualifications*). Then ask Sts to write six sentences using the gapped words, and compare with a partner.

3A Phrases with *get*

A rewriting activity

Sts replace words and phrases using phrases with *get*. Copy one worksheet per student.

LANGUAGE
expressions, idioms, and phrasal verbs with *get*

- Give out the worksheets to individual Sts or to pairs. Focus on **1** and elicit that you could substitute *growing older* for *getting on*. Point out that Sts must use the correct form of *get* (gerund, past simple, etc.) depending on the sentence.
- Set a time limit. If Sts worked individually, get them to compare with a partner, and then check answers.

2 get on with **3** got together **4** get around **5** get rid of
6 got the wrong end of the stick **7** get a move on
8 get on my nerves **9** get through to him
10 get her own way **11** gets me down **12** get her own back
13 got the chance **14** get the message
15 get your act together **16** get hold of **17** getting by
18 get out of the / my way

- Now focus on **Activation**. Tell Sts to cover the column on the right and read the sentences. Can they remember the missing words?

3B Conflict and warfare

A gap-fill activity

Sts complete sentences using *Conflict and warfare* vocabulary. Copy one worksheet per student.

LANGUAGE
conflict and warfare: people and events, conflict verbs, metaphorical uses of conflict verbs

- Give out the worksheets to individual Sts or to pairs. Focus on the instructions and set a time limit for Sts to complete as many sentences as possible.
- If Sts worked individually, get them to compare with a partner, and then check answers. The first student or pair to write all the words correctly wins, or the student or pair with the most correct answers at the end of the time limit wins.

2 executed **3** blow up **4** broke out **5** treaty
6 commander **7** defeated **8** sniper **9** wounded
10 Civil War **11** civilians **12** ceasefire **13** casualties
14 captured **15** survivors **16** declared **17** released
18 surrender **19** forces **20** refugees

- Now focus on **Activation**. Tell Sts to cover the column on the right and read the sentences. Can they remember the missing words?

EXTRA IDEA Ask Sts which fact(s) they found most interesting or surprising.

4B Sounds and the human voice

A pairwork question and answer activity

Sts ask each other questions about sounds and the human voice. Copy one worksheet per pair and cut into **A** and **B**.

> **LANGUAGE**
> sounds and the human voice

- Put Sts in pairs, **A** and **B**, ideally face to face, and give out the worksheets. Give Sts time to read their questions. Tell them that they have example answers in brackets, but that they should accept any answer that they agree with.
- Sts take turns to ask each other questions. Remind Sts to keep note of their partner's score, one point for each correct answer.
- Monitor and help if necessary.
- When Sts have finished, get feedback to see who got the most points and to see if anyone came up with different answers to those on the worksheet.
- Find out if any Sts got all the answers correct.

5A Expressions with *time*

A pairwork vocabulary race

Sts complete sentences with time expressions. Copy one worksheet per pair.

> **LANGUAGE**
> expressions with time: verbs, prepositional phrases, expressions

- Put Sts in pairs and give out the worksheets. Ask Sts to complete as many sentences as they can within the time limit of four minutes. The pair who completes all the sentences correctly first is the winner.
- Check answers.

2 short of   3 her hands   4 for, being   5 on   6 off
7 before   8 at   9 lives   10 spare   11 take   12 in
13 ran out   14 giving, hard   15 This   16 waste your
17 matter   18 from, to   19 save   20 up

- Now focus on **Activation**. Tell Sts to work in pairs and ask and answer the questions. Then ask them to write three more questions of their own to practise the vocabulary.
- Get feedback on the most interesting questions.

5B Money

An information gap activity

Sts define words and phrases to help their partner complete a crossword. Copy one worksheet per pair and cut into **A** and **B**.

> **LANGUAGE**
> money: nouns, adjectives, colloquial language, and expressions related to money

- Put Sts in pairs, **A** and **B**, ideally face to face, and give out the worksheets. Make sure that Sts can't see each other's crosswords. Explain that **A** and **B** have the same crossword, but with different words missing. They have to describe / define words to each other to complete their crosswords.
- Give Sts a minute to read their words and phrases. If they don't know what a word or phrase means, they can look it up in **Vocabulary Bank** Money p.168.
- Sts take turns to ask each other for their missing words (e.g. *What's 1 down? What's 5 across?*). Their partner must describe / define the word until the other student is able to write it in his / her crossword. Sts should help each other with other clues if necessary.
- Monitor and make sure Sts are pronouncing the words and phrases correctly.
- When Sts have finished, get them to compare their crosswords to make sure they have the same words and have spelled them correctly.

7A Prefixes

A gap-fill activity

Sts complete sentences with the correct form of the given word. Copy one worksheet per student.

> **LANGUAGE**
> prefixes: negative prefixes and prefixes which add other meanings

- Put Sts in pairs and give out the worksheets. Focus on the instructions. Set a time limit for Sts to complete the sentences.
- Check answers. Elicit or model the pronunciation of any words your Sts find difficult to pronounce.

2 irrational   3 misunderstood   4 illiterate   5 impractical
6 overslept   7 inappropriate   8 dehydrated
9 monolingual   10 outvoted   11 underestimate
12 rewrite   13 antisocial   14 uphill   15 supernatural
16 multinational / international   17 ill-prepared / unprepared
18 autobiography   19 co-founders   20 prematurely

- Now focus on **Activation**. Get Sts to write example sentences using the words from the list. When Sts have finished, get them to compare with a partner.

EXTRA SUPPORT   Sts could work in pairs to write their sentences, then compare with another pair.

- Get feedback on the most interesting sentences.

8B Travel and tourism
An error correction activity

Sts correct vocabulary mistakes related to travel and tourism. Copy one worksheet per pair.

LANGUAGE

travel and tourism: describing places, verb phrases

- Put Sts in pairs and give out the worksheets. Focus on the instructions and then on sentence **1**, and elicit that it is correct.
- Give Sts time to complete the task.
- Check answers.

2 ✗ picturesque   3 ✓   4 ✗ go on   5 ✓
6 ✗ setting off / out   7 ✗ touristy   8 ✗ chill out   9 ✓
10 ✗ remote   11 ✓   12 ✓   13 ✗ soak up
14 ✗ recharge   15 ✗ overrated   16 ✓   17 ✓
18 ✗ lively   19 ✗ get away   20 ✗ off the beaten track

EXTRA SUPPORT   Give Sts a few minutes to review **Vocabulary Bank** Travel and tourism p.170 before they start.

- Now focus on **Activation**. Get Sts to take it in turns to cover the wrong sentences and say the correct sentence to a partner.

9A Animal matters
A gap-fill activity

Sts complete sentences related to animal matters. Copy one worksheet per student.

LANGUAGE

animal matters: animals, birds and insects; animal issues

- Give out the worksheets either to individual Sts or to pairs. Set a time limit for Sts to complete the sentences.
- If Sts worked individually, get them to compare with a partner, and then check answers.

2 hooves   3 calf   4 hives   5 in captivity
6 Animal rights activists   7 kennel, barked
8 endangered species   9 neighed   10 claws, meow
11 horns   12 beak   13 cruelly, inhumane
14 hunt, for sport   15 goldfish, tank   16 twittering
17 shell   18 cubs

EXTRA IDEA   You could make this activity a race by setting a time limit (e.g. three minutes) and telling Sts they have to complete as many sentences as they can within the time. The first pair to complete all the sentences correctly wins.

- Now focus on **Activation**. Get Sts to cover the sentences and say as much as possible about the photos to a partner.

9B Preparing food
An information gap activity

Sts define words to help their partner complete a crossword. Copy one worksheet per pair and cut into **A** and **B**.

LANGUAGE

preparing food: how food is prepared, utensils

- Put Sts in pairs, **A** and **B**, ideally face to face, and give out the worksheets. Make sure Sts can't see each other's crosswords. Explain that **A** and **B** have the same crossword, but with different words missing. They have to describe / define words to each other to complete their crosswords.
- Give Sts a minute to read their words. If Sts don't know what a word means, they can check in **Vocabulary Bank** Preparing food p.172.
- Sts take turns asking each other for their missing words (e.g. *What's 6 across? What's 3 down?*). Their partner must describe / define the word until the other student is able to write it in his / her crossword. Sts should help each other with clues if necessary.
- Monitor and make sure Sts are pronouncing the words and phrases correctly.
- When Sts have finished, get them to compare their crosswords to make sure they have the same words and have spelled them correctly.

Revision 1: Describing game
A group card game

Sts define words and phrases for others to guess. Copy and cut up one worksheet per pair or small group.

LANGUAGE

vocabulary from all Files of the Student's Book

- Put Sts in pairs or small groups and give each pair / group a set of cards face down or in an envelope.
- Tell Sts that they have to pick a card and explain as many of the words to their partner or group as they can in a given time. Highlight that they are not allowed to use any form of the word they are describing.
- Start by setting a time limit (e.g. two minutes). Get one student from each pair or group to pick a card, and then say *Go!* Sts describe / define as many words from the card as they can. After two minutes, stop them and find out how many words or phrases each pair or group managed to guess.
- Now get another student from each pair or group to pick a card and describe the words. Continue until all the cards have been used.

NON-CUT ALTERNATIVE   Put Sts in pairs. Copy one worksheet per student and fold it down the middle. Sts take turns to describe the groups of words and phrases for their partner.

Revision 2: Phrasal verbs

A gap-fill activity

Sts complete sentences. Copy one worksheet per student.

LANGUAGE

phrasal verbs from all Files of the Student's Book

- Give out the worksheets and explain that this activity revises phrasal verbs Sts have learned throughout the course. Focus on **a** and set a time limit (e.g. five minutes) for Sts to complete the **PARTICLE** column.
- Get Sts to compare with a partner, and then check answers.
- Focus on **b**. Get Sts to cover the **PARTICLE** column and try to remember the phrasal verbs for all the sentences.

a
2 off   **3** across   **4** out   **5** through   **6** on   **7** up   **8** out
9 off   **10** behind   **11** out   **12** away   **13** on   **14** up   **15** by

- Now focus on **c** and set the same time limit for Sts to complete the **VERB** column.
- Get Sts to compare with a partner, and then check answers.

c
1 break   **2** grow   **3** find   **4** hang   **5** keep   **6** come
7 run   **8** dress   **9** top   **10** get   **11** turn   **12** go   **13** pick
14 set   **15** get

- Focus on **d**. Get Sts to cover the **VERB** column and try to remember the phrasal verbs for all the sentences.

Revision 3: Idioms

A gap-fill activity

Sts complete sentences using idioms. Copy one worksheet per student.

LANGUAGE

idioms from all Files of the Student's Book

- Give out the worksheets either to individual Sts or to pairs. Explain that this activity revises the idioms Sts have learned throughout the course. Set a time limit (e.g. ten minutes) for Sts to complete the sentences.
- If Sts worked individually, get them to compare with a partner, and then check answers.

2 letter   **3** eye   **4** head-on   **5** gut   **6** white   **7** heart
8 hold   **9** blue   **10** nose   **11** gold   **12** wrong
13 picture   **14** mind   **15** grey   **16** move   **17** belts
18 tape   **19** finger   **20** beyond   **21** smell   **22** dream
23 arm, leg   **24** next   **25** bark

1A VOCABULARY Personality

● Look at the clues and fill in the crossword.

Across →

5 Despite being really famous, I couldn't believe how ____ ____ ____ he was. He was just so 'normal'.

7 Louisa's very ____. She's great at solving problems.

8 Be ____ with your sister. Just stay calm and be kind to her.

10 Mark was very ____ when I lost my job. He really tried to understand how I was feeling.

12 He's a really ____ child – he's intelligent and quick to learn.

13 Eliza's so ____. You never know what she's going to do next.

14 She's totally ____-____. She never asks anyone for help.

Down ↓

1 He seems quite outgoing, but ____ ____ he's quite shy.

2 I'm sure you can get Mum to lend you the car. She's usually a ____ ____.

3 My new PA is really ____. He does his work really carefully and pays attention to detail.

4 Tim's so ____. He never forgets to do his homework, and he usually gets all the answers right!

6 I know I can always rely on Sarah. She's really ____ and sensible.

9 My English teacher at school was very ____. She always used to say 'What a brilliant answer!' when we had said something stupid.

11 I think Tom will go far. He's so ____ – nothing will stop him from doing what he wants.

Cover the crossword. In pairs, take turns reading out a clue. Try to remember the answers.

1B VOCABULARY Work

● Complete the second sentence with one or two words so that it means the same as the first.

1 Anna isn't at work for now because she's just had a baby.
Anna isn't at work for now because she's on _maternity_ _leave_.

2 I didn't get the job because I hadn't worked in marketing before.
I didn't get the job because I didn't have any _____ _____ in marketing.

3 I'm not working right now because I'm ill.
I'm _____ _____ right now because I'm ill.

4 My contract's only from March to June.
I've only got a _____-_____ contract.

5 He worked briefly as a sales assistant and now he's been promoted to area manager.
He worked briefly as a sales assistant and now he's moving up the _____ _____.

6 My sister's a journalist and she writes articles for lots of different newspapers.
My sister's a journalist and has a number of different _____ contracts.

7 I don't enjoy my job very much, but I get on well with the people that I work with.
I don't enjoy my job very much, but I get on well with my _____.

8 She's got a degree and a PhD.
She has good _____ _____.

9 I lost my job last year, as the company I was working for wasn't making a profit.
I was _____ _____ last year.

10 The nurses who work at this hospital are fantastic.
The nursing _____ at this hospital are fantastic.

11 Apart from my salary, I also get a company car and free lunches, which is brilliant!
The _____ are brilliant in this job. I get a company car and free lunches.

12 I decided to tell my boss I was leaving because I'd had a better offer from another company.
I decided to _____ from my job because I'd had a better offer from another company.

13 My friend's been unemployed for over a year now.
My friend's been _____ _____ _____ for over a year now.

14 Adriana graduated from university and got a job in local government.
Adriana graduated from university and became a _____ _____.

15 Stuart's going nowhere in his job.
Stuart's in a _____-_____ job.

16 He works on a car production line and does exactly the same thing every day.
His job on a car production line is very monotonous and _____.

Write six sentences about people you know using as many of the words from the gaps as you can.

3A VOCABULARY Phrases with *get*

● Read the sentences. Replace the **bold** words or phrases with the correct form of a phrase with *get*. Write your answers in the column on the right.

1 Both of my parents are **growing older**, but they still lead very active lives.   *getting on*

2 Can you stop annoying me and just let me **continue** my work?   _____

3 My husband and I **met** at school and we've been together ever since.   _____

4 What's the best way to **move from one place to another** in this city?   _____

5 Could you please **throw away** all the old clothes you don't wear anymore?   _____

6 I thought we'd made it clear that we'd meet at the restaurant, but somehow she **misunderstood** and was waiting for us to pick her up.   _____

7 Come on! We'll be late if you don't **hurry up**.   _____

8 I liked him to begin with, but he's now really starting to **annoy me**.   _____

9 I tried to explain the problem to my father, but I just can't **make him understand**.   _____

10 My parents always let my little sister **do whatever she wants** – that's why she's so spoilt.   _____

11 Not having enough time for myself really **depresses me**.   _____

12 Martha was dumped by her ex-boyfriend and now she wants to **take revenge** on him.   _____

13 If I **had the opportunity** to go and live abroad, I think I'd probably take it.   _____

14 I've told my mum time after time that I can't afford to move out, but she just doesn't seem to **hear what I'm saying**!   _____

15 You need to **change your attitude and work harder** or you'll fail all your exams.   _____

16 It's difficult to **contact** George because he never has his phone switched on.   _____

17 It's not easy **managing to live** on a student grant, especially in a big city.   _____

18 I tried to walk past her, but she wouldn't **move to the side to let me pass**.   _____

ACTIVATION

Test your memory. Cover the column on the right. Read the sentences aloud with the correct phrase with *get*.

3B VOCABULARY Conflict and warfare

● Complete the sentences with the correct word or phrase. Write your answers in the column on the right.

1 After the siege of Constantinople in 1204, the Crusaders ▮▮▮ the city and transferred its riches to Italy.

l_ooted_

2 Two of Henry VIII's six wives were ▮▮▮, two he divorced, one died following childbirth, and the last one survived.

e_____

3 In 1605, a man called Guy Fawkes attempted to ▮▮▮ the Houses of Parliament in London with barrels of gunpowder.

bl____ _____

4 The Great Fire of London ▮▮▮ in a bakery on 2nd September 1666 and wasn't extinguished until four days later.

br____ _____

5 On 3rd September 1783, a peace ▮▮▮ was signed between the United States and Britain that ended the American War of Independence.

tr_____

6 In 1805, naval ▮▮▮ Horatio Nelson led the British Royal Navy to destroy the French-Spanish fleet at the Battle of Trafalgar.

c_____

7 The French army under Napoleon was ▮▮▮ at the Battle of Waterloo by the British-led and Prussian armies.

d_____

8 A ▮▮▮ is a soldier who usually works alone and specializes in shooting from very long distances. The word originates from the British occupation of India in the 1800s.

sn_____

9 Florence Nightingale and Mary Seacole were nurses who improved the treatment of the ▮▮▮ in the Crimean War from 1853–6.

w_____

10 The ▮▮▮ in the United States – fought between the Northern and Southern States – lasted from 1861 to 1865.

C____ _____

11 Although the Anglo-Zanzibar War of 1896 lasted only 38 minutes, over 500 people, both combatants and ▮▮▮, were killed or injured.

c_____

12 In December 1914, Pope Benedict XV suggested a temporary break in World War I for the celebration of Christmas. While an official ▮▮▮ was refused, many soldiers declared their own unofficial truce.

c_____

13 The total number of ▮▮▮ (people killed or injured) caused directly by the First World War was around 40 million.

c_____

14 In the early 1930s, the divorced American socialite Wallis Simpson ▮▮▮ the heart of the heir to the British throne, who soon after became King Edward VIII. Their intended marriage caused a constitutional crisis and ultimately led to Edward's abdication.

c_____

15 The battleship *Bismarck* was sunk during the Second World War. Of a crew of 2,200, there were only 114 ▮▮▮.

s_____

16 On 8th December 1941, President Roosevelt ▮▮▮ war on Japan following the Japanese attack on Pearl Harbor the previous day.

d_____

17 Nelson Mandela was ▮▮▮ in 1990 after having been imprisoned for 27 years.

r_____

18 In 2018, convicted British football hooligans had to ▮▮▮ their passports to police to prevent them from travelling to the World Cup in Russia.

s_____

19 In Sweden, compulsory service in the armed ▮▮▮ – army, navy, or air force – was abolished in 2010, but then reintroduced in 2018.

f_____

20 In 2019, there were 26 million ▮▮▮ globally, the majority of whom had fled their home countries due to war and persecution.

r_____

ACTIVATION

Test your memory. Cover the column on the right. Read the sentences aloud with the correct word or phrase.

4B VOCABULARY Sounds and the human voice

Ask your partner the questions. Give one point for each correct answer.

1 Can you name two things that drip?
   (*e.g. a tap, an ice cream*)
2 How do people often close the door when they're angry?
   (*They slam it.*)
3 Can you name two animals that hiss?
   (*e.g. a snake, a cat*)
4 What noise do lions and tigers make?
   (*They roar.*)
5 Give two reasons why someone might whisper.
   (*e.g. so as not to be overheard, so as not to disturb other people in a cinema, etc.*)
6 What unpleasant noise do some people make when they eat soup?
   (*They slurp.*)
7 Why might you start stammering?
   (*e.g. because you're nervous or frightened*)
8 What sound would you hear if someone jumped into a swimming pool?
   (*A splash.*)
9 What do people sometimes hum?
   (*A tune.*)
10 What sound might you make if you were feeling very disappointed or sad?
   (*A sigh.*)

- -

Ask your partner the questions. Give one point for each correct answer.

1 What noise does a balloon make when it bursts?
   (*A bang.*)
2 Can you name two parts of the body we use to tap with?
   (*e.g. your fingers, your foot*)
3 Give two situations when a driver might hoot.
   (*e.g. when the driver in front is slow to move at traffic lights, when another driver has done something dangerous*)
4 What noise does a time bomb make?
   (*It ticks.*)
5 If someone's mumbling, what might you say to them?
   (*Can you please speak more clearly?*)
6 What noise does a door make when it needs oil?
   (*It creaks.*)
7 Can you name two situations where people giggle?
   (*e.g. when they think something is funny, when they're nervous*)
8 What noise do people sometimes make when they have a cold, but they don't have a tissue?
   (*They sniff.*)
9 Name two insects that buzz.
   (*e.g. a mosquito, a wasp*)
10 What noise do you often hear if somebody who is driving brakes suddenly?
   (*A screech.*)

5A VOCABULARY Expressions with *time*

● Work with a partner. You have four minutes to complete the sentences. Don't run out of time!

1 We were very late and the wedding ceremony had finished _by the time_ we got there.

2 Sorry, I can't help you now. I'm a bit _____ _____ **time**.

3 Now that Linda's been made redundant, she's got too much **time** on _____ _____ .

4 We're going to keep our old television _____ **the time** _____ , until we can afford a new one.

5 My sister's never _____ **time**. She's the least punctual person I know.

6 It's been a long year! I'm looking forward to a bit of **time** _____ work to relax.

7 My niece was born in the nineties, so The Beatles were _____ **her time**.

8 Generally speaking, I enjoy living on my own, but _____ **times** I miss having someone to talk to.

9 Our honeymoon was fantastic! We had **the time of our** _____ .

10 I don't suppose you could _____ **the time** to give me a hand with this report, could you? I'd be eternally grateful.

11 I'm not in a hurry for an answer, so you can _____ **your time** and think it over for a while.

12 We thought we were going to miss our connecting flight, but we made it just _____ **time**.

13 I couldn't answer the last question because I _____ _____ **of time**.

14 My parents are _____ **me a** _____ **time** because they think I'm going out too much.

15 _____ **time last year** we were in the middle of moving house.

16 Don't _____ _____ **time** trying to convince him. He'll never change his mind.

17 They're always arguing. It's only **a** _____ **of time** before they split up.

18 I only see my half-brother _____ **time** _____ **time**.

19 We can cut across the park to _____ **time**.

20 OK, **time's** _____ ! Stop writing now.

ACTIVATION

Ask and answer the questions below with a partner. Then write three more questions to ask them using some of the expressions above.

What were you doing this time last year?

Do you waste a lot of time doing things you shouldn't?

Have you ever done anything which seemed like a good idea at the time, but turned out not to be?

5B VOCABULARY Money

Student A

a Look at your crossword and make sure you know the meaning of all the words you have.

b Ask **B** to define one of your missing words for you. Ask for example, *What's 5 across?* Write the word in.

c Now **B** will ask you to define a word.

Crossword grid (Student A):

- 1 down: L O A N
- 2 across: H A R D U P
- 3 down: D
- 7 across: M O R T G A G E
- 8 down: B A N K R U P T
- 9 across: I N S T A L M E N T
- 10 down: A
- 11 down: B U C K
- 14 down: S H A R E S
- 15 across: D E P O S I T
- 16 across: F A R E

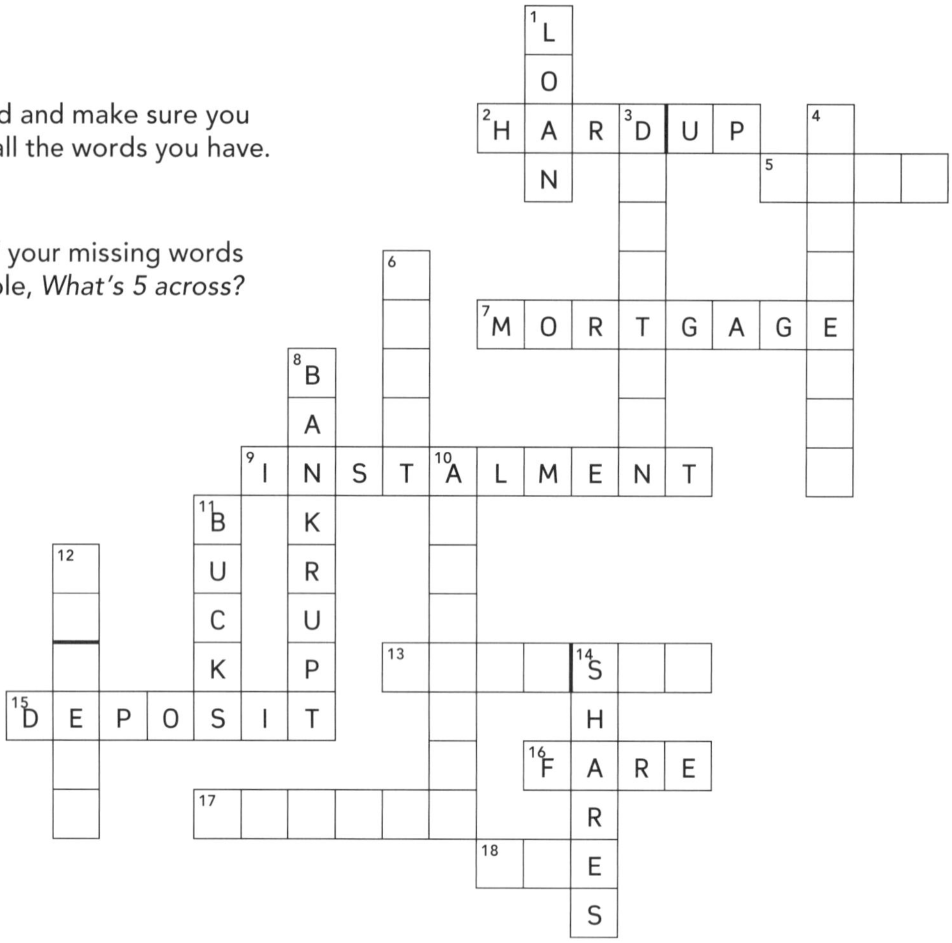

Student B

a Look at your crossword and make sure you know the meaning of all the words you have.

b **A** will ask you to define a word.

c Now ask **A** to define one of your missing words for you. Ask for example, *What's 1 down?* Write the word in.

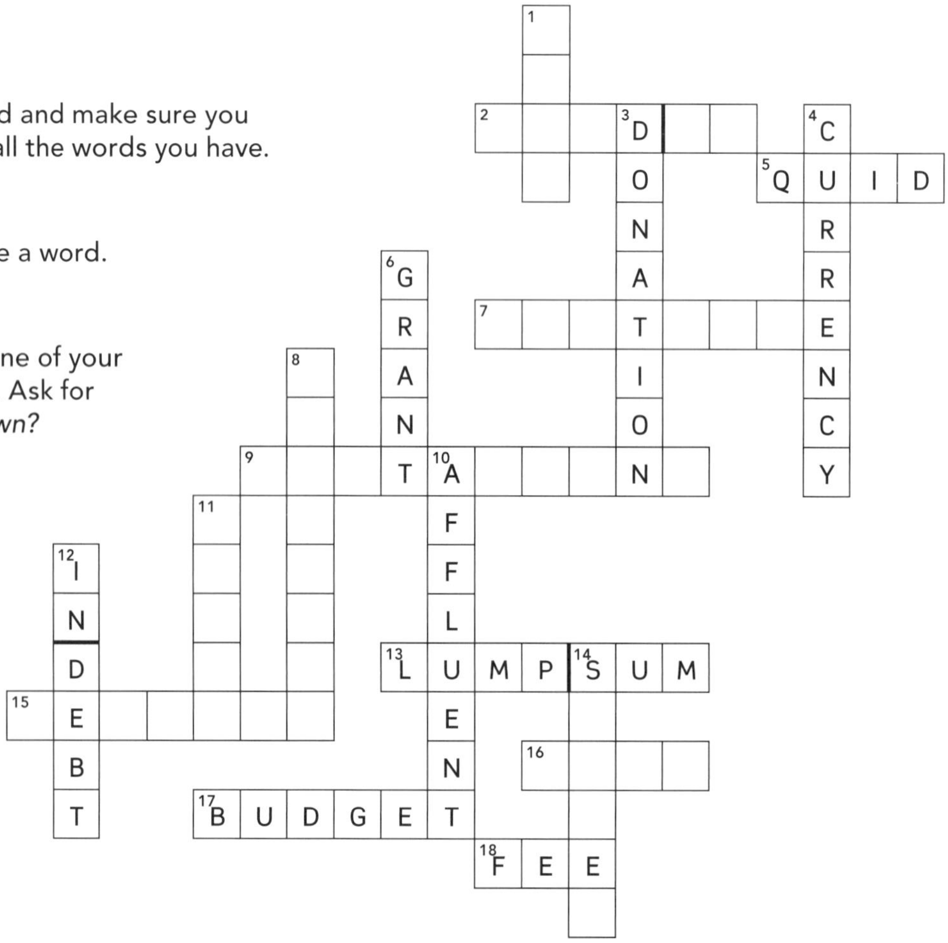

Crossword grid (Student B):

- 3 down: D O N A T I O N
- 4 down: C U R R E N C Y
- 5 across: Q U I D
- 6 down: G R A N T
- 12 down: I N D E B T
- 13 across: L U M P S U M
- 14 down: S
- 17 across: B U D G E T
- 18 across: F E E

English File fourth edition Teacher's Guide Advanced   Photocopiable © Oxford University Press 2020

7A VOCABULARY Prefixes

● Complete the sentences by adding a prefix (e.g. *anti-*, *dis-*, *re-*, etc.) to the word in **bold**, and make any other necessary changes.

1 I wouldn't believe a word he says. He's completely ▨▨▨.
(**honest**) *dishonest*

2 It's very difficult to reason with you when you are behaving in such an ▨▨ manner.
(**rational**) _____

3 You weren't paying attention so you completely ▨▨ what I said.
(**understand**) _____

4 Despite the fact that the rest of her family was ▨▨, she managed to learn to read, and eventually went on to become a nurse.
(**literate**) _____

5 Paul came up with some absolutely amazing ideas, but they were all completely ▨▨.
(**practical**) _____

6 Sorry I'm late this morning. I didn't get to bed until midnight and then I ▨▨.
(**sleep**) _____

7 He was severely reprimanded at work for making ▨▨ comments in an email.
(**appropriate**) _____

8 In hot weather it's easy to become ▨▨ if you don't drink enough liquids.
(**hydrate**) _____

9 Being ▨▨ can be a real disadvantage in the world of business.
(**lingual**) _____

10 I proposed having the office Christmas party on 23rd December, but I was ▨▨ by my colleagues.
(**vote**) _____

11 He might look tired now, but don't ▨▨ him. He could still win this match.
(**estimate**) _____

12 My boss has asked me to make a lot of changes to my report, so now I've basically got to ▨▨ it.
(**write**) _____

13 The government is introducing new measures to try to control ▨▨ behaviour in young people.
(**social**) _____

14 The walk to the monastery was exhausting. It was ▨▨ all the way.
(**hill**) _____

15 I don't believe in ghosts or other ▨▨ phenomena.
(**natural**) _____

16 My brother works for a(n) ▨▨ company, which has offices all over Europe and in South America.
(**national**) _____

17 The first candidate was very ▨▨ for the interview. She didn't know anything about the company at all.
(**prepared**) _____

18 The singer is only 23 and he's already written his ▨▨.
(**biography**) _____

19 Geoff and his sister were ▨▨ of a successful online business.
(**founder**) _____

20 An unhealthy lifestyle can make you look ▨▨ old.
(**mature**) _____

ACTIVATION

Write sentences using the words from the list. Then compare with a partner.

biannual   irreplaceable   postgraduate   substandard   unofficial

8B VOCABULARY Travel and tourism

● Right (✓) or wrong (✗)? If you think the **bold** word or phrase is wrong, write the correct word or phrase in the space provided.

1 In the winter, only a few people come here, but in the summer it gets seriously **overcrowded**. ✓ _____

2 I think Salzburg is one of the most **pictureful** cities in Europe. ☐ _____

3 Have you ever spent a whole day just **wandering round** a city you've never visited before? ☐ _____

4 If you could **go in** holiday anywhere in the world, where would you choose? ☐ _____

5 I hate **tacky** souvenirs, but the kids always manage to find something cheap and plastic to take home from our holiday. ☐ _____

6 What time are you **setting away** tomorrow morning? ☐ _____

7 The resort was far too **touristic** for us. ☐ _____

8 Relaxing by the pool is the perfect way to **chill down** after a busy day sightseeing. ☐ _____

9 It used to be quite a pretty town, but they've really **spoilt** it with all those high-rise buildings. ☐ _____

10 There are some very **removed** beaches on the island that you can only reach by boat. ☐ _____

11 We're going to have to **postpone** our trip until the end of the month. ☐ _____

12 The views from the top of the mountain are **breathtaking**. ☐ _____

13 What do you think is the best way to **soak** the local atmosphere when you visit a place for the first time? ☐ _____

14 He's been working very long hours recently, so he can't wait to go on holiday and **renew** his batteries. ☐ _____

15 I think the cathedral is **overstated**. It's not nearly as beautiful as people say. ☐ _____

16 I've decided to **extend** my trip to Australia by a week, so that I can visit the Great Barrier Reef. ☐ _____

17 They're going to **hit the shops** as soon as they arrive in New York. ☐ _____

18 The town is very **lifely** at this time of year because it's packed with holidaymakers. ☐ _____

19 We're going to our friends' house on the coast for the weekend because we really need to **go away** from it all. ☐ _____

20 Our hotel is up in the hills and completely **off the bitten track**. ☐ _____

ACTIVATION

Cover the wrong sentences one by one and try to say them correctly.

9A VOCABULARY Animal matters

● Complete the missing words in the sentences.

1 If it weren't for _a n i m a l c h a r i t i e s_, lots of abandoned dogs would be on the streets.

2 On race day, you can hear the sound of horses' __ __ __ __ __ __ from miles away.

3 Look at that cow with her __ __ __ __. It's just been born.

4 Beekeepers have to open the __ __ __ __ __ several times a year to collect the honey.

5 Some animals bred __ __ __ __ __ __ __ __ __ struggle to cope when they are reintroduced into the wild.

6 __ __ __ __ __ __ __ __ __ __ __ __ __ __ __ __ __ __ __ __ __ __ believe in justice for animals and do whatever they can to get it.

7 We bought a __ __ __ __ __ __ for our dog because we didn't want it to sleep in the house. It __ __ __ __ __ __ all night though, so we changed our minds.

8 The white rhino became an __ __ __ __ __ __ __ __ __ __ __ __ __ __ __ __ __ __ __ because of poaching and the destruction of its habitat.

9 When we reached the gate, my horse __ __ __ __ __ __ __ loudly and refused to jump.

10 The kitten got its __ __ __ __ __ stuck in a ball of wool and started to __ __ __ __ so loudly that I thought something terrible had happened.

11 One way to tell the difference between a male and a female goat is by looking at the shape of their __ __ __ __ __: the male's are more curved.

12 I always wondered how much water a pelican can carry in its __ __ __ __.

13 If you know of an animal that is being treated __ __ __ __ __ __ __ or kept in __ __ __ __ __ __ __ __ __ conditions, please call our 24-hour hotline.

14 In spite of protests, some people still __ __ __ __ rabbits and other small animals __ __ __ __ __ __ __.

15 They often have __ __ __ __ __ __ __ __ in a __ __ __ __ in dentists' waiting rooms – they are said to be very calming.

16 I love waking up to the sound of the birds __ __ __ __ __ __ __ __ __ __ outside.

17 Turtles can be identified by the pattern on their __ __ __ __ __.

18 Lions give birth to up to six __ __ __ __ at a time.

Cover the sentences and talk about the photos, trying to use the words or phrases above.

9B VOCABULARY Preparing food

Student A

a Look at your crossword and make sure you know the meaning of all the words you have.

b Now ask **B** to define one of your missing words for you. Ask e.g. *What's 6 across?* Write the word in.

c Now **B** will ask you to define a word.

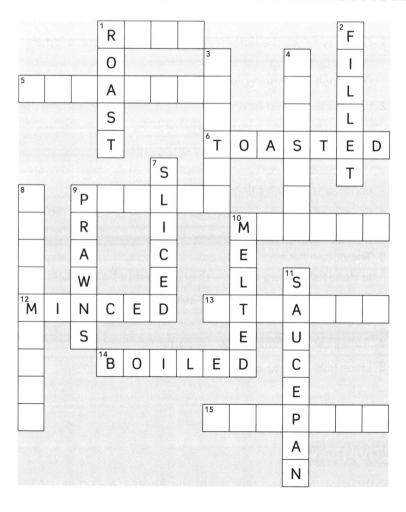

Student B

a Look at your crossword and make sure you know the meaning of all the words you have.

b **A** will ask you to define a word.

c Now ask **A** to define one of your missing words for you. Ask e.g. *What's 3 down?* Write the word in.

English File fourth edition Teacher's Guide Advanced   Photocopiable © Oxford University Press 2020

VOCABULARY   Revision 1: Describing game

Personality

conscientious	a cold fish
sympathetic	down to earth
straightforward	a pain in the neck
thorough	a heart of gold
bright	a very quick temper

Conflict and warfare

troops	an ally
a coup	loot v.
a commander	retreat v.
casualties	surrender v.
snipers	shell v.

Money

a recession	the balance n.
a will	go bankrupt
interest rates	exchange rate
inflation	well-off
a quote	five grand

Travel and tourism

breathtaking	set off
iconic	pricey
dull	chill out
unimposing	recharge your batteries
run-down	wander round

Work

demanding	workforce
rewarding	get a pay rise
fast track	be laid off
qualifications	compassionate leave
a part-time contract	a zero-hours contract

Sounds and the human voice

yell	tick
snore	hoot
click	whistle
groan	hum
whisper	rattle

Animal matters

a foal	paws
a puppy	a fin
a stable	squeak v.
a nest	grunt v.
a cage	bred in captivity

Phrases with get

get your own back on sb	get into trouble
get to know sb	get away with sth
get your act together	get out of doing sth
get the joke	get back to sb
get on your nerves	get over sth

Expressions with time

time-consuming	make up for lost time
from time to time	have time on your hands
short of time	kill time
for the time being	give sb a hard time
one thing at a time	behind the times

Prefixes

an outpatient	substandard
a postgraduate	understaffed
biannual	upgraded
illiterate	outgrow
undo	coexist

Preparing food

a poached egg	a toasted sandwich
sliced bread	a frying pan
stuffed chicken breast	a baking tray
chopped parsley	a chopping board
melted chocolate	a spatula

Phones and technology

a touch screen	coverage
a keyboard	stream v.
a password	swipe v.
broadband	unplug
a pop-up	hang up

VOCABULARY   Revision 2: Phrasal verbs

a Complete the **PARTICLE** column with a word from the list.

across   away   behind   by   off (x2)   on (x3)   out (x3)   through   up (x2)

PARTICLE

1 I'm not sure if I want to carry ▉ with my degree; I've found this year really challenging. _on_

2 My in-laws want to come and stay next month, but I'm going to put them ▉ until we've finished redecorating. _____

3 Rita comes ▉ as straightforward, but she's actually a very complicated person when you get to know her. _____

4 The first applicant we interviewed turned ▉ to be unsuitable as he had no experience. _____

5 If you ring this number, an operator will put you ▉ to the relevant person. _____

6 Can you pass a message ▉ to Louise for me, please? _____

7 When I'm on holiday, I love just sitting in a café and soaking ▉ the atmosphere. _____

8 Sarah gets so stressed about the tiniest things – she really needs to chill ▉ a bit. _____

9 If I have a problem with my laptop, I usually just switch it ▉ and try again. _____

10 I haven't been feeling too well lately and I've got a bit ▉ with my work. _____

11 Amy wanted to get ▉ of going to the party, so she said she had an interview the next day. _____

12 He cheated in an exam, but he got ▉ with it as the teacher didn't see him. _____

13 We went ▉ a cruise with some friends last year. _____

14 The soldiers blew ▉ the bridge to stop the enemy from crossing the river. _____

15 Although I've only studied Italian for a year, I think I could get ▉ if I went there on holiday. _____

b Cover the **PARTICLE** column. Say the full sentences.

c Complete the **VERB** column with a verb from the list.

~~break~~   come   dress   find   get (x2)   go   grow   hang   keep   pick   run   set   top   turn

VERB

1 People were afraid that a civil war might ▉ out between government supporters and the rebels. _break_

2 So Johnnie, what do you want to be when you ▉ up? A footballer? _____

3 If you want to ▉ out which places to visit on holiday, do plenty of research before you leave. _____

4 If a helpline keeps me on hold for ages, in the end I usually ▉ up. _____

5 I read the newspapers online every day to ▉ up with current affairs. _____

6 Tom is so resourceful! He can ▉ up with brilliant solutions to most problems. _____

7 I always ▉ out of time in exams; I need to speed up. _____

8 It was a Halloween party, so we had to ▉ up. _____

9 How often do you ▉ up your pay-as-you-go phone? _____

10 It's taken Steve three weeks to ▉ over his cold. _____

11 If you ▉ up late for an interview, it'll give a very bad impression. _____

12 Shall we stop now or do you want to ▉ on for a bit longer? _____

13 Experts say that children ▉ up foreign languages much faster than adults. _____

14 Our flight leaves at 9.00, so we'll need to ▉ off for the airport at 6.00. _____

15 We're going to stay in a remote cottage in the mountains – we want to ▉ away from it all. _____

d Cover the **VERB** column. Say the full sentences.

English File fourth edition Teacher's Guide Advanced   Photocopiable © Oxford University Press 2020

VOCABULARY Revision 3: Idioms

● Complete the **bold** idioms with the correct word.

1 When I'm reading in English, I sometimes **get st**<u>uck</u> on a word and have to look it up.

2 Do you usually **follow** recipes **to the l**_____ when you're cooking, or do you like to improvise?

3 The dress **caught my e**_____ as soon as I walked into the shop. It was stunning!

4 We have to face this problem **h**_____-_____ and find a solution as quickly as possible.

5 The more you think about it, the harder it can be to decide what to do. Just go with **your g**_____ **feeling** and see what happens.

6 Mark didn't really want to go to the theatre, so he told a **wh**_____ **lie** and said he wasn't feeling very well.

7 The government's proposal to deal with the rise in homelessness has been criticized for not **getting to the h**_____ **of** the problem.

8 There was a lot of competition, but she was able to **h**_____ **her own**.

9 We were so surprised by Sally's decision to resign. It came completely **out of the bl**_____.

10 If I **keep my n**_____ **to the grindstone**, I'm sure I'll get that pay rise.

11 Suzie is probably the kindest person I know. She has a real **heart of g**_____.

12 I got **the wr**_____ **end of the stick**. I thought the meeting was next week, but it turns out we're actually meeting tomorrow.

13 For the time being, you really need to focus on **the big p**_____ and ignore the details.

14 I took up yoga and it really helped to **keep my m**_____ **off** all my problems.

15 Whether this technology is legal or not is still a bit of a **gr**_____ **area**.

16 If you don't **get a m**_____ on, we'll miss the start of the film.

17 Consumers are being encouraged to **tighten their b**_____ as the cost of living rises.

18 You wouldn't believe the amount of **red t**_____ that was involved in getting this permit.

19 What do you mean, I never **lift a f**_____ around the house? I did the washing-up last week!

20 If you carry on **living b**_____ **your means**, you'll get further and further into debt.

21 When the online company didn't answer any of my emails, I began to **sm**_____ **a rat**.

22 That cream you suggested **worked like a dr**_____. The rash was gone in a day or two.

23 Wow! Nice car. That must have **cost an a**_____ **and a l**_____.

24 Beth bought her flat for **n**_____ **to nothing** 15 years ago, but it's worth a fortune now.

25 Don't be scared of my mother! Her **b**_____ **is worse than her bite**!

OXFORD
UNIVERSITY PRESS

Great Clarendon Street, Oxford, OX2 6DP, United Kingdom

Oxford University Press is a department of the University of Oxford.
It furthers the University's objective of excellence in research, scholarship,
and education by publishing worldwide. Oxford is a registered trade
mark of Oxford University Press in the UK and in certain other countries

ACKNOWLEDGEMENTS

Back cover photograph: Oxford University Press building/David Fisher

*The authors would like to thank all the teachers and students round the world
whose feedback has helped us to shape* English File.

The authors would also like to thank: all those at Oxford University Press
(both in Oxford and around the world) and the design team who have
contributed their skills and ideas to producing this course.

*A very special thanks from Clive to Maria Angeles, Lucia, and Eric, and from
Christina to Cristina, for all their support and encouragement. Christina would also
like to thank her children Joaquin, Marco, and Krysia for their constant inspiration.*

*The publisher and authors would also like to thank the following for their
invaluable feedback on the materials:* Krysia Mabbott, Magdalena Muszyńska,
and Philip Drury.

Illustrations by: Sophie Joyce pp.184, 213; Adam Larkum pp.169, 177, 180,
226; Roger Penwill pp.171, 174, 223; Gavin Reece p.179; Colin Shelbourn
p.207.

*The publisher would like to thank the following for their permission to reproduce
photographs:* Alamy Stock Photo pp.170 (punting/Oxford Picture Library),
172 (Guy Fawkes/Pictorial Press Ltd), 198 (LBJ/Atlaspix), 205 (sports day/
Shepic), 212 (fans/Agencja Fotograficzna Caro), 227 (rescue kennels/
ZUMA Press Inc), 227 (seal/Inga Spence); DACS p.206 (Incommunicado/
Mona Hatoum); Getty Images pp.185 (Migrant mother,1936/Dorothea
Lange/SSPL), 193 (1940's family/Popperfoto), 193 (parents/Betsie Van der
Meer), 204 (woman with glasses/Peter Dazeley), 206 (armchair/Mariia
Masich), 212 (footballers/Tim Clayton/Corbis); Oxford University Press
pp.167 (eye test/13/Heath Korvola), 168 (businessman/Blue Jean Images),
168 (student/wavebreakmedia), 168 (senior woman/Gareth Boden),
173 (young man/photolibrary.com), 173 (monster/Albert Ziganshin),
173 (baby/fStop), 173 (donut eyes/artemisphoto), 173 (cat/George Doyle
& Ciaran Griffin), 173 (woman/Bevan Goldswain), 173 (male student/
michaeljung), 173 (stone stack/Michele Constantini), 182 (father & son/
Olix Wirtinger), 195 (washing up/Chris King), 195 (reading/Sparkling
Moments Photography), 196 (woman/Jutta Klee), 196 (young man/Tetra
Images), 196 (woman/Adrian Weinbrecht), 196 (happy man/Sarah Kastner),
196 (smiling man/racorn), 199 (books/Dean Ryan), 200 (bells/SuperStock),
200 (fireworks/Creatas), 200 (blowing bubbles/amanaimages), 204 (girl with
coffee/lightwavemedia), 204 (young man/Holger Winkler), 204 (footballer/
Image Source), 204 (young man/Boryana Manzurova), 204 (Asian woman/Ni
Qin), 206 (drawers/Folio Images), 209 (butterfly/Lukas Gojda), 210 (elephant/
Ingram), 210 (fly/r.classen), 211 (gazpacho/hfng), 211 (Birthday cupcake/
Ruth Black), 211 (sub/Markus Mainka), 211 (broccoli/Nik Merkulov), 222 (tap/
Serg64), 222 (balloon/Hurst Photo), 227 (rhino/Scott Ward), 227 (pelican/
Ivan Kuzmin); Shutterstock pp.170 (Wellington/FiledIMAGE), 172 (barrels/
Fernando Macias Romo), 182 (ribbon cutting/Motortion Films), 196 (woman/
digitalskillet), 196 (smiling woman/Nadino), 196 (young man/AJR_photo),
200 (bee/Bildagentur Zoonar GmbH), 200 (dog/pirita), 200 (barn owl/
Anan Kaewkhammul), 200 (dirty dishes/sirtravelalot), 200 (underground/
VanderWolf Images), 204 (teen boy/Shell114), 205 (grading/Pixsooz),
205 (classroom/wavebreakmedia), 206 (toy blocks/Jiri Hera), 206 (rubber
duck/Danny Smythe), 209 (octopus/Yellow Cat), 212 (horse race/gabriel12),
219 (baby/Syda Productions), 219 (healthcare workers/Monkey Business
Images), 219 (assembly line/Irina Borsuchenko), 227 (lion cubs/Charl A
Stafleu); Shutterstock Editorial pp.198 (The Butler 2013/Follow Through
Prods/Salamander/Laura Ziskin Prods/Kobal), 198 (Vice 2018/Matt Kennedy/
Annapurna/Kobal), 198 (Lincoln 2012/Dreamworks/20th Century Fox/Kobal),
198 (Hyde Park On Hudson 2012/Daybreak/Kobal); Studio Florentijn Hofman
p.206 (Kobe Frog/Florentijn Hofman).